SAXON MATH™
Intermediate 3

Student Edition

Stephen Hake

A Harcourt Achieve Imprint

www.SaxonPublishers.com
800-531-5015

ACKNOWLEDGEMENTS

This book was made possible by the significant contributions of many individuals and the dedicated efforts of talented teams at Houghton Mifflin Harcourt Publishing Company.

Special thanks to Chris Braun for conscientious work on Power Up exercises, Problem Solving scripts, and student assessments. The long hours and technical assistance of John and James Hake were invaluable in meeting publishing deadlines. As always, the patience and support of Mary is most appreciated.

– Stephen Hake

2012 Edition

Copyright © by Houghton Mifflin Harcourt Publishing Company and Stephen Hake

Printed in the U.S.A.

ISBN 978-1-600-32534-2

9 10 0868 20 19 18 17 16 15 14 13 12 11

4500308333 ^ B C D E F G

ABOUT THE AUTHOR

Stephen Hake has authored six books in the **Saxon Math** series. He writes from 17 years of classroom experience as an elementary and secondary teacher, and as a math specialist in El Monte, California. As a math coach, his students won honors and recognition in local, regional, and statewide competitions.

Stephen has been writing math curriculum since 1975 and for Saxon since 1985. He has also authored several math contests including Los Angeles County's first Math Field Day contest. Stephen contributed to the 1999 National Academy of Science publication on the Nature and Teaching of Algebra in the Middle Grades.

Stephen is a member of the National Council of Teachers of Mathematics and the California Mathematics Council. He earned his BA from United States International University and his MA from Chapman College.

CONTENTS OVERVIEW

TABLE OF CONTENTS

Integrated and Distributed Units of Instruction

Section 1   *Lessons 1–10, Investigation 1*

Strands Key:
NO = Number and Operations
A = Algebra
G = Geometry

M = Measurement
DAP = Data Analysis and Probability
PS = Problem Solving

CM = Communication
RP = Reasoning and Proof
C = Connections
R = Representation

TABLE OF CONTENTS

Section 3 *Lessons 21–30, Investigation 3*

Strands Key:
NO = Number and Operations
A = Algebra
G = Geometry

M = Measurement
DAP = Data Analysis and Probability
PS = Problem Solving

CM = Communication
RP = Reasoning and Proof
C = Connections
R = Representation

TABLE OF CONTENTS

Section 5 *Lessons 41–50, Investigation 5*

Strands Key:
NO = Number and Operations
A = Algebra
G = Geometry
M = Measurement
DAP = Data Analysis and Probability
PS = Problem Solving
CM = Communication
RP = Reasoning and Proof
C = Connections
R = Representation

TABLE OF CONTENTS

Section 7 *Lessons 61–70, Investigation 7*

Strands Key:
NO = Number and Operations
A = Algebra
G = Geometry
M = Measurement
DAP = Data Analysis and Probability
PS = Problem Solving
CM = Communication
RP = Reasoning and Proof
C = Connections
R = Representation

TABLE OF CONTENTS

Section 9 — *Lessons 81–90, Investigation 9*

Strands Key:
NO = Number and Operations
A = Algebra
G = Geometry

M = Measurement
DAP = Data Analysis and Probability
PS = Problem Solving

CM = Communication
RP = Reasoning and Proof
C = Connections
R = Representation

TABLE OF CONTENTS

Section 11 — *Lessons 101–110, Investigation 11*

Strands Key:
NO = Number and Operations
A = Algebra
G = Geometry
M = Measurement
DAP = Data Analysis and Probability
PS = Problem Solving
CM = Communication
RP = Reasoning and Proof
C = Connections
R = Representation

Place Value

Thousands			,	Ones		
Hundred Thousands	Ten Thousands	Thousands	,	Hundreds	Tens	Ones
___	___	___	,	___	___	___

Comparison Symbols

>	greater than
<	less than
=	equal to

Time

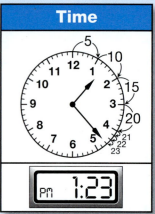

Length

Metric

1 kilometer = 1000 meters

1 meter = 100 centimeters

Customary

1 yard = 3 feet

1 foot = 12 inches

Mass and Weight

Metric

1 kilogram = 1000 grams

Customary

1 ton = 2000 pounds

1 pound = 16 ounces

Capacity

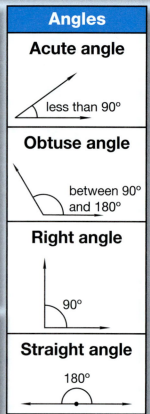

Arithmetic with Two Numbers

Addition	addend + addend = sum	$\begin{array}{r} addend \\ + addend \\ \hline sum \end{array}$
Subtraction	greater − lesser = difference	$\begin{array}{r} greater \\ - lesser \\ \hline difference \end{array}$
Multiplication	factor × factor = product	$\begin{array}{r} factor \\ \times factor \\ \hline product \end{array}$
Division	dividend ÷ divisor = quotient	$divisor\overline{)dividend}$ quotient

Angles

Acute angle

less than 90°

Obtuse angle

between 90° and 180°

Right angle

90°

Straight angle

180°

Lines and Segments

line	segment	parallel lines	perpendicular
A B	D E		

Dear Student,

We study mathematics because it plays a very important role in our lives. Our school schedule, our trip to the store, the preparation of our meals, and many of the games we play involve mathematics. The word problems in this book are often drawn from everyday experiences.

When you become an adult, mathematics will become even more important. In fact, your future may depend on the mathematics you are learning now. This book will help you to learn mathematics and to learn it well. As you complete each lesson, you will see that similar problems are presented again and again. *Solving each problem day after day is the secret to success.*

Your book includes daily lessons and investigations. Each lesson has three parts.

1. The first part is a Power Up that includes practice of basic facts and mental math. These exercises improve your speed, accuracy, and ability to do math *in your head.* The Power Up also includes a problem-solving exercise to help you learn the strategies for solving complicated problems.

2. The second part of the lesson is the New Concept. This section introduces a new mathematical concept and presents examples that use the concept. The Lesson Practice provides a chance for you to solve problems using the new concept. The problems are lettered a, b, c, and so on.

3. The final part of the lesson is the Written Practice. This section reviews previously taught concepts and prepares you for concepts that will be taught in later lessons. Solving these problems will help you practice your skills and remember concepts you have learned.

Investigations are variations of the daily lesson. The investigations in this book often involve activities that fill an entire class period. Investigations contain their own set of questions but do not include Lesson Practice or Written Practice.

Remember to solve every problem in each Lesson Practice, Written Practice, and Investigation. Do your best work, and you will experience success and true learning that will stay with you and serve you well in the future.

Temple City, California

HOW TO USE YOUR TEXTBOOK

Saxon Math Intermediate 3 is unlike any math book you have used! It doesn't have colorful photos to distract you from learning. The Saxon approach lets you see the beauty and structure within math itself. You will understand more mathematics, become more confident in doing math, and will be well prepared when you take high school math classes.

Power Yourself Up

Start off each lesson by practicing your basic skills and concepts, mental math, and problem solving. Make your math brain stronger by exercising it every day. Soon you'll know these facts by memory!

Learn Something New!

Each day brings you a new concept, but you'll only have to learn a small part of it now. You'll be building on this concept throughout the year so that you understand and remember it by test time.

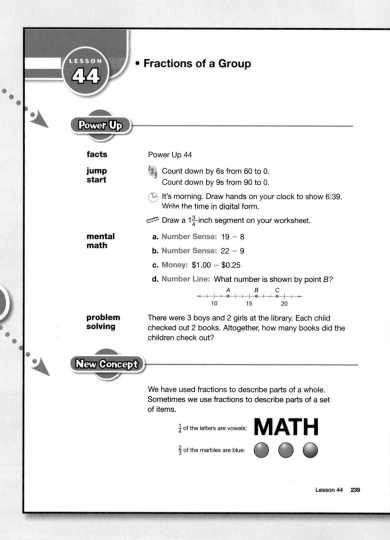

LESSON 44

• Fractions of a Group

Power Up

facts	Power Up 44
jump start	Count down by 6s from 60 to 0. Count down by 9s from 90 to 0.
	It's morning. Draw hands on your clock to show 6:39. Write the time in digital form.
	Draw a $1\frac{3}{4}$-inch segment on your worksheet.
mental math	**a.** Number Sense: $19 - 8$
	b. Number Sense: $22 - 9$
	c. Money: $\$1.00 - \$0.25$
	d. Number Line: What number is shown by point *B*?

problem solving
There were 3 boys and 2 girls at the library. Each child checked out 2 books. Altogether, how many books did the children check out?

New Concept

We have used fractions to describe parts of a whole. Sometimes we use fractions to describe parts of a set of items.

$\frac{1}{4}$ of the letters are vowels: **MATH**

$\frac{2}{3}$ of the marbles are blue:

You will measure the next two objects or distances in feet. These should be larger objects like the length of a row of desks or the distance from your seat to the chalkboard.

You will measure the final two objects or distances in yards. These should be several yards such as the length or width of the classroom.

Activity
Estimating and Measuring Lengths

Materials: ruler, yardstick

Copy the chart below on a piece of paper. With your partner, decide on six objects to measure and record them in the first column of the chart.

Object to be measured	Estimated length	Measured length
1.	inches	inches
2.	inches	inches
3.	feet	feet
4.	feet	feet
5.	yards	yards
6.	yards	yards

Before you measure with a ruler or yardstick, estimate the measure of each object or distance you choose. We estimate by making a careful guess. You may want to take small steps by placing one foot just in front of another to help you estimate feet. You can take big steps to help you estimate yards. You should discuss your estimates with your partner. Write down your estimate before you measure with a ruler or yardstick.

When measuring yards, you can use three rulers instead of a yardstick. Record the closest whole number of inches, feet, or yards for each object measured.

Analyze Find 2 items in the classroom that would measure about 1 foot together.

Get Active!

Dig into math with a hands-on activity. Explore a math concept with your friends as you work together and use manipulatives to see new connections in mathematics.

Check It Out!

The Lesson Practice lets you check to see if you understand today's new concept.

Exercise Your Mind!

When you work the Written Practice exercises, you will review both today's new concept and also math you learned in earlier lessons. Each exercise will be on a different concept — you never know what you're going to get! It's like a mystery game — unpredictable and challenging.

As you review concepts from earlier in the book, you'll be asked to use higher-order thinking skills to show what you know and why the math works.

The mixed set of Written Practice is just like the mixed format of your state test. You'll be practicing for the "big" test every day!

Lesson Practice

a. Draw a parallelogram that does *not* have right angles.

b. What is the perimeter of the parallelogram?

3 in.
4 in.

c. **Multiple Choice** Which shape below is *not* a parallelogram?

A   B   C   D

d. Which shapes in problem **c** are rectangles?

e. Which angles in this parallelogram are obtuse?

Q   R
T   S

f. Which side of this parallelogram is parallel to side *QT*?

Written Practice
Distributed and Integrated

1. **Formulate** Gwen has 3 boxes of tiles with 40 tiles in each box. Write a number sentence to show how many tiles are in all 3 boxes.
(60, 24)

2. **Multiple Choice** Gwen sees this tile pattern around the edge of a shower. What are the next two tiles in the pattern?
(2)

A   B   C   D

3. Write two addition facts and two subtraction facts using 7, 8, and 15.
(8)

4. **Multiple Choice** Which shape is *not* a parallelogram?
(66)
A   B   C   D

5. One square yard equals 9 square feet. How many square feet is 9 square yards?
(60, 64)

Become an Investigator!

Dive into math concepts and explore the depths of math connections in the Investigations.

Continue to develop your mathematical thinking through applications, activities, and extensions.

INVESTIGATION 9

Focus on

• Symmetry, Part 2

Recall from Investigation 7 that a line of symmetry divides a figure into mirror images.

Visit www. SaxonMath.com/ Int3Activities for an online activity.

A figure may have one line of symmetry, two lines of symmetry, or more. A figure may also have no lines of symmetry.

No lines of symmetry   One line of symmetry   Two lines of symmetry

A line of symmetry also shows where a figure could be folded in half so that one half exactly fits onto the other half. In the following activity, you will create shapes with one or two lines of symmetry by folding and cutting paper.

Activity 1

Creating Symmetrical Figures

Materials: two sheets of paper, scissors

Fold a sheet of paper in half. While the paper is folded, cut a shape out of the paper starting from one end of the folded edge to the other end.

Investigation 9   491

Focus on

• Problem Solving

Problem solving is a part of daily life. We can become powerful problem solvers by using the tools we store in our minds. When we study mathematics we increase the number of tools we can use. In this book we will practice solving problems every day.

Four-Step Problem Solving Process

Solving a problem is like arriving at a new location. So problem solving is similar to taking a trip.

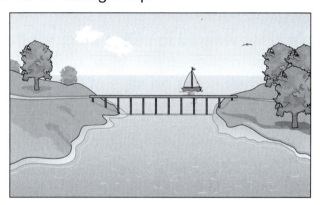

Step	Problem-Solving Process	Taking a Trip
1	**Understand** Know where you are and where you want to go.	We are on the mainland and want to go to the island.
2	**Plan** Decide how you will get to the island. This is your route.	We can walk or ride our bike across the bridge. We can also use the boat.
3	**Solve** Follow your plan.	Go to the island.
4	**Check** Be sure that you have reached the right place.	Verify. We are now on the island.

When we solve a problem, it helps to ask ourselves some questions along the way.

Step	Follow the Process	Ask Yourself Questions
1	Understand	What do I know? What do I need to find out?
2	Plan	How can I use what I know? What strategy can I use?
3	Solve	Am I following my plan? Is my math correct?
4	Check	Did I answer the question that was asked? Is my answer reasonable?

The example below shows how we follow the four-step process to solve a word problem.

Example 1

Ms. Tipton's class wanted to pick a color for their class t-shirts. They could choose red, blue, or yellow. The students wrote their votes on slips of paper. Use a tally chart to display the votes. Which color did the class choose?

blue	red	blue	yellow	red	blue
red	blue	yellow	blue	yellow	red
yellow	red	blue	red	blue	yellow

Step 1: Understand the problem. Votes for three t-shirt colors are shown on the slips of paper. I need to **tally** the votes and find which color was chosen.

Step 2: Make a plan. I can make a **table** to tally the votes. Then I can count the tallies to see which color was chosen.

Step 3: Solve the problem.
We make one tally mark in the table for each vote. The color blue has the most votes. So, blue was the color chosen by the class.

Our Votes

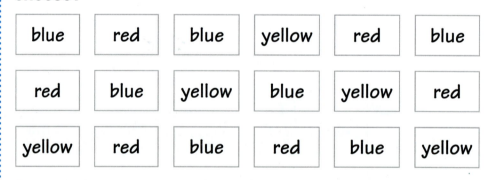

Color	Tally
red	ⅢⅠ Ⅰ
blue	ⅢⅠ ⅠⅠ
yellow	ⅢⅠ

Step 4: Check your answer. I can check the tallies in the table to be sure they match the slips of paper shown. I can verify that the color blue has the most votes.

Example 2

Four students line up at the water fountain. Eric is behind Katie. Zachary is in front of Katie. Marcela is behind Eric. Who is first in line?

Step 1: Understand the problem. I know the following:

- There are four students.
- Eric is behind Katie.
- Zachary is in front of Katie.
- Marcela is behind Eric.

I need to find who is first in line.

Step 2: Make a plan. I can act out this problem. I can make a nametag for each student—Eric, Katie, Zachary, and Marcela. Then I can use what I know to put the nametags in the correct order.

Step 3: Solve the problem. I put the nametags in order starting with Eric and Katie. Since Eric is behind Katie, I 0place Katie in front of Eric.

Katie	Eric

Zachary is in front of Katie. So, I move him to the front.

Marcela is behind Eric. So, I move her to the very back.

The order is Zachary, Katie, Eric, Marcela. I can look at the line of nametags and see that Zachary is first.

Step 4: Check your answer. I can check the order of the nametags by reading the question again.

- There are four students.
- Eric is behind Katie.

- Zachary is in front of Katie.
- Marcela is behind Eric.

The order is correct. I answered the question asked. Zachary is first in line.

1. List the four steps in the problem solving process.

2. What two questions do we answer to understand the problem?

Refer to the following problem to answer problems **3–8.**

Denzel arranges his rock collection into 5 rows. Each row has one more rock than the row above it. The bottom row has 6 rocks. How many rocks are in Denzel's collection?

3. What do we know?

4. What do we need to find?

5. **Connect** Which step of the four-step process did you complete in problems **3** and **4?**

6. Describe your plan for solving the problem.

7. Solve the problem by following your plan.

8. **Explain** Check your answer.

Problem-Solving Strategies

Problem-solving **strategies** are types of plans we can use to solve problems. In example 1 we made a table and in example 2 we acted out the problem. The list below shows the problem-solving strategies that we will use in this book.

Draw a Picture. We can use the information in a problem to draw a picture of the problem. Then we can use our picture to help us find the solution.

Look for a Pattern. Sometimes the order of a list of numbers or shapes follows a pattern. If we study the list we can find the pattern. Then we can predict what number or shape will come next.

Make a Table. We can organize what we know in a table. Then we study the table to see a pattern or relationship that will help us solve the problem.

Guess and Check. We can guess a reasonable answer and then check to see if our guess is correct. If the guess is not correct, we use the information we learned from the guess to make a better guess. We continue to guess until we find the correct answer.

Act It Out. We can use objects or people to represent the actions in a problem.

Make a Table. We can organize what we know in a table. Then we study the table to see a pattern or relationship that will help us solve the problem.

Work a Simpler Problem. Some problems contain large numbers. Sometimes we can use smaller numbers to see how to work the problem. Then we use the same plan to solve the harder problem.

Work Backwards. Some problems are easier to solve if we start at the end of the problem. Then we use what we know to get to the missing information at the beginning of the problem.

Write a Number Sentence. We can solve many word problems by using the numbers in the problem to write a number sentence.

Use Logical Reasoning. All problems require reasoning. However, for some problems we use the given information to rule out certain answer choices. We can use a picture or an organized list to help us as we work.

Make an Organized List. We can organize the given information in a list. Then we use the information in the list to solve the problem.

The chart below shows where each strategy is first introduced in this textbook.

Strategy	Lesson
Draw a Picture	7
Look for a Pattern	1
Guess and Check	18
Act It Out	13
Make a Table	4
Work a Simpler Problem	67
Work Backwards	59
Write a Number Sentence	20
Use Logical Reasoning	30
Make an Organized List	45

Writing and Problem Solving

Sometimes a problem will ask us to explain our thinking or our answer. This helps us measure how well we understand the problem. When we do this, we describe how we solved the problem or why our answer is correct.

LESSON 1

- • **Months and Years**
- • **Calendar**

Power Up

facts	Power Up 1
jump start	Count up by 1s from 0 to 10.
	Draw hands on your clock to show 9:00.
mental math	**a. Number Sense:** 1 + 0 1
	b. Number Sense: 1 + 1 2
	c. Number Sense: 0 + 0 0
	d. Number Sense: 0 + 2 2
problem solving	**Focus Strategy: Find and Continue a Pattern**

What shape comes next in this pattern?

(**Understand**) We are asked to find the shape that comes next in the pattern.

(**Plan**) We will find a pattern and then continue it.

(**Solve**) The pattern is "triangle, square, triangle, square" and so on. The last shape we see is a triangle, so we expect the next shape to be a square.

△, □, △, □, △, □, △, □, ...

(**Check**) Our answer makes sense because a square comes after every triangle in the pattern.

Months and Years

The table below shows the months of the year in order. It also shows the number of days in each month. A **common year** is 365 days long. A **leap year** is 366 days long. The extra day in a leap year is always added to February.

Number	Month	Number of days
1	January	31
2	February	28 (29 in leap years)
3	March	31
4	April	30
5	May	31
6	June	30
7	July	31
8	August	31
9	September	30
10	October	31
11	November	30
12	December	31

Notice that February has 28 or 29 days. April, June, September, and November have 30 days. The other months have 31 days. The following rhyme helps us remember which months have 30 days. Then we can easily remember the numbers of days in the other months.

Thirty days hath September,

April, June, and November.

We can write a date several ways. Usually, we name the month first, then the day and year.

July 4, 1776

We can write the number of the month instead of its name. We call this the "month/day/year" form. Since July is the seventh month, we write

7/4/1776

We also can write the day first, then the month and year.

Fourth of July, 1776

When we read a date, we use an ordinal number to name the day of the month. An **ordinal number** names a position or an order. The first ten ordinal numbers are: first, second, third, fourth, fifth, sixth, seventh, eighth, ninth, and tenth.

We read July 4, 1776, as

July fourth, seventeen seventy-six

The word *fourth* is an ordinal number. It refers to the fourth day in the month. We can also write fourth as 4th.

(**Conclude**) What ordinal number comes before 4th? What ordinal number comes after 4th?

Calendar

A monthly **calendar** is a chart that relates the days of the month to the days of the week. A calendar has seven **columns,** one for each day of the week. It has six **rows** for the weeks. Not all of the rows are filled with numbers. For example, if the first day of the month is a Saturday, the only number in the first row is 1.

\	\	JULY	2006	\	\	\
S	M	T	W	T	F	S
						1
2	3	4	5	6	7	8
9	10	11	12	13	14	15
16	17	18	19	20	21	22
23	24	25	26	27	28	29
30	31					

Activity

Make a Calendar

Materials: **Lesson Activity 1,** class calendar

1. Write the name of this month at the top of your calendar.

2. Use the class calendar to find the column and the row for the first day of the month.

3. Write the number 1 on your calendar to show the first day.

4. Write the dates for the rest of the month. Use the rhyme you learned or the table to find the number of days in this month. Remember to stop writing when you get to this number.

5. Record on your calendar special events for this month such as holidays and birthdays.

Example 1

How many days are there from the 4th of the month to the 12th of the month? Use your calendar.

We will count up from the 4th through the 12th. When we count up from the 4th, we do not count the 4th. We begin counting with the first day as the 5th and the last day as the 12th. We find there are **8 days** from the 4th through the 12th.

Example 2

What date is one week after the 6th?

First we find the 6th on our calendar. One week after the 6th will be on the same day of the week. The date below the 6th is the 13th. The date one week after the 6th is the **13th.**

Generalize What date is two weeks after the 10th?

Lesson Practice Answer problems **a–f** aloud as a class.

a. Repeat aloud the rhyme that tells the months that have 30 days.

b. On which day of the week did this month begin?

c. How many days are there in this month?

d. On which day of the week will this month end?

e. How many rows did we need for the calendar this month? Why?

f. How many columns did we need? Why?

For problems **g–k** write your answers.

g. How many days are in a leap year?

h. What month is the tenth month of the year?

i. How many months have 31 days?

j. How many days are there from the 16th of the month through the 21st?

k. What date is two weeks after the 3rd?

Written Practice

Distributed and Integrated

1. How many years old are you?

2. **Represent** Write your birth date in two different ways.

3. What month is the ninth month of the year?

4. Name the four months that complete this rhyme:

Thirty days hath _____,

_____, _____, and _____.

5. A week has how many days?

6. This month has four weeks plus how many days?

7. How many days are there from the 5th through the 11th?

8. **Analyze** You are the seventh person in a line of 12 people.
   a. How many people are in front of you?

   b. How many people are behind you?

9. Michael is the third person in line and Janet is the tenth person in line. How many people are standing between them?

10. List the missing ordinal numbers.

first, _second,_ third, fourth, _fifth_, sixth, _seventh,_ _eighth,_ ninth, _tenth_

11. What date is one week after the 9th?

12. What date is two weeks after the 11th?

13. What date is three weeks before the 27th?

14. Which month has less than 30 days?

15. On what day of the week does next month begin?

Early Finishers

Real-World Connection

Bianca takes piano lessons every Wednesday. If the first of March falls on a Thursday, how many days would Bianca have piano lessons for the month of March? What would the dates be?

LESSON 2

• Counting Patterns

Power Up

facts

Power Up 2

jump start

Count up by 2s from 0 to 20.
Count up by 5s from 0 to 30.

Draw hands on your clock to show 11:00.

mental math

a. **Calendar:** What date is 1 week after the 5th?

b. **Calendar:** What date is 7 days before the 9th?

c. **Number Sense:** 2 + 0

d. **Number Sense:** 2 + 1

problem solving

Draw the next two shapes in this pattern.

○, △, ○, △, ○, △, ___, ___ ...

New Concept

Counting is a math skill we learn early in life. Counting by ones we say, "One, two, three, four, five, . . ."

$$1, 2, 3, 4, 5, \ldots$$

We often count by other numbers. For example, we can count in these ways.

by twos: 2, 4, 6, . . .

by fives: 5, 10, 15, . . .

by tens: 10, 20, 30, . . .

These are examples of **counting patterns.** A counting pattern is a kind of **sequence** that follows a rule. The three dots (…) mean that the counting pattern continues without end.

A counting pattern may count up or down. We may study the pattern to discover its rule. Then we can find more numbers in the sequence.

Example 1

Find the column on the calendar that starts with 7. What are the four numbers in this column?

The numbers in the column are **7, 14, 21,** and **28.**

Example 2

Find the next three numbers in this sequence:

7, 14, 21, 28, _____, _____, _____, …

We study the sequence and see this pattern:

$$\overset{+7}{\frown}\ \overset{+7}{\frown}\ \overset{+7}{\frown}$$
$$7,\ 14,\ 21,\ 28$$

To reach each number, we count up by seven. The rule is "Count up by seven."

Counting this way we find the next three numbers:

$$28 + 7 = \mathbf{35} \qquad 35 + 7 = \mathbf{42} \qquad 42 + 7 = \mathbf{49}$$

Generalize Will the rule for any column of a calendar be to count up by seven? Why?

Activity

Skip Counting

Materials: monthly calendar

We can use a calendar to help us practice skip counting. For example, when we count by twos from 2, we say two, skip over three, then say four, skip over five, then say six …

FEBRUARY						
S	M	T	W	T	F	S
						1
2	3	4	5	6	7	8
9	10	11	12	13	14	15
16	17	18	19	20	21	22
23	24	25	26	27	28	

To count by threes we say three, then skip over four and five, then say six, then skip over seven and eight, then say nine...

1. Skip count by threes from 3 to 30.

2. Skip count by fours from 4 to 28.

3. Skip count by twos from 30 down to 2.

Lesson Practice   Find the next 3 numbers in each pattern and write the rule.

a. 3, 6, 9, 12, _____, _____, _____, · · ·

b. 10, 9, 8, 7, _____, _____, _____, · · ·

c. 80, 70, 60, 50, _____, _____, _____, · · ·

d. Skip count by sevens from 7 to 35.

Written Practice   *Distributed and Integrated*

1.
(1) How many days are in two weeks?

2.
(1) What month is the last month of the year?

3.
(1) Which four months of the year have exactly 30 days?

4.
(1) What month is the shortest month of the year?

5.
(1) What month is the seventh month of the year?

6.
(1) What day is the fourth day of the week?

Conclude   Write the next 3 numbers in the sequence and then write the rule.

7. 7, 14, 21, _____, _____, _____, · · ·
(2)

8. 5, 10, 15, _____, _____, _____, · · ·
(2)

---

[1] The italicized numbers within parentheses underneath each problem number are called *lesson reference numbers.* These numbers refer to the lesson(s) in which the major concept of that particular problem is introduced. If additional assistance is needed, refer to the discussion, examples, or practice problems of that lesson.

9. 50, 60, 70, _____, _____, _____, ...
(2)

10. 4, 8, 12, _____, _____, _____, ...
(2)

Use the calendar to answer problems **11–14**.

11. Write the circled date in two ways.
(1)

12. On what day of the week did the month begin?
(1)

13. Write the date of the first Saturday of the month in
(1) month/day/year form.

14. On what day of the week did April, 2007, begin?
(1)

MARCH 2007						
S	M	T	W	T	F	S
				1	2	3
4	5	6	7	8	9	10
11	12	(13)	14	15	16	17
18	19	20	21	22	23	24
25	26	27	28	29	30	31

15. a. Twenty students lined up for a fire drill. Brad was tenth in line.
(1)   How many students were in front of him? How many students
were behind him?

    b. John was sixth in line. Beth was fifteenth in line. How many
people were between them in the line?

Early Finishers
Real-World Connection

Pablo earned $3 in January for helping do chores around the
house. In February he earned $6 and in March he earned $9. If the
pattern continues, how much money will Pablo earn in June?

LESSON 3

• Reading a Clock to the Nearest Five Minutes

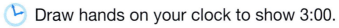
facts   Power Up 3

jump start   Count up by 5s from 0 to 60.
Count up by 10s from 0 to 100.

Draw hands on your clock to show 3:00.

mental math   **a. Calendar:** What date is 7 days before the 11th?

b. Calendar: What date is 8 days before the 11th?

c. Pattern: Find the missing number: 2, 4, _____, 8, 10

d. Pattern: Find the missing number: 10, 9, _____, 7, 6

problem solving   Suzi has 6 nickels. Count up by fives to find the total value of Suzi's nickels.

5¢   10¢   15¢   ___¢   ___¢   ___¢

New Concept

Two types of clocks are analog clocks and digital clocks. An analog clock shows time by the position of "hands" on a circular face. The numbers on an analog clock represent hours. The tick marks between the numbers represent minutes.

To tell time on an analog clock, we begin with the shorter hand, which is called the hour hand. On the analog clock below, the hour hand points to the space between 12 and 1. It is after 12:00 but before 1:00.

The longer hand is called the minute hand. The minute hand moves from one small tick mark to the next in one minute. There are 5 minutes between each hour number. We can skip count by fives from the 12 to the 6 to find the minute: 5, 10, 15, 20, 25, 30. The clock above shows twelve thirty.

To write the time of day in digital form, we write the hour followed by the colon sign (:). Then we write the number of minutes after the hour. We can write the time shown above this way.

12:30

We refer to 12:00 in the middle of the day as **noon.** We refer to 12:00 at night as **midnight.** The abbreviation **a.m.** is for the twelve hours before noon. The abbreviation **p.m.** is for the twelve hours after noon. Noon begins the p.m. hours and is written "12:00 p.m." Midnight begins the a.m. hours and is written "12:00 a.m."

Most digital clocks show a.m. or p.m. in the display to tell if the time is in the morning or afternoon. The digital clock below shows 12:30 p.m.

Verify Is 12:30 p.m. in the morning or in the afternoon?

If it is evening, what time is shown by the clock?

The hour hand is between the 9 and the 10. It is after 9 p.m. We skip count by fives from the 12 to the 4: 5, 10, 15, 20. It is **9:20 p.m.**

Analyze What time will it be in one hour?

Setting a Clock

Materials: **Lesson Activity 2**

Read the time on each digital clock. Then draw hands on the analog clock face to show the same time. Write each time in digital form, including either a.m. or p.m.

Lesson Practice If it is morning, what time is shown by each clock?

a.   b.   c.

Written Practice   *Distributed and Integrated*

1. It is morning. Write the time in digital form.
(3)

2. What month is the eighth month of the year?
(1)

3. The year 1776 was a leap year. How many days were
(1) in the year 1776?

4. Which two letters are between the seventh and tenth letters of the
(1) alphabet?

Write the next four numbers in each sequence. Then write the rule.

5. 7, 14, 21, ____, ____, ____, ____, · · ·
(2)

6. 15, 20, 25, ____, ____, ____, ____, · · ·
(2)

7. 3, 6, 9, ____, ____, ____, ____, · · ·
(2)

*__8.__ The minute hand of a clock points to what number at 5:45?
(3)

*__9.__ What month comes just before the tenth month of the year?
(1)

10. How many days are in three weeks?
(1)

(**Analyze**) Refer to the clock to answer problems **11–13.**

11. It is evening. Write the time in digital form.
(3)

12. What time will the clock show in 1 hour?
(3)

13. What time will the clock show in 2 hours?
(3)

14. What day is four days after Saturday?
(1)

15. Sam's birth date was 7/15/99. In what month was Sam born?
(1)

Real-World Connection

Marcus is studying for his math test. He likes to study for 15 minutes, then take a 5-minute break. If Marcus starts studying at 5:00 p.m., what time would he start his first break? What time would he start his second break? What time would he start his third break? Use a clock to help you find the answers.

LESSON 4

- **Number Line**
- **Thermometer**

Power Up

facts   Power Up 4

jump start   Count up by 7s from 0 to 35.
Count up by 100s from 0 to 1000.

Draw hands on your clock to show 6:30. It is morning.
Write the time in digital form.

mental math

a. Time: What is the time 1 hour after 3:00 p.m.?

b. Patterns: 10, 20, _____, 40, 50

c. Patterns: 10, 15, _____, 25, 30

d. Money: Find the value of these coins:

problem solving

Focus Strategy: Make a Table

Find the number of days in one week, two weeks, three weeks, and four weeks.

(**Understand**) We are asked to find how many days are in 1 week, 2 weeks, 3 weeks, and 4 weeks.

(**Plan**) We can make a two-column table. We will label one column "Weeks" and the other column "Days."

(**Solve**) We place the numbers 1 through 4 in the "Weeks" column. We can count by 7s to find the numbers for the "Days" column: 7, 14, 21, 28.

(**Check**) The numbers in the "Days" column increase by 7. There are 7 days in a week, so our answers make sense.

Weeks	Days
1	7
2	14
3	21
4	28

Number Line

A **number line** shows numbers on a line in counting order. The spaces between the **counting numbers** are the same. The number line below goes from 0 to 15. Each **tick mark** represents a number. The tick marks between the 0 and the 5 stand for 1, 2, 3, and 4.

Number Line

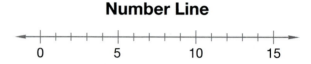

What do the tick marks between the 5 and the 10 stand for?

Number lines are a useful tool for measuring and comparing things in our daily lives.

We can use number lines to locate and display numbers, and to see the relationships between numbers. We can use an arrow or a **point** to show a number's location.

On the first number line, the arrow points to 4. On the second number line, the point is on the number 7.

Example 1

What numbers do the points labeled a–c represent?

a. Each tick mark represents one counting number. We can count up from 0 by 1s to find the number: 1, 2, **3.**

b. We can count up from 10 by 1s to find the number: 11, **12.**

c. We can count down from 10 by 1s to find the number: 10, **9.**

On some number lines, each tick mark represents an increase of more than one counting number.

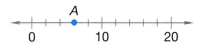

On this number line, each tick mark represents an increase of 2. We can count up by 2s from 0 to find the value of point *A*: 2, 4, 6. Point *A* represents the number 6.

Generalize How can we find the value of each unlabeled tick mark?

Example 2

What numbers do the points labeled a–c represent?

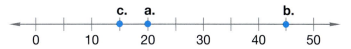

a. The point is on the tick mark labeled **20.**

b. Each tick mark represents an increase of 5. We can count up by 5s from 40: **45.**

c. We can count up by 5s from 10: **15.**

Thermometer

A thermometer uses a type of number line called a **scale.** We use a thermometer to measure temperature.

Thermometers measure temperature in units called **degrees.** Some thermometers show the temperature in degrees **Fahrenheit** (°F). Others show the temperature in degrees **Celsius** (°C). Some thermometers show both scales.

When it is hot enough for water to boil, it is 212°F and 100°C. When it is cold enough for water to freeze, it is 32°F and 0°C.

Normal body temperature is about 98.6°F and 37°C.

Fahrenheit Scale   **Celsius Scale**

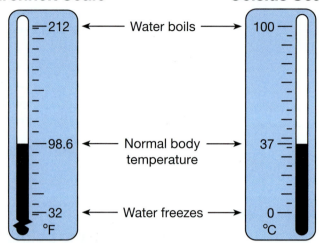

The thermometer on the right shows the Fahrenheit and Celsius scales. There are five spaces between each number on both scales. On the Fahrenheit scale, there are five tick marks for each increase of 10. If we skip count by twos, we can see that each space equals two degrees. On the Celsius scale, there are five tick marks for each increase of 5. Each space equals one degree.

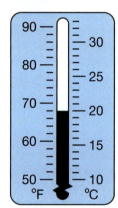

To read a thermometer, we look at the number on the scale next to where the temperature mark ends. The thermometer on the right shows 68°F and 20°C.

Example 3

What is the temperature on each thermometer?

a.
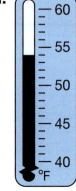

b.

a. The temperature marker is between 50°F and 55°F. We count up by 1s from 50. The temperature is **54°F.**

b. The temperature marker is between 20°C and 30°C. We count up by 2s from 20: 22, 24, 26, 28. The temperature is **28°C.**

Reading and Recording Temperature

Materials: **Lesson Activity 3,** classroom thermometer, clock

In this activity we will read an outside temperature in degrees Fahrenheit several times during the day. Each time we will follow these steps to record the temperature on our activity sheet.

1. Read the temperature on the outside thermometer.

2. Mark the temperature on the activity sheet.

3. Write the temperature.

4. Write the time the temperature is recorded.

5. Write whether the outside temperature feels cold, cool, warm, or hot.

Lesson Practice For **a–c,** write the number that each point represents.

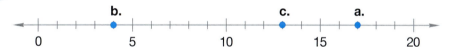

What temperature is shown on each thermometer?

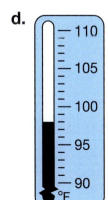

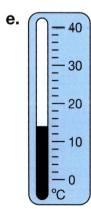

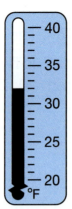

f.

g. The temperature is 35°F. Is it a hot or a cold day?

Written Practice · *Distributed and Integrated*

1. Name the middle two months of the year.
(1)

2. It is morning. Write the time in digital form.
(3)

3. **Generalize** The clock on the right is a digital clock. Is it 9:30 in the morning or 9:30 in the evening?
(3)

Write the next four numbers in each sequence:

4. 14, 21, 28, _____, _____, _____, _____, ...
(2)

5. 4, 8, 12, _____, _____, _____, _____, ...
(2)

6. What day is six days after Friday?
(1)

7. It is 8:35. The minute hand points to what number?
(3)

8. **Represent** Trevor was born on July 5, 2001. Write this date in month/day/year form.
(1)

9. At what temperature does water freeze on the Fahrenheit scale?
(4)

10. What temperature is shown on this thermometer?
(4)

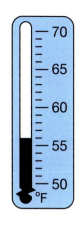

11. Jan's birthday is May 12. Ivan's birthday is exactly
(1) one week after Jan's. What is the date of Ivan's
birthday?

12. (**Analyze**) Dan was seventh in line. Jan was twelfth in
(1) line. How many people were in line between Dan and
Jan?

13. Look at the number line. The dot is on what number?
(4)

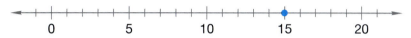

14. Name the last three months of the year.
(1)

15. **Multiple Choice** Which could be the temperature on a cool
(4) day?

  A 60°F   **B** 90°F   **C** 100°F   **D** 80°F

• Fractions of an Hour

Power Up

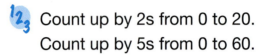

facts   Power Up 5

**jump
start**   Count up by 2s from 0 to 20.
            Count up by 5s from 0 to 60.

            Draw hands on your clock to show 8:15. It is morning.
            Write the time in digital form.

**mental
math**   **a. Time:** What is the time 1 hour after 8:00 p.m.?

           b. Calendar: What date is 7 days after the 1st?

           c. Patterns: 10, _____, 14, 16, 18

           d. Money: Find the value of these coins:

**problem
solving**   The table shows that the value of
            one dime is 10¢. Find the value of
            2 dimes, 3 dimes, and 4 dimes.
            Then fill in the missing values in the
            "Value" column.

Dimes	Value
1	10¢
2	
3	
4	

We know how to say the time in words using hours and minutes.

7:00   seven o'clock

7:15   seven fifteen

7:30   seven thirty

7:45   seven forty-five

We also use hours and the **fractions** one half and one quarter of an hour to name time.

One Full Hour   One Half Hour   One Quarter Hour

The minute hand moves from 12 all the way around to 12 again in one whole hour. One whole hour is 60 minutes.

One **half** hour is $\frac{1}{2}$ of 60 minutes, or 30 minutes. If we count the minutes by 5s, we see that when the minute hand points to the 6, it is "half past" the hour.

6:30
"Half past 6"

When we talk about time, we call $\frac{1}{4}$ of an hour "one quarter hour." One **quarter** hour is 15 minutes. When the minute hand points to the 3, it is a "quarter after" or a "quarter past" the hour. When the minute hand points to the nine, it is a "quarter to" or a "quarter of" the hour.

6:15   5:45
"A quarter after 6"   "A quarter to 6"

Example 1

Write each time in digital form.

    a. nine o'clock in the morning

    b. half past nine in the morning

    a. Nine o'clock is the whole hour. Since it is morning, the time is **9:00 a.m.**

    b. Half past nine is 30 minutes after nine o'clock. Since it is morning, the time is **9:30 a.m.**

Example 2

Write each time in digital form.

    a. a quarter after four in the afternoon

    b. a quarter to five in the afternoon

    a. A quarter after four is 15 minutes after four. Since it is afternoon, the time is **4:15 p.m.**

    b. A quarter to five is fifteen minutes before five. Since it is evening, the time is **4:45 p.m.**

Fractions of an Hour

Materials: **Lesson Activity 4**

On your activity sheet, draw hands on the clock faces for these times. Then write each time in digital form.

    1. A quarter to three

    2. Half past four

    3. A quarter after ten

    4. A quarter of eight

Lesson Practice

a. The clock says 1:15. Write the time in words using a fraction of an hour.

b. Write a quarter to eight in the evening in digital form.

c. Cory gets up at half past six in the morning. Write that time in digital form.

Written Practice — *Distributed and Integrated*

1. How many minutes are in half an hour?
(5)

2. The date on the letter is 6/23/07. In what month was the letter
(1) written?

3. The first day of the week is Sunday. How many days of the week
(1) are left after Wednesday?

Write the next four numbers in each sequence. Then write the rule for the sequence.

4. 18, 24, 30, _____, _____, _____, _____, ...
(2)

5. 7, 14, 21, _____, _____, _____, _____, ...
(2)

6. 50, 45, 40, _____, _____, _____, _____, ...
(2)

7. It is morning. Write the time in digital form.
(3)

8. Look at the number line. The dot is on what number?
(4)

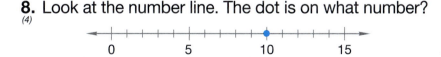

9. Write a number sequence with five numbers. Start with the
(2) number 5. Use the rule "count up by 5."

10. Ana came home at a quarter past four in the afternoon. Write that
(5) time in digital form.

11. What temperature is shown on this thermometer?
(4)

12. In degrees Fahrenheit, at what temperatures does water freeze? At what temperatures does it boil?
(4)

13. **Multiple Choice** Which counting pattern shows counting by sevens?
(2)

    A 8, 6, 4, 2   **B** 5, 7, 9, 11

    C 21, 28, 35, 42   **D** 25, 20, 15, 10

14. It is evening. Write the time on the clock in digital form.
(3)

15. Look at the number line. The dot is on what number?
(4)

```
<---+--+--+--+--●--+--+--+--+--+--+--+--+--+--+--+--+--+--->
    0        5        10        15
```

 Real-World Connection

Cori was assigned a book report on Monday. The teacher told the class that their reports were due ten days after the report was assigned. On what day of the week are the reports due? Cori waited three days to start her report after it was assigned. On which day did she start her report? How many days does she have left to work on it? You can use a calendar to help find the answers.

• Addition

Power Up

facts   Power Up 6

jump   Count up by 10s from 0 to 100.
start   Count up by 25s from 0 to 200.

Draw hands on your clock to show 12:45.
It is afternoon. Write the time in digital form.

Read the temperature on the outside thermometer.
Record the temperature on your worksheet.

mental   **a. Time:** What is the time 1 hour before 1:00 a.m.?
math
b. Number Sense: $4 + \_\_\_\_ = 10$

c. Patterns: 50, 60, ____, 80, 90

d. Money: Find the value of these coins:

problem   Draw the two missing shapes in this pattern:
solving

One way to combine two or more groups is to use **addition.**

$$4 + 3 = 7$$

This picture shows "Four plus three **equals** seven."

We call $4 + 3 = 7$ a number sentence. A **number sentence** is a complete sentence that uses numbers and symbols but not words.

The symbol **+** is a plus sign. The numbers that are added are called **addends.** The answer or total is called the **sum.** Here we show two ways to add 4 and 3.

4	addend	3
+ 3	addend	+ 4
7	sum	7

Notice that the two sums above are the same. This is true for any two numbers that are added. **When we add two or more numbers, the numbers can be added in either order and the sum is the same.**

We can write addends side by side or one above the other. To show 4 plus 3 equals 7 we can write:

$$4 + 3 = 7 \quad \text{or} \quad \begin{array}{r} 4 \\ + 3 \\ \hline 7 \end{array}$$

One way to add is to count up from one of the addends. For example, to add 4 and 3, we start at 4 and count three more numbers.

When 0 is one of the addends, the sum is the same as the other addend. **Adding 0 to a number does not increase the total.**

$$6 + 0 = 6$$

Analyze Which numbers are addends in $6 + 0 = 6$? What is the sum?

The fastest way to add is to remember the addition facts. The addition facts are all the combinations of one digit numbers from $0 + 0$ to $9 + 9$. We will practice the addition facts during the Power Ups. This will help you remember them quickly.

Example 1

Use words and numbers to show this addition.

Two plus four equals six. $2 + 4 = 6$

Example 2

Use color tiles to show this addition.

$8 + 6 = 14$

We combine a group of 8 tiles and a group of 6 tiles to make a group of 14 tiles.

Lesson Practice

a. Use words and numbers to show this addition.

b. Use color tiles to show this addition.

$$6 + 4 = 10$$

c. What is the name for numbers that are added?

d. What is the name for the total when we add?

Find each sum.

e. $4 + 0$ **f.** $2 + 8$

g. $\begin{array}{r} 9 \\ + 6 \\ \hline \end{array}$ **h.** $\begin{array}{r} 7 \\ + 5 \\ \hline \end{array}$

1. **Analyze** What temperature is shown on this
(4) thermometer? Would this be a cool day or a hot day?

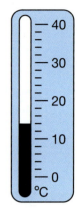

2. Frank left for school at half past seven in the morning.
(5) Write that time in digital form.

Write the next four numbers in each sequence:

3. 7, 14, 21, 28, _____, _____, _____, _____, . . .
(2)

4. 3, 6, 9, 12, _____, _____, _____, _____, . . .
(2)

5. It is the afternoon. Write the time on the clock in digital
(3) form.

6. Look at the number line. The dot is on what number?
(4)

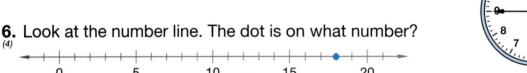

7. What day is five days after Thursday?
(1)

8. What month is five months after July?
(1)

9. Jose went to a movie at a quarter to three in the afternoon. Write
(5) that time in digital form.

10. **Multiple Choice** Which answer is the freezing point of water
(4) in °F?

   A 0°F   **B** 32°F   **C** 212°F   **D** 100°F

11. Look at your classroom clock or use a student clock to help you
(3) answer these questions.

   a. The short hand of a clock points between the 2 and the 3.
   What is the hour?

   b. The long hand points to the 5. How many minutes is it past
   the hour?

   c. It is dark outside. Write the time in digital form.

12. **Formulate** Write a number sentence that shows this addition.
₍₆₎

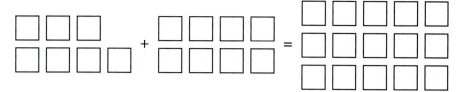

13. **Represent** Draw circles to show this addition.
₍₆₎

$$6 + 6 = 12$$

14. Cory gets up at half past six in the morning. Write that time in digital form.
₍₅₎

15. Look at this number sentence.
₍₆₎

$$5 + 4 = 9$$

a. Which numbers are the addends?

b. Which number is the sum?

LESSON 7

• Subtraction

facts	Power Up 7
jump start	Count up by 2s from 0 to 20 and then back down to 0.
	Draw hands on your clock to show "half past 2." It is afternoon. Write the time in digital form.
	Mark your thermometer to show 30°C.
mental math	**a. Time:** What is the time 2 hours after 3:30 p.m.?
	b. Number Sense: 8 + _____ = 10
	c. Number Sense: _____ + 3 = 10
	d. Calendar: What date is 7 days before the 17th?
problem solving	**Focus Strategy: Draw a Picture or Diagram**

Tina has 3 nickels and her sister has 2 pennies. How much money do they have altogether?

(**Understand**) We will combine 3 nickels and 2 pennies.

(**Plan**) We can *draw a diagram* of the coins. Then we can count up by fives for the nickels and by ones for the pennies.

(**Solve**) We draw a picture of the coins.

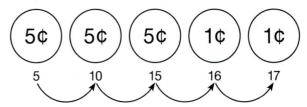

For each nickel, we count up by fives: 5¢, 10¢, 15¢. Then we continue counting by ones for the pennies: 16¢, 17¢.

(**Check**) We found that **3 nickels and 2 pennies have a total value of 17¢.** We drew a diagram to help us find the value.

To subtract we take away a part of the group. For example, if we take 2 marbles from 6 marbles, then 4 marbles are left. Here is one way to show this **subtraction.**

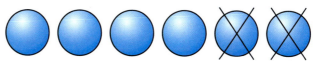

We can also show subtraction on a number line. To subtract 6 − 2 we start at 6 and count down two numbers.

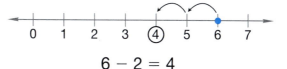

$$6 - 2 = 4$$

"Six minus two equals four."

The symbol − is a minus sign. The answer when we subtract is called the **difference**.

$$\begin{array}{r} 6 \\ -\ 2 \\ \hline 4 \end{array} \rightarrow \text{difference}$$

Order matters when we subtract.

2 − 6 does not equal 6 − 2.

We can write subtraction side by side or one above the other. To show 6 minus 2 equals 4 we write:

$$6 - 2 = 4 \quad \text{or} \quad \begin{array}{r} 6 \\ -\ 2 \\ \hline 4 \end{array}$$

(**Connect**) Why do the arrows on the number line above point to the left?

Example 1

There are 12 months in a year. How many months are left in a year after August? Write a subtraction number sentence that shows the answer.

We can draw a picture to help us solve the problem. We show the first letter of each month.

August is the eighth month, so after August there are **4 months.** We write the number sentence this way.

$$12 - 8 = 4$$

Example 2

Find the difference.

$$10 - 3$$

Here are 2 ways to subtract 3 from 10. In each example we start with 10.

1. Draw 10 circles and mark out 3 circles.

2. Find 10 on the calendar and count back 3 days.

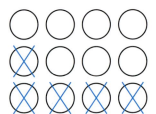

S	M	T	W	T	F	S
4	5	6	⑦	8	9	10

Example 3

Use words and numbers to write the subtraction shown.

Twelve minus five equals seven: $12 - 5 = 7$.

Example 4

Draw circles to show this subtraction.

$$14 - 6 = 8$$

We draw 14 circles and cross out 6 circles. There are 8 circles left.

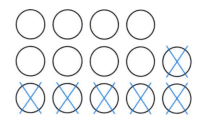

The fastest way to subtract is to remember the subtraction facts. We will practice the subtraction facts during the Power Ups. This will help you remember the facts quickly.

Lesson Practice

a. There are 7 days in a week. Five days have passed. How many days of the week are left?

b. There are 12 months in a year. How many months are left in a year after February? Write a subtraction number sentence that shows the answer.

c. Use words and numbers to write the subtraction shown.

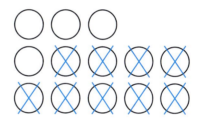

d. Draw circles to show this subtraction.

11 − 5 = 6

Find each difference.

e. 5 − 1   **f.** 10 − 2

g. 4 − 3   **h.** 6 − 4

1. **Explain** How would you use this number line to find $8 - 2$?
(7)

2. **Represent** Draw circles to show the addition $7 + 5$.
(6)

Write the next four numbers in each sequence:

3. 18, 24, 30, _____, _____, _____, _____, …
(2)

4. 18, 27, 36, _____, _____, _____, _____, …
(2)

5. What month has an extra day in leap years?
(1)

6. It is morning. Write the time on the clock in digital
(3) form.

Find each sum and name the addends.

7. $7 + 3$ **8.** $8 + 5$
(6)   (6)

9. Draw a number line with one tick mark for each number 0–10.
(4) Label 0, 5, and 10. Draw a point to represent the number 8.

10. What temperature is shown on this thermometer?
(4)

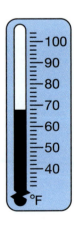

11. If the time is a quarter to noon, how do we write the
(5) time in digital form?

12. Yesterday afternoon, Tamara's mom picked her up
(5) from the movie at half past four. Write that time in
digital form.

13. Look at the number line. The dot is on what number?
(4)

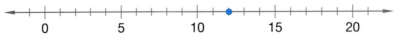

14. The clock shows the time Ashlee leaves for school
every morning. Write the time in digital form.

₍₃₎

15. Jamal goes to football practice at 6:15 p.m. Write the
time in words using a fraction of an hour.

₍₅₎

*Real-World
Connection*

Jade is reading a 14-page book. If she reads 4 pages before
dinner and seven pages after dinner, how many pages does she
need to read to get to the end of the book?

LESSON 8

• Addition and Subtraction Fact Families

 **Power Up**

facts   Power Up 8

jump start   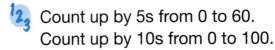 Count up by 5s from 0 to 60.
                   Count up by 10s from 0 to 100.

                   Draw hands on your clock to show 1:15. It is morning.
                   Write the time in digital form.

                   Mark your thermometer to show 100°F.

mental math   **a. Number Sense:** Use a calendar to add: 14 + 7

                   b. Time: It is night. What time will it be 3 hours after the
                   time on this clock?

                   c. Patterns: 20, 18, _____, 14, 12

                   d. Number Sense: 10 + 3

problem solving Berto has 3 dimes, 1 nickel, and 3 pennies. How much
                    money does he have in all?

The three numbers that make an addition fact also make a subtraction fact.

$$3 + 4 = 7 \qquad 7 - 4 = 3$$

Using 3, 4, and 7 we can write another addition and subtraction fact.

$$4 + 3 = 7 \qquad 7 - 3 = 4$$

Together, these four facts are called an addition and subtraction fact family. A **fact family** is a group of related facts.

Discuss How are the four facts shown related?

Example 1

Write two addition facts and two subtraction facts with the numbers 3, 7, and 10.

Addition facts: The addends 3 and 7 equal 10. We can write the addends in either order.

$$3 + 7 = 10$$

$$7 + 3 = 10$$

Subtraction facts: We start with the sum above, 10. We can subtract 7 or we can subtract 3.

$$10 - 7 = 3$$

$$10 - 3 = 7$$

Example 2

Which of these sets of numbers *cannot* be used to make a fact family?

A 1, 2, 3   B 2, 4, 6   C 2, 3, 4

Choice A	Choice B	Choice C
1 + 2 = 3	2 + 4 = 6	2 + 3 does not equal 4
2 + 1 = 3	4 + 2 = 6	3 + 2 does not equal 4
3 − 2 = 1	6 − 4 = 2	4 − 3 does not equal 2
3 − 1 = 2	6 − 2 = 4	4 − 2 does not equal 3
fact family	fact family	*not* a fact family

We see that **choice C** is not a fact family.

Lesson Practice

a. Write two addition facts and two subtraction facts using the numbers 2, 5, and 7.

b. Write two addition facts and two subtraction facts using the numbers 4, 6, and 10.

c. Three months plus 9 months total 12 months. Write two addition facts and two subtraction facts using 3, 9, and 12.

d. **Multiple Choice** Which of these sets of numbers can be used to make an addition and subtraction fact family?

A 3, 4, 5 **B** 3, 6, 9 **C** 6, 8, 10

Written Practice *Distributed and Integrated*

1. How many months of the year are left after September?
(1)

2. Look at the number line. The dot is on what number?
(4)

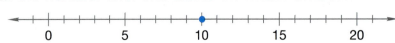

3. Jenny's alarm went off at a quarter to seven in the morning. Write
(5) the time in digital form.

Find the next four numbers in each sequence.

4. 60, 55, 50, _____, _____, _____, _____, …
(2)

5. 4, 8, 12, _____, _____, _____, _____, …
(2)

Find each answer.

6. 7 + 8
(6)

7. 9 + 9
(6)

8. 10 − 1
(7)

9. 8 − 7
(7)

10. ⟨ **Conclude** ⟩ Bob came home from school at a quarter after four.
(5)   His sister came home at half past four. Who came home first?

11. Write two addition facts and two subtraction facts using 1, 4,
(8)   and 5.

12. **Multiple Choice** Which of these sets of numbers **cannot** be
(8)   used to make a fact family?

    A 2, 7, 9   **B** 3, 5, 8   **C** 2, 4, 7   **D** 2, 9, 11

13. Mariah got home from school at the time shown. Write
(3)   the time in digital form.

14. Andrew was born on 7/11/01. In what month was
(1)   Andrew born?

15. ⟨ **Justify** ⟩ The temperature outside is 32°F. Dave said that
(4)   it is a hot day. Do you agree? Why or why not?

*Real-World
Connection*

Tyrone had three baseball cards and bought four more from the
card shop. Brittany had four baseball cards and bought three from
the card shop. Who had more baseball cards?

LESSON

9

• **Unknown Addends**

facts   Power Up 9

jump start   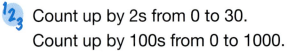 Count up by 2s from 0 to 30.
Count up by 100s from 0 to 1000.

Draw hands on your clock to show "quarter to 11."
It is night. Write the time in digital form.

Read the temperature on the outside thermometer.
Record the temperature on your worksheet.

mental math

a. Time: What is the time 3 hours after 8:15 p.m.?

b. Number Sense: Use a calendar to add: 8 + 7

c. Number Sense: Use the numbers 2, 4, and 6 to write two addition facts and two subtraction facts.

d. Money: Find the value of these coins:

problem solving   There are six chairs at a table in the school library. Each chair has four legs. Find the total number of legs on all six chairs.

Some of the addition examples in this book will have an addend missing. We can use a letter or a box to represent the missing number.

$$3 + m = 8$$

$$3 + \square = 8$$

When an addend is missing and the sum is given, the problem is to find the missing addend.

Example 1

Find each missing addend.

a. $4 + m = 7$

b. $\square + 4 = 9$

a. Think "Four plus what number equals seven?"

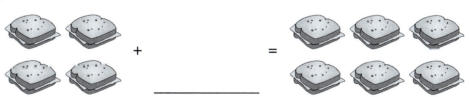

Since $4 + 3 = 7$, **m = 3.**

b. Since $5 + 4 = 9$, $\square$ = **5.**

Example 2

John and Monica made a total of 6 sandwiches for the picnic. John made 4 of the sandwiches.

How many sandwiches did Monica make?

We want to find out how many sandwiches Monica made. We know that there are a total of 6 sandwiches and that John made 4 of them.

Think "Four plus what number equals 6?"

We write $4 + \square = 6$. The $\square$ stands for the number of sandwiches Monica made.

Since $4 + 2 = 6$, we know that Monica made **2 sandwiches**.

Formulate What subtraction number sentence could we use to solve example 2?

Lesson Practice Find the missing addend:

a. $3 + \square = 7$

b. $5 + a = 9$

c. $9 + \square = 16$

d. $2 + n = 7$

e. Maria had 5 pencils. Her friend gave her some more. Then she had 9 pencils. How many pencils did Maria's friend give her?

Written Practice Distributed and Integrated

1. Use the numbers 3, 3, and 6 to write an addition fact and a
(8) subtraction fact.

2. **Analyze** What fraction of an hour is shaded on this
(5) clock?

Add:

3. $6 + 3$
(6)

4. $2 + 5$
(6)

5. **Evaluate** Amy wrote an addition fact and a subtraction fact.
(8)

$$7 + 4 = 11 \qquad 7 - 4 = 3$$

She said the facts belong in the same fact family. Is she correct? Explain your answer.

Find the missing addend:

6. $6 + \square = 10$
(9)

7. $3 + m = 12$
(9)

8. At what number does the minute hand point when it is 7:10 p.m.?
(3)

Subtract:

9. $9 - 3$
(7)

10. $4 - 4$
(7)

11. To what number is the arrow pointing?
₍₄₎

12. One whole hour is equal to how many minutes?
₍₅₎

13. Danielle was born on February 24, 1992. Show how to write this
₍₁₎ date in month/day/year form.

14. Show how to write noon in digital form.
₍₃₎

15. **Predict** If you counted by nines starting with 9, what is the
₍₂₎ fourth number you would say?

Real-World Connection

At the beginning of the week Shannon had 15 pencils. She gave one each to four of her friends and lost two. How many pencils did she give to her friends altogether? How many pencils does she have left?

LESSON 10

• Adding Three Numbers

facts   Power Up 10

jump start   Count up by 5s from 0 to 60 and then back down to 0.

Draw hands on your clock to show "quarter past 3." It is afternoon. Write the time in digital form.

Mark your thermometer to show 20°C.

mental math

a. **Number Sense:** Write a number sentence using the numbers 3, 7, and 10.

b. **Number Sense:** _____ + 2 = 10

c. **Number Sense:** Use a calendar to subtract: 10 − 7

d. **Money:** Find the value of these coins:

problem solving

The table shows the value of one quarter. Find the value of 2 quarters, 3 quarters, and 4 quarters and fill in the table with the correct values.

Quarters	Value
1	25¢
2	
3	
4	

To add three numbers we use two steps.

Step 1: We add two of the numbers.

Step 2: We add the third number to the sum of the first two numbers.

Here we use these steps to add 4 + 3 + 5.

Step 1: Add 4 + 3.   4 + 3 + 5
                              └──┘
                                7

Step 2: Add 7 + 5.   7   + 5 = 12

We can add 4, 3, and 5 in any order. The sum is always 12.

   4 + 3 + 5 = 12   3 + 5 + 4 = 12   5 + 4 + 3 = 12

(**Represent**) Draw circles to show all three number sentences.

Example 1

Show three ways to add 3 + 6 + 5.

We show all three ways using the two-step method we learned above.

First way:

Step 1: Add 3 + 6.   3 + 6 + 5
                                     └──┘
Step 2: Add 9 + 5.   9 + 5 = **14**

Second way:

Step 1: Add 6 + 5.   3 + 6 + 5
                                         └──┘
Step 2: Add 3 + 11.   3 + 11 = **14**

Third way:

Step 1: Add 3 + 5.   3 + 6 + 5
                                     └──────┘
Step 2: Add 8 + 6.   8 + 6 = **14**

Example 2

Sara walked for 5 minutes, jumped rope for 1 minute, and jogged for 4 minutes. How many minutes did Sara exercise?

We add the minutes in two steps

Walked	5
Jumped	+ 1 ⌐
Jogged	+ 4 ⌐ 5
Total	10 minutes

For step 1 we add $1 + 4 = 5$.

For step 2 we add $5 + 5 = 10$.

Sara exercised for **10 minutes.**

Lesson Practice Add.

a. $1 + 3 + 2$ **b.** $4 + 4 + 4$

c. $6 + 5 + 4$ **d.** $5 + 4 + 1$

e. Carol has 8 sheets of orange paper, 5 sheets of black paper, and 2 sheets of blue paper on her desk. How many sheets of paper does she have in total?

Written Practice *Distributed and Integrated*

1. Name the last three months of the year. Which of these three months has only 30 days?
(1)

2. **Analyze** The short hand of a clock points between the 1 and the 2. The long hand points to the 8. It is dark outside. What time is it?
(3)

Write the next four numbers in each sequence.

3. 7, 14, 21, 28, _____, _____, _____, _____, ...
(2)

4. 3, 6, 9, 12, _____, _____, _____, _____, ...
(2)

Analyze Write the missing numbers in this sequence.

5. 6, 12, 18, _____, 30, _____, 42, _____, ...
(2)

Find each missing addend in problems **6** and **7**.

6. $8 + n = 14$
(9)

7. $1 + \square = 9$
(9)

8. How many days are in five weeks?
(1)

Add.

9. $9 + 2 + 7$
(10)

10. $6 + 3 + 5$
(10)

Find each answer.

11. $8 - 3$
(7)

12. $7 - 1$
(7)

13. Write two addition facts and two subtraction facts using the numbers 1, 5, and 4.
(8)

14. Use words and numbers to write the addition shown.
(6)

$$\begin{matrix} \bigcirc\ \bigcirc \\ \bigcirc\ \bigcirc \end{matrix} + \begin{matrix} \bigcirc\ \bigcirc \\ \bigcirc\ \bigcirc\ \bigcirc \end{matrix} = \begin{matrix} \bigcirc\ \bigcirc\ \bigcirc\ \bigcirc \\ \bigcirc\ \bigcirc\ \bigcirc\ \bigcirc\ \bigcirc \end{matrix}$$

15. **Analyze** Look at this number sentence.
(6, 10)

$$5 + 4 + 3 = 12$$

a. Which numbers are the addends?

b. Which number is the sum?

Early Finishers
Real-World Connection

Kaycie scored 8, 11, and 9 points in her first three basketball games. She scored 7, 6, and 10 points in her last three games. What is the total number of points she scored in the first three games? What is the total number of points she scored in the last three games?

Focus on

• Pictographs and Bar Graphs

A meteorologist is a person who studies the weather. Meteorologists measure the weather and keep careful records. The records help them predict the weather.

Jan wants to be a meteorologist. She recorded information about the weather near her home for many months. For example, she counted the number of sunny days in each month of the year. She made a tally mark for each sunny day. Here is her tally for the first three months.

Sunny Days

Month	Tally
January	||||| ||||| ||
February	||||| |||
March	||||| ||||| ||||

The information Jan collected is called **data.** To display this data, she made a type of **graph** called a pictograph. A **pictograph** uses a small image on the graph to show data. Jan chose a picture of the sun to stand for sunny days. Here is Jan's pictograph.

Sunny Days	
January	☼ ☼ ☼ ☼ ☼ ☼
February	☼ ☼ ☼ ☼
March	☼ ☼ ☼ ☼ ☼ ☼ ☼

Key
☼ = 2 days

The **key** shows us that each sun picture stands for 2 days. To count the number of sunny days we count by 2.

1. The row for March shows how many sun pictures?

2. How many sunny days did Jan count in March?

3. (Conclude) If Jan counts 10 sunny days in April, how many suns will she draw?

Jan recorded the high temperature in degrees Celsius every day during the first five days of March.

High Temperatures in March

Date	1st	2nd	3rd	4th	5th
°C	8	10	14	12	10

To display her data Jan made a **bar graph.**

High Temperatures in March

(bar graph showing Temperature (°C) on the y-axis from 0 to 16 and Date on the x-axis: 3/1 = 8, 3/2 = 10, 3/3 = 14, 3/4 = 12, 3/5 = 10)

4. What is the title of the graph?

5. Read the labels on the bottom and the side of the bar graph. What two kinds of information does the graph show?

6. What was the high temperature on March 4? How do you know?

7. Looking at the graph, how can you tell which day was warmest?

Pictograph and Bar Graph

Materials: **Lesson Activity 5**

Pictograph: Create a pictograph titled *Rainy Days* from this data.

Rainy Days

Month	Number of Days
January	9
February	12
March	6

Use the symbol ☁ to stand for 3 rainy days.

Bar Graph: Make a graph titled *Sunny Days in Spring*.

8. Label the bottom of the graph *Months*.

9. Write April, May, and June in order.

10. Label the scale going up the left side *Number of Days*.

11. Look at the **scale**. There is a 0 at the bottom and a 30 at the top. Count by 5s from zero to label the other five **tick marks**.

12. Use the following data to make your graph.

Sunny Days in Spring

Month	Number of Days
April	10
May	15
June	25

Investigate Further

a. In November, Jan recorded 16 sunny days, 8 rainy days, and 6 cloudy days. Follow the models in this lesson to sketch a bar graph to display this data using three bars and a scale that increases by twos.

b. Jan counted 8 cloudy days in October, 6 cloudy days in November, and 10 cloudy days in December. Follow the models in this lesson to make a pictograph to display this data. Draw a picture of a cloud to represent two days.

LESSON 11

• Place Value

Power Up

facts	Power Up 11
jump start	Count up by 10s from 0 to 100. Count up by 25s from 0 to 200.

Draw hands on your clock to show "quarter to 10." It is night. Write the time in digital form.

Mark your thermometer to show 36°F.

mental math

a. Number Sense: Use the numbers 4, 5, and 9 to write a subtraction fact.

b. Number Sense: 9 + 1 + 3

c. Number Sense: 8 + 2 + 3

d. Money: Find the value of these coins:

problem solving

Kaniyah drew this number line.

0   5   20

She forgot to label two of the tick marks. What two numbers are missing? Explain your answer.

There are ten **digits** in our number system:

0, 1, 2, 3, 4, 5, 6, 7, 8, 9.

These 10 digits can be used to make any number. The number 247 has three digits, 2, 4, and 7.

Each digit in a number has a place value. The **place value** of a digit is decided by its position in the number. We can write the number 247 in a place value chart.

Hundreds	Tens	Ones
2	4	7

The 2 in the hundreds place has a value of 2 hundreds or 200.

The 4 in the tens place has a value of 4 tens or 40.

The 7 in the ones place has a value of 7 ones or 7.

Money can help us understand our number system. For example, we can use $100 bills, $10 bills, and $1 bills to show place value.

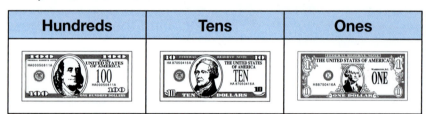

Hundreds	Tens	Ones

Read this story and see if you can figure out how much money Cindy had.

Cindy played a board game with her friends. At the end of the game, Cindy counted all of her money. She had three $10 bills, seven $1 bills, and five $100 bills. How much money did Cindy have?

We will place the bills in three groups. The $100 bills have the greatest value. We place the $100 bills on the left. Next we place the $10 bills beside them. Then we place the $1 bills to the right.

5

3

7

We see that Cindy had five hundreds, three tens, and seven ones. She had 537 dollars, which we can write as $537 or $537.00.

Activity

Place Value

Materials: **Lesson Activity 6** and **Lesson Activities 7–9** or money manipulatives (bills only)

Cindy's friend counted her money at the end of the game. She had eight $1 bills, four $100 bills, and nine $10 bills. How much money did Cindy's friend have?

Use your place value chart and bills to show how much money Cindy's friend has. Write this amount of money using a dollar sign.

Example 1

Matt counted his money. He had six $1 bills, four $100 bills, and three $10 bills. How much money did Matt have?

We arrange the money mentally: first hundreds, then tens, then ones.

4 hundreds, 3 tens, 6 ones

Matt had $436.

We can also show place value using base-10 blocks.

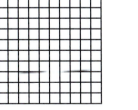  ☐

A flat has 100 cubes.
It has a value of 100.

A 10-stick has 10 cubes.
It has a value of 10.

A unit cube is 1 cube.
It has a value of 1.

Example 2

Write the number shown using digits.

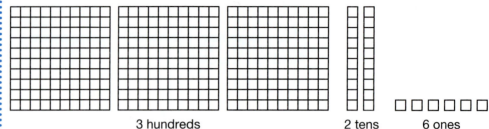

3 hundreds   2 tens   6 ones

The number shown is **326.**

Model Use money manipulatives to show the number 326.

When we show the value of each place of a number, we are writing the number in **expanded form.** The place value chart below shows the number 362.

Hundreds	Tens	Ones
3	6	2

300   +   60   +   2

The three is in the hundreds place. It has a value of 3 hundreds or 300.

The six is in the tens place. It has a value of 6 tens or 60.

The two is in the ones place. It has a value of 2 ones or 2.

The expanded form of 362 is **300 + 60 + 2.**

Example 3

Use bills to show $320. Then write 320 in expanded form.

3   2

Expanded form: **300 + 20**

Model Use base-10 blocks to show the number 320.

Lesson Practice

a. Nate had seven $10 bills, three $100 bills, and two $1 bills. How much money did Nate have?

b. Add: $200 + $5 + $70

Use bills to show each number. Then write each number in expanded form.

c. 54   **d.** 230

e. 403   **f.** 324

Written Practice
Distributed and Integrated

1. In expanded form, 250 is 200 + 50. Write 520 in expanded form.
(11)

2. How much money is five $10 bills and four $1 bills?
(11)

3. (Analyze) How much money is three $100 bills, six $1 bills, and
(11) five $10 bills? What digit is in the hundreds place?

4. Multiple Choice How many minutes is a quarter of an hour?
(5)
   A 15 minutes   **B** 30 minutes   **C** 45 minutes   **D** 60 minutes

5. Write 365 in expanded form.
(11)

(Generalize) Write the next four numbers in each sequence. Write the
rule for each.

6. 7, 14, 21, 28, _____, _____, _____, _____, . . .
(2)

7. 30, 27, 24, _____, _____, _____, _____, . . .
(2)

8. Find the sum of 5, 9, and 5.
(10)

9. To what number is the arrow pointing?
(4)

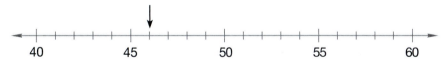

10. The minute hand of a clock points to what number at 8:10?
(3)

Find each answer:

11. $200 + $30 + $5   **12.** 8 + 2 + 3
(11)   (10)

13. $6 + 4 + 2$
(10)

14. $10 - 6$
(7)

15. Use 2, 7, and 9 to write two addition facts and two subtraction
(8)   facts.

Find the missing addend:

16. $6 + m = 14$
(9)

17. $7 + m = 10$
(9)

18. What temperature is shown on this thermometer?
(4)

19. Write a quarter after six in the morning in digital
(5)   form.

20. Use the words "addend" and "sum" to name each
(6)   number in this addition problem: $3 + 7 = 10$.

Early Finishers

Real-World Connection

Jin was asked to solve this riddle.

What number am I? I have three digits. There is a 6 in the tens place, a 9 in the ones place, and a 4 in the hundreds place.

Jin said the answer to the riddle was 694. Did Jin give the correct answer? Explain.

LESSON 12

• Reading and Writing Numbers Through 999

facts   Power Up 12

jump start   Count up by 2s from 0 to 30.
Count up by 5s from 0 to 60.

Draw hands on your clock to show "half past 5." It is morning. Write the time in digital form.

Mark your thermometer to show 12°F.

mental math

a. Time: It is morning. What time will it be 2 hours after the time shown on this clock?

b. Number Sense: 7 + 3 + 4

c. Number Sense: 7 + 7

d. Number Sense: 8 + 10

problem solving   Beth had 4 coins in her hand. As she counted up to find the total value of the coins, she said, "10¢, 15¢, 16¢, 17¢." What coins does Beth have in her hand?

New Concept

We can write numbers using words or digits. To write the names of whole numbers through 999 (nine hundred ninety-nine), we need to know number words and how to put them together.

We can use the following number words to write all 1,000 numbers from 0–999:

0	zero	10	ten	20	twenty
1	one	11	eleven	30	thirty
2	two	12	twelve	40	forty
3	three	13	thirteen	50	fifty
4	four	14	fourteen	60	sixty
5	five	15	fifteen	70	seventy
6	six	16	sixteen	80	eighty
7	seven	17	seventeen	90	ninety
8	eight	18	eighteen	100	one hundred
9	nine	19	nineteen		

We write a hyphen between two number words that are combined to name a two-digit number. Here are some examples of numbers that are written with a hyphen.

24	twenty-four
37	thirty-seven
568	five hundred sixty-eight

Analyze What is the place value of the number word before the hyphen?

Example 1

Use digits to write two hundred seventy-five.

275

Example 2

Use words to name $384.

Notice that we do not use the word "and" when we name the number.

Three hundred eighty-four dollars

Example 3

Write the total amount of money shown using words and numbers.

$231, two hundred thirty-one dollars

Lesson Practice

Use numbers and a dollar sign to write the following.

a. six hundred twenty-five dollars

b. two hundred eight dollars

Use words to write each amount.

c. $648   **d.** 706

e. Write the amount of money shown with numbers and words.

Written Practice   *Distributed and Integrated*

1. Look at the number line. The dot represents what number?
(4)

2. **Analyze** In expanded form, 360 is 300 + 60. Write 640 in
(11)   expanded form. What digit is in the ones place?

3. Joan has five $10 bills and nine $1 bills. Name that amount using
(11, 12)   words and using a dollar sign and digits.

4. **Formulate** How many months of the year are left after
(1, 7)   the fifth month? How would you write this as a subtraction
number sentence?

Generalize Write the next four numbers in each sequence. Write the rule for each.

5. 6, 12, 18, 24, ____, ____, ____, ____, …
(2)

6. 44, 40, 36, ____, ____, ____, ____, …
(2)

7. Use words to write $683.
(12)

8. The greatest three-digit counting number is nine hundred ninety-nine. Use digits to write that number.
(12)

Find each answer:

9. $600 + $7 + $50
(11)

10. 6 + 8
(6)

11. 4 + 2 + 7
(10)

12. 9 + 7
(6)

13. 9 − 5
(7)

14. 8 − 5
(7)

15. Draw a number line with a tick mark for each number from 1 to 5. Draw a dot on the number 2.
(4)

16. Find the missing addend: $5 + x = 9$
(9)

17. On Monday morning Larry arrived at school at the time shown on this clock. What time was it?
(3)

18. Use 3, 5, and 8 to write two addition facts and two subtraction facts.
(8)

19. Ben was eighth in line. Brenda was twelfth in line. How many people were between Ben and Brenda?
(1)

20. **Multiple Choice** What is the total number of days in two weeks and two days?
(1, 10)

   A 14 days   **B** 15 days   **C** 16 days

• Adding Two-Digit Numbers

Power Up

facts	Power Up 13
jump start	Count up by 10s from 0 to 100 and back down to 0.
	Draw hands on your clock to show "quarter past 4." It is afternoon. Write the time in digital form.
	Mark your thermometer to show 8°C.
mental math	**a. Time:** What is the time 4 hours before 9:30 p.m.?
	b. Patterns: 60, 50, _____, 30, 20
	c. Number Sense: 8 + 6
	d. Number Sense: $3 + $10

problem solving

Focus Strategy: Act It Out or Make a Model

Sam has six $1 bills. He makes two equal groups with the bills. How much money is in each group?

(**Understand**) We are asked to find how much money is in each group that Sam made.

(**Plan**) We can use money manipulatives to act out the problem.

(**Solve**) We make two equal groups of $1 bills:

$3

$3

We see that there are three $1 bills in each group.

(**Check**) It makes sense that each group contains $3, because $3 + $3 = $6.

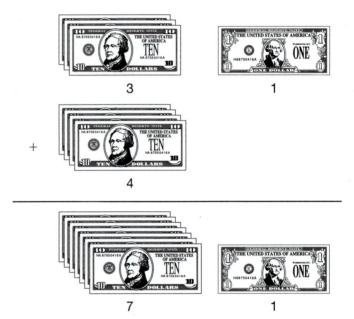 New Concept

We can use money manipulatives to help us add two-digit numbers. We will use $10 bills to show the digits in the tens place. We will use $1 bills to show the digits in the ones place.

We can use $10 bills and $1 bills to add $31 to $40. First, we show $31. Next, we show $40. Then, we combine the bills.

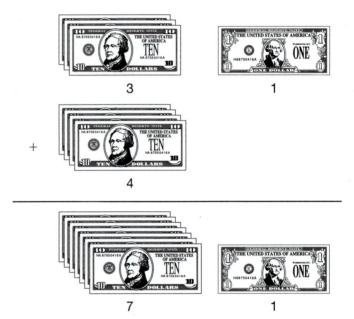

The total is 7 tens and 1 one, which is **$71.**

To add the numbers with pencil and paper, we line up the digits by their place value. Next, we add the digits in the ones place. Then, we add the digits in the tens place.

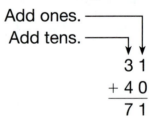

Add ones.

Add tens.

$$\begin{array}{r} 31 \\ + 40 \\ \hline 71 \end{array}$$

Discuss Why is it important to keep the digits lined up when we add?

Regrouping

Materials: $10 bills and $1 bills, **Lesson Activity 6**

Malik has five $10 bills and twelve $1 bills. How much money does he have?

1. Place five $10 bills in the tens column on the place value chart.

2. Place twelve $1 bills in the ones column on the place value chart. Use your remaining money manipulatives as the "bank."

3. We cannot write a 12 in the ones place. We need to trade ten of the $1 bills for one $10 bill.

4. When we trade, we call this regrouping.

   a. Take ten of the $1 bills to the bank and trade them for one $10 bill.

   b. Add the $10 bill to the tens column.

5. Count the number of tens and the number of ones. How much money does Malik have?

Discuss When do we regroup $1 bills?

Example

Use money manipulatives to add 36 and 27.

First, we show $36. Next, we show $27. Then, we combine the $10 bills and the $1 bills.

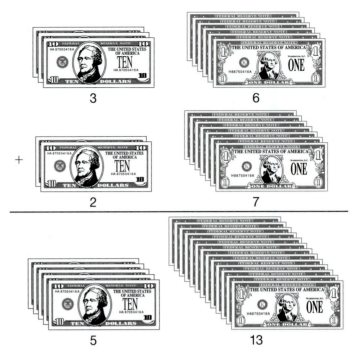

Since there are thirteen $1 bills, we regroup ten of the $1 bills into one $10 bill.

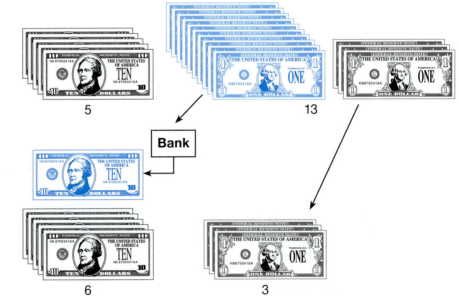

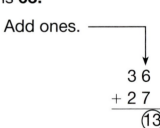

Now we have 6 tens and 3 ones, which is **63.**

To add the numbers with pencil and paper, we line up the digits. Next, we add the ones and get 13.

Add ones.

$$\begin{array}{r} 3\,6 \\ +\,2\,7 \\ \hline ⑬ \end{array}$$

Thirteen ones is the same as 1 ten and 3 ones. We write the 3 in the ones place and add the 1 ten to the other tens. We show this by writing a 1 above the column of tens. Then we add the tens.

Add ones. ⎯⎯⎯⎯⎯⎤
Add tens. ⎯⎯⎯⎯⎯⎯⎯⎤
$$\begin{array}{r} 1 \\ 3\,6 \\ +\,2\,7 \\ \hline 6\,3 \end{array}$$

Lesson Practice

Model Use your money manipulatives to add:

a. $60 + $22

b. 10 + 49 + 30

c. 30 + 20 + 5

d. $20 + $20

e. How much money is four $10 bills and eleven $1 bills?

Add:

f. $39 + $23   **g.** 26 + 52   **h.** 35 + 16

Written Practice

Distributed and Integrated

1. (11, 12) **Analyze** Use words to write $526. What digit is in the tens place?

2. (13) Add $30 + $30.

3. (11) Write 256 in expanded form.

4. (1, 7) How many months are left in the year on the last day of September?

Generalize Write the next four numbers in each sequence. Write the rule for each.

5. (2) 55, 50, 45, 40, _____, _____, _____, _____, …

6. (2) 14, 21, 28, 35, _____, _____, _____, _____, …

7. Add $53 and $10.
(13)

8. Use digits and a dollar sign to write five hundred twenty-four
(12) dollars.

9. How many minutes are equal to half an hour?
(5)

Find each answer.

10. $60 + $20
(13)

11. 15 + 19
(13)

12. $80 + $500
(11)

13. $5 + $300 + $40
(11)

14. 12 − 2
(7)

15. 9 − 2
(7)

16. Three pennies plus 7 pennies equals 10 cents. Use 3, 7, and 10 to
(8) write two addition facts and two subtraction facts.

17. How do you write a quarter to eight in the morning in digital form?
(5)

Find the missing addend:

18. 6 + g + 7 = 14
(9)

19. 45 + m = 55
(9)

20. (Analyze) Write November 10, 1998, in month/day/year form.
(1) How many months are before November in the year?

*Real-World
Connection*

Smithfield Elementary is having a fall festival. The festival begins at 4:00 p.m. and ends at 7:00 p.m. Every fifteen minutes a student's name will be drawn to win a pumpkin. The last student's name will be drawn when the festival ends. How many students will win a pumpkin before the festival is over? You may wish to use a clock to help find the answer.

• Subtracting Two-Digit Numbers

Power Up

facts	Power Up 14
jump start	Count up by 7s from 0 to 35. Count up by 100s from 0 to 1000. Draw hands on your clock to show a "quarter of noon." Write the time in digital form. Mark your thermometer to show 48°F.

mental math

a. Fact Family: Find the missing number in this fact family:

$$3 + \square = 7 \qquad 7 - \square = 3$$
$$\square + 3 = 7 \qquad 7 - 3 = \square$$

b. Time: It is morning. What time was it 3 hours before the time shown on this clock?

c. Number Sense: $6 + 10 + 1$

d. Number Sense: $6 + 9$

problem solving

Sharon and Letrisa are planning a nature hike. If Sharon brings 4 bottles of water to share, how many bottles can each girl have?

In this lesson we will use money manipulatives and pencil and paper to subtract two-digit numbers.

Read this story and see if you can figure out how much money Daniel has.

Daniel had saved $35. He spent $12 on a birthday present for his sister. How much money does Daniel have left?

First we show $35. Then we take away $12.

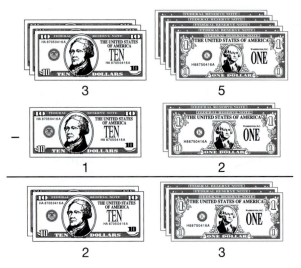

We see that Daniel has **$23** left.

To subtract the numbers with pencil and paper, we line up the digits by their place value. First, we subtract the digits in the ones place. Then we subtract the digits in the tens place.

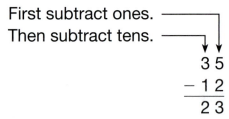

First subtract ones.
Then subtract tens.

$$
\begin{array}{r}
3\,5 \\
-\ 1\,2 \\
\hline
2\,3
\end{array}
$$

Regrouping for Subtraction

Materials: $10 bills and $1 bills, **Lesson Activity 6**
Subtract: $75 − $28

1. Place seven $10 bills in the tens column on the place value chart.

2. Place five $1 bills in the ones column on the place value chart.

3. Can we take away eight $1 bills?

4. What can we do since we can't take away $8?

5. Take one $10 bill and trade it for ten $1 bills. Add the ten $1 bills to the ones column.

6. Can we take away eight $1 bills now?

7. How many $10 bills do we have now?

8. Can we take away two $10 bills?

9. What is $75 − $28?

Example

Use money manipulatives to subtract 61 and 15.

First, we regroup $61 into 5 tens and 11 ones. Next, we take away $15.

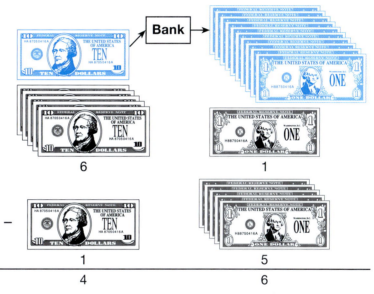

We have 4 tens and 6 ones left over, which is **46.**

$$\begin{array}{r} \overset{5}{\cancel{6}}\overset{1}{1} \\ -\ 1\ 5 \\ \hline 4\ 6 \end{array}$$

To subtract with paper and pencil, we write the first number on top. Next, we rewrite 61 as 5 tens and 11 ones. Then, we subtract the digits in the ones place and the digits in the tens place.

Discuss When do we need to regroup to subtract?

Lesson Practice Subtract. You may use your money manipulatives.

a. 81 − 30

b. $97 − $55

c. 14 − 10

d. $56 − $27

e. 35 − 19

f. $43 − $35

1. Use words to write $247.
(12)

2. Write 247 in expanded form.
(11)

3. List the months of the year that have exactly 30 days.
(1)

Generalize Write the first four numbers in each sequence:

4. ____, ____, ____, ____, 90, 100, 110, 120, ...
(2)

5. ____, ____, ____, ____, 54, 63, 72, 81, ...
(2)

Add or subtract, as shown.

6. $50 − $40   **7.** $50 + $20
(14)   (13)

8. $46 − $32   **9.** $37 + $20
(14)   (13)

10. Use digits and a dollar sign to write eight hundred nineteen dollars.
(12)

11. **Connect** A nickel plus a dime is 15 cents. Use the value of the
(8) coins to write two addition facts and two subtraction facts.

Add or subtract, as shown:

12. $27 + $28   **13.** 7 + 5 + 2
(13)   (10)

14. $55 − $27   **15.** 5 + 5 + 5
(14)   (10)

16. Write "a quarter after four in the morning" in digital form.
(5)

17. **Multiple Choice** Which problem has a sum of 10?
(6)
   A 5 + 10 = 15   **B** 10 = 6 + 4   **C** 10 + 3 = 13   **D** 10 + 10 = 20

Analyze Find the missing addend:

18. $90 + m + 10 = 110$ **19.** $5 + m + 10 = 25$
(9)   (9)

20. Subtract: 11 − 4
(7)

• Rounding to the Nearest Ten and Hundred

facts

Power Up 15

jump start

Count up by 5s from 50 to 100.
Count up by 25s from 0 to 200.

Draw hands on your clock to show "half past 1." It is afternoon. Write the time in digital form.

Mark your thermometer to show 24°F.

mental math

a. Fact Family: Find the missing number in this fact family:

$$\square + 6 = 8 \quad 8 - \square = 6$$
$$6 + \square = 8 \quad 8 - 6 = \square$$

b. Expanded Form: Write 47 in expanded form.

c. Number Sense: $7 + 9$

d. Money: Find the value of these coins:

problem solving

Draw a square on your paper. Then draw a straight line across the square from one corner to the opposite corner. What shapes do you see inside the square?

One of the sentences below states exactly how much a radio costs. The other sentence states about how much the radio costs. Can you tell which sentence uses a rounded price?

The radio costs about $50.

The radio costs $47.

The first sentence uses a rounded price. We often **round** exact numbers to nearby numbers that are easier to work with and to understand.

In this lesson we will practice rounding amounts of money to the nearest ten dollars and the nearest hundred dollars.

To round an exact number to the nearest ten, we find the closest number that ends in zero. Those are the numbers we say when we count by tens (10, 20, 30, 40, and so on).

We will use this number line to round 47 to the nearest ten.

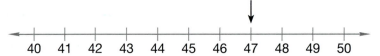

We see that 47 is between 40 and 50. Since 47 is closer to 50 than to 40, we round 47 to 50. We say that 47 is "about" 50. When rounding to the nearest ten, we look at the ones place. If the digit is 5 or greater, we round up.

Example 1

The price of the jacket is $63. What is the price to the nearest ten dollars?

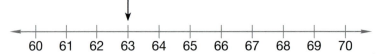

We know that $63 is between $60 and $70. Since $63 is closer to $60 than to $70, we round $63 down to **$60.** We can say that $63 is about $60.

Now we will learn to round numbers to the nearest hundred. To round an exact number to the nearest hundred, we find the closest number that ends in two zeros. Those are the numbers we say when we count by hundreds (100, 200, 300, 400, and so on). When rounding to the nearest hundred, we look at the tens place. If the digit is 5 or greater, we round up.

Example 2

The camera cost $367. What is the price to the nearest hundred dollars?

The number 367 is between 300 and 400. Halfway between 300 and 400 is 350. Since 367 comes after 350, it is closer to 400 than it is to 300. We see this on the number line below.

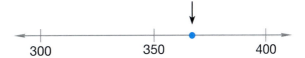

The number line shows why $367 rounded to the nearest hundred is **$400.** We can say that $367 is about $400.

Example 3

Jasmine bought a computer game that cost $49 and a new baseball glove that cost $28. Round the prices to help you find about how much money she spent.

This is a some and some more story. Jasmine spent some money and then spent some more money. We are asked to find "about" how much money she spent.

We begin by writing the addition problem from the story.

$$\begin{array}{r} \$49 \\ + \$28 \\ \end{array} \quad \begin{array}{l} \text{rounds to} \\ \text{rounds to} \\ \end{array} \quad \begin{array}{r} \$50 \\ + \$30 \\ \hline \$80 \\ \end{array}$$

The word "about" in the question tells us that the answer may be a rounded number. To answer the question, we may round the numbers in the story.

Last, we add the rounded numbers.

Since $50 + $30 = $80, we know that the total is $80. **Jasmine spent about $80.**

Verify Add 49 + 28. How can rounding help you decide if your answer is reasonable?

Lesson Practice Round these prices to the nearest ten dollars:

a.  $27

b.  $83

c.  $49

Round these prices to the nearest hundred dollars:

d.  $317

e.  $168

f.  $729

g. Write a number sentence for this story after rounding the numbers. Then write a complete sentence to answer the question.

> *Last weekend Frank made muffins to sell at the carnival. He made 38 muffins on Saturday and 23 muffins on Sunday. About how many muffins did Frank make on Saturday and Sunday? (Hint: To find the answer, first round both numbers to the nearest ten.)*

Written Practice *Distributed and Integrated*

1. The refrigerator cost $894. Use words to write $894.
(12)

2. Write 894 in expanded form.
(11)

3. **Multiple Choice** Jamal bought a shirt for $28 and pants for
(15) $33. About how much did the shirt and pants cost? (*Hint:* Round
the prices before adding.)

  A $50   **B** $60   **C** $70   **D** $80

4. Round these amounts to the nearest ten.
(15)
  a. $24   **b.** $36

5. Round these amounts to the nearest hundred.
(15)
  a. $621   **b.** $876

Add or subtract as shown.

  6. $75 − $50   **7.** $500 + $50
  (14)   (11)

  8. $31 − $15   **9.** $35 + $16
  (14)   (13)

10. Use 5, 6, and 11 to write two addition facts and two subtraction
(8) facts.

11. (Represent) Draw a number line from 50–60 with one tick mark
(4) for each number. Label 50, 55, and 60. Draw dots at 52, 54,
and 57.

12. Is $768 closer to $700 or $800?
(15)

13. Use digits and a dollar sign to write seven hundred eighty-six
(12) dollars.

Add or subtract, as shown:

  14. $30 + $30 + $30   **15.** $42 − $12
  (10, 13)   (14)

16. (Generalize) What are the next four numbers in this sequence?
(15) Write the rule.

        8, 16, 24, 32, _____, _____, _____, _____, …

Find the missing addend:

  17. 100 = 60 + m **18.** 4 + q = 11
  (9)   (9)

19. Verify $27 rounds to 30. Explain why this is correct.
(2)

20. It is morning. What time is shown on this clock? Write the time twice, once with digits and once with words.
(3, 5)

Real-World Connection

Austin walks his neighbor's dog every day for three months to earn money for a new scooter. Would he make more money if he walks his neighbor's dog for the months of February, March, and April, or June, July, and August? Explain your answer.

LESSON 16

• Adding Three-Digit Numbers

facts   Power Up 16

jump start    Count up by 10s from 100 to 200.
                 Count up by 100s from 0 to 1000.

                 Draw hands on your clock to show "quarter to 8." It is morning. Write the time in digital form.

                 Mark your thermometer to show 18°C.

mental math **a. Calendar:** How many days are in 3 weeks?

                 b. Number Sense: 13 − 10

                 c. Time: What is the time 2 hours after midnight?

                 d. Number Sense: 9 + 8

problem solving   Draw the next two shapes in this pattern:

New Concept

Visit www. SaxonMath.com/ Int3Activities for a calculator activity.

In Lesson 13 we used money manipulatives to add two-digit numbers. In this lesson we will use money manipulatives to help us add three-digit numbers. We will use $100 bills to show digits in the hundreds place, $10 bills to show digits in the tens place, and $1 bills to show digits in the ones place.

Example 1

Use money manipulatives to add $472 and $216.

We show $472 and $216. Then we combine the $1 bills, $10 bills, and $100 bills.

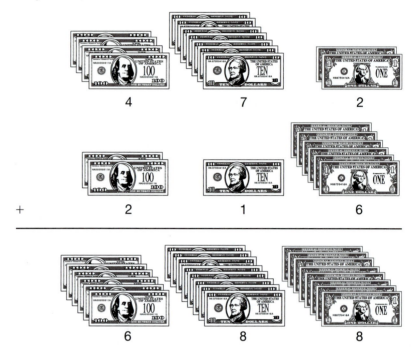

The sum is 6 hundreds, 8 tens and 8 ones. That equals **$688.**

We can also use pencil and paper to calculate the sum. First we add the digits in the ones place. Then we add the digits in the tens place. Last we add the digits in the hundreds place.

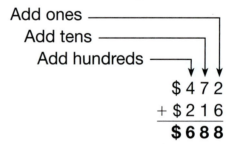

Add ones ─────────────────┐
Add tens ──────────────┐ │
Add hundreds ───┐   │ │
                ▼   ▼ ▼
        $ 4 7 2
      + $ 2 1 6
        $ 6 8 8

Example 2

Use money manipulatives to add $365 and $427.

We show $365 and $427. Then we combine the $1 bills, the $10 bills, and the $100 bills.

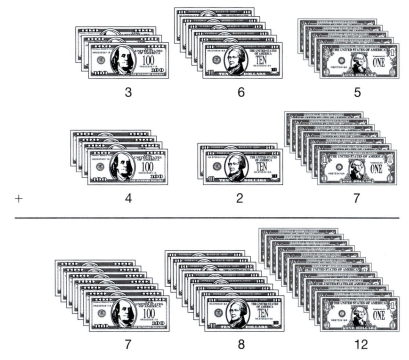

Since there are twelve $1 bills, we can regroup ten of the $1 bills into one $10 bill. Now we have 7 hundreds, 9 tens, and 2 ones. That equals **$792.**

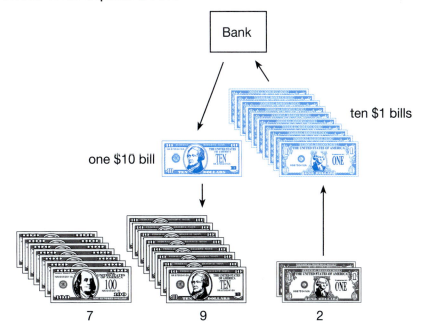

We can also use pencil and paper to find the sum. First we add the digits in the ones place and get 12. Twelve ones is the same as 2 ones and 1 ten. We write 2 in the ones place and add the 1 ten to the other tens. Then we add the digits in the tens place and get 9. Last we add the digits in the hundreds place and get 7.

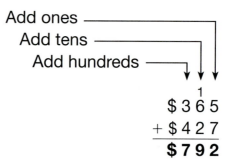

Add ones
Add tens
Add hundreds

$$
\begin{array}{r}
\overset{1}{} \\
\$365 \\
+\ \$427 \\
\hline
\$792
\end{array}
$$

Example 3

Use money manipulatives to add $154 and $382.

We show $154 and $382. Then we combine the $1 bills, the $10 bills, and the $100 bills.

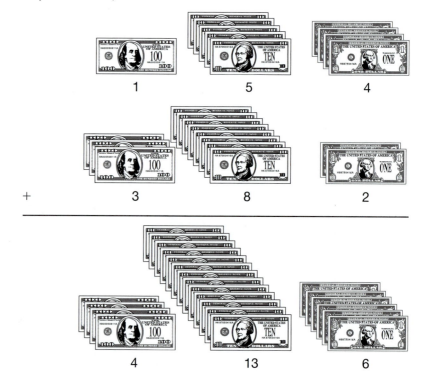

There are a total of six $1 bills so we do not regroup in the ones place. Since there are thirteen $10 bills, we can regroup ten of the $10 bills into one $100 bill.

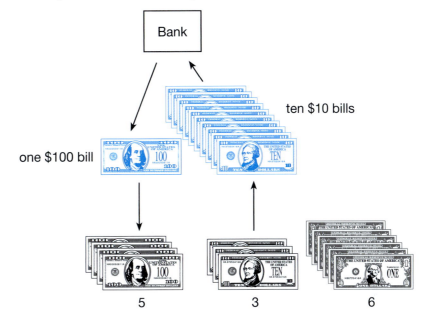

Now we have **5 hundreds, 3 tens** and **6 ones.** That equals **$536.**

We can also use pencil and paper to find the sum. First we add the digits in the ones place. Then we add the digits in the tens place. Last we add the digits in the hundreds place. The sum in the tens column, 13, is the same as 3 tens and 1 hundred. We write 3 in the tens place and add 1 hundred to the other hundreds. Then we add the digits in the hundreds place and get 5.

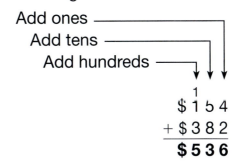

(**Discuss**) You will find that some 3-digit addition problems need regrouping in the ones place and the tens place. How could you show regrouping for both columns?

(**Lesson Practice**) (**Model**) Use your money manipulatives to add:

a. $430 + $120   **b.** 123 + 245

c. 249 + 325   **d.** $571 + $364

e. How much money is five $100 bills, three $10 bills and thirteen $1 bills?

Add:

f. 431 + 263   **g.** $648 + $237   **h.** 362 + 194

Written Practice · Distributed and Integrated

1. Use manipulatives to find the sum of $162 and $253.
(16)

2. Use words to write $444.
(12)

3. Miguel had five $10 bills. How much money did Miguel have?
(11)

4. Write 560 in expanded form.
(11)

Conclude What are the next four numbers in each sequence?

5. 3, 6, 9, 12, _____, _____, _____, _____, ...
(2)

6. 6, 12, 18, 24, _____, _____, _____, _____, ...
(2)

7. **Analyze** Jess had one $100 bill, three $10 bills, and nine
(11, 16) $1 bills. Gayle had four $100 bills, two $10 bills, and three $1 bills. How much money did Jess and Gayle have altogether?

8. Round these amounts to the nearest hundred:
(15)
   a. $872   **b.** $463

9. Round these numbers to the nearest ten:
(15)
   a. 81   **b.** 16

10. The bus arrives each morning at a quarter to eight. The minute
(3, 5) hand of a clock points to what number when the bus arrives?

11. **Multiple Choice** Which expression below is equal to the
(5, 6) number of minutes in a quarter of an hour plus the number of minutes in a half hour?

   A 4 + 30   **B** 25 + 30   **C** 15 + 30   **D** 25 + 50

Add or subtract, as shown:

12. $16 − $5
₍₁₄₎

13. 58 + 10
₍₁₃₎

14. 8 + 8 + 8
₍₁₀₎

15. $25 − $17
₍₁₄₎

16. 127 + 631
₍₁₆₎

17. $58 − $30
₍₁₄₎

Find the missing addend:

18. 35 + m = 55
₍₉₎

19. 100 = ☐ + 30
₍₉₎

20. Brock wrote the addition fact 8 + 2 = 10. Use the numbers 8,
₍₈₎ 2, and 10 to write one more addition fact and two subtraction facts.

Real-World Connection

Fernanda's school was having a carnival to raise money for a new playground. Fernanda was in charge of collecting money at the ticket booth. When the carnival was over she had collected twelve $10 bills and seven $1 bills. Name the amount that Fernanda collected twice, once using words and once using a dollar sign and digits.

• Comparing and Ordering, Part 1

Power Up

facts	Power Up Worksheet 17
jump start	Count up by 2s from 0 to 30. Count up by 5s from 0 to 60.
	Draw hands on your clock to show "quarter after 8." It is evening. Write the time in digital form.
	Mark your thermometer to show the freezing point of water, 32°F.

mental math

a. Number Sense: $13 - 9$

b. Number Sense: $16 - 9$

c. Money: $\$3 + \$9$

d. Money: Find the value of these coins:

problem solving

Use your money manipulatives to help you act out this problem:

Darrin had $25. He went to the carnival and spent some of the money. After the carnival, Darrin had $10. How much money did Darrin spend at the carnival?

New Concept

Sometimes we need to compare the costs of different items to find the lowest price. In this lesson we will compare amounts of money and arrange amounts of money in order.

We can use **comparison symbols** to show how we compare money. If two amounts are equal, we write an equal sign between the two numbers. If the amounts are not equal, we write < or > so that the small end points to the number that is less. We read the symbol > as "**greater than**." We read the symbol < as "**less than**."

Example 1

Samantha saved her birthday money to buy new skates. She found skates she liked at The Super Store for $58. She found the same skates at Bob's Sporting Goods for $72. Write the two prices with a comparison symbol. Where should Samantha buy her skates?

Samantha wants to buy the skates that cost less. We can use money to compare the two prices.

First we will look at the $10 bills. There are five $10 bills in $58 and seven $10 bills in $72. Since five is less than seven, we know that $58 is less than $72. We write $58 < $72.

We can also use a number line to compare 58 and 72. Remember that a number line shows numbers on a line in counting order.

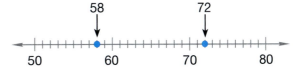

We see on the number line that 58 comes before 72. We say that 58 is less than 72. We write 58 < 72. Since $58 is less than $72, Samantha should buy her skates at **The Super Store.**

Example 2

Mr. Jung is shopping for an airline ticket. A ticket from Blue Skies Airline costs $475. A ticket from World Wide Airlines costs $425. Which ticket costs more? Write < or > in the circle to complete the comparison.

$475 ◯ $425

We will use money to compare $475 and $425.

| 4 | 7 | 5 |
| 4 | 2 | 5 |

First we will look at the $100 bills. There are four $100 bills in $475 and four $100 bills in $425. Since the $100 bills in each number are the same, we look next at the $10 bills. There are seven $10 bills in $475 and two $10 bills in $425. We know that 7 is more than 2, so $475 is greater than $425.

$475 > $425

We can also use the number line below to compare 475 and 425.

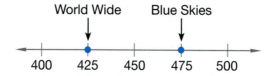

We see that 475 comes after (is farther right than) 425 on the number line. So 475 is greater than 425.

$475 > $425

Example 3

Columbus Elementary School third graders sold magazines to raise money for their school. The three students who raised the most money won prizes. Li raised $261. Bud raised $172. Ashley raised $285. Show the total raised by each of these students in order from least to greatest.

We will use money manipulatives to find the order of these three amounts. Show $261, $172, and $285 on your desk using money manipulatives.

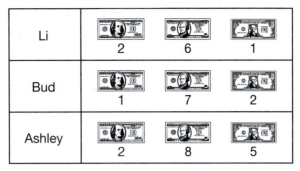

Li	2	6	1
Bud	1	7	2
Ashley	2	8	5

We will look at the $100 bills first. Since one $100 bill is less than two $100 bills, we know that $172 is the least number.

Now we will compare $261 and $285. In $261 and $285 the number of $100 bills is equal, so we look at the $10 bills. Since six $10 bills are less than eight $10 bills, $261 is less than $285.

The total amount of money raised by each student in order from least to greatest is **$172, $261, $285.**

Analyze Which has the greater value, two $10 bills or four $1 bills?

Lesson Practice

a. Choose < or > to compare $29 and $57.

b. Which costs less, a basketball for $15 or a baseball bat for $30?

c. Choose < or > to compare $193 and $163.

d. Write these numbers in order from least to greatest: 273, 615, 480

Written Practice *Distributed and Integrated*

1. Add $524 and $112.
(16)

2. Which is greater, $432 or $423?
(17)

3. Use words to write $405.
(12)

4. **Analyze** Round three hundred forty-seven dollars to the nearest
(12, 15) hundred.

5. Add $119 and $119.
(16)

Conclude What are the next four numbers in each sequence?

6. 6, 12, 18, 24, _____, _____, _____, _____, . . .
(2)

7. 60, 70, 80, 90, _____, _____, _____, _____, . . .
(2)

8. Round these numbers to the nearest ten:
(15)
   a. 92   **b.** 68

9. Round these amounts to the nearest hundred:
(15)
   a. $438   **b.** $398

10. **Analyze** Gia checked the outside thermometer
(4) while getting ready for school. Should she wear a
T-shirt or a sweater? Explain your choice.

Add or subtract, as shown. Use manipulatives for
problem **11:**

11. $248 + $300   **12.** $36 − $12
(16)   (14)

13. 7 + 7 + 7   **14.** 36 − 34
(10)   (14)

15. 52 + 28   **16.** $26 − $23
(13)   (14)

Find the missing addend:

17. $25 + m = 100$ **18.** ☐ $+ 36 = 66$
(9)   (9)

19. It is almost time for dinner. What time is shown on
(3, 5) this clock? Write the time twice, once using digits
and once using words.

20. **Multiple Choice** Altogether, how many days are in
(1, 13) December and January?

   A 60 days   **B** 61 days   **C** 62 days

LESSON 18

- • Some and Some
  More Stories, Part 1

Power Up

facts	Power Up 18
jump start	Count up by 100s from 0 to 1000 and back.
	Draw hands on your clock to show "half past midnight." Write the time in digital form.
	Mark your thermometer to show 51°F.
mental math	**a. Expanded Form:** 100 + 20 + 3
	b. Patterns: 20, 15, _____, 5, 0
	c. Number Sense: 14 − 9
	d. Measurement: 6 inches + 6 inches
problem solving	**Focus Strategy:** Guess and Check

Tyler and Chad have 10 toy cars altogether.

Tyler has 2 more cars than Chad. How many toy cars does each boy have?

(Understand) We are told the total number of toy cars. We are asked to find how many toy cars each boy has.

(Plan) We can *guess* an answer and then *check* our guess.

Solve We look for two numbers whose sum is 10 and whose difference is 2. We can guess 7 cars for Tyler and 5 cars for Chad. The total is 12 cars, which is too high. We can guess 6 cars for Tyler and 4 cars for Chad. The total is 10 cars.

Check There are 10 cars altogether, and $6 + 4 = 10$. Six is 2 more than 4 ($6 - 4 = 2$). Our guess of 6 cars for Tyler and 4 for Chad is correct.

New Concept

Many word problems tell a story. If we understand what is happening in the story, it is easier to solve the problem. Look at this story.

John had $5. Then he earned $7. Now John has $12.

Notice what is happening in this story. John had some money. Then he earned some more money. We call a story like this a **some and some more** story.

A some and some more story is an addition story.

Some + some more = total

$5 + $7 = $12

We can also write the information this way.

Some	$\longrightarrow$	$5
+ Some more	$\longrightarrow$	+ $7
Total	$\longrightarrow$	$12

Generalize Why is a some and some more story an addition story?

Example 1

Write a number sentence for this story.

Nolan threw 25 baseballs. Later, he threw 62 baseballs. Altogether, Nolan threw 87 baseballs.

25 baseballs + 62 baseballs = 87 baseballs

Example 2

Here is a some and some more story with a missing number. Find the missing number. Then answer the question.

Mickey saw 15 rabbits. Then he saw 7 more rabbits. How many rabbits did he see in all?

Mickey saw some, and then he saw some more.

Some + some more = total

15 rabbits + 7 rabbits = ☐ rabbits

Since 15 + 7 = 22, we know the total is 22 rabbits. We answer the question with a complete sentence. **Mickey saw 22 rabbits in all.**

Example 3

Make up a some and some more story for this number sentence.

$$\$5 + \$3 = \$8$$

Write a story and tell it to a classmate or to your teacher. One story for this number sentence is:

Tasha had $5. Her mom gave her $3. Then she had $8.

Lesson Practice

a. Write a number sentence for the following story.

Gus had seven dollars. He received five dollars more in a birthday card. Then Gus had twelve dollars.

b. The following story has a missing number. Write a number sentence for this story. Then write a complete sentence to answer the question.

Diane ran 5 laps in the morning. She ran 8 laps in the afternoon. How many laps did she run in all?

c. Write a number sentence for this story. Then write a complete sentence to answer the question.

Dan had some play money in his pockets. He had $50 in his left pocket and $25 in his right pocket. How much play money did Dan have in both pockets?

d. Make a some and some more story with a question for this number sentence.

7 birds + 8 birds = ? birds

Written Practice *Distributed and Integrated*

1. Write a number sentence for this some and some more story.
(18) Then write a complete sentence to answer the question.

Sergio had $12. He earned $5 more. Then how much money did Sergio have?

2. (Analyze) Round seven hundred sixty-seven to the nearest
(12, 15) hundred.

3. (Formulate) Write a number sentence for this story. Then write a
(18) complete sentence to answer the question.

Nate had $37. He earned $20 more. Then how much money did Nate have?

4. Use words to write $919.
(12)

5. Write 919 in expanded form.
(11)

6. Find the sum of $167 and $528.
(16)

(Connect) What are the four missing numbers in each sequence?

7. 4, 8, 12, _____, _____, _____, _____, 32, ...
(2)

8. 9, 18, _____, _____, _____, _____, 63, 72, ...
(2)

9. Is $248 closer to $200 or $300?
(15)

10. (Analyze) Marisol's music class starts at a quarter to one in the
(3, 5) afternoon. At a quarter to one, the minute hand is pointing to what number?

Add or subtract, as shown:

11. $65 − $24
(14)

12. 56 − 54
(14)

13. 38 − 15
(14)

14. 6 + 6 + 6
(10)

15. $56 − $32
(14)

16. $100 + $60 + $4
(11)

Find the missing addend:

17. 52 = m + 32
(9)

18. ☐ + 10 = 100
(9)

19. Show how to write a quarter to nine o'clock in the morning in
(5) digital form.

20. Multiple Choice What is the total number of minutes in a
(5) quarter of an hour plus half of an hour?

    A 15   **B** 30   **C** 45   **D** 60

Real-World Connection

Susan went on a field trip to an alligator farm in Jacksonville. A worker told the children that an alligator clutch on the farm had hatched 70 alligators. Twelve babies were male. How many babies were female?

LESSON 19

• Subtracting Three-Digit Numbers, Part 1

Power Up

facts   Power Up 19

jump start   Count up by 10s from 100 to 200.
                 Count up by 25s from 0 to 200.

Draw hands on your clock to show "five o'clock." It is afternoon. Write the time in digital form.

Mark your thermometer to show normal body temperature, 37°C.

mental math

a. Fact Family: Find the missing number in this fact family:

$$\square + 9 = 11 \quad 11 - 9 = \square$$
$$9 + \square = 11 \quad 11 - \square = 9$$

b. Time: It is evening. What time will it be 4 hours after the time shown on this clock?

c. Number Sense: $2 + 10 + 1$

d. Number Sense: $3 + 11$

problem solving

Sylvia has 3 coins. The total value is 12¢. What coins does Sylvia have?

New Concept

Visit www. SaxonMath.com/ Int3Activities for a calculator activity.

In this lesson we will use money manipulatives to help us subtract three-digit numbers. We will also subtract using pencil and paper.

Predict What bills should we use to help us subtract three-digit numbers?

Example 1

Matt and Cindy were playing a board game. Cindy had $537. When she landed on Matt's property, she had to pay $125. How much money did Cindy have left?

Cindy had $537. To show this we put on our desk five $100 bills, three $10 bills, and seven $1 bills.

5   3   7

She had to pay Matt $125. We show this by taking from the desk one $100 bill, two $10 bills, and five $1 bills. Then we count how much money Cindy has left.

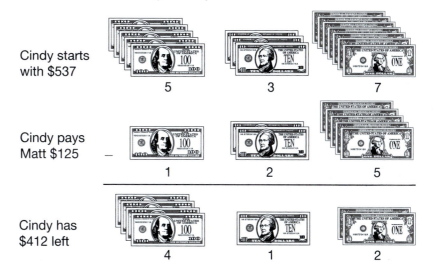

Cindy starts with $537

5   3   7

Cindy pays Matt $125

—   1   2   5

Cindy has $412 left

4   1   2

After paying Matt, Cindy had four $100 bills, one $10 bill, and two $1 bills. She had **$412.**

We can also subtract with pencil and paper. First we subtract the digits in the ones place. Next we subtract the digits in the tens place. Last we subtract the digits in the hundreds place.

Start
↓

$537
− $125
$412

Sometimes we need to trade one $10 bill for ten $1 bills or one $100 bill for ten $10 bills when subtracting. Read this example to see how Matt used the bank to regroup his money.

Example 2

Matt has $430. If he pays Cindy $70 rent, how much money will Matt have left?

Matt's money equals four $100 bills and three $10 bills.

He needs to pay $70, which is seven $10 bills. He does not have enough $10 bills, so he can trade one $100 bill for ten $10 bills.

one $100 bill 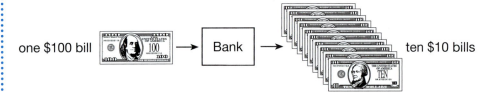 ten $10 bills

After regrouping, Matt has three $100 bills and thirteen $10 bills. Now he can pay Cindy $70 with seven $10 bills.

Matt has $430

Matt pays Cindy $70

Now Matt has

After paying Cindy, Matt will have three $100 bills and six $10 bills, which is **$360.**

We can also subtract with pencil and paper. First we subtract the **digits** in the ones place. We know that 0 ones from 0 ones is zero. Next we look at the digits in the tens place.

Start
↓

$$\begin{array}{r} \$430 \\ -\ \$\ 70 \\ \hline 0 \end{array}$$

We cannot subtract 7 from 3, so we trade one of the hundreds for 10 tens. We show that we are trading one of the hundreds by drawing a line through the 4 and writing a 3 above it. We now have 3 hundreds and 13 tens. We show the 13 tens by placing a small 1 in front of the 3.

$$\begin{array}{r} \overset{3}{ } \\ \$4\!\!\!/\,30 \\ -\ \$\ 70 \\ \hline 0 \end{array}$$

Now we are ready to subtract.

$$\begin{array}{r} \overset{3}{ } \\ \$4\!\!\!/\,30 \\ -\ \$\ 70 \\ \hline \$360 \end{array}$$

Example 3

Cindy had $472. She had to pay Matt $238 for a new property. How much money did Cindy have left?

We will subtract using pencil and paper. First we look at the **digits** in the ones place. We cannot subtract 8 ones from 2 ones so we trade one of the tens for 10 ones. Now we have 6 tens and 12 ones. We are ready to subtract.

$$\begin{array}{r} \overset{6}{ } \\ \$47\!\!\!/\,2 \\ -\ \$238 \\ \hline \$234 \end{array}$$

Lesson Practice

Model Solve problems **a** and **b** using money manipulatives. Then show the subtraction with pencil and paper.

a. Cindy had $843. She landed on a property that had a house. She had to pay Matt $125. How much money did she have left?

b. Matt had $720. He had to pay Cindy $250. How much money did he have left?

Use pencil and paper to subtract.

c. $63 − $47

d. $354 − $182

Written Practice
Distributed and Integrated

1. Find the sum of $321 and $123.
(16)

Formulate Write number sentences for the stories in problems **2** and **3.** Then write a complete sentence to answer each question.

2. Nellie has $25. Julie has $20. How much money do Nellie and Julie have together?
(18)

3. Yolanda had $450. She earned $120 more from babysitting. Then how much money did Yolanda have? Use manipulatives to help you find the answer.
(16, 18)

4. Is $67 closer to $60 or $70? Is $670 closer to $600 or $700?
(15)

5. Write 330 in expanded form.
(11)

6. Use manipulatives to find the difference of $567 and $232.
(19)

What are the next four numbers in each sequence?

7. 14, 21, 28, 35, _____, _____, _____, _____, ...
(2)

8. 25, 50, 75, 100, _____, _____, _____, _____, ...
(2)

9. Round $91 to the nearest ten. Round $910 to the nearest hundred.
(15)

10. **Conclude** Terrance has a doctor's appointment at a quarter past nine in the morning. He arrived at the doctor's office at 9:30 a.m. Was he on time for his appointment? Explain your answer.
(5)

Add or subtract, as shown:

11. $56 + $43
(13)

12. $59 − $35
(14)

13. 6 + 8 + 10
(10)

14. $14 − $4
(14)

15. 5 + 7 + 3
(10)

16. $35 − $20
(14)

Find the missing addend:

17. **Connect** $10 = m + 6 + 4$
(9, 10)

18. ☐ + 36 = 40
(9)

19. Martin's clock looked like the clock at right when he woke up in the morning. What time was it?
(3)

20. **Multiple Choice** Which is *not* a way to say 9:45 a.m.?
(3, 5)

    A a quarter after nine in the morning

    B nine forty-five in the morning

    C a quarter of ten a.m.

    D a quarter to ten in the morning

Real-World Connection

Preston took a tour of an art museum in Dallas. For every exhibit he viewed, Preston received a sticker to put in his museum guide. After the first hour Preston had 4 stickers. By the end of the tour Preston had 19 stickers in his museum guide. How many stickers did Preston get after the first hour of the museum tour?

• **Some Went Away Stories, Part 1**

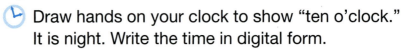

facts	Power Up 20
jump start	Count up by 2s from 0 to 30 and then back down to 0.
	Draw hands on your clock to show "ten o'clock." It is night. Write the time in digital form.
	Mark your thermometer to show 15°C.
mental math	**a. Number Sense:** 4 + 11
	b. Number Sense: 8 + 8
	c. Money: $7 + $10
	d. Money: Find the value of these coins:

problem solving	**Focus Strategy: Write a Number Sentence**

Tim started with $6. Then he earned some money doing chores. After getting paid for the chores, Tim had $16. How much money did Tim earn?

Understand We are given a beginning amount and a total amount. We are asked to find how much money Tim earned.

Plan We can *write a number sentence.*

Solve We can write this number sentence: $6 + ☐ = $16.

Now we need to find the missing number. We know that 6 + 10 = 16, so **Tim earned $10.**

Check Our answer makes sense, because $6 + $10 = $16. This is the total Tim had after getting paid.

Word problems often tell a story. We carefully read the story to understand what is happening. We have practiced some and some more stories. Here is another kind of story.

John had $12. He spent $5 for a book. Then he had $7.

Notice what is happening in this story. John had some money. Then some of John's money "went away" because he spent it. This is a **some went away** story.

A some went away story is a subtraction story.

Some − some went away = what is left

$12 − $5 = $7

We can also write the information this way.

$$
\begin{array}{rr}
\text{Some} & \$12 \\
- \text{ Some went away} & - \$\ 5 \\
\hline
\text{What is left} & \$\ 7 \\
\end{array}
$$

(**Generalize**) What is another name for the number that tells "what is left"?

Rebecca had $65. Then she spent $13. How much money did Rebecca have left?

At the beginning of the story, Rebecca had $65. Then $13 "went away." We are asked how much money she had left. We write a number sentence for this story.

$$\$65 - \$13 = \square$$

Since $65 − $13 is $52, we know the difference is $52. We answer the question with a complete sentence.

Rebecca had $52 left.

(**Formulate**) Show another way to write the information in this story.

Write a number sentence for each story. You may use your money manipulatives to help you find the answer. Answer each question with a complete sentence.

a. Donald had $26. He spent $12 on a new game. How much money did he have left?

b. Sarah had $43. Then she bought a new coat for $36. How much money did Sarah have after she bought the coat?

c. Jim had $40. He bought a shirt that cost $25. How much change did he get?

Written Practice
Distributed and Integrated

1. List the first three months of the year and the number of days in each of those months in a common year.
(1)

Formulate Write number sentences for the stories in problems **2** and **3.** Then write a complete sentence to answer each question.

2. Mike had $450. Rita paid him $140 more. Then how much money did Mike have?
(16, 18)

3. Jenny had $36. She spent $12 for a class party. Then how much did Jenny have?
(20)

4. Use words to write $647.
(12)

5. Write 647 in expanded form.
(11)

6. Write the amount of money shown using numbers.
(12)

Generalize What are the next four numbers in each sequence? Write the rule for each.

7. 18, 27, 36, 45, _____, _____, _____, _____, ...
(2)

8. 18, 24, 30, 36, _____, _____, _____, _____, ...
(2)

9. Use money to help you with this subtraction:
(19)
$$\$340 - \$126$$

10. Use 7, 8, and 15 to write two addition facts and two subtraction
(8)   facts.

Add or subtract, as shown:

11. $57 − $52   **12.** 25 + 73
(14)   (13)

13. 340 − 140   **14.** $279 + $119
(19)   (16)

15. 5 + 7 + 4 + 10   **16.** $34 + $51
(10)   (13)

17. Alan, Kalia, and Alita went on a fishing trip. Alan caught 3 fish.
(10)   Kalia caught 5 fish. Alita caught 2 fish. How many fish did they
       catch in all?

Find the missing addend:

18. 8 + m = 15   **19.** 56 + ☐ = 86
(9)   (9)

20. (**Justify**) Gina bought a pair of shoes for $27 and a pair of socks
(11. 17,   for $6. She gave the cashier three $10 bills and three $1 bills.
18)   Did she give the cashier the right amount of money? How do you
          know?

Early Finishers
Real-World Connection

DeMario is saving his money for a new telescope so he can learn more about space. The telescope costs $76. Demario had saved $23 and earned $14 more doing chores around the neighborhood. How much more does DeMario need to buy the telescope? You may wish to use money manipulatives to help you find the answer.

Focus on

• Working with Money

In this investigation you will work with a partner to practice **exchanging** money. You will record the results of the exchange on an activity sheet.

Getting Started

Sit with your partner. You and your partner should each take three $100 bills, four $10 bills and five $1 bills from the bank. Now you each have $345. Leave the rest of the money in the bank so both partners can reach it.

Each money exchange needs a Student A and a Student B. Decide with your partner who will be A and who will be B. You will keep this letter for the whole activity.

Money Exchanges

Materials: **Lesson Activity 10**

Record each exchange on your worksheet.

First Exchange

Be sure each partner begins with $345.

- Student A gives Student B $32.
- Count how much money each student has. Record your answer on your worksheet. Begin the second exchange.

Second Exchange

- Student B gives Student A $43.
- Count how much money each student has. Record your answer on your worksheet. Begin the third exchange.

Third Exchange

- Student A gives Student B $128. Student A needs eight $1 bills but only has six.

Go to the bank. Student A trades one $10 bill for ten $1 bills.

Now Student A can give $128 to Student B.

- After the exchange, B has twelve $1 bills.

Go to the bank. Student B trades ten $1 bills for one $10 bill.

- Count how much money each student has. Record your answer on your worksheet. Include the regrouping. Begin the fourth exchange.

Fourth Exchange

- Student B gives Student A $114. Student B needs four $1 bills but only has two.

Go to the bank. Student B trades one $10 bill for ten $1 bills. Now Student B can give $114 to Student A.

- After the exchange, Student A has twelve $1 bills.

Go to the bank. Student A trades ten $1 bills for one $10 bill.

- Count how much money each student has. Record your answer on your worksheet. Include the regrouping. Begin the fifth exchange.

Fifth Exchange

- Student A gives Student B $161. Student A needs six $10 bills but only has four.

Go to the bank. Student A trades one $100 bill for ten $10 bills. Now Student A can give $161 to Student B.

- After the exchange, Student B has ten $10 bills.

Go to the bank. Student B trades ten $10 bills for one $100 bill.

- Count how much money each student has. Record your answer on your worksheet. Include the regrouping. Begin the sixth exchange.

Sixth Exchange

- Student B gives Student A $164. Student B needs six $10 bills but has none.

Go to the bank. Student B trades one $100 bill for ten $10 bills. Now Student B can give $164 to Student A.

- After the exchange, Student A has fourteen $10 bills.

Go to the bank. Student A trades ten $10 bills for one $100 bill.

- Count how much money each student has. Record your answer on your worksheet. Include the regrouping.

What do you notice about the final sum and difference?

• **Naming Dollars and Cents**
• **Exchanging Dollars, Dimes, and Pennies**

facts   Power Up 21

jump start   Count up by 3s from 0 to 30.
                  Count up by 7s from 0 to 35.

                  Draw hands on your clock to show "half past four."
                  It is morning. Write the time in digital form.

                  Mark your thermometer to show 1°C.

                  Write "forty cents" using digits and a dollar sign.

mental math   a. **Number Sense:** 6 + 11

                  b. **Number Sense:** 15 − 10

                  c. **Expanded Form:** 100 + 70 + 6

                  d. **Number Line:** Which point represents the number 6?

problem solving   Ms. Spurlin asked her students to name their favorite meal of the day. This pictograph shows how the students voted. Write a number sentence to find the total number of students.

Students' Favorite Meal

Meal	Number of Students
Breakfast	🙂 🙂 🙂 🙂 🙂
Lunch	🙂 🙂 🙂 🙂 🙂 🙂 🙂
Dinner	🙂 🙂 🙂 🙂 🙂 🙂

Key
🙂 = 1 student

Naming Dollars and Cents

We can use a number followed by a cent sign (¢) to show an amount of money. A number followed by a cent sign shows the value in cents (pennies).

    324¢   20¢   4¢

We can show a value in cents or in dollars. The dollar sign ($) is written in front of the numbers to show a value in dollars. We use a **decimal point** followed by two places to show cents. Here we show the same amounts of money using a dollar sign instead of a cent sign.

    $3.24 $0.20 $0.04

We read $3.24 by saying, "3 dollars and 24 cents." To read $0.20 we say, "20 cents." We do not read the zero in the dollars place. To read $0.04 we just say "4 cents."

Notice that we do not use a dollar sign and a cent sign together.

        $3.24¢   **INCORRECT**

Exchanging Dollars, Dimes, and Pennies

We can gain a better understanding of money exchange by practicing with bills and coins. For this lesson's activities we will use only the $1 bills, dimes, and pennies from the money kit. These items are traded or grouped by tens.

Activity

Exchange Pennies for Dimes

Materials: **Lesson Activity 11,** money manipulatives

Cut apart the dimes and pennies on **Lesson Activity 11.** Put these with your other money manipulatives. We will call this play money your "money kit."

Take 12 pennies from your money kit and place them on your desk. We will call the money still in your kit "the bank."

1. Name the money on your desk using digits and a cent sign.

2. How can we make the same amount of money using fewer coins?

Trade 10 of the pennies on your desk for 1 dime from the bank.

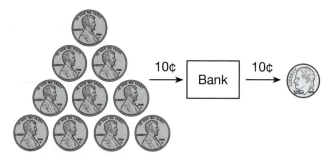

Put the dime on your desk with the remaining pennies.

3. How much money is on your desk now?

4. How do the digits in 12¢ describe the number of coins on your desk?

Exchange Dimes for Dollars

Put 14 dimes and 5 pennies on your desk.

5. How much money is on your desk?

6. How can we make the same amount of money using fewer coins?

Trade 10 of the dimes on your desk for a $1 bill from the bank. Place the $1 bill on your desk with the remaining coins. Arrange the money so that the $1 bill is on the left, the dimes are in the middle, and the pennies are on the right.

7. Now how much money is on your desk?

8. How do the digits 1, 4, and 5 in $1.45 describe the money on your desk?

(**Generalize**) If you add 3 dimes to the money on your desk, how much money will you have?

(**Lesson Practice**)

a. Describe three ways to make 21¢ using coins from the money kit.

b. Describe how to make $3.45 from the money kit using the fewest number of bills and coins.

c. How much money is three $1 bills, 11 dimes, and 12 pennies? Describe how to make the same amount of money using the fewest number of bills and coins.

(**Written Practice**) *Distributed and Integrated*

1. List the last three months of the year and the number of days in
(1) each of those months.

(**Formulate**) Write number sentences for the stories in problems **2** and **3**. Then write a complete sentence to answer each question.

2. Mike had $450. He paid Rita $140. Then how much money did
(20) Mike have?

3. Jenny had $36. She earned $12 more. Then how much did Jenny
(18) have?

4. (**Model**) Use money to show this subtraction. Then subtract
(14) using pencil and paper.

$$\$62 - \$28$$

5. Use words to write $873.
(12)

6. (**Model**) Use money to show this subtraction. Then subtract
(14) using pencil and paper.

$$\$80 - \$54$$

What are the next four numbers in each sequence?

7. 8, 16, 24, _____, _____, _____, _____, …
(2)

8. 4, 8, 12, _____, _____, _____, _____, …
(2)

9. (Analyze) Show how to write ten minutes before midnight in
(3) digital form.

Add or subtract, as shown:

10. 8 + 9 + 10
(10)

11. $54 − $12
(14)

12. $36 + $47
(13)

13. $56 − $21
(14)

14. 495 + 10
(16)

15. 34 − 25
(14)

16. The sign is incorrect. Show two ways to write 99 cents.
(21)

Apples

0.99¢

Find the missing addend:

17. 9 + 4 + m = 15
(9, 10)

18. 100 = 75 + ☐
(9)

19. The sun rose at 5:40 a.m. The minute hand points to what number
(3) at 5:40 a.m.?

20. Finish this rhyme: "Thirty days hath September…"
(1)

Early Finishers

Real-World Connection

An odometer shows you how many miles you've driven in your car. The Changs' car had 347 miles on the odometer when they left for a 148-mile trip to Port Aransas. What did the odometer read when they got to Port Aransas?

LESSON 22

• Adding Dollars and Cents

facts   Power Up 22

jump start
 Count up by 5s from 50 to 100.
Count up by 10s from 100 to 200.

Draw hands on your clock to show "quarter to seven."
It is evening. Write the time in digital form.

Mark your thermometer to show 43°F.

 Use the numbers 3, 6, and 9 to write one addition fact
and one subtraction fact.

mental math

a. **Number Sense:** $9 + 9$

b. **Number Sense:** $12 - 9$

c. **Estimation:** Is $43 closer to $40 or $50?

d. **Time:** It is night. What time will it be
3 hours after the time shown on this
clock?

problem solving

Jim kept a table to show how many
books he read each month. How
many more books did Jim read in
May than in February?

Month	Number of Books
January	3
February	5
March	4
April	4
May	7

Visit www.
SaxonMath.com/
Int3Activities for
an online activity.

In the following "some and some more" story, we need to add dollars and cents to answer the question. We will show how to find the answer by using money manipulatives and by using pencil and paper.

Example

Clara bought a book for $4.85 and a game for $3.72. What was the total price of the book and the game?

On one side of the desk we count out $4.85 for the book. On the other side of the desk we count out $3.72 for the game.

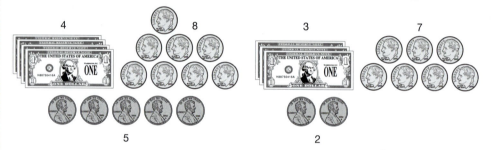

Now we combine the bills and coins to find out how much the items cost altogether. This is what we have.

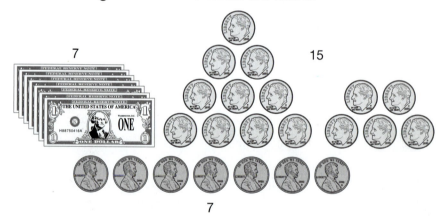

We see that we need to regroup the dimes. We take ten dimes to the "bank" and trade them for one $1 bill. This gives us eight $1 bills and five dimes.

8

5

7

We see that the book and the game together cost **$8.57.**

We can use pencil and paper to find the total price. We start with the digits on the right.

$$
\begin{array}{r}
1 \\
\$4.85 \\
+ \ \$3.72 \\
\hline
.57
\end{array}
$$

We add 5 pennies and 2 pennies and get 7 pennies. Then we add 8 dimes and 7 dimes and get 15 dimes. Since 10 of the 15 dimes make 1 dollar, we write a 5 in the dimes column, and we write a 1 in the dollar column. We place the decimal point to separate dollars from cents. Next we add 4 dollars and 3 dollars and the 1 dollar from the 10 dimes. This makes 8 dollars. Again, the total is **$8.57.**

$$
\begin{array}{r}
1 \\
\$4.85 \\
+ \ \$3.72 \\
\hline
\$8.57
\end{array}
$$

(**Formulate**) If the game cost just 72 cents, show how to write the addition problem and then find the total price.

Lesson Practice Add using money manipulatives. Then add using pencil and paper.

a.
$$
\begin{array}{r}
\$6.44 \\
+ \ \$3.38 \\
\hline
\end{array}
$$

b.
$$
\begin{array}{r}
\$2.72 \\
+ \ \$5.18 \\
\hline
\end{array}
$$

c. Nathan bought a game for $6.29 plus $0.44 tax. What was the total price?

1. How much money is five $1 bills, twelve dimes, and fifteen
(21) pennies?

2. On his first turn, Tom scored 164 points. On his second
(18) turn he scored 200 points. How many points did Tom score
altogether?

3. Tania had three $100 bills and four $10 bills. She had to pay
(20) Latisha $30. Then how much money did Tania have?

4. (Model) Use money to show this subtraction. Then subtract
(14) using pencil and paper.

$$\$81 - \$27$$

5. Use digits and a dollar sign to write one hundred five dollars.
(12)

6. What month is four months after the tenth month?
(1)

7. (Conclude) What are the next four numbers in this sequence?
(2)

18, 24, 30, _____, _____, _____, _____, . . .

8. **Multiple Choice** The price of a jacket is about $80. Which price
(15) below rounds to $80?

    A $73   **B** $93   **C** $82   **D** $89

Add or subtract, as shown:

9. $79
(13) $- \$55$

10. 25
(13) $+ 25$

11. $46 − $35
(14)

12. 48 + 63
(13)

13. $52 − $32
(14)

14. 4 + 7 + 10
(10)

15. (Model) Use money to show this subtraction. Then subtract
(14) using pencil and paper.

$$\$60 - \$24$$

Find the missing addend:

16. $350 + m = 450$
(9)

17. $\square + 10 + 15 = 30$
(9, 10)

18. Sandra looked at the clock after dinner. What time
(3) was it?

19. Write 2¢ using a dollar sign, and write $0.10 using
(21) a cent sign.

20. (**Model**) Draw a number line from 10 to 30 with tick marks
(4) representing each counting number. Label the tick marks for
10, 20, and 30 on your number line and place a point at 25.

Real-World Connection

Marcus brought 6 dimes, 3 nickels, and 4 pennies to school. He gave 2 dimes to the lunch lady for a snack. How much money does he have left?

LESSON 23

• **Subtracting Three-Digit Numbers, Part 2**

Power Up

facts   Power Up 23

jump start   Count up by 3s from 0 to 30.
Count up by 7s from 0 to 35.

 Draw hands on your clock to show "quarter after two."
It is morning. Write the time in digital form.

Mark your thermometer to show 29°F.

Use the numbers 5, 6, and 11 to write one addition fact
and one subtraction fact.

mental math   **a. Money:** 70¢ + 20¢

b. Patterns: 100, 200, 300, 400, _____

c. Calendar: The year 2000 was a leap year. Which of
the following years is also a leap year?

1999   **2004**   **2005**   **2007**

d. Number Line: Which point represents the
number 2?

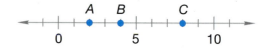

problem solving   Together, Jennie and Laura picked 8 flowers. Laura picked
2 more flowers than Jennie. How many flowers did each
girl pick?

New Concept

When we subtract money, we often need to "go to the
bank" to trade a larger bill for ten smaller bills.

Example 1

Roger has $520. He needs to give his brother $50. Then how much money will Roger have?

We will find the answer two ways. First we will use money. Roger has $520. We show five $100 bills and two $10 bills.

5   2

To give his brother $50, he will give him five $10 bills. Since Roger only has two $10 bills, we will need to trade one $100 bill for ten $10 bills.

one $100 bill   ten $10 bills

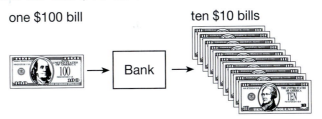

After we regroup, Roger has four $100 bills and twelve $10 bills, but he still has $520.

12

4

Now Roger can give his brother five $10 bills. After giving his brother the money, Roger has four $100 bills and seven $10 bills. **Roger will have $470 left.**

Now we show a pencil-and-paper solution. We start with the ones place. We know that 0 ones from 0 ones is zero. Next we look at the tens place.

Start
$\downarrow$
520
$- \ \ 50$

We cannot subtract 5 from 2, so we trade one of the hundreds for 10 tens. We show that we are trading one of the hundreds by drawing a line through the 5 and writing a 4 above it. We now have 4 hundreds and 12 tens, which we show by placing a small 1 in front of the 2, like this:

$$
\begin{array}{r}
^{4}\!\!\!\not{5}\,^{1}2\,0 \\
-\ \$\ \ 5\,0 \\
\hline
\end{array}
$$

We are ready to subtract.

$$
\begin{array}{r}
\$\,^{4}\!\!\!\not{5}\,^{1}2\,0 \\
-\ \$\ \ 5\,0 \\
\hline
\$4\,7\,0
\end{array}
$$

Roger had $470 left.

(**Generalize**) How many $10 bills are equal to $520?

Example 2

Mrs. Jones had $465. She paid $247 for her new microwave oven. How much money did she have left?

First we will show the solution using money. Mrs. Jones started with $465.

4	6	5

She spent $247, or two $100 bills, four $10 bills, and seven $1 bills. Since she only had five $1 bills, we will trade one $10 bill for ten $1 bills. That leaves four $100 bills, five $10 bills, and fifteen $1 bills.

4	5	15

Now we can take away seven $1 bills, four $10 bills, and two $100 bills. **Mrs. Jones had $218 left.**

Now we will show a pencil and paper solution.

Start

$$\begin{array}{r} \overset{5}{\$4\cancel{6}5} \\ - \$247 \\ \hline 218 \end{array}$$

We start with the ones place.

We cannot subtract seven from five so we trade 1 ten for 10 ones. Then we subtract.

$$\begin{array}{r} \overset{5\ 1}{\$4\cancel{6}5} \\ - \$247 \\ \hline \mathbf{\$218} \end{array}$$

Lesson Practice

Perform each subtraction in **a–c** using money manipulatives and using pencil and paper.

$$\begin{array}{r} \overset{3}{\cancel{4}}\overset{}{12}6 \\ - 176 \\ \hline 250 \end{array}$$

a.
$$\begin{array}{r} \$426 \\ - \$176 \\ \hline 250 \end{array}$$

b.
$$\begin{array}{r} \overset{7}{\$5}\cancel{8}4 \\ - \$126 \\ \hline 458 \end{array}$$

c.
$$\begin{array}{r} \overset{6}{\$\cancel{7}}14 \\ - \$342 \\ \hline 372 \end{array}$$

d. The groceries cost $70. The customer has $130. How much money will the customer have left?

e. Margie went to the mall with $242. She spent $28. Then how much money did Margie have?

Written Practice   *Distributed and Integrated*

Formulate   Write number sentences for the stories in problems **1–3**. Then write a complete sentence to answer each question.

1. Matt spent $160 on Saturday and $45 on Sunday. How much
(18) money did he spend in all?

$$205$$

2. Christie gave the clerk $45. The clerk kept $32 and gave the rest
(20) of the money back to Christie. How much money did the clerk give Christie?

3. Anita has a big box of 516 raisins. She put 150 raisins in a bag
(20) and packed it in her lunch. How many raisins are left in the box?

4. (Model) Use money to show this addition. Then add using pencil and paper.
(22)

$$\begin{array}{r} \$6.45 \\ + \$5.35 \\ \hline \end{array}$$

11.80

5. Write 375 in expanded form.
(11)

6. Use 2, 7, and 9 to write two addition facts and two subtraction facts.
(8)

What are the next four numbers in each sequence?

7. 9, 12, 15, _18_, _21_, _24_, _27_, ...
(2)

8. 21, 28, 35, _42_, _49_, _56_, _63_, ...
(2)

9. (Analyze) How much money is six $1 bills, eleven dimes, and sixteen pennies?
(21)

Add or subtract, as shown:

10. $24 + $50
(13)

11. $330 − $250
(23)

12. 5 + 8 + 6
(10)

13. $516 − $70
(23)

446

14. 463 + 250
(16)

15. $687 − $500
(23)

187

Find the missing addend:

16. *m* + 45 = 50
(9)

17. ☐ + 40 = 100
(9)

18. To what number is this arrow pointing?
(4)

85   90   95   100

19. (Interpret) Kiana has pen pals in four different countries. She
(17)   wants to send each pen pal a book. The table below shows the
cost to send a book to each country.

Country	Cost
Guatemala	$62
Canada	$38
India	$58
France	$47

Order the costs from least to greatest.

20. Use words to write $202.
(12)
two hundred two

Early Finishers

Real-World Connection

Cori and Austin are buying a new remote control car together.
Austin has $17 and Cori has $13. If the remote control car
costs $56, how much more money do Austin and Cori need to
buy the car? *16*

• **Column Addition**

Power Up

facts   Power Up 24

jump
start
     Count down by 2s from 30 to 0.
     Count down by 5s from 60 to 0.

     The school bell rang at 8:25 in the morning. Draw hands on your clock to show this time. Write the time in digital form.

     Mark your thermometer to show 27°C.

     Write 341 in expanded form.

mental
math
     a. Number Sense: $8 + 11 = 19$

     b. Estimation: Is $86 closer to $80 or $90?

     c. Money: 30¢ + 40¢   70   86

     d. Money: Write the total value of these coins with a cent sign.

38¢

problem
solving
     As Kara walked through the auditorium, she counted the number of people in each row of seats. If the pattern continues, predict the number of people in the fifth and sixth rows.

12, 22, 32, 42, 52, 62

Arranging numbers in columns helps us to add when we use pencil and paper.

Example 1

Mr. Jones paid a $25 gas bill, a $72 electric bill, and a $46 water bill. Add to find the total amount he paid.

$$\begin{array}{r} \$25 \\ \$72 \\ + \$46 \\ \hline \end{array}$$

When we add with pencil and paper, we start with the digits with the least place value. So we add the digits in the ones column first.

Start

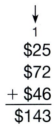

$$\begin{array}{r} {}^{1} \\ \$25 \\ \$72 \\ + \$46 \\ \hline 3 \end{array}$$

The sum of 5, 2, and 6 is 13. Remember that the number 13 is 1 ten plus 3 ones. We write the 3 in the ones column and the 1 in the tens column. Next we add the digits in the tens column.

$$\begin{array}{r} \downarrow \\ 1 \\ \$25 \\ \$72 \\ + \$46 \\ \hline \$143 \end{array}$$

The sum of 2, 7, 4, and 1 is 14. This is 14 tens, which is the same as 1 hundred and 4 tens. So the total is **$143.**

Analyze Show two more ways to add $25, $72, and $46.

Example 2

Write in a column and add:

$$\$345 + \$76 + \$120$$

We arrange the numbers so that digits with the same place value are in a column. Then we add

$$
\begin{array}{r}
^{1\,1} \\
\$345 \\
\$\ 76 \\
+\ \$120 \\
\hline
\$541
\end{array}
$$

Lesson Practice Arrange in columns and add. You may use your money manipulatives.

a. $42 + $56 + $25 = 123   **b.** $24 + $35 + $60 /29

c. $25 + $25 + $25 75   **d.** $125 + $50 + $25 200

Written Practice *Distributed and Integrated*

1. Christine had $87. She gave $25 to her brother. Then how much money did Christine have?
(20)

2. Daniel paid $2.65 for a sandwich plus $0.21 tax. Altogether, how much did he pay?
(18, 22)

3. Write these numbers in order from least to greatest: 58, 52, 63.
(17)

4. **Model** Use money to show this addition. Then add using pencil and paper.
(22)

$$\$3.54 + \$8.65$$

5. **Formulate** Kane bought a bag of dog food for $21, a dog house for $83 and a dog toy for $16. Round these numbers to the nearest ten. Write a number sentence using the rounded amounts to find about how much Kane spent on his dog.
(15, 24)

6. Is the temperature outside closer to 80°F or 90°F?
(4, 15)

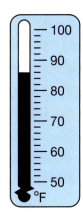

7. Use words to write $450.
(12)

8. Use 10, 2, and 8 to write two addition facts and two subtraction facts.
(8)

9. Show how to write half past noon in digital form.
(5)

What are the next four numbers in each sequence?

10. 14, 21, 28, 35, _____, _____, _____, _____, ...
(2)

11. 8, 12, 16, 20, _____, _____, _____, _____, ...
(2)

Add or subtract, as shown:

12. $384 − $70
(23)

13. 8 + 7 + 5 + 10
(10)

14. 450 − 400
(23)

15. $587 − $100
(23)

16. $875 − $250
(23)

17. $15 + $25 + $35
(24)

Find the missing addend:

18. $37 + m = 137$
(9)

19. $\square + 25 = 75$
(9)

20. The dot represents what number?
(4)

Real-World Connection

Gene moved to a new school on the 24th day of the 2nd month of a common year. When his new teacher introduced him to the class, Gene told them that his birthday was only seven days away. When is Gene's birthday? How many days away would Gene's birthday be if it were a leap year?

• Counting Dollars and Cents

facts   Power Up 25

**jump
start**   Count up by 7s from 0 to 35.
            Count up by 25s from 0 to 200.

The class will visit the library at 1:40. Draw hands on your clock to show this time. Write the time in digital form.

The temperature in the classroom was 20°C. Mark your thermometer to show this temperature.

Write a fact family using the numbers 4, 6, and 10.

**mental
math**   **a. Patterns:** 25, 50, 75, _____, 125

          b. Time: 10 minutes − 8 minutes

          c. Money: $6 + $7

          d. Money: Write the total value of these coins with a dollar sign.

problem solving

The pizza is cut into 8 slices. Dewayne, Emma, Franki, and Gem will share the pizza. Act out this problem to find how many slices of pizza each student can have.

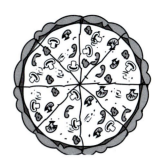

There are many ways to count the value of a group of bills and coins. We will practice counting the money by starting with the coins with the greatest value.

Example 1

What is the value of these coins?

We will count the coins in groups according to their value. We can skip count to find the total.

The total is **$1.04.**

Example 2

Find the total value of these bills and coins.

We start with $2, add 50¢ to make $2.50, add 10¢ to make $2.60, then add 5¢ and 2¢ to make **$2.67.**

Example 3

Write a number sentence that states the total value of a quarter plus a half-dollar.

Remember that a number sentence uses digits and other symbols to make a statement. Since a quarter is twenty-five cents and a half-dollar is fifty cents, we can write

25 cents + 50 cents = 75 cents

Instead of the word *cents*, we can use a cent sign or a dollar sign.

25¢ + 50¢ = 75¢

$0.25 + $0.50 = $0.75

Each of these is a number sentence.

Example 4

This table shows the values of certain numbers of dimes. Continue and complete the table through six dimes.

Number of dimes	1	2	3	4	5	
Value in cents	10	20	30			

Number of dimes	1	2	3	4	5	**6**
Value in cents	10	20	30	**40**	**50**	60

Generalize What is the rule for each row in the above table?

Counting Money

Find the total value of the play money given to you by your teacher. Then select a set of bills and coins for others in your group to count. For more practice, count the coins shown on **Lesson Activity 12.**

Lesson Practice

a. What is the total value of these coins?

b. What is the total value of these bills and coins?

Write number sentences that state the total value of the following:

c. a quarter plus a dime plus a nickel

d. two quarters and three dimes

e. This table shows the values of certain numbers of nickels. Copy and complete the table through six nickels.

Number of nickels	1	2	3	4	5	
Value in cents	5	10	15			

Written Practice
Distributed and Integrated

Formulate Write number sentences for the stories in problems **1** and **2**. Write a complete sentence to answer each question.

1. The bus ride cost $2.50. The taxi ride cost $4.50. What was the cost of both rides?
(18, 22)

2. Karen had $87. She gave her friend $25. Then how much money did Karen have?
(20)

3. Write a number sentence that states the total value of two quarters, a dime, and 3 pennies.
(25)

4. **Model** Use money to show this addition. Then add using pencil and paper.
(22)

$$\begin{array}{r} \$\,7.27 \\ +\ \$\,1.45 \\ \hline \end{array}$$

5. Round these prices to the nearest ten dollars:
(15)

a.  $28.00

b.  $11.00

6. Round these prices to the nearest hundred dollars:
(15)

a.

$185.00

b.

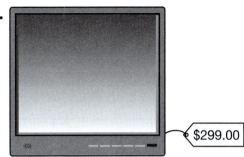

$299.00

7. Use digits and a dollar sign to write two hundred three
(12) dollars.

8. After May 10, how many days are left in May?
(1, 20)

9. Use 8, 9, and 1 to write two addition facts and two subtraction
(8) facts.

What are the next four numbers in each sequence?

10. 18, 27, 36, _____, _____, _____, _____, ...
(2)

11. 18, 24, 30, 36, _____, _____, _____, _____, ...
(2)

Add or subtract, as shown:

12. $89 − $11
(14)

13. $4.25 + $3.50
(22)

14. $387 − $55
(23)

15. 570 + 25
(16)

16. $865 − $330
(23)

17. 8 + 10 + 2
(10)

Find the missing addend:

18. $65 + m = 75$
(9)

19. $5 + 8 + \square = 15$
(9)

20. (**Explain**) Sarah woke up from a dream. It was dark
(3, 15) outside. She looked at the clock. Was the time closer
to 11:15 p.m. or 11:20 p.m.? How do you know?

• Subtracting Dollars and Cents

Power Up

facts	Power Up 26
jump start	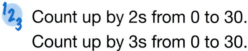 Count up by 2s from 0 to 30. Count up by 3s from 0 to 30.
	The swimming lesson ends at 4:25. Draw hands on your clock to show this time. Write the time in digital form.
	The temperature of the water in the swimming pool was 87°F. Mark your thermometer to show this temperature.
	Write 42¢ using words.

mental math

a. **Number Sense:** 15 + 10

b. **Time:** What is the time 2 hours after 1:15 p.m.?

c. **Estimation:** Is $220 closer to $200 or $300?

d. **Number Line:** Which point represents the number 9?

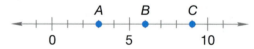

problem solving

Zach has 7 books. He will make two stacks with the books. Each stack will have at least 2 books. Complete this table to show the ways Zach could stack the books.

Stack 1	Stack 2
2 books	5 books
	4 books
4 books	
	2 books

In this lesson we will practice subtracting dollars and cents using money and using pencil and paper. Read this "some went away" story.

Example 1

Maribel took $7.50 on the field trip. She paid $3.80 for her lunch. How much money did she have left?

We put $7.50 on the desk to show how much money Maribel started with.

We need to take away $3.80, which is three $1 bills and eight dimes. There are not enough dimes on the desk so we will regroup.

We trade one $1 bill for ten dimes.

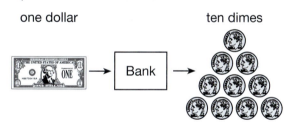

After we regroup, there are six $1 bills and 15 dimes, which is still $7.50.

Now we subtract $3.80 by taking away three $1 bills and 8 dimes. Maribel had **$3.70** left.

To subtract with pencil and paper, we start from the right.

Start
↓

$7.50
− $3.80

We know that 0 pennies from 0 pennies is zero. Next, we look at the dimes. We cannot take 8 dimes from 5 dimes so we trade one $1 bill for ten dimes. Then we subtract.

Start
6 ↓
$7̸.¹50
− $3.80
$3.70

Example 2

Theresa went to the store with $4.32. She bought a gallon of milk for $2.48. Then how much money did she have?

We put $4.32 on the desk to show how much money Theresa took to the store.

We need to take away $2.48, which is two $1 bills, four dimes, and eight pennies. Since there are not enough dimes and pennies on the desk, we will regroup.

We trade one $1 bill for ten dimes.

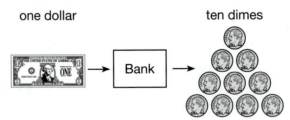

one dollar   ten dimes

We will also trade one dime for ten pennies.

one dime   ten pennies

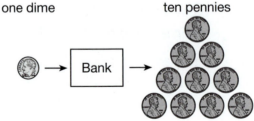

After we regroup there is still $4.32 on the desk in the form of three $1 bills, 12 dimes, and 12 pennies.

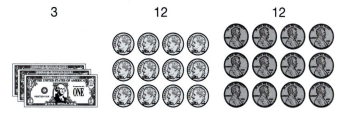

Now we subtract $2.48 by taking away two $1 bills, 4 dimes, and 8 pennies.

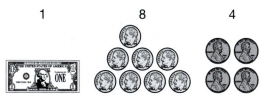

We see that Theresa has **$1.84** left.

To subtract with pencil and paper, we start from the right.

Start
↓

$4.32
− $2.48

We cannot subtract eight pennies from two pennies, so we trade one dime for ten pennies. Now we have 2 dimes and 12 pennies, so we can subtract the pennies.

$\overset{2}{\$4.\overset{1}{\cancel{3}}2}$
− $2.48
4

We do not have enough dimes to subtract, so we trade one $1 bill for ten dimes. Now we have three $1 bills and 12 dimes, so we can finish subtracting.

$\overset{3\ \ 12}{\$\cancel{4}.\overset{1}{\cancel{3}}2}$
− $2.48
$1.84

The bottom number shows us how much Theresa has left. Theresa has **$1.84.**

Verify How can you prove that $1.84 is correct?

Lesson Practice Perform each subtraction using money manipulatives. Then solve using pencil and paper.

a. $4.30
   − $1.17

b. $6.28
   − $3.56

c. $5.25
   − $3.78

d. Karen had $6.25. She paid the taxi driver $4.50. Then how much money did Karen have?

Written Practice *Distributed and Integrated*

1. Linda had 64 cents. She spent 36 cents. Then how much money did she have?
(14, 20)

2. Paul put a 39-cent stamp and a 25-cent stamp on the envelope. What was the total value of the stamps on the envelope?
(13, 18)

3. **Model** Use money to show this subtraction. Then subtract using pencil and paper.
(26)

$$\$5.75 − \$4.56$$

4. **Model** Use money to show this addition. Then add using pencil and paper.
(22)

$$\$6.89 + \$4.56$$

5. Round $12 to the nearest ten dollars.
(15)

6. Round $322 to the nearest hundred dollars.
(15)

7. Use words to write $24.
(12)

8. **Explain** Li wants to buy a snack that costs $1.00. He has one quarter, two dimes, one nickel and four pennies. His friend gave him a quarter. Does Li have enough money to buy the snack? Explain your answers.
(17, 25)

9. Class started at a quarter to nine in the morning. Write this time in
(5)   digital form.

What are the next four numbers in each sequence?

10. 48, 44, 40, 36, _____, _____, _____, _____, ...
(2)

11. 70, 63, 56, _____, _____, _____, _____, ...
(2)

Add or subtract, as shown:

12. $3.48 + $2.60
(22)

13. $385 − $250
(23)

14. 38 + 47 + 10
(24)

15. $346 − $34
(23)

16. 8 + 7 + 5 + 9
(10)

17. $1.77 − $1.25
(21, 26)

Find the missing addend:

18. $m + 5 = 25$
(9)

19. $6 + \square + 3 = 19$
(9, 10)

20. **Multiple Choice** Which of these does NOT equal one dollar?
(25)
 A four quarters   **B** ten dimes
 C fifteen nickels   **D** one hundred pennies

Real-World Connection

Ashton had a treasure hunt at his birthday party. His father hid 130 small prizes for the children to find. Team 1 found 26 items, Team 2 found 35, and Team 3 found 48. How many of the small prizes were not found?

• Comparing and Ordering, Part 2

Power Up

facts   Power Up 27

jump start   Count down by 5s from 60 to 0.
                   Count down by 10s from 100 to 0.

                   Music class begins at 9:20 in the morning. Draw hands on your clock to show this time. Write the time in digital form.

                   The high temperature was 95°F. Mark your thermometer to show this temperature.

                    Write a fact family using the numbers 3, 9, and 12.

mental math   **a. Money:** 25¢ + 10¢

                   b. Time: It is morning. What time will it be 4 hours after the time shown on this clock?

                   c. Number Sense: 8 + 9

                   d. Estimation: Is $525 closer to $500 or $600?

problem solving   Copy this picture on your paper. Then trace each triangle in your picture. How many different triangles can you find?

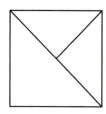

New Concept

In this lesson, we will compare numbers. We will arrange groups of 3 or more numbers in order from least to greatest **or** from greatest to least.

Visit www. SaxonMath.com/ Int3Activities for an online activity.

To write a group of numbers from least to greatest, we start with the least (smallest) number and then write the other numbers in order. To write a group of numbers from greatest to least, we start with the greatest (or largest) number and then write the other numbers in order.

Example 1

Karen has $261. Jamal has $237. Who has more money? Write < or > in place of the circle to complete the comparison.

$$\$261 \bigcirc \$237$$

We will use place value to compare $261 and $237. First, we look at the hundreds place. There are 2 hundreds (two $100 bills) in $261 and 2 hundreds in $237. Since the amount of hundreds in each number is the same, we look next at the tens place. There are 6 tens in $261 and 3 tens in $237. We know that 6 is more than 3, so $261 is greater than $237.

$$\$261 > \$237$$

Example 2

Amado looked at three remote control airplanes at the toy store. The planes cost $149, $123, and $158. Arrange these numbers in order from greatest to least.

We will use money manipulatives to find the order of these three amounts. First, we show $149, $123, and $158 on your desk using money from the money kit.

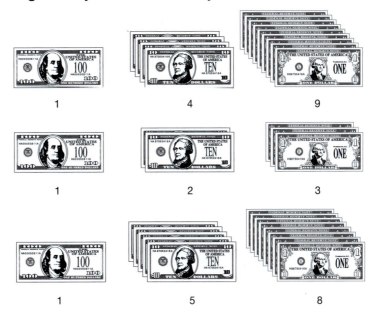

We will look at the $100 bills first. The $100 bills are equal in all three amounts. Next we look at the $10 bills. The number of $10 bills in order from greatest to least is 5, 4, 2. We will start with $158, which is the greatest number. The cost of the remote control airplanes from greatest to least is **$158, $149, $123.**

Example 3

The third grade classes at Cook Elementary collected aluminum cans. Mr. Brown's class collected 324 cans, Mrs. Jones's class collected 291 cans, and Ms. Hardy's class collected 215 cans. Write the number of cans each class collected in order from least to greatest.

We can compare the place value of the digits in these numbers to help us write them in order.

Hundreds	Tens	Ones
3	2	4
2	9	1
2	1	5

First, we look at the digits in the hundreds place. We see that 324 has 3 in the hundreds place, so we know that 324 is the greatest of the three numbers.

Hundreds	Tens	Ones
3	2	4
2	**9**	1
2	**1**	5

Next, we look at the digits in the tens place of 291 and 215. We know that 1 ten is less than 9 tens, so 215 is less than 291. We will start with 215, which is the least. The numbers in order from least to greatest are **215, 291, 324.**

Example 4

The students at Hardy Elementary keep track of how many minutes they read at home each week. The table below shows how many minutes some of the students read in one week. Write the numbers in order from greatest to least.

Minutes Read in One Week

Student	Minutes
Cindy	327
Juan	432
Mikel	321
Marissa	486

First we compare the digits in the hundreds place. We see that 432 and 486 both have 4 hundreds so we look at the tens place. Since 8 tens is more than 3 tens, 486 is greater than 432.

We see that 327 and 321 both have 3 hundreds and 2 tens. Next we compare the ones place in those two numbers. We know that 7 ones is more than 2 ones, so 327 is greater than 321. We write 486 first because it is the greatest number. The numbers in order from greatest to least are **486, 432, 327, 321.**

Justify A group of students were asked to write numbers in order from greatest to least. One student wrote the following order: 317, 392, 398. Was the student correct? Why or why not?

Lesson Practice

Use the table below to answer problems **a–d**.

Minutes Read in One Week

Student	Minutes
Alana	470
Diego	473
Kita	312
Loc	486

a. Which student read the greatest number of minutes?

b. Which student read the least number of minutes?

c. Write the numbers in order from least to greatest.

d. Write the names of the students in order from greatest to least number of minutes read.

Written Practice
Distributed and Integrated

1. Angel spent $3.56 for lunch and $6.24 for dinner. How much did
(18, 22) Angel spend for both lunch and dinner?

2. **Analyze** Willie had nine dimes and three pennies. He spent
(20, 26) $0.43. How much money did he have left?

3. **Model** Use money to show this subtraction. Then subtract
(26) using pencil and paper.

$$\$1.52 - \$1.48$$

4. **Model** Use money to show this addition. Then add using pencil
(22) and paper.

$$\$3.58 + \$2.94$$

5. The gas bill was $39. Round $39 to the nearest ten dollars.
(15)

6. The hammock cost $69. Round $69 to the nearest ten
(15) dollars.

7. **Interpret** The table below shows the temperature in four
(27) different cities one day last spring.

City	Temperature
Austin	74°F
Boston	66°F
Los Angeles	68°F
Miami	86°F

Write the temperatures in order from least to greatest.

8. How many days is 5 weeks?
(1, 2)

9. Draw a number line from 10 through 15 with one tick mark for
(4) each counting number. Label 10 and 15. Draw a dot on the
number line at 11.

Conclude What are the next four numbers in each sequence?

10. 16, 20, 24, 28, _____, _____, _____, _____, · · ·
(2)

11. 16, 24, 32, 40, _____, _____, _____, _____, · · ·
(2)

Add or subtract, as shown:

12. $52 − $48   **13.** 8 + 5 + 10
(14)   (10)

14. $796 − $790   **15.** $4.25 + $2.50
(23)   (22)

16. $786 − $76   **17.** 58 + 76 + 30
(23)   (24)

Find the missing addend:

18. $m + 8 + 7 = 20$ **19.** $\square + 45 = 60$
(9, 10)   (9, 13)

20. **Analyze** Audrey has 1 quarter, 6 dimes, and 2 pennies. Kai has
(17, 25) 2 quarters, 2 nickels, and 3 pennies. Who has more money? Write
the two amounts of money with a comparison symbol.

Early Finishers
Real-World Connection

Cesar and Paul were playing a board game using play money. The
player with the most money at the end of the game wins. When
the game ended, Cesar had fourteen $10 bills, three $5 bills, and
six $1 bills. Paul ended the game with eleven $10 bills, nine $5 bills,
and eight $1 bills. How much money did each player have? Who
won? How much more money does the winner have?

LESSON 28

• Subtracting Across Zeros

facts	Power Up 28
jump start	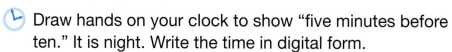 Count up by 25s from 0 to 200. Count up by 100s from 0 to 1000.
	Draw hands on your clock to show "five minutes before ten." It is night. Write the time in digital form.
	The temperature at sunrise was 50°F. It was 10 degrees warmer at sunset. Mark your thermometer to show the temperature at sunset.
	Write "one hundred twenty dollars" using digits.
mental math	**a. Number Sense:** 9 + 11
	b. Number Sense: 17 − 9
	c. Money: Write the total value of these coins with a dollar sign.

d. Patterns: What number is missing from the pattern below?

95	85	75	_____	55

problem solving	Alex, Bailey, and Chandra lined up to get on the bus. Bailey stood right in front of Alex. How many different ways could the children have lined up? Act out the problem to find the ways.

Think about this story.

> *Simon is playing a board game. He needs to pay another player $157. Simon has three $100 bills. How can Simon trade with the bank so that he can pay the other player? How much money will Simon have after he pays?*

Simon starts with a total of $300. He needs to trade a $100 bill to the bank for $10 bills and $1 bills. Simon can trade one $100 bill for ten $10 bills. Then, he can trade one $10 bill for ten $1 bills.

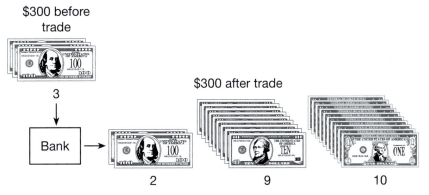

$300 before trade

3

Bank

$300 after trade

2   9   10

Verify Write and solve a number sentence to show that two $100 bills, nine $10 bills, and ten $1 bills are equal to three $100 bills.

After Simon pays $157, he will have $143. We can also subtract using pencil and paper.

$$\begin{array}{r} \$300 \\ -\ \$157 \end{array} \longrightarrow \begin{array}{r} \$\overset{2}{\cancel{3}}\overset{1}{0}\ 0 \\ -\ \$1\ 5\ 7 \end{array} \longrightarrow \begin{array}{r} \$\overset{2}{\cancel{3}}\overset{9}{\cancel{0}}\overset{1}{0} \\ -\ \$1\ 5\ 7 \\ \hline \$1\ 4\ 3 \end{array}$$

First we trade 1 hundred for 10 tens. That trade leaves 2 hundreds. Then we trade 1 ten for 10 ones. That trade leaves 9 tens. After the two trades we are ready to subtract.

Activity

Subtracting Across Zeros

Work with a partner to complete these two exchanges.

1. Student A starts with four $100 bills from the bank. Then Student A pays Student B $163 by first trading one $100 to the bank for $10 bills and $1 bills. Then both partners should subtract with pencil and paper.

$$\$400 - \$163$$

2. Student B starts with one $100 bill. Student B pays Student A $74 by first trading the $100 bill to the bank for $10 bills and $1 bills. Then both partners should subtract with pencil and paper.

$$\$100 - \$74$$

Example

The grocery bill was $127. Malia paid for the groceries with two $100 bills. How much money should she get back?

We subtract $127 from $200. First we trade 1 hundred for 10 tens. Then we trade 1 ten for 10 ones. →

$$
\begin{array}{r} \$200 \\ -\$127 \\ \hline \end{array}
\longrightarrow
\begin{array}{r} \$\overset{1}{2}\overset{1}{0}0 \\ -\$127 \\ \hline \end{array}
\longrightarrow
\begin{array}{r} \$\overset{1}{2}\overset{1}{\cancel{0}}\overset{9}{\cancel{0}}0 \\ -\$127 \\ \hline \$\ \ 73 \end{array}
$$

Malia should get back **$73.**

Lesson Practice Use your money manipulatives to help you with each subtraction.

a. $500
   − $371

b. $200
   − $144

c. $200
   − $ 56

d. $100
   − $ 38

Written Practice *Distributed and Integrated*

1. Darren took $100 to the department store. He spent $89 on a
(20, 28)   breadmaker. Then how much money did he have?

2. Write the total price in problem **1** using words.
(12)

3. **Analyze** The umbrella was on sale for $8.95. Tax was 70¢. What
(18, 22) was the total price of the umbrella with tax?

4. What is the total value of two quarters, a dime, a nickel, and three
(25) pennies?

5. **Model** Use money to show this addition. Then add using pencil
(22) and paper.

$$\$5.48 + \$3.64$$

6. Round $18 to the nearest ten dollars.
(15)

7. Round $781 to the nearest hundred dollars.
(15)

8. How many nickels equal a dollar?
(25)

9. Marty bought some juice for 66¢. What coins might Marty have
(25) used to buy the juice?

Conclude What are the next four numbers in each sequence?

10. 12, 18, 24, _____, _____, _____, _____, ...
(2)

11. 99, 90, 81, _____, _____, _____, _____, ...
(2)

Add or subtract, as shown:

12. 876 + 100
(16)

13. $489 − $50
(23)

14. 25 + 35 + 45
(24)

15. $279 − $119
(23)

16. 6 + 5 + 4 + 10
(10)

17. $280 − $180
(19)

Find the missing addend:

18. 25¢ + m = 75¢
(9)

19. 30 = 24 + ☐
(9)

20. **Multiple Choice** Deshawn went to the carnival with his father.
(22) The price of an adult ticket was $4.75. The price of a child's
ticket was $3.25. How much did Deshawn and his father spend
on tickets?

    A $7.00   **B** $7.75   **C** $8.00   **D** $8.25

• Fractions of a Dollar

---

facts   Power Up 29

jump start

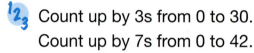 Count up by 3s from 0 to 30.
Count up by 7s from 0 to 42.

Draw hands on your clock to show "ten minutes past six." It is evening. Write the time in digital form.

The temperature at noon was 50°F. It was 10 degrees cooler at midnight. Mark your thermometer to show the temperature at midnight.

 Write 135 in expanded form.

mental math

a. **Number Sense:** 50 + 30

b. **Money:** Which has greater value, 2 dimes or 15¢?

c. **Estimation:** Is $47 closer to $40 or to $50?

d. **Time:** It is afternoon. The train will arrive 1 hour after the time shown on the clock. What time will the train arrive?

problem solving

Lydia is placing beads on a string. In this picture, R stands for red and B stands for blue. If Lydia continues the pattern of beads, what will be the color of the tenth bead?

We can name parts of a whole with a **fraction.** The bottom number in the fraction tells the number of equal parts in the whole. The top number in the fraction tells the number of parts we are naming.

The value of a coin is a fraction of a whole dollar.

4 quarters equal $1, so

1 quarter is $\frac{1}{4}$ ("one fourth") of a dollar.

10 dimes equal $1, so

1 dime is $\frac{1}{10}$ ("one tenth") of a dollar.

20 nickels equal $1, so

1 nickel equals $\frac{1}{20}$ ("one twentieth") of a dollar.

100 pennies equal $1, so

1 penny equals $\frac{1}{100}$ ("one hundredth") of a dollar.

Notice that each of these fractions has two parts. The bottom number tells how many of that coin equal one whole dollar. The top number shows how many of that coin we are naming.

Example 1

What fraction of each shape is shaded?

a.
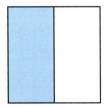

b.

a. The square is divided into two equal parts, so the bottom number of the fraction will be 2. One part is shaded, so the top number in the fraction will be 1. The fraction is $\frac{1}{2}$.

b. The circle is divided into three equal parts, so the bottom number of the fraction will be 3. Two parts are shaded so the top number of the fraction will be 2. The fraction is $\frac{2}{3}$.

Example 2

Draw a circle and shade $\frac{1}{4}$.

First we draw a circle. Next, we divide it into four equal parts. Then we shade one of the parts.

Example 3

Tom held 3 quarters in his hand. What fraction of a dollar is 3 quarters?

A whole dollar is 4 quarters, so 3 quarters is $\frac{3}{4}$ (**"three fourths"**) of a dollar.

Example 4

Mia has 7 dimes. What fraction of a dollar is 7 dimes?

A whole dollar is 10 dimes, so 7 dimes is $\frac{7}{10}$ (**"seven tenths"**) of a dollar.

Analyze Name a fraction of a dollar that is equal to 50¢.

Lesson Practice

a. What fraction of the circle is shaded?

b. What fraction of the rectangle is shaded?

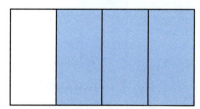

c. Which coin is $\frac{1}{4}$ of a dollar?

d. Three dimes is what fraction of a dollar?

1. Freddy ordered a sandwich for $4.29 and a drink for $1.29. What was the total price?
(18, 22)

2. Analyze The item cost $4.19. Elizabeth gave the clerk a $5 bill and a quarter. How much money did Elizabeth give the clerk? How much money did she get back?
(20, 26)

3. Write "nine hundred thirty dollars" using numbers and a dollar sign.
(12)

4. Sam has three quarters, two dimes, and a penny in his pocket. What is the total value of the coins?
(25)

5. The price of the refrigerator was $389. Round the price to the nearest hundred dollars.
(15)

6. The price of the computer game was $28. Round the price to the nearest ten dollars.
(15)

7. Max received $75 in cash for washing cars and a check for $82 for mowing lawns. For which job did Max earn more money? Write the two amounts with a comparison symbol.
(17)

8. Dina saw these three prices for a television she wants to buy: $287, $293, and $279. Write the prices in order from least to greatest.
(17)

What are the next five numbers in each sequence?

9. 8, 16, 24, _____, _____, _____, _____, _____, ...
(2)

10. 4, 8, 12, _____, _____, _____, _____, _____, ...
(2)

Add or subtract, as shown:

11. $31 + 26 + 15$
(24)

12. $6 + 6 + 6 + 6$
(10)

13. $375 + $375
(16)

14. $625 − $125
(23)

15. $3.45 − $1.50
(26)

16. $250 − $10
(23)

Find the missing addend:

17. $30 + m = 90$
(9)

18. $37 + \square = 100$
(9. 13)

19. (Analyze) Minh spent 15 minutes eating his lunch and another 15
(5. 29)   minutes playing on the monkey bars. What fraction of an hour did
he spend eating and playing?

20. Multiple Choice Which shaded circle shows the fraction $\frac{3}{4}$?
(29)

A

B

C

D

Early Finishers
Real-World Connection

Danielle jumps rope faster than anyone on her street. She can
jump five times every four seconds. How long would it take
Danielle to jump 25 times? You may wish to make a table that
shows the numbers of jumps and seconds to help you find the
answer.

• Estimating Sums and Differences

facts	Power Up 30
jump start	Count up by 25s from 0 to 200 and then back down to 0.
	Draw hands on your clock to show "ten minutes before four." It is afternoon. Write the time in digital form.
	A normal low temperature in January in Houston, Texas is 41°F. Mark your thermometer to show this temperature.
mental math	**a. Number Sense:** $18 - 10$
	b. Number Sense: $8 + 7$
	c. Money: Which has greater value, $0.46 or 48¢?
	d. Place Value: What digit is in the tens place in the number 264?

problem solving

Focus Strategy: Use Logical Reasoning

Cheyenne has five coins that are worth 18¢ altogether. What are the coins?

(**Understand**) We are asked to find five coins worth 18¢.

(**Plan**) We can use logical reasoning to solve the problem.

(**Solve**) We cannot make 18¢ without some pennies. This is because combinations of quarters, dimes, and nickels always have values that end in 0 or 5. Eighteen cents is 3 pennies more than 15¢, so we know that Cheyenne has 3 pennies.

Now we need to find two more coins that are worth 15¢. We know that 1 dime plus 1 nickel is 15¢.

We can show our coin combination in a table.

Check Our table shows 1 dime, 1 nickel, and 3 pennies, which is a total of five coins. If we add the values, we get 18¢, so our answer fits the problem.

Coin	Number
Q	0
D	1
N	1
P	3

New Concept

We often use addition or subtraction to solve math problems. Sometimes we need to know the exact answer. Sometimes we only need to find a number that is close to the exact answer. When we only need to know *about* how much, we **estimate.**

In Lesson 15 we learned to round numbers to the nearest ten and hundred. In this lesson we will add and subtract rounded numbers to estimate sums and differences.

Example 1

At the pet store, Jonah picked out an aquarium for $52 and a turtle for $26. About how much money will Jonah need to pay for his items? Will you add or subtract to find the answer?

This is a "some and some more" story, so we will **add** to find the answer.

We are asked *about* how much money Jonah needs, so we will estimate the sum. We begin by rounding $52 and $26 to the nearest ten dollars.

$$
\begin{array}{lll}
\$52 & \text{rounds to} & \$50 \\
+\ \$26 & \text{rounds to} & +\ \$30 \\
\hline
& & \$80
\end{array}
$$

Then we add the rounded numbers to estimate the sum: $50 + $30 = $80. Jonah will need **about $80** to pay for his items.

Example 2

Cass had 92 balloons. She used 39 balloons to decorate for a friend's party. About how many balloons does Cass have left? Will you add or subtract to find the answer?

This is a "some went away" story, so we will **subtract** to find the answer.

We are asked *about* how many balloons Cass has left, so we will estimate the difference. We begin by rounding 92 and 39 to the nearest ten.

$$
\begin{array}{rll}
92 & \text{rounds to} & 90 \\
-\ 39 & \text{rounds to} & -\ 40 \\
\hline
& & 50
\end{array}
$$

Then we subtract the rounded numbers to estimate the difference: $90 - 40 = 50$. Cass has **about 50 balloons** left.

Example 3

What is the best estimate of the sum of 287 and 529?

　A 700　　　**B 900**　　　**C 800**　　　**D 600**

We begin by rounding 287 and 529 to the nearest hundred. Then we add the rounded numbers to estimate the sum: $300 + 500 = 800$. The sum of 287 and 529 is about 800, so the correct answer choice is **C**.

Discuss Is estimating sums and differences easier or harder than finding exact numbers?

Lesson Practice For problems **a–c,** first say whether you will add or subtract. Then find the answer.

a. Rodney's worksheet has 96 subtraction facts. After one minute he has worked 57 facts. About how many facts does he have left to work?

b. Mr. Neustadt drove 278 miles on Monday and 429 miles on Tuesday. About how many miles did he travel in all?

c. Joni wants a pair of cleats that cost $53 and a pair of kneepads that cost $18. About how much money does Joni need to pay for her items?

d. What is the best estimate of the difference of 687 and 312?

A 900   **B** 300   **C** 1000   **D** 400

Written Practice

Distributed and Integrated

1. **Explain** Silvia has 3 quarters and 2 dimes. She wants to buy a
(17, 25) bagel that costs 79 cents. Does she have enough money? Explain your answer.

2. For breakfast Jimmy bought cereal for 85 cents, juice for 65 cents,
(27) and toast for 45 cents. List the items in order of price from least to greatest.

3. **Analyze** Find the total price of the items in problem **2** and write
(21, 24) the answer with a dollar sign.

4. The new video tape costs $16. Round the price to the nearest ten
(15) dollars.

5. The baseball glove costs $61. Round the price to the nearest ten
(15) dollars.

6. Use words to write $849.
(12)

7. What fraction of a dollar is nine dimes?
(29)

Conclude What are the next four numbers in each sequence?

8. 99, 90, 81, _____, _____, _____, _____, …
(2)

9. 20, 24, 28, _____, _____, _____, _____, …
(2)

Add or subtract, as shown:

10. $250 − $150
(19)

11. 31 + 28 + 31
(24)

12. $465 − $420
(23)

13. 6 + 4 + 8 + 2
(10)

14. $875 − $500
(19)

15. $4.35 + $2.65
(22)

Find the missing addend:

16. 55 + *m* = 66
(9)

17. 20 + 30 + ☐ = 100
(9, 10)

18. There are 163 third graders and 117 fourth graders at Vargas
(30) Elementary School. About how many third and fourth graders
are there?

19. As the sun began to set, Stella glanced at the clock.
(3) What time was it?

20. Write 875 in expanded form.
(11)

Real-World Connection

It takes Roseanna 50 minutes to get ready for school. If the
bus comes at 7:00 a.m., about what time should she get up?
Her sister rides the same bus but it only takes her 20 minutes
to get ready. What time should Roseanna's sister get up in the
morning?

Focus on

• More About Pictographs

Recall from Investigation 1 that a pictograph uses pictures to show data.

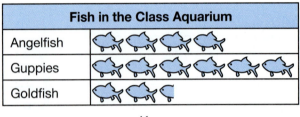

Fish in the Class Aquarium

Angelfish	
Guppies	
Goldfish	

Key
= 2 fish

The title at the top tells what the graph is about. Labels along the side tell what is counted. The pictures tell us how many of each type there are. The key tells us how many each picture represents.

Look at the pictograph above to answer problems **1–6.**

1. What is the title of the pictograph?

2. How many guppies are in the class aquarium?

3. Read the key. How many fish does each picture represent?

4. **Interpret** How many fish does the last picture in the "goldfish" row represent? How many goldfish are in the class aquarium?

5. Are there more goldfish or more angelfish in the aquarium?

6. If the teacher removed 2 angelfish from the class aquarium, how many angelfish would be left?

We can make pictographs from data we are given or from data we collect. In this investigation we will work as a class to collect data. Then we will organize our data and display it using a pictograph.

Activity

Class Pictograph

Materials: **Lesson Activity 14**

Our pictograph will show how many students in the class were born in each season. There are four seasons in a year: fall, winter, spring, and summer. In most years, the seasons begin and end on these dates:

Fall:	September 23 to December 20
Winter:	December 21 to March 19
Spring:	March 20 to June 20
Summer:	June 21 to September 22

Go around the class one student at a time saying aloud the season in which you were born. After each student's turn, make a tally mark at the top of **Lesson Activity 14** next to the season named. Here is a sample tally:

Fall: ||||| ||
Winter: ||||
Spring: ||||| |
Summer: |||||

After each student has had a turn, answer problems **7–13** to plan your pictograph. Use the tally you made on **Lesson Activity 14** to help you plan.

7. What will you title your pictograph? Write your title in the correct place on your worksheet.

8. Choose a picture to use in your pictograph. Draw the picture in the key on your worksheet.

9. As a class, decide whether each picture on your pictographs will represent one, two, or more students. Record your answer in the correct place for the key on your worksheet.

10. How many pictures will you need to represent the students with fall birthdays?

11. How many pictures will you need to represent the students with winter birthdays?

12. How many pictures will you need to represent the students with spring birthdays?

13. How many pictures will you need to represent the students with summer birthdays?

Use your answers to problems **8–13** to fill in the pictograph on **Lesson Activity 14.**

a. Olivia enjoys watching birds at summer camp. One week she counted 4 blue jays. The next week she counted 7 blue jays. The third week she counted 6 blue jays. Make a pictograph to display this data. Begin by choosing a title and making a key for your pictograph.

b. Collect data about your classmates or objects in your classroom and make a pictograph to display your data. Here are some sample subjects you might use:

- hair colors of students
- colors of students' shirts
- favorite foods of students
- favorite sports of students

LESSON 31

• Writing Directions

Power Up

facts	Power Up 31
jump start	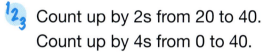 Count up by 2s from 20 to 40. Count up by 4s from 0 to 40. Write a fact family using the numbers 4, 7, and 11. Write "three dollars and fifty cents" using a dollar sign and digits.
mental math	**a. Calendar:** How many days are in 4 weeks? **b. Number Sense:** 90 − 20 **c. Money:** $100 − $50 **d. Number Line:** What number does point *A* represent? 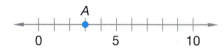
problem solving	Donna has four coins that are worth 32¢ altogether. What coins does she have?

New Concept

When we tell how to go from one place to another, we describe both the direction and the distance.

Maps are usually drawn so that the top of the map is north. The directions north, east, south, and west are often marked on the map's legend with the capital letters N, E, S, W.

Below is a map of the United States with a compass rose showing north, east, south, and west.

Connect If you face south, which direction will be to your right?

Example

The X on the map shows where Robert and his sister live. Robert says he lives on the left side of Oak Street. His sister says she lives on the right side of Oak Street. Who is correct? Is there a better way to describe where they live?

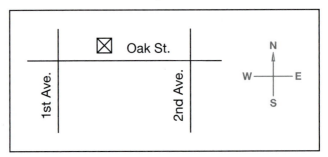

The words *left* and *right* can be confusing because they depend on the direction a person is facing. The map above shows that the house is on the left side of Oak Street when a person is traveling from 1st Avenue toward the house. However, the house is on the right side of the street if a person is coming from 2nd Avenue.

It would be less confusing to state that Robert and his sister live on the **north side of the street** because the directions of the compass do not depend on which way a person is facing. Left and right may be used if the direction of travel is clearly understood.

In the following activity you will practice giving directions. Describe the direction to travel using compass directions. Describe the distance to travel by stating the number of blocks.

Giving Directions

There are five locations labeled A-E on the map below. With a partner, take turns giving oral directions from one location to another. While one person speaks the directions, the other person follows the directions.

Here is an example:

Start at A. Travel east one block. Turn right and travel south two blocks. Where are you?

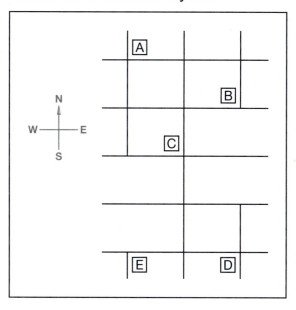

The directions lead to location **C**.

Lesson Practice Using the map in this lesson, write directions for traveling from:

a. Location B to location E.

b. Location D to location B.

c. Choose two locations on the map. Name the locations and then write directions from one location to the other.

1. Freddy spent 75¢ playing a video game and 85¢ for a snack.
(18, 22) Altogether, how much did Freddy spend? Write the answer using digits and a dollar sign.

2. Cindy owed Matt $45. She gave Matt a $100 bill. How much
(20, 28) money should Matt give back to Cindy?

3. Alvin had $92. He spent $76 at the grocery store. About how
(30) much money does Alvin have left?

4. The price of the shirt was $16. Round the price to the nearest
(15) ten dollars.

5. Pallu wrote a check to *Sharp Shirts* for $169. Write that amount
(12) using words.

6. (**Connect**) A penny is what fraction of a dollar? A penny is what
(21, 29) fraction of a dime?

7. Estimate the sum of 231 and 529.
(30)

(**Predict**) What is the tenth number in each sequence?

8. 36, 33, 30, 27, 24, 21, 18 …
(2)

9. 12, 24, 36, 48, 60, 72, 84 …
(2)

Add or subtract as shown:

10. $3.49 + $2.83
(22)

11. 200 − 150
(28)

12. 8 + 9 + 4
(10)

13. $4.65 − $3.75
(26)

14. 36¢ + 45¢ + 60¢
(21, 24)

15. $450 − $30
(19)

16. Find the missing addend: $25 + 50 + m = 100$
(9, 24)

17. Write 860 in expanded form.
(11)

18. **Model** Fred bought an eraser for 18¢ and paid for it with two
(21, 28) dimes. What coins should he get back in change? Show the
subtraction using money manipulatives.

19. This thermometer shows the temperature inside a
(4) refrigerator. What is the temperature on the Fahrenheit
and Celsius scales?

20. Show how to write a quarter to four o'clock in the
(5) afternoon in digital form.

Early Finishers

*Real-World
Connection*

Paulina and her friends are making posters for
the school bake sale. Paulina can buy a pack
of seven markers for $1.00. If she buys three
packs of markers, can she give two markers to each of her eight
friends? Explain. You may use manipulatives to find the
answer.

• **Reading and Writing Numbers Through 999,999**

 **Power Up**

facts   Power Up 32

jump start   Count down by 5s from 60 to 0.
                 Count down by 10s from 100 to 0.

                  Write 296 in expanded form.

                 Write 132 using words.

mental math

a. **Number Sense:** 80 − 50

b. **Money:** $1.00 − $0.30

c. **Time:** It is morning. The class will eat lunch 2 hours after the time shown on this clock. What time will the class eat lunch?

d. **Number Sense:** 6 + 5 + 4

problem solving

This is a square pattern that contains 4 tiles. It has 2 rows, and each row has 2 tiles.

Jim has 9 tiles. If he makes 3 rows of tiles, how many tiles will be in each row?

New Concept

Visit www. SaxonMath.com/ Int3Activities for an online activity.

In Lesson 11 we learned about digits and place value to the hundreds place. In this lesson, we will learn about place value to the hundred-thousands place.

Remember that the **place value** of a digit is decided by its position in the number. We can write the number 7,596 in a place value chart.

Hundred Thousands	Ten Thousands	Thousands	,	Hundreds	Tens	Ones
___	___	7	,	5	9	6

The expanded form of 7,596 is 7,000 + 500 + 90 + 6.

The 7 in the thousands place has a value of 7 thousands or 7,000. The 5 in the hundreds place has a value of 5 hundreds or 500. The 9 in the tens place has a value of 9 tens or 90. The 6 in the ones place has a value of 6 ones or 6.

To write a number in the thousands, we use a comma so that the number is easier to read. We start from the ones place and count to the left three digits. The comma should be between the hundreds place and the thousands place.

We read this number as "seven thousand, five hundred ninety-six."

Example 1

Write each of these numbers with a comma.

a. 1760   b. 25000   c. 125000

Starting from the ones place, we count three digits to the left and write a comma.

a. 1,760   b. 25,000   c. 125,000

The odometer on the dashboard of a car can help us understand place value. An odometer shows how far the car has been driven. The odometers of most cars in the United States measure the distance traveled in miles.

Most odometers can count through hundreds of thousands of miles.

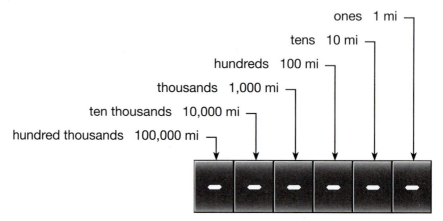

ones 1 mi
tens 10 mi
hundreds 100 mi
thousands 1,000 mi
ten thousands 10,000 mi
hundred thousands 100,000 mi

Example 2

The Johnsons bought a new car two years ago. The odometer shows this display.

a. How far has the car been driven?

b. Use words to name the number of miles shown.

To read an odometer, we ignore the zeros in front and begin reading with the first digit that is not a zero. We name a number in the thousands by first reading the digits to the left of the comma. We say "thousand" at the comma. Then we name the digits to the right of the comma.

ignore   miles

We can also show this number on a place value chart.

Hundred Thousands	Ten Thousands	Thousands	,	Hundreds	Tens	Ones
0	2	5	,	4	7	3

a. The car has been driven 25,473 miles.

b. twenty-five thousand, four hundred seventy-three miles

Example 3

a. A mile is five thousand, two hundred eighty feet. Write that number with digits.

b. Write 5,280 in expanded form.

a. We write five, then the thousands comma, then two hundred eighty.

5,280

b. The 5 in 5,280 has a value of 5,000:

5,000 + 200 + 80

Generalize There are 10 ones in a ten and 10 tens in a hundred. How many hundreds are in one thousand? How many ten thousands are in a hundred thousand?

Example 4

Compare:

35,498 ◯ 33, 882

We can use place value to compare the numbers. We begin with the digits in the ten thousands place. Both have 3s, so we move to the thousands place. Five thousands is greater than three thousands, so we replace the circle with a greater than symbol:

35, 498 > 33, 882

Reading and Writing Big Numbers

Work with a partner to read and write numbers greater than 999 and less than 999,999. Take turns writing numbers for your partner to read.

Lesson Practice

Write these numbers with a comma. Then name the numbers.

    a. 24800

    b. 186000

Use digits to write these numbers.

    c. six thousand, four hundred

d. sixty-four thousand

Write each of these odometer displays with digits. Then use words to name the miles shown.

e.

f.

g. Compare: 68, 329 $\bigcirc$ 69, 235

 *Distributed and Integrated*

1. **Analyze** Ann earned three hundred forty dollars. Tina earned
(16, 18) two hundred ninety-five dollars. How much did they earn
altogether? Who earned more?

2. Juan bought a tent for $65. He paid for the tent with a $100 bill.
(28) How much money should Juan get back?

3. Hugo bought a windbreaker for $39. Round the price to the
(15) nearest ten dollars.

4. Write $9.12 using words.
(21)

5. Look at this map and write directions for traveling from location A
(31) to location B.

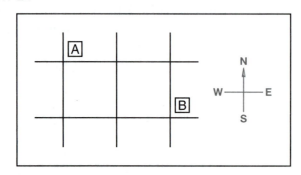

6. **Analyze** How many cents is $\frac{2}{4}$ of a dollar?
(29)

7. Write the number 35694 using a comma. Then name the number
(32) using words.

8. Write the next four numbers in this sequence:
(2) 7, 14, 21, _____, _____, _____, _____ ···

9. Compare: 354, 382 ◯ 352, 847
(32)

Add or subtract, as shown:

10. $300 − $150
(28)

11. $6.47 + $0.98
(22)

12. $7.25 − $5.35
(26)

13. 8 + 8 + 8 + 8
(10)

14. 375 − 250
(19)

15. 38¢ + 53¢ + 72¢
(21, 24)

Find the missing addend:

16. $12 + 12 + m = 36$
(9, 24)

17. ☐ + 100 = 900
(9, 16)

18. While eating lunch, Jaime glanced at the clock.
(3) What time was it?

19. (Analyze) The price of the toy car was 53¢. Sam gave
(14, 25) the clerk one quarter, one dime, one nickel and three
pennies. How much more does Sam need to pay?

20. (Represent) Draw a picture of this story. Then answer the
(31) question with a complete sentence:

*Pedro started his walk. He walked one block north, then one block east,
then one block south. In which direction and how far should Pedro walk
to return to where he started?*

*Real-World
Connection*

Tyrone and his 3 friends won 30 fun tickets playing video games
at the Game Palace. Since they won them as a team, they
decided to share the tickets equally. How many tickets should
each person get? How many extra tickets will they have? You may
use manipulatives to find the answer.

• **More About Number Lines**

facts	Power Up 33
jump start	Count up by 10s from 5 to 95. Count up by 7s from 0 to 42.
	The piano recital will begin at half past 5 in the afternoon. Draw hands on your clock to show this time. Write the time in digital form.
	A normal low temperature in July in Washington, D.C., is 19°C. Mark your thermometer to show this temperature.
mental math	**a. Number Sense:** $2 + 7 + 8$
	b. Number Sense: $19 + 10$
	c. Estimation: Is $345 closer to $300 or to $400?
	d. Patterns: What number is missing from the pattern shown below?

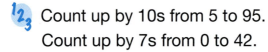

	problem solving	There are 4 goldfish in the first tank. There are 8 goldfish in the second tank. Chad wants an equal number of goldfish in each tank. How can he move some goldfish to do this?

4 goldfish

8 goldfish

We remember from Lesson 4 that a **number line** shows numbers on a line in counting order. Each point on a number line stands for a number. The number line below shows tick marks that represent numbers. Point *A* on this number line stands for 25 and Point *B* stands for 45.

Generalize What is the rule for the pattern shown by the first 4 numbers on the number line above?

Example

Which point on this number line stands for 126? Which point stands for 138?

The numbered tick marks on a number line help us find what other points stand for. On this number line we see that there are 5 tick marks from 120 to 130. The pattern for this number line is "count up by twos." We can use this pattern to see that **point *C* stands for 126** and **point *H* stands for 138.**

Activity

Making a Timeline

A **timeline** is like a number line. Points on a timeline stand for dates. This timeline shows some important dates in the history of flight.

Flight Timeline

| 1903 Wright Brothers' powered flight | 1927 Lindberg's transatlantic flight | 1947 Yeager's supersonic flight | 1969 Armstrong/ Aldrin moon landing |

In 1932, Amelia Earhart became the first woman to fly solo across the Atlantic Ocean. We can use the dates on the timeline to figure out where to place this event.

1932 is between 1927 and 1947. Earhart's flight across the Atlantic happened between Lindberg's flight and Yeager's flight. We draw a point on the timeline between 1927 and 1947.

Flight Timeline

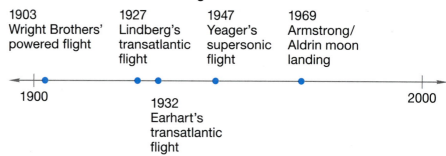

1903	1927	1947	1969
Wright Brothers' powered flight	Lindberg's transatlantic flight	Yeager's supersonic flight	Armstrong/ Aldrin moon landing

1900   2000

1932
Earhart's
transatlantic
flight

With a partner, create a timeline for the following inventions:

    1876: Telephone   1975: Personal Computer

    1927: Television   1844: Telegraph

1. Begin by sketching a segment that you will use for the timeline. Then order the years from least to greatest.

2. Mark the year 1800 near the left end of the segment and mark 2000 near the right end of the segment.

3. Draw a mark halfway between the marks for 1800 and 2000. What year would the middle mark represent?

4. Draw four dots on the timeline at the proper places for the dates shown above.

5. Near each dot write the year and the name of the invention.

Lesson Practice   Use this number line for **a–d.**

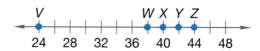

24   28   32   36   40   44   48

a. What number does *X* stand for?

b. Which point stands for 24?

c. What number does *W* stand for?

d. Which point stands for 44?

e. Some highways are marked with mileage markers to show the number of miles from the state line. Draw a number line to represent a 10-mile stretch of highway. Make equally spaced tick marks to stand for mileage markers. Label the tick mark on the left 130. Then label each tick mark to its right until you get to 140.

Written Practice

Distributed and Integrated

1. **Analyze** Rosemarie bought a glass of juice for 65¢. She gave
(20, 25) the clerk three quarters. What coins should Rosemarie get back in change?

2. James is reading a book that has 184 pages. He has read 52 pages.
(20) How many more pages does James have to read?

3. Julie bought a pony for $685. Round $685 to the nearest hundred
(15) dollars.

4. Estimate the difference of 923 and 688.
(30)

5. What number does point *Y* represent on the number line?
(33)

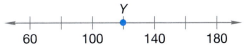

6. **Analyze** List the names of these coins in order from least to
(17, 21) greatest value.

dime, penny, quarter, nickel

7. What fraction of a dollar is eight dimes?
(29)

What are the next four numbers in each sequence?

8. 18, 24, 30, 36, _____, _____, _____, _____, …
(2)

9. 375, 400, 425, _____, _____, _____, _____, …
(2)

Add or subtract, as shown:

10. 35¢ + 48¢ + 65¢
(21, 24)

11. $100 − $77
(28)

12. $4.58 + $4.49
(22)

13. 885 − 850
(19)

14. 12 + 12 + 12
(25)

15. $746 + $74
(16)

16. Find the missing addend: $6 + m + 8 = 15$
(9, 10)

17. Write 605 in expanded form.
(11)

18. What is the value of these coins?
(25)

19. The odometer display shows how many miles? Write your answer
(32) with digits and with words.

20. **Represent** Draw a picture of this story. Then answer the
(31) question with a complete sentence.

> *Glenda walked five steps south. She turned and walked eight steps west. Then she turned and walked five steps north. In which direction and how far should Glenda walk to return to where she started?*

• **Length: Inches, Feet, and Yards**

Power Up

facts   Power Up 34

jump start    Count up by 2s from 0 to 30.
Count up by 4s from 0 to 40.

🕐 The zoo opened at a quarter of nine in the morning. Draw hands on your clock to show this time. Write the time in digital form.

🌡 The temperature inside the refrigerator was 3°C. Mark your thermometer to show this temperature.

mental math

a. **Number Sense:** $14 + 9$

b. **Number Sense:** $60 - 30$

c. **Money:** Which has the greater value?

$0.20 or $2.00

d. **Money:** Find the value of these bills and coins:

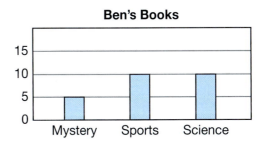

problem solving   This bar graph shows the different kinds of books Ben owns. If Ben bought 5 more mystery books to add to his collection, how many books would he have altogether?

Ben's Books

The odometer of a car measures distances in miles. To measure shorter distances we use other units. **Inches, feet,** and **yards** are smaller units for measuring length in the U.S. Customary System of measure. You might have a ruler in your desk that is 12 inches long. Twelve inches equals one foot. There might be a yardstick in your classroom. Three rulers laid end to end measure about a yard because 3 feet equals a yard. One yard also equals 36 inches.

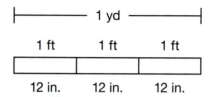

Abbreviations	
inch	in.
foot	ft
yard	yd

It helps to have a mental image of these units so you can estimate lengths. In this table we list some items that measure about 1 inch or 1 foot or 1 yard.

Unit	Example
1 inch	the distance across a quarter
1 foot	the length of a man's shoe
1 yard	the length of a big step

Justify Would you measure the distance around the block in inches? Why?

Inches, Feet, Yards

Make a table like the one above using objects in the room. Use your ruler to find at least two items to represent each unit of measure. Work with a partner or in a small group. Each person should make his or her own table.

Example 1

This table shows the number of inches in 1, 2, and 3 feet. Copy the table. Continue the pattern to 4 feet and 5 feet to find how many inches tall a 5-foot step ladder would be.

Feet	1	2	3	4	5
Inches	12	24	36		

Each additional foot adds 12 inches.

Feet	1	2	3	4	5
Inches	12	24	36	48	60

A 5-foot step ladder is **60 inches** tall.

Example 2

Use a ruler to measure the length of the pencil below in inches.

We place our ruler so that the 0 inch mark is at one end of the pencil. Then we look at the number on the ruler that is even with the other end of the pencil. We see that the pencil is **3 inches** long.

Example 3

Use the ruler to measure the length of the arrow below to the nearest inch.

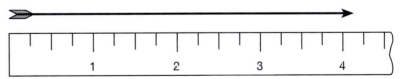

We see that the arrow is between 4 and 5 inches long. It is closer to 4 inches than 5 inches. Measured to the nearest inch, the arrow is 4 inches long.

Lesson Practice

a. Hold your ruler flat, and then balance it on the side of your forefinger. How many inches of the ruler are on each side of your finger?

b. Six rulers, each 12 inches long, are laid end to end. How many yards do they reach?

c. Use your ruler to find the distance from point *A* to point *B* to the nearest inch.

A   *B*
●   ●

d. Use a ruler to find the distance from point *C* to point *D* to the nearest inch.

C   *D*
●   ●

e. This table shows how many feet equal 1, 2, or 3 yards. The lines across a football field are five yards apart. Extend the table to find how many feet equal 5 yards.

Yards	1	2	3	4	5
Feet	3	6	9		

Written Practice *Distributed and Integrated*

1. Use a ruler to measure the length of the eraser below in inches.
(34)

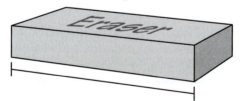

2. **Analyze** Gina paid seven dollars and fifty cents for a movie ticket and two dollars and fifty cents for snacks. Altogether, how much did Gina spend?
(21, 22)

3. The binoculars were on sale for $49. Round the price to the nearest ten dollars.
(15)

4. Write 549 using words.
(12)

5. This map shows Tracy's house and school. Describe how to go from Tracy's house to school.
(31)

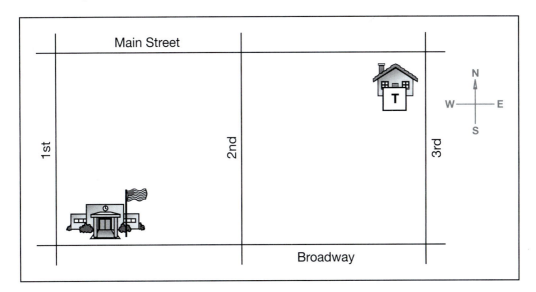

6. **Analyze** The price of a box of cereal is $3.97. Norman has a coupon for 50¢ off the regular price. If Norman uses the coupon, how much will the cereal cost?
(20, 21, 26)

7. What temperature is shown on this thermometer?
(4)

8. What are the next four numbers in this sequence?
(2)

12, 24, 36, _____, _____, _____, _____, ...

9. **Multiple Choice** Which set of coins is $\frac{3}{100}$ of a dollar?
(29)

A 3 quarters   **B** 3 dimes

C 3 nickels   **D** 3 pennies

Add or subtract, as shown:

10. $200 − $44
(28)

11. 7 + 7 + 7 + 7
(10)

12. 463 − 200
(19)

13. $567 + $32
(16)

14. $2.50 − $1.49
(26, 28)

15. 47¢ + 38¢ + $1.00
(21, 24)

Find the missing addend:

16. 10 + m + 14 = 36
(9, 24)

17. 100 = 30 + ☐
(9)

18. A mile is 5,280 feet. Use words to write that number.
(32)

19. Before leaving for school, Ruben looked at the clock.
(3) What time was it?

20. (Formulate) A toll road charges 10¢ per mile.
(10) What is the charge to drive 8 miles on the toll road?
Write a number sentence to answer the question.

Real-World Connection

Jenny and Olivia wanted to find out how old they are in days. Jenny calculated that she is 3,657 days old while Olivia figured she is 4,387 days old. How many days older is Olivia than Jenny? How many years older is Olivia than Jenny? (Hint: There are 365 days in a year.)

LESSON 35

• Measuring to the Nearest Quarter Inch

Power Up

facts	Power Up 35
jump start	Count up by 3s from 0 to 30. Count up by 9s from 0 to 90. Write a fact family using the numbers 8, 2, and 10. Write "five hundred forty" using digits.
mental math	**a. Number Sense:** $18 + 9$ **b. Estimation:** Is $12 closer to $10 or $20? **c. Money:** $1.00 - $0.10 **d. Number Line:** What number does point *B* stand for?

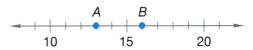

problem solving	Mai has four coins that are worth 22¢ altogether. What are the coins?

New Concept

In this lesson we will draw an inch ruler and divide it into half inches and quarter inches. Then we will use the ruler to measure.

In the last lesson we measured objects to the nearest inch. The length of most objects is between inch marks. We can name these measures with the number of whole inches plus the fraction of an inch.

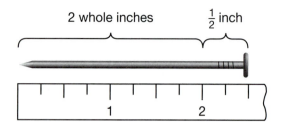

2 whole inches $\frac{1}{2}$ inch

The nail measures 2 whole inches plus $\frac{1}{2}$ inch. We say the nail is $2\frac{1}{2}$ inches long.

Activity

Inch Ruler

Materials: inch ruler, pencil, strip of card stock about 6 inches long

You will make your own ruler. You need a strip of card stock about 6 inches long, a pencil, and a ruler. Lay the strip of card stock sideways on your desk. Lay the ruler on top of it so that you can read the number of inches. Match the left end of the ruler to the left end of the strip. Then slide the ruler toward you a little bit so that you can mark on the strip.

Strip of Card Stock

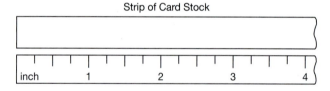

Step 1: At each inch mark on your ruler, make a mark on the strip of paper. The inch marks should all be the same size. Then number the marks as they are numbered on your ruler. When you are done, the strip of paper should look like this.

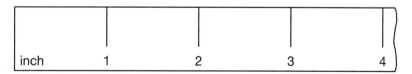

Step 2: Now set the ruler aside and use just your pencil and the strip of paper. Find the halfway point between the inch marks and make the half-inch marks. The half-inch marks should be shorter than the inch marks.

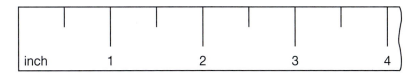

Step 3: We will make one more set of marks on the ruler. Find the halfway point between each pair of marks and make the quarter-inch marks. These are the shortest marks.

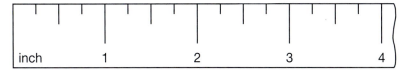

Save this ruler as a bookmark. We will use it for measuring. First we will use it for counting.

- Point to the marks on the ruler as you count by half-inches. Counting by half-inches is like counting by half-dollars.

- Point to the marks on the ruler as you count by quarter-inches (fourths of an inch). Counting by quarter-inches is like counting by quarters with money.

(**Analyze**) Justin measured the lengths of 3 pieces of ribbon. The red ribbon was $2\frac{1}{2}$ inches long, the blue ribbon was $\frac{1}{2}$ inch long, and the white ribbon was $3\frac{3}{4}$ inches long. Write the colors of ribbon in order from shortest length to longest length.

Example

Use your ruler to find the distance between Danbury and Waterbury on the map in inches.

We place the 0 inch mark of the ruler at the dot for Danbury. The dot for Waterbury is at the mark halfway between 2 inches and 3 inches. So the distance between the towns on the map is **$2\frac{1}{2}$ in.**

Use the ruler you made and this map to find the distance in inches between the cities on this map.

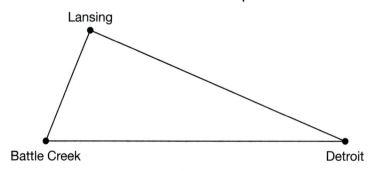

a. From Battle Creek to Detroit

b. From Battle Creek to Lansing

c. From Detroit to Lansing

d. Use your ruler to draw a segment that is $1\frac{1}{2}$ inches long.

Written Practice — *Distributed and Integrated*

1. All stuffed animals were on sale for $5.00 off the regular price. The
(20, 26) regular price of a stuffed lion was $9.99. What was the sale price of the lion?

2. Alison bought a stuffed animal on sale for $4.99. Sales tax was
(18, 22) $0.35. What was the total price, including sales tax?

3. **Interpret** The table below shows the height in inches of four
(17) students. Write the names of the students in order from shortest to tallest.

Student	Height
Lindsay	72
Iva	59
Chad	66
Nash	76

4. Round $26 to the nearest ten dollars.
(15)

5. This map shows that Paula lives 3 blocks from school. Describe a
(31) way to go to Paula's house from school.

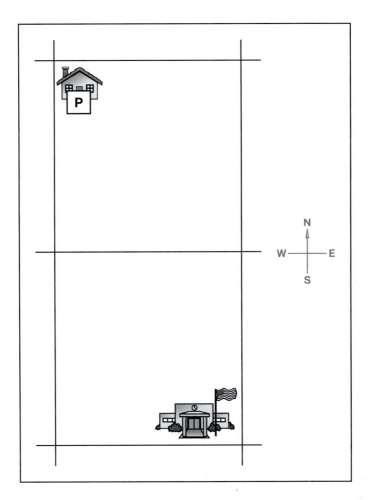

6. a. One foot is equal to how many inches?
(34)

b. Two feet is equal to how many inches?

7. **Represent** Use a ruler to draw a line segment that is $2\frac{1}{4}$ inches
(35) long.

What are the next four numbers in each sequence?

8. 9, 18, 27, _____, _____, _____, _____, ...
(2)

9. 33, 44, 55, _____, _____, _____, _____, ...
(2)

Add or subtract, as shown:

10. 64¢ + 46¢ + $1.00
(21, 24)

11. $4.58 − $2.50
(26)

12. $649 + $350
(16)

13. 100 − 33
(28)

14. 9 + 8 + 7
(10)

15. $625 − $175
(19)

16. Find the missing addend: 10 + 15 + ☐ = 75
(9, 24)

17. (**Analyze**) Sarah paid for a 58¢ item with three quarters. What is
(14, 25) the fewest number of coins she should get back in change?

18. A mile is 1,760 yards. Use words to write that number.
(32)

19. To what number is the arrow pointing?
(33)

750   770   790

20. (**Represent**) Draw a picture of this story. Then answer the
(31) question with a complete sentence.

Simpson walked 3 yards south, then 2 yards west,
then 3 yards south, then 4 yards east, then 6 yards
north. In which direction and how far should Simpson
walk to return to where he started?

LESSON 36

• Some and Some More Stories, Part 2

facts   Power Up 36

jump start

 Count up by 10s from 1 to 91.
Count up by 7s from 0 to 49.

✏️ Write 413 in expanded form.

📏 Draw a segment that is 1 inch long.

mental math

a. **Number Sense:** $11 + 10$

b. **Measurement:** How many inches are in 1 foot?

c. **Time:** Mike started his homework at 3:25 in the afternoon. He finished it 2 hours later. What time did Mike finish his homework?

d. **Patterns:** What number is missing from the pattern shown below?

| 12 | 14 | 16 | 18 | _____ |

problem solving

Four children can sit on each park bench. If there are 3 benches, how many children can sit on the benches?

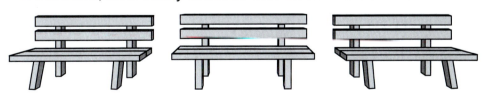

New Concept

Recall that some and some more stories have three (or more) numbers.

$$\text{Some} + \text{some more} = \text{total}$$

Usually, one number will be missing. If we know the other numbers, we can figure out the missing number. A story may ask a question about any one of the numbers.

Example 1

John rode his bike nine miles in the morning. He rode his bike some more in the afternoon. In all, John rode his bike fifteen miles. How many miles did he ride in the afternoon?

This is a some and some more story.

$$\text{Some} + \text{some more} = \text{total}$$

$$\underset{\text{(morning)}}{9 \text{ miles} +} \quad \underset{\text{(afternoon)}}{? \text{ miles}} \quad \underset{\text{(all)}}{= 15 \text{ miles}}$$

Instead of using a question mark, we can use a letter to stand for the unknown number.

$$9 + m = 15$$

We can also write the information this way.

$$\begin{array}{r} \text{Some} \\ + \text{ Some more} \\ \hline \text{Total} \end{array} \qquad \begin{array}{r} 9 \\ + \ m \\ \hline 15 \end{array}$$

How many miles did John ride in the afternoon? Since $9 + 6 = 15$, we answer, **"John rode his bike 6 miles in the afternoon."**

Example 2

Pasadena is on the road between Glendale and Azusa. It is 13 miles from Pasadena to Azusa and 18 miles from Glendale to Azusa. How far is it from Glendale to Pasadena?

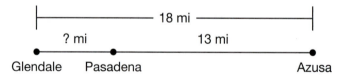

This is a some and some more story. From Glendale to Pasadena is some of the distance. From Pasadena to Azusa is some more of the distance. From Glendale to Azusa is the total distance.

$$\text{Some} + \text{some more} = \text{total}$$

$$\square \text{ mi} + \quad 13 \text{ mi} \quad = 18 \text{ mi}$$

We will use ☐ to stand for the unknown distance from Glendale to Pasadena.

$$☐ + 13 = 18$$

Since $5 + 13 = 18$, **from Glendale to Pasadena is 5 miles.**

Connect How would you write $☐ + 13 = 18$ as a related subtraction problem? How do you know your answer is correct?

Lesson Practice

a. Refer to the map to answer the question. How far is it from Jackson to Denton?

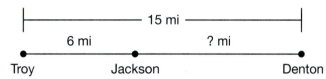

b. A biathlon is a race that includes running and biking. In a biathlon, Jeff ran and biked a total of 36 miles. He biked 24 miles. How many miles did he run?

c. Write a some and some more story with a question for this number sentence.

$$☐ \text{ mi} + 6 \text{ mi} = 10 \text{ mi}$$

Written Practice *Distributed and Integrated*

1. Nelson bought a pair of stilts for $199. The sales tax was $16.
(16) What was the total price of the stilts, including tax?

2. **Analyze** On stilts, Nelson stood 12 inches taller. If Nelson was
(36) 68 inches tall standing on stilts, how tall was Nelson when he was not standing on stilts?

3. Round the total price of the stilts in problem **1** to the nearest
(15) hundred dollars.

4. Nelson wrote a check to *Joys of Toys* for the total price of the
(12) stilts in problem **1**. Write the total price of the stilts using words.

5. **Verify** The distance from Tan's house to the park is 100 yards.
(34) Is 100 yards equal to 30 feet or 300 feet?

6. **Explain** Which has greater value, three quarters or seven
(17, 25) dimes? How do you know?

7. Mr. Simms is 6 feet tall. Continue this table to find how many
(34) inches tall Mr. Simms is.

Feet	1	2	3	4	5	6
Inches	12	24	36	48		

What are the next four numbers in each sequence?

8. 14, 21, 28, _____, _____, _____, _____, ⋯
(2)

9. 8, 16, 24, _____, _____, _____, _____, ⋯
(2)

Add or subtract, as shown:

10. $987 − $245
(19)

11. $650 + $250
(16)

12. $7.95 − $1.50
(26)

13. 6 + 6 + 6 + 6
(10)

14. 200 − 122
(28)

15. $5.49 + $0.86
(22)

16. Find the missing addend: $100 = m + 25$
(9)

17. Write "six-hundred three thousand, six hundred forty" using digits.
(32)

18. What fraction of a dollar is 3 quarters?
(29)

19. Use a ruler to measure the distance from Davis to Fairfield on
(35) this map.

Davis

Fairfield

20. This odometer display shows how many miles? Write the number
(32) with digits and with words.

LESSON 37

• Estimating Lengths and Distances

facts   Power Up 37

jump start

 Count up by 2s from 0 to 40.
Count up by 4s from 0 to 40.

 Write "twenty-five dollars and ninety cents" using a dollar sign and digits.

Draw a segment that is 3 inches long.

mental math

a. Money: Which has the greater value?

3 nickels or 30¢

b. Number Sense: 40 + 40

c. Number Sense: 3 + 9 + 7

d. Time: It is night. What time will it be 3 hours after the time shown on this clock?

problem solving   The years 2000 and 2004 were leap years. The year 2028 will also be a leap year. Use a pattern of counting by 4s to list the leap years between 2004 and 2028.

New Concept

In this lesson, you will measure lengths and distances. You and a partner will choose six objects or distances to measure.

You will measure two of the objects in inches. These should be small objects like the length of a pencil or the width of a book.

You will measure the next two objects or distances in feet. These should be larger objects like the length of a row of desks or the distance from your seat to the chalkboard.

You will measure the final two objects or distances in yards. These should be several yards such as the length or width of the classroom.

Estimating and Measuring Lengths

Materials: ruler, yardstick

Copy the chart below on a piece of paper. With your partner, decide on six objects to measure and record them in the first column of the chart.

Object to be measured	Estimated length	Measured length
1.	inches	inches
2.	inches	inches
3.	feet	feet
4.	feet	feet
5.	yards	yards
6.	yards	yards

Before you measure with a ruler or yardstick, estimate the measure of each object or distance you choose. We estimate by making a careful guess. You may want to take small steps by placing one foot just in front of another to help you estimate feet. You can take big steps to help you estimate yards. You should discuss your estimates with your partner. Write down your estimate before you measure with a ruler or yardstick.

When measuring yards, you can use three rulers instead of a yardstick. Record the closest whole number of inches, feet, or yards for each object measured.

Analyze Find 2 items in the classroom that would measure about 1 foot together.

a. Estimate the height of your classroom in yards. (Hint: Imagine taking big steps up the wall.)

b. Use your answer to problem **a** to estimate the height of your classroom in feet.

Written Practice

Distributed and Integrated

Formulate Write number sentences for the stories in problems **1** and **2**. Then answer each question.

1. Bill spent a dollar and a half for a salad and a dollar and a half for a sandwich. Altogether, how much did Bill spend on the salad and sandwich?
_(21, 22)

2. Sherry rode her bike 11 miles in the morning. She rode again in the afternoon. Altogether, Sherry rode 25 miles. How many miles did she ride in the afternoon?
₍₃₆₎

3. Sherman bought four pirate costumes for $165 plus $13 tax. What was the total price of the costumes with tax?
_(16, 18)

4. Write the answer to problem **3** using words.
₍₁₂₎

5. Connie walks 5 blocks to school. This map shows Connie's house and school. Write directions that describe one route to Connie's house from school.
₍₃₁₎

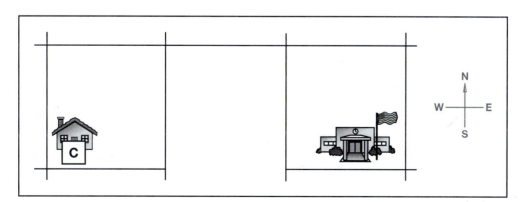

6. Write 5,280 in expanded form.
_(11, 32)

7. _(2, 13) (Justify) It takes about 20 minutes to walk a mile. About how long would it take to walk two miles? Explain how you found your answer.

8. ₍₃₅₎ Use your ruler to measure the length of each segment.

A   B   C

     a. From point *A* to point *B*

     b. From point *B* to point *C*

     c. From point *A* to point *C*

9. ₍₃₎ Daniel hurried home from school. He saw a clock through a store window. What time was it?

10. _(15, 27)   **a.** Write these amounts in order from least to greatest: $116, $120, $110.

     b. Is $116 closer to $100 or $200?

11. _(14, 25) Sara owed 83¢. She paid with nine dimes. List the coins she should get back.

12. ₍₂₎ A week is 7 days. Copy and extend this table to find the number of days in 8 weeks.

Weeks	1	2	3	4				
Days	7	14	21					

Add or subtract, as shown:

13. ₍₁₀₎ $4 + 5 + 6 + 7$

14. ₍₂₈₎ $300 - 95$

15. _(21, 24) 50¢ + 48¢ + 92¢

16. ₍₁₉₎ $360 - $150

17. ₍₁₆₎ $547 + $20

18. ₍₂₆₎ $2.80 - $2.75

19. ₍₉₎ Find the missing addend: $100 = m + 25$

20. (35) **Represent** Use a ruler to draw the line and points from problem **8** on your paper. Include point *D* so that the length from point *A* to point *D* is $3\frac{1}{4}$ inches.

Real-World Connection

Kyle collects baseball cards. He collected 250 cards the first year and gave 94 away. The following year he collected 36 cards and gave away 17. How many cards did Kyle have at the end of the second year? Write number sentences to show your answer.

LESSON 38

• **Reading a Clock to the Nearest Minute**

jump start   Count up by halves from 0 to 5.
Count up by 5s from 25 to 75.

 Write a fact family using the numbers 4, 9, and 13.

Draw a segment that is $1\frac{1}{2}$ inches long.

mental math

a. **Number Sense:** $13 - 8$

b. **Number Sense:** $200 + 50 + 8$

c. **Money:** $\$1.00 - \$0.75$

d. **Money:** Find the value of these bills and coins:

problem solving   The grocery store sells juice boxes in packages of 2 boxes. Joy bought 8 juice boxes altogether. How many packages did she buy?

In Lesson 3 we learned to read an analog clock to the nearest 5 minutes. We recall that the analog clock is a circular "scale" showing the numbers 1 through 12. There are tick marks between the numbers.

The short hand is the hour hand and it moves all the way around the clock in twelve hours. The long hand is the minute hand and it moves from one tick mark to the next tick mark in one minute. The minute hand moves all the way around the clock in one hour.

Example 1

It is afternoon. Write the time shown on the clock in digital form.

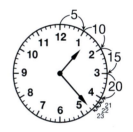

The hour hand is between the 1 and the 2, so it is after 1 p.m. The minute hand is between the 4 and the 5. We skip count by fives until we get to the number before the minute hand: 5, 10, 15, 20. Then, we count the tick marks by ones until we get to the mark the minute hand is pointing to: 21, 22, 23. The time to the minute is **1:23 p.m.**

Example 2

Use your student clock to show this time:

Another way to say 4:36 is thirty-six minutes after four. Since we know it is after 4, we show the hour hand between 4 and 5. To show the minute hand, we start at 12 and move the minute hand as we skip count by fives to 35. Then we move the hand 1 tick mark to get to 36.

Example 3

The clock shows the time Donald started his homework after school. Write the time in digital form.

Donald started his homework at 4:17 p.m.

Discuss What are some situations when it would be important to know the time to the exact minute?

Lesson Practice If it is morning, what time is shown by each clock?

a.    b.    c.

Written Practice
Distributed and Integrated

1. **Formulate** Delia spent $10.00 at the show. She paid $7.50 for
(22, 36) the ticket and spent the rest for snacks. How much did Delia spend for snacks? Write a number sentence and then the answer.

2. Neil bought a five-foot-long sled for $399. Sales tax was $32. Find
(16, 18) the total price of the sled with tax.

3. Write the answer to problem **2** using words.
(12)

4. What fraction of a dollar is a 50¢ coin?
(29)

5. Round these prices to the nearest ten or hundred dollars:
(15)   **a.** nearest hundred dollars   **b.** nearest ten dollars

6. Use your ruler to measure the segments in inches:
(35)

    a. From point *A* to point *B*

    b. From point *B* to point *C*

    c. From point *A* to point *C*

7. **Multiple Choice** The length of your arm is nearly
(34, 37)
    A 2 inches   **B** 2 feet   **C** 2 yards   **D** 2 miles

8. Write the number of miles on this odometer display with digits
(32)
and with words.

$$1\ 1\ 2\ 3\ 0\ 0$$

9. The folder cost 78¢. Tom paid for it with three quarters and one
(25)
nickel. List the coins he should get back.

Conclude   Find the next four numbers in each sequence:

10. 8, 12, 16, _____, _____, _____, _____, . . .
(2)

11. 8, 16, 24, _____, _____, _____, _____, . . .
(2)

12. Extend this table to find the value of 6 quarters.
(25)

Quarters	1	2	3	4		
Value	$0.25	$0.50	$0.75	$1.00		

13. The bicycle tire cost $12.
(15, 30)
    a. Round the price to the nearest ten dollars.

    b. Use the rounded price to find about how much two tires
    would cost.

Add or subtract, as shown:

14. 3 + 3 + 3 + 3
(10)

15. 200 − 38
(28)

16. 75¢ + 75¢
(21, 24)

17. $4.50 − $0.25
(26)

18. **Analyze** If a table is 2 yards long, then it is how many inches
(34) long?

19. The sun rose at the time shown on the clock. Write the
(3, 38) time in digital form.

20. Three cities lie on a road as shown. From Vaughn to
(36) Fort Sumner is 58 miles. From Yeso to Fort Sumner is
22 miles. How far is it from Vaughn to Yeso?

Vaughn   Yeso   Fort Sumner

Real-World
Connection

Samantha had a party. She invited 10 friends. Each of her friends
invited 2 more friends. If everyone invited came to the party, how
many people, including Samantha, were there? You may use
manipulatives to help you find the answer.

LESSON 39

• Stories About Comparing

facts   Power Up 39

jump start    Count up by 3s from 0 to 30.
Count up by 9s from 0 to 90.

It's night. Draw hands on your clock to show 9:04.
Write the time in digital form.

Draw a segment that is $2\frac{1}{2}$ inches long.

mental math

a. **Number Sense:** $15 - 8$

b. **Money:** $50¢ - 40¢$

c. **Calendar:** The year 2008 is a leap year. Which of the following years is a common year?

> **2000**   **2004**   **2009**   **2012**

d. **Patterns:** What number is missing from the pattern shown below?

| 3 | 6 | _____ | 12 | 15 |

problem solving   Josh has two rulers that are each 12 inches long. He placed them as shown in the picture. What is the length from end to end?

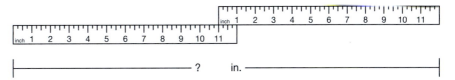

We have learned to solve problems about combining and problems about separating. In this lesson we will learn how to solve two kinds of problems about comparing:

Later − earlier = difference

Greater − lesser = difference

First we will look at problems about comparing two dates. We can subtract to find the number of years between two dates.

Later − Earlier = Difference

We start with the later date, and we subtract the earlier date. The difference is the number of years between the two dates.

Example 1

How many years were there from Charles Lindbergh's flight across the Atlantic in 1927 until Armstrong and Aldrin walked on the moon in 1969?

The later date is 1969. The earlier date is 1927. We subtract.

$$
\begin{array}{rr}
\text{Later} & 1969 \\
-\ \text{Earlier} & -\ 1927 \\
\hline
\text{Difference} & \mathbf{42}
\end{array}
$$

There were **42 years** between the two events.

Example 2

How old was Gloria on her birthday in 2007 if she was born in 1992?

We will use a timeline to solve this problem. Since Gloria was born in 1992, we will start at 1992 on the timeline. We will count up to 2007.

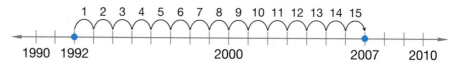

Gloria was **15** on her birthday in 2007.

Connect When you count up on a number line, are you adding or subtracting? What is the relationship between $2007 - 1992 = \square$ and $1992 + \square = 2007$?

We can also subtract to find the difference between two amounts being compared.

Greater − lesser = difference

We start with the greater amount, and we subtract the lesser amount. The difference tells how much greater the bigger number is (or how much smaller the lesser number is).

Example 3

Frederick and his brother played a board game. Frederick scored 354 points. His brother scored 425 points. How many more points did Frederick's brother score than Frederick?

The greater amount is 425. The lesser amount is 354. We subtract.

Greater	425 points
− Lesser	− 354 points
Difference	**71 points**

Frederick's brother scored **71 more points** than Frederick.

Lesson Practice

Write later − earlier = difference number sentences for problems **a** and **b**. Then answer each question.

a. The telephone was invented in 1876. This was how many years after the telegraph was invented in 1844?

b. The bar code that is printed on products was invented in 1974. The laser that is used to read the bar codes was invented in 1960. The bar code was invented how many years after the laser?

Write a greater − lesser = difference number sentence for problem **c.** Then answer the questions.

c. Rose saved her money and bought a stereo that cost $238. Hans saved his money and bought a stereo that cost $255. Whose stereo cost more? How much more?

1. Cindy spent a dollar and a quarter for a milk shake and a dollar
(22, 29) and a half for a chicken sandwich. Altogether, how much did
Cindy spend on the milk shake and the sandwich?

2. Twelve of the 28 children in the class were boys. How many girls
(36) were in the class? Write a number sentence and then answer the
question.

3. The grocery bill was $116. Write that amount using words.
(12)

4. Rounded to the nearest hundred dollars, what is the grocery bill in
(15) problem **3**?

5. This map shows Bill's house and school.
(31)
  a. Bill lives how many blocks from school?

  b. Write directions to Bill's house from school.

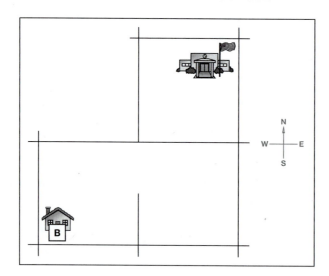

6. Which coin is $\frac{1}{10}$ of a dollar?
(29)

7. (**Represent**) Draw a line that is $2\frac{1}{2}$ inches long.
(35)

8. Driving along the highway, Nathan saw the tens digit of the trip
(2, 11) odometer change about every ten minutes. He saw 150, 160, and
170. What are the next four numbers in this sequence?

150, 160, 170, _____, _____, _____, _____, . . .

9. The ice cream sandwich cost 64¢. Bret paid for it with three
(25) quarters. List the coins he should get back.

10. A ticket to the amusement park cost $38.
(15, 30)
 a. Round $38 to the nearest ten dollars.

 b. Use the rounded price to find about how much two tickets
  would cost.

11. How much money is five quarters, four dimes, three nickels, and
(25) two pennies?

Add or subtract, as shown:

12. $76 + $284
(16)

13. 100 − 63
(28)

14. 37¢ + 48¢ + $1
(21, 24)

15. $8.50 − $6.30
(26)

16. **Multiple Choice** Your classroom door is about how wide?
(34, 37)
 A 1 inch   **B** 1 foot   **C** 1 yard   **D** 1 mile

17. (**Analyze**) Arrange these amounts of money in order from least to
(21, 27) greatest: $2, $0.08, 12¢.

18. Write nine hundred thousand, three hundred thirty-two using
(32) digits.

19. Albert was eager for lunch. He glanced at the clock on
(38) the wall. What time was it?

20. Emma has four quarters and three dimes. Angela has
(25, 39) nineteen dimes. Which girl has more money? Write and
  solve a greater − lesser = difference problem to show
  how much more.

Real-World Connection

The odometer on the Allgood's car reads 3,632 miles. Mr. Allgood
wants to get a tune-up for the car when the odometer reads 5,000
miles. How many more miles can Mr. Allgood drive before he has
to take his car in for a tune-up?

- **Missing Numbers in Subtraction**

- **Some Went Away Stories, Part 2**

facts   Power Up 40

jump start    Count up by 10s from 2 to 92.
Count up by 7s from 0 to 49.

It's morning. Draw hands on your clock to show 7:33. Write the time in digital form.

Write "one thousand three hundred" using digits.

mental math

a. Money: 60¢ + 20¢

b. Number Sense: 20 − 8

c. Money: Which of these amounts has the greatest value?

$1.23 $1.45 $1.20

d. Number Line: Which point stands for the number 17?

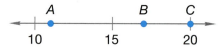

problem solving   Copy this picture on your paper. Then trace each triangle in your picture. How many different triangles can you find?

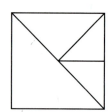

Missing Numbers in Subtraction   We have solved subtraction problems to find the difference between two numbers. In this lesson we will solve problems that are missing a different number.

$19 - m = 7$ "Nineteen minus what number equals seven?"

$\square - 30 = 42$ "What number minus thirty equals forty-two?"

Remember that subtraction is separating one larger group into two smaller groups. The first number is always the greatest and the other two numbers are smaller. If the first number is missing, we can add the other two numbers to find the answer. If the second number is missing, we can subtract the difference from the first number to find the missing number.

Connect Think of the second number sentence above as a member of a fact family and write the family's two addition facts. How can these addition facts help us find the answer?

Example 1

Find each missing number:

a. $80 - \square = 45$ b. $m - 13 = 18$

a. The second number is missing. We can subtract 45 from 80 to find the answer: $80 - 45 = $ **35.**

b. The first number is missing. We can add the other two numbers to find the answer: $18 + 13 = $ **31.**

Some Went Away Stories, Part 2

Remember that some went away stories can be written two ways:

Some $-$ some went away $=$ what is left

$$\begin{array}{r} \text{Some} \\ - \text{ Some went away} \\ \hline \text{What is left} \end{array}$$

We have solved several problems to find "what is left." In this lesson we will learn to solve problems in which one of the other numbers is missing.

Example 2

Read the following story and write a some went away number sentence. Then find the missing number.

Estelle went into the store with $150. She bought some items and left with $62. How much money did Estelle spend in the store?

Estelle had $150. After spending some, she had $62.

$$\$150 - \square = \$62$$

We can subtract $62 from $150 to find the answer:
$150 − $62 = $88. **Estelle spent $88 in the store.**

Example 3

Carson had a big bag of marbles. He gave his best friend 54 marbles. Carson had 80 marbles left. How many marbles did Carson have before he gave any marbles to his friend? Write and solve a some went away number sentence to find the answer.

Carson had some marbles. Then 54 went away. He had 80 marbles left.

$$m - 54 = 80$$

We can add to find the missing number: 54 + 80 = 134.
Carson had 134 marbles.

Lesson Practice

Find each missing number in problems **a–c.**

a. $\square - 16 = 16$ **b.** $66 - m = 24$

c. $\square - 388 = 125$

d. Before the carnival, Angus had $21.50. He spent some money on rides and food. After the carnival, Angus had $9.00. How much did Angus spend at the carnival? Write and solve a some went away problem to find the answer.

Written Practice

Distributed and Integrated

1. The blender cost $37. Debbie gave the clerk a $50 bill. How much
(14) money should Debbie get back?

2. Nicole found 5 quarters in her purse and 5 more quarters in a
(25) drawer. Altogether, how much money did she find?

3. Four new tires cost two hundred eighty-nine dollars. Use digits
(12) and a dollar sign to write that amount.

4. Is the cost of the four tires in problem **3** closer to $200 or $300?
(15)

5. John lives two blocks from Mike's house and two blocks from
(31) school. John stops at Mike's house before he goes to school.
Describe a way John could walk to Mike's house and on to
school without walking twice on the same street.

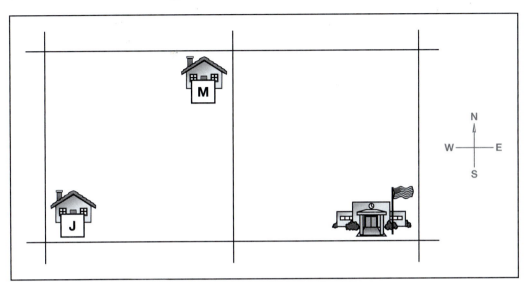

6. (Justify) It takes about 20 minutes to walk a mile. About how
(29) long would it take to walk half a mile? Explain how you found your
answer.

7. Use your ruler to measure the segments.
(35)

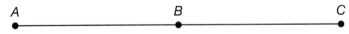

A   B   C

   a. From point *A* to point *B*

   b. From point *B* to point *C*

   c. From point *A* to point *C*

8. (Analyze) Denzel was born in 1987. His sister Angie was born in
(39) 1972. What is the age difference between Denzel and Angie? Who
is older?

9. The carton of milk cost 55¢. Derek paid for the milk with two
(14, 25) quarters and a dime. List the coins he should get back.

10. (List) Count by nines from 9 to 99. Write the list on your paper.
(2) Start like this: 9, 18, ...

11. **Represent** Draw a map to solve this problem. Mac lives
(31) 2 blocks west of school and Jason lives 3 blocks east of school.
In which direction and how far does Mac walk from his home to
Jason's home?

12. To make a "first down" in football, the team needs to move the
(34) ball forward at least 10 yards. Copy and extend this table to find
the number of feet in 10 yards.

Yards	1	2	3	4	5	6	7	8	9	10
Feet	3	6	9							

Add or subtract, as shown:

13. $5.48 + $3.27
(22)

14. $450 − $150
(19)

15. 4 + 4 + 4 + 4
(10)

16. 500 − 75
(28)

17. Find the missing addend: $25 + m = 75$
(9)

18. As Della swam laps, she paused to check the pool
(4) thermometer. What temperature was the water?

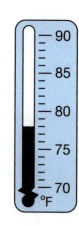

19. **Represent** Draw two line segments. Make one
(35) segment $1\frac{1}{4}$ inches and the other $1\frac{3}{4}$ inches.

20. Marco has 35 stickers. After decorating his notebook,
(39) he had 29 stickers left. How many stickers did Marco
use to decorate his notebook? Write a some went away
number sentence to help you find the answer.

Focus on

• Scale Maps

When you draw a map from school to home, you want the distance on the map to accurately represent the distance you travel. We call this drawing the map to **scale.** On a map drawn to scale, each inch on the map equals a certain number of miles.

Each inch on this map equals one mile. To find the actual distance from Robin's house to the school, use your ruler to measure the distance on the scale map. The **line segment** between Robin's house and school measures 2 inches. Since one inch equals one mile, two inches equal two miles. So the actual distance from Robin's house to the school is 2 miles.

We can also describe the streets as either parallel or perpendicular to each other. Line segments are **perpendicular** if they **intersect** and make square corners, like Birch Avenue and 2nd Street. Line segments are **parallel** if they do not intersect and stay in the same distance apart, like 1st Street and 2nd Street.

Use your ruler and this map to answer problems **1–8.**

1. How far is it from Todd's house to school if he travels along the lines (roads)?

2. If Todd wants to take the shortest route to school, how many choices does he have?

3. How far does Todd ride his bike each day traveling from home to school and back home?

4. How far is it from Marcy's house to school?

5. How many miles is it from Todd's house to Marcy's house along the roads?

6. Todd rode his bike from school straight to Marcy's house. Then he rode home. How far did Todd ride?

7. Name two streets **parallel** to Oak Avenue.

8. Name two streets **perpendicular** to Oak Avenue.

Scale Map

Material: ruler

Draw a map that matches the directions below. Let each mile be one inch on the map.

Jaime lives on the northeast corner of Maxwell St. and Grand Ave. On his way to school, Jaime rides two miles east on Maxwell. Then he turns south on Lime Ave. and rides one mile to Newton St. The school is on the southwest corner of Newton and Lime. Lime is parallel to Grand, and Newton is parallel to Maxwell. All streets are straight and Newton and Grand intersect.

Then write directions that describe how Jaime can get home from school by riding on Newton and Grand.

• Modeling Fractions

facts	Power Up 41
jump start	Count up by 25s from 0 to 200. Count up by fourths from 0 to 2.
	It's morning. Draw hands on your clock to show 8:59. Write the time in digital form.
	The afternoon temperature was 16°C. At night it was 9 degrees cooler. Mark your thermometer to show the temperature at night.
mental math	**a. Estimation:** Round $175 to the nearest hundred dollars.
	b. Number Sense: $18 - 8$
	c. Time: A decade is 10 years. How many years are in 2 decades?
	d. Money: Find the value of these bills and coins:

problem solving

Ted wrote this sequence to help him find the number of feet in 1 yard, 2 yards, 3 yards, and so on. Which number is incorrect in his sequence? Why?

3, 6, 9, 12, 15, 17, 21, 24, 27

We have used fractions to describe parts of an hour and parts of a dollar.

Thirty minutes is $\frac{1}{2}$ of an hour.

A quarter is $\frac{1}{4}$ of a dollar.

We have also used models to illustrate fractions.

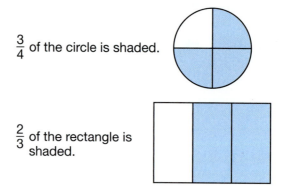

$\frac{3}{4}$ of the circle is shaded.

$\frac{2}{3}$ of the rectangle is shaded.

In this lesson we will make fraction manipulatives. First, we will learn some vocabulary.

- The **denominator** of a fraction shows how many equal parts make the whole.

- The **numerator** shows how many parts we are describing.

numerator $\longrightarrow$ $\frac{3}{4}$ is shaded.
denominator $\longrightarrow$

Activity

Fraction Manipulatives

Materials: **Lesson Activities 15 and 16,** crayons or colored pencils, scissors, paper envelope or locking plastic bag

1. Your teacher will give you four fraction circles on two sheets of paper.

2. Use crayons or colored pencils to color each circle a different color. Use only one color for a circle. Color both the front and back of the circle.

3. After you color all the circles, cut out each one. Then cut each circle into pieces by cutting on the lines.

4. You will use your fraction manipulatives for the examples and for later lessons and problem sets.

5. Store your fraction manipulatives in an envelope or plastic bag when you are not using them.

Example 1

Name the fraction of a circle shown using digits and words.

We see that the circle is divided into 4 equal parts. One of the parts is shaded. We find the fraction piece that is one of four equal parts. The fraction is $\frac{1}{4}$, which we read **"one fourth."**

Analyze What is the denominator of the fraction? What does it tell you?

Example 2

Name the fraction shown.

We see that the circle is divided into 5 equal parts. Three of the parts are shaded. The fraction shown is $\frac{3}{5}$, which we read **"three fifths."**

Analyze What is the numerator of the fraction? What does it tell you?

Lesson Practice

a. What is the denominator of the fraction $\frac{4}{5}$?

b. What is the numerator of the fraction $\frac{2}{3}$?

Use your fraction manipulatives to model each fraction shown below. Then name the fraction using digits and words.

c.   **d.**   **e.**

1. Rosa's ticket cost $4.75. Her brother's ticket cost $3.25. What
(18, 22) was the total price of the two tickets?

2. Bradley read 32 pages before dinner. He read some more pages
(36) after dinner. Bradley read 58 pages in all. How many pages did he
read after dinner? Write a number sentence, and then answer the
question.

3. There were 238 fans at the game. Write that number using words.
(12)

4. Round the number of fans in problem **3** to the nearest hundred.
(15)

5. This map shows John's house, Mike's house, and school. Today
(31) Mike is stopping at John's house before going to school. If Mike
does not retrace his steps or return to his house, what route will
Mike take to John's house and on to school?

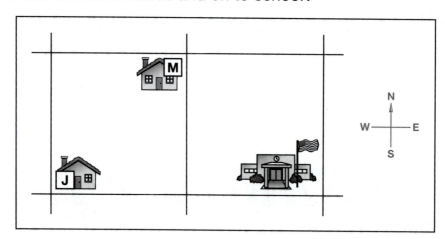

6. This map shows three towns on a highway. Use your ruler to
(35) measure the distance in inches:

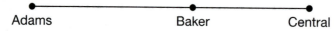

Adams   Baker   Central

   a. From Adams to Baker

   b. From Baker to Central

   c. From Adams to Central

7. If each inch on the map in problem **6** represents ten miles, then
(inv. 4) how many miles is it from Adams to Central?

8. What number is indicated on this number line?

350   400   450

9. The ride cost 65¢. Nick paid with three quarters. List the coins he
(14, 25) should get back.

10. To find the number of feet in 8 yards, Shannon said the following
(2) sequence of numbers. What is the eighth number of the sequence?

3, 6, 9, 12, …

11. An insect has 6 legs. Andy found the number of legs on 7 insects
(2) by making a table. Copy and extend the table to find Andy's
answer.

Insects	1	2	3	4	5	6	7
Legs	6	12	18				

12. Name the fraction shown using digits and words.
(41)

13. (**Represent**) Draw two perpendicular lines that are
(35,
Inv. 4) each $3\frac{1}{4}$ inches long.

Add or subtract, as shown:

14. 200 + 300 + 400
(24)

15. $5.25 + $3.17
(22)

16. 45 + 92 + 11
(24)

17. $800 − $225
(28)

18. Find the missing number: ☐ − 20 = 55.
(40)

19. (**Analyze**) Arrange these collections of coins in order from lowest
(17, 25) value to highest value.

6 dimes   9 nickels   2 quarters

20. (**Represent**) Sketch a map to help you with this problem:
(31)

*Bill and Ted rode their bikes home from school in opposite
directions. Bill rode seven blocks east. Ted rode five blocks
west. How many blocks and in what direction would Bill ride
from his home to Ted's home?*

LESSON 42

• Drawing Fractions

facts

Power Up 42

jump start

Count down by 2s from 30 to 0.
Count up by 4s from 0 to 40.

It's afternoon. Draw hands on your clock to show 12:25. Write the time in digital form.

The temperature inside the movie theater was 65° F. It was 20 degrees warmer outside the theater. Mark your thermometer to show the outside temperature.

mental math

a. Money: Raj bought a marker for 80¢. He paid $1.00. How much change did he receive? Write your answer with a cent sign.

b. Number Sense: 40 + 50

c. Measurement: How many inches are in 2 feet?

d. Time: It is morning. What time will it be 3 hours after the time shown on the clock?

problem solving

How many different ways can you place three Xs in a row on a tic-tac-toe board? Draw the ways.

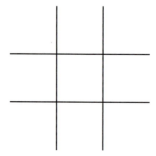

When we draw pictures to show fractions, we are careful to divide the picture into equal parts.

Example 1

Draw a figure and shade $\frac{1}{2}$ of it.

We are careful to divide the figures into two equal parts before shading. Here we show a few examples of $\frac{1}{2}$.

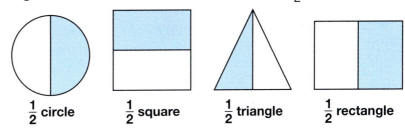

$\frac{1}{2}$ circle $\frac{1}{2}$ square $\frac{1}{2}$ triangle $\frac{1}{2}$ rectangle

The shapes below do not show $\frac{1}{2}$ because the parts are not equal.

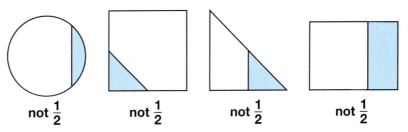

not $\frac{1}{2}$ not $\frac{1}{2}$ not $\frac{1}{2}$ not $\frac{1}{2}$

Generalize   Show other ways to shade $\frac{1}{2}$ of a square.

Example 2

Draw and shade $\frac{1}{3}$ of a rectangle.

We draw a rectangle and divide it into three equal parts. Then we shade one of the parts.

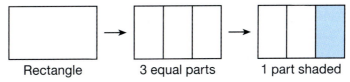

Rectangle   3 equal parts   1 part shaded

Here is another way we could shade $\frac{1}{3}$ of the rectangle:

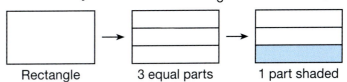

Rectangle   3 equal parts   1 part shaded

Example 3

> **Draw and shade $\frac{3}{4}$ of a circle.**
>
> First we draw a circle. Next we divide the circle into four equal parts. Then we shade three of the parts.

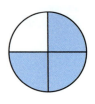

Lesson Practice

   a. Draw a square and shade $\frac{1}{2}$ of it.

   b. Draw a circle and shade $\frac{1}{4}$ of it.

   c. Draw a rectangle and shade $\frac{2}{3}$ of it.

   d. Is $\frac{1}{3}$ of this circle shaded? Why or why not?

Written Practice   *Distributed and Integrated*

1. **Formulate** Simon was running a marathon, which is a 26-mile
(36) race. After running 12 miles he stopped to drink some water. How many miles did he have to go to finish the marathon? Write a number sentence, and then answer the question.

2. The keyboard cost $385. Sales tax was $21. Find the total price
(16, 18) of the keyboard with tax.

3. Round the total price in problem **2** to the nearest hundred dollars.
(2A)

4. To what number is the arrow pointing on the number line below?
(33)

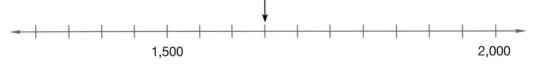

5. **Explain** What does the number 5 in the fraction $\frac{2}{5}$ tell you?
(41, 42)

6. One wall of Mac's bedroom is 4 yards long. How many feet is
(34) 4 yards?

Yards	1	2	3	4
Feet	3	6		

7. **Represent** Draw a rectangle and shade $\frac{1}{4}$ of it.
(42)

8. This map shows three towns on a highway. One-quarter inch
(35, on the map represents one mile. Use your ruler to measure the
Inv. 4) distance between towns. Then answer the questions.

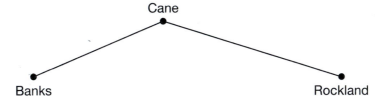

   a. How many miles is it from Rockland to Cane?

   b. How many miles is it from Cane to Banks?

   c. Joyce drove from Rockland to Banks. On her way she drove
   through Cane. How many miles did Joyce drive?

9. Write 800,744 using words.
(32)

10. Stella owed 59¢. She paid with one quarter, three dimes, and a
(25) nickel. List the coins she should get back.

11. The distance around the earth at the equator is about 25,000
(32) miles. Use words to write that number.

12. **Predict** There are 4 quarters in a dollar. Stella counted by 4s to
(2) find the number of quarters in $12. What is the 12th number in this
sequence?

$$4, 8, 12, 16, \ldots$$

13. Simon counted by 12s to find the number of inches in 4 ft. What
(2) is the 4th number that we say when counting by 12s?

14. Find the missing number: $100 - \square = 30$.
(40)

Add or subtract, as shown.

15. 93 + 47 + 58
(24)

16. $300 − $250
(28)

17. 400 + 400
(16)

18. $500 − $336
(28)

19. **Multiple Choice** How much money is $\frac{1}{4}$ of a dollar plus $\frac{1}{10}$ of a
(29) dollar?

    A 25¢   **B** 10¢   **C** 35¢   **D** 40¢

20. After dinner, Sam sat down to read a book and noticed
(38) the clock. What time was it?

Early Finishers
Real-World Connection

Mark needs to buy crayons for his science project. He needs at least 48 crayons to complete the project. He has $6.00 to spend. One store is selling a box of 64 crayons for $3.98. A different store is selling a box of 24 crayons for $1.99. Which is the better buy? Explain your answer.

• Comparing Fractions, Part 1

Power Up

facts

Power Up 43

jump start

 Count up by 100s from 0 to 1,000.
Count up by 7s from 0 to 56.

It's morning. Draw hands on your clock to show 3:46. Write the time in digital form.

Write a fact family using the numbers 5, 9, and 14 in the workspace on your paper.

mental math

a. Money: Which has greater value?

2 dimes or 24¢

b. Number Sense: 25 − 10

c. Number Sense: 7 + 14

d. Patterns: What number is missing from the pattern shown below?

60	____	50	45	40

problem solving

Mr. Ogburn put the oranges into 4 bags. He put 3 oranges in each bag. Altogether, how many oranges did he put into bags? Write a number sentence for this story.

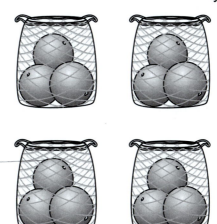

We compare two fractions by deciding if the fractions are equal or if one fraction is greater than the other fraction. For example, $\frac{1}{2}$ is greater than $\frac{1}{4}$.

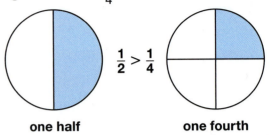

$\frac{1}{2} > \frac{1}{4}$

one half   **one fourth**

Notice that $\frac{1}{2}$ is greater than $\frac{1}{4}$ even though the denominator of $\frac{1}{4}$ is greater than the denominator of $\frac{1}{2}$. This makes sense because 1 out of 2 parts is a larger fraction than 1 out of 4 parts.

Activity

Comparing Fractions

Use your fraction manipulatives to find which fraction of each pair is greater or whether the fractions are equal.

1. $\frac{1}{2}$ and $\frac{1}{3}$ **2.** $\frac{2}{3}$ and $\frac{2}{5}$

3. $\frac{2}{3}$ and $\frac{3}{4}$ **4.** $\frac{1}{2}$ and $\frac{2}{4}$

Example 1

Draw two rectangles the same size. Shade $\frac{1}{2}$ of one rectangle and $\frac{3}{4}$ of the other rectangle. Look at your drawing to compare $\frac{1}{2}$ and $\frac{3}{4}$.

First we draw and shade two rectangles.

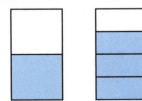

Next we look at the rectangles. We compare *how much* of the whole rectangle is shaded, not the number of parts that are shaded. We see that more than half of the rectangle is shaded when $\frac{3}{4}$ is shaded. We show two ways to write the comparison.

$$\frac{3}{4} > \frac{1}{2} \quad \text{or} \quad \frac{1}{2} < \frac{3}{4}$$

Example 2

The class is painting a mural on a sheet of plywood. Look at the part of the mural that is painted in each answer choice below. Which shows the greatest part painted?

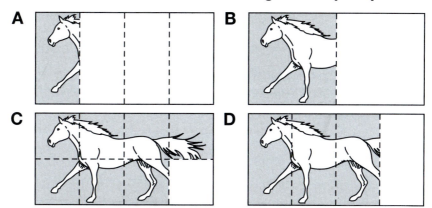

A B

C D

Figure **C** shows the greatest part painted.

Connect For choices **A** through **D**, what fraction of each figure is painted?

Lesson Practice

a. Draw two circles that are the same size. Shade $\frac{1}{2}$ of one circle and $\frac{2}{4}$ of the other circle. Look at your drawings to compare $\frac{1}{2}$ and $\frac{2}{4}$. Use your fraction manipulatives to check your work.

b. Use your fraction manipulatives to compare $\frac{1}{4}$ and $\frac{1}{5}$. Then write the comparison.

c. Draw two rectangles the same size. Shade $\frac{1}{4}$ of one rectangle and $\frac{1}{2}$ of the other rectangle. Then write the comparison. Use your fraction manipulatives to check your work.

1. **Formulate** Sally drove to visit her grandmother who lived
(36) 385 miles away. She stopped after 160 miles to get gas. How
much farther did she have to drive? Write a number sentence
and then answer the question.

2. Gas for her car cost $28. Sally paid with a $20 bill and a $10 bill.
(18, 20) How much money should Sally get back?

3. Sally's grandmother lives 385 miles away. Sally's cousin lives
(27) 326 miles away. Sally's older brother is at college 410 miles away.
Which of the three relatives lives nearest Sally? Which of the
relatives lives farthest from Sally?

4. Sally's grandmother was born in 1945. How old was she in 1995?
(39)

5. The odometer on Sally's car shows this display.
(32)

   a. How far has the car been driven? Write the number using a
   comma.

   b. Use words to state the number of miles the car has been
   driven.

6. The Martins bought a house that cost three hundred eighty
(12, 32) thousand dollars. Use digits and a dollar sign to write that amount
of money.

7. Sarina picked a big basket of peaches. She gave 14 peaches to
(40) her grandmother for a peach pie. Then Sarina had 52 peaches
left. How many peaches did Sarina pick in all? Write and solve a
some went away number sentence to find the answer.

8. **List** Count by eights from 8 to 96. Write the list on your paper.
(2)

This map shows where Leslie and Jenny live. Use this map for problems **9–11.**

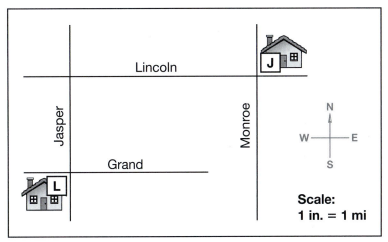

9. The map is drawn so that one inch represents one mile. If Leslie drives from her house to Jenny's house, about how far does she drive?
(Inv. 4)

10. Write directions that describe how to get to Jenny's house from Leslie's house using compass directions and miles.
(31)

11. Look at the map and name a street parallel to Grand.
(Inv. 4)

12. 62 + 32 + 22
(24)

13. 650 − 70
(19)

14. $8.45 + $0.70
(22)

15. $250 − $200
(19)

16. **Analyze** Sketch a map to help you with this problem.
(31, 36)

From Colorado Springs, Ivan drove north 100 miles to Boulder, passing through Denver. From Denver to Boulder is 30 miles. From Denver to Colorado Springs is which direction and how far?

17. Use your fraction manipulatives to show $\frac{2}{3}$. Then draw a picture of the model on your paper.
(41)

18. Use your fraction manipulatives to compare $\frac{2}{3}$ and $\frac{3}{4}$. Write the comparison.
(43)

19. Find the missing number: $175 - \square = 32$.
(40)

20. What is the value of the 4 in 342,891?
(32)

Real-World Connection

In parts of Texas the temperature can have big changes in a single day. On a day in February the temperature rose 47°F. The high temperature was 82°F. What was the low temperature that day? Write a number sentence to show how you found your answer.

44

• **Fractions of a Group**

Power Up

facts   Power Up 44

jump start   Count down by 6s from 60 to 0.
Count down by 9s from 90 to 0.

It's morning. Draw hands on your clock to show 6:39.
Write the time in digital form.

Draw a $1\frac{3}{4}$-inch segment on your worksheet.

mental math
a. **Number Sense:** $19 - 8$

b. **Number Sense:** $22 - 9$

c. **Money:** $\$1.00 - \$0.25$

d. **Number Line:** What number is shown by point *B*?

problem solving   There were 3 boys and 2 girls at the library. Each child checked out 2 books. Altogether, how many books did the children check out?

New Concept

We have used fractions to describe parts of a whole. Sometimes we use fractions to describe parts of a set of items.

$\frac{1}{4}$ of the letters are vowels: **MATH**

$\frac{2}{3}$ of the marbles are blue:

In the examples above, the **denominator** shows the number of items in the set. The **numerator** shows the number of items that are described.

Example 1

What fraction of the marbles in the bag are blue? Use words and digits to name the fraction.

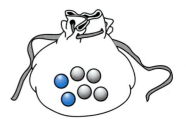

There are 6 marbles in the bag. Two of the 6 marbles are blue. So **two sixths** $\left(\frac{2}{6}\right)$ of the marbles in the bag are blue.

Analyze Are more or less than half of the marbles blue? Explain.

Example 2

Toni has finished $\frac{7}{8}$ of an addition quiz. Which quiz below could be Toni's?

A

3	5	6	3
+ 4	+ 7	+ 4	+ 2
7	12	10	5

4	7	2	7
+ 7	+ 8	+ 6	+ 6
			13

B

3	5	6	3
+ 4	+ 7	+ 4	+ 2
7	12	10	5

4	7	2	7
+ 7	+ 8	+ 6	+ 6
11	15	8	13

C

3	5	6	3
+ 4	+ 7	+ 4	+ 2
7	12	10	5

4	7	2	7
+ 7	+ 8	+ 6	+ 6
11	15		

D

3	5	6	3
+ 4	+ 7	+ 4	+ 2
7	12	10	5

4	7	2	7
+ 7	+ 8	+ 6	+ 6
11	15	8	

Each addition quiz has 8 questions. Since Toni has finished $\frac{7}{8}$ of the test, she has answered 7 of the 8 questions. So Toni's quiz could be **D**.

Lesson Practice

a. What fraction of the names of the days of the week begin with the letter *S*?

> Sunday
> Monday
> Tuesday
> Wednesday
> Thursday
> Friday
> Saturday

b. What fraction of the marbles in the bag are blue?

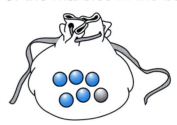

c. Brad has 3 red shirts, 4 blue shirts, and 1 green shirt. What fraction of his shirts are red?

d. What fraction of the letters in the word SAXON are vowels? Use words and digits to name the fraction.

Written Practice   *Distributed and Integrated*

1. Shoes are on sale at *Sam's Shoes*. All shoes regularly priced at
(20) $49 are on sale for $10 off the regular price. What is the sale price of the shoes? Write a number sentence, and then answer the question.

2. Ginger is buying two pairs of shoes for the sale price in problem **1.**
(18)   What is the total price of the shoes?

3. Nita had $70. She bought a pair of gloves and got $32 back from
(40)   the cashier. How much did Nita spend on the gloves? Write a some went away number sentence to find the answer.

4. Find the missing number in each number sentence:
(9, 40)
   a. $\square + 35 = 149$ **b.** $49 - \square = 28$

   c. $m - 200 = 567$

5. When the Olsens' car was four months old, its odometer showed
(32) this display.

    a. How far has the car been driven? Write the number using
    a comma.

    b. Use words to name the number of miles.

6. **Represent** Draw a square and shade $\frac{1}{2}$ of it.
(42)

Use the clock shown for problems **7** and **8.**

7. **Multiple Choice** What time is shown on the clock?
(3, 5)

    A 7:45   **B** 7:15

    C A quarter to 7   **D** A quarter after 7

8. What fraction of the names of the months of the year
(1, 44) begin with the letter J?

9. The paper cost 63¢. Nathan paid with two quarters and 3 nickels.
(25) List the coins he should get back.

10. The population of Durant is sixteen thousand, four hundred sixty.
(32) Use digits to write that number.

11. **List** Count by 25s from 25 to 250. Write the list on your paper.
(2)

Add or subtract, as shown:

12. 41 + 42 + 23   **13.** $150 − $90
(24)   *(19)*

14. 8 + 8 + 8 + 8   **15.** $250 − $237
(10)   *(19)*

16. Draw a circle and divide it into thirds. Shade $\frac{1}{3}$.
(42)

17. Room A collected 458 aluminum cans for the recycling drive.
(39) Room B collected 724 cans. How many more cans did Room B
collect? Write a greater-lesser-difference number sentence to
find the answer.

18. Brooke has 42 crayons. Jason has 84 crayons. About how many
(30) crayons do they have altogether?

19. Use your ruler to draw a line $3\frac{1}{2}$ inches long.
(34)

20. What fraction of the students in your class have names that begin
(44) with the letter M?

Real-World Connection

Mrs. Sullivan's third grade class is having a party. Mrs. Sullivan needs to buy enough balloons for each of the 20 students in the class. The store sells 8 balloons in a bag. How many bags of balloons should Mrs. Sullivan buy?

LESSON 45

• Probability, Part 1

Power Up

facts   Power Up 45

jump start   Count up by 3s from 0 to 30 and back down to 0.

It's night. Draw hands on your clock to show 11:11. Write the time in digital form.

Write these money amounts in order from least to greatest.

$5.80 $5.60 $6.15

mental math   a. **Number Sense:** 23 + 9

b. **Number Sense:** 5 + 12 + 5

c. **Calendar:** How many days are in 3 weeks?

d. **Money:** Find the value of these bills and coins:

problem solving   **Focus Strategy: Make an Organized List**

Rob has a red shirt, a white shirt, blue pants, and tan pants. List the combinations of 1 shirt and 1 pair of pants Rob can wear.

(**Understand**) We will list the different combinations of 1 shirt and 1 pair of pants.

(**Plan**) We can use a **tree diagram** to make an organized list.

Solve For each shirt color, Rob can choose between two different pant colors. We use two branches from each shirt color to connect to each pant color.

Shirt	Pants	Combination
R	B	R, B
	T	R, T
W	B	W, B
	T	W, T

Check We read from left to right along the branches to find the 4 combinations: 1. red shirt and blue pants; 2. red shirt and tan pants; 3. white shirt and blue pants; or 4. white shirt and tan pants.

New Concept

Amy likes to play board games. One game she plays has a spinner that looks like this.

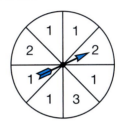

Most of the times Amy spins the spinner, it stops on 1. We say that stopping on 1 is **more likely** because it happens on more spins.

The spinner does not stop on 3 very often. We say that stopping on three is **less likely** because it happens on fewer spins.

Explain Why is it most likely that the spinner will stop on 1, and least likely that the spinner will stop on 3?

Activity
Probability Demonstration

Watch your teacher's demonstration. Decide which outcomes are more likely or less likely to occur.

Example 1

There are 7 marbles in a bag. Two marbles are blue and 5 are gray. Jason reaches into the bag and takes a marble without looking.

    a. Which color marble is Jason more likely to pick? Why?

    b. Which color marble is Jason less likely to pick? Why?

    a. There are more gray marbles than blue marbles, so Jason is more likely to pick **gray.**

    b. There are less blue marbles than gray marbles, so Jason is less likely to pick **blue.**

Example 2

If Nathan spins the spinner one time, is it less likely to stop on 1 or 2?

The part of the spinner with 1 is much larger than the part with 2. So the spinner is more likely to stop on 1 and **less likely to stop on 2.**

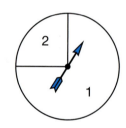

Lesson Practice

For problems **a** and **b** look at the picture of the bag of marbles.

    a. If one marble is taken from the bag, which color is more likely to be picked, blue or white?

    b. If one marble is picked, is it more likely or less likely to be gray?

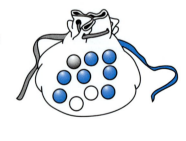

For problems **c** and **d** look at the spinner.

    c. If Dwayne spins the spinner one time, which number is the spinner less likely to stop on, 1 or 3?

    d. If Isabel spins the spinner one time, what number is it most likely to stop on?

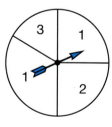

1. All dresses at *Fair Apparel* were on sale for half price. Cheryl
(29) bought a dress regularly priced at $60. What was the sale price?
(*Hint*: Think of the number of minutes in half of an hour.)

2. Jimmy bought a box of 60 dog treats. He used some of the treats to
(40) train his dog to roll over. When he was finished, there were 48 treats
left in the box. How many treats did Jimmy use to train his dog?
Write a some went away number sentence to find the answer.

3. Find the missing number in each number sentence:
(9, 40)
   a. $\square + 26 = 49$ **b.** $700 - \square = 280$

4. What fraction of these stars are blue?
(44)

5. When Jefferson's car was one year old, its odometer showed this
(33) display.

   a. How far had the car been driven? Write the number using a comma.

   b. Use words to write the number of miles.

6. There are 10 dimes and 3 pennies in a bag. Is Kale more likely or
(45) less likely to pick a penny from the bag?

This map shows were Andrew and Tony live. Use this map to answer
problems **7–9.**

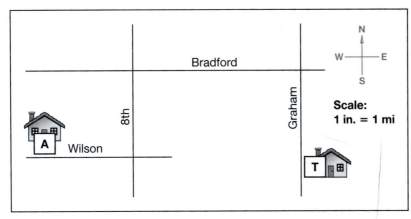

7. The map is drawn so that one inch represents one mile. Traveling on the streets, about how many miles is it from Tony's home to Andrew's home?
(Inv. 4)

8. Write directions for Tony that describe how to get to Andrew's home. Use compass directions and number of miles.
(31)

9. Look at the map and name a street perpendicular to Wilson.
(Inv. 4)

10. Use words to write 412,600.
(32)

11. **List** To find the number of days in 12 weeks, count by sevens. Write the twelve numbers you say on your paper.
(2)

12. **Represent** Draw a figure and shade $\frac{2}{4}$ of it.
(42)

13. **Analyze** Write the fractions in order from least to greatest.
(43)

$$\frac{1}{3}, \frac{1}{5}, \frac{1}{2}, \frac{1}{4}$$

Add or subtract, as shown:

14. $5 + 8 + 7 + 4$
(10)

15. $\$125 - \$100$
(19)

16. $95 + 76 + 52$
(24)

17. $\$350 - \$284$
(23)

18. Find the missing number: $37 - \square = 18$.
(40)

19. Brenda looked at the clock. It was almost time for morning recess. What time was it?
(3)

20. Anh has 5 quarters and 7 pennies. What fraction of the coins are pennies?
(44)

- **Fractions Equal to 1**
- **Mixed Numbers**

facts   Power Up 46

jump start

 Count up by halves from 0 to 5.
Count up by fourths from 0 to 2.

 Write a fact family using the numbers 8, 4, and 12 in the workspace on your paper.

 Write the year "nineteen ten" using digits.

mental math

a. Money: Which has greater value?

3 quarters or 72¢

b. Number Sense: 60 minutes − 20 minutes

c. Time: It is 11:30 in the morning. The track meet began 2 hours ago. What time did it begin?

d. Patterns: What number is missing from the pattern shown below?

| 200 | 175 | _____ | 125 | 100 |

problem solving

The numbers we say when we count by 2s are **even numbers.** Even numbers have a ones digit of 2, 4, 6, 8, or 0. Counting numbers that are not even are **odd numbers.** Odd numbers have a ones digit of 1, 3, 5, 7 or 9.

In many neighborhoods, even-numbered addresses are on one side of the street and odd-numbered addresses are on the other side of the street.

All the addresses on Anna's side of the street are two-digit odd numbers that begin with 6. What are the possible address numbers on Anna's side of the street?

Fractions Equal to One

We have used fractions to name parts of a whole shape. We can also use a fraction to name a whole shape. Each of the circles below represents 1. Each is named with a different fraction.

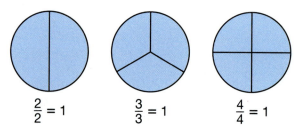

$$\frac{2}{2} = 1 \qquad \frac{3}{3} = 1 \qquad \frac{4}{4} = 1$$

Notice that the numerator and denominator are the same when a fraction equals 1.

Example 1

Write the fraction equal to 1 represented by each shaded figure.

a.   b.   c.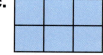

a. Five of five equal parts are shaded, $\frac{5}{5}$.

b. Four of four equal parts are shaded, $\frac{4}{4}$.

c. Six of six equal parts are shaded, $\frac{6}{6}$.

Example 2

Use your fraction manipulatives to show that $\frac{3}{3}$ equals 1. Then draw and shade a circle to illustrate $\frac{3}{3}$.

We use three $\frac{1}{3}$ pieces to build the fraction. The whole circle represents 1. Notice that we do not divide a circle in half to make thirds. Instead, starting from the center, we draw three segments.

Mixed Numbers

In Lesson 35 we learned to name lengths that are between whole numbers of inches with a whole number plus a fraction.

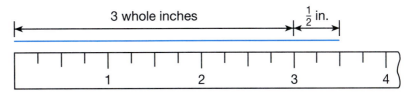

We can name amounts that are between whole numbers using a whole number plus a fraction.

There are more than three whole circles, but fewer than four whole circles. We can name this number with the whole number of circles plus the fraction number of circles: $3\frac{1}{2}$. We read the number as "three and one half." A whole number plus a fraction is called a **mixed number.**

Example 3

Name the number of circles shown using numbers and using words.

There are 4 whole circles plus $\frac{3}{4}$ circle: **$4\frac{3}{4}$.** We read $4\frac{3}{4}$ as **"four and three fourths."**

Lesson Practice

a. Multiple Choice Which of these fractions equals 1?

A $\frac{1}{2}$ **B** $\frac{2}{3}$ **C** $\frac{3}{4}$ **D** $\frac{5}{5}$

b. Draw and shade a square to represent the fraction $\frac{4}{4}$.

c. Compare: $\frac{3}{3}$ ◯ $\frac{4}{4}$

d. What fraction equal to 1 is represented by this shaded figure?

e. Write $5\frac{3}{10}$ using words.   **f.** Draw circles to show $2\frac{1}{2}$.

1. What fraction of a dollar is represented by 10 dimes?
(46)

2. *Sputnik,* the first man-made satellite, was launched in Russia in
(39) 1957. The first space shuttle flight was in 1981. How many years
were there from *Sputnik* to the first space shuttle flight?

3. To what number is the arrow pointing on this number line?
(33)

4. Sammy bought a CD for $19 plus $2 tax. Write the total price of
(12, 18) the CD with tax using digits and again using words.

5. There are three basketballs and four footballs in the bag. What
(44) fraction of the balls in the bag are basketballs?

6. There are 1,440 minutes in a day. Write 1,440 in expanded
(32) form.

7. In the fraction $\frac{8}{9}$, which number is the numerator? Which number
(41) is the denominator?

8. (**Represent**) Draw a line segment that is $5\frac{1}{4}$ inches long.
(35)

9. Estimate the height of your desk in inches. Then use your ruler to
(37) measure the height of your desk.

10. (**Analyze**) What fraction of the marbles in the bag
(44, 46) are **NOT** grey?

11. Morgan turned 9 years old. Copy and continue the table to find
(2) the number of months in 9 years.

Years	1	2	3	4	5	6	7	8	9
Months	12	24	36						

Add or subtract, as shown:

12. $976 - 200$
(19)

13. $812 + 30$
(16)

14. $\$4.38 + \$1.52$
(22)

15. $65 + 48 + 21$
(24)

16. $200 - 143$
(28)

17. $6 + 7 + 5 + 4$
(10)

18. $5 + 5 + 5 + 5 + 5 + 5 + 5 + 5 + 5 + 5$
(10)

19. Find the missing number: $180 - \square = 50$.
(40)

20. **Analyze** There are 10 apples in a bag. Four of the apples are
(44) green and the rest are red. What fraction of the apples are red?

LESSON 47

• Equivalent Fractions

facts

Power Up 47

jump start

Count down by 7s from 56 to 0.
Count down by 10s from 93 to 3.

It's afternoon. Draw hands on your clock to show 2:02. Write the time in digital form.

Draw a 2-inch segment on your worksheet.

mental math

a. **Number Sense:** 200 + 400 + 200

b. **Number Sense:** 27 + 10

c. **Money:** Mrs. Timm bought one apple for 60¢. She paid $1.00. How much change did she receive? Write your answer with a dollar sign.

d. **Number Line:** Which point shows the number 59?

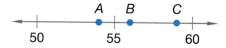

problem solving

Bret has a total of 9 coins in his left and right pockets. He has at least 3 coins in each pocket. Complete this table to show the different ways he could have the coins in his pockets.

Left	Right
3	6

New Concept

In Lesson 46 we found that there are different fractions that equal 1, such as $\frac{2}{2}$, $\frac{3}{3}$, and $\frac{4}{4}$. Equal fractions are called **equivalent fractions.**

Below we show some fractions equivalent to $\frac{1}{2}$.

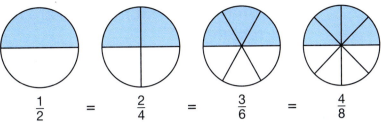

$$\frac{1}{2} \quad = \quad \frac{2}{4} \quad = \quad \frac{3}{6} \quad = \quad \frac{4}{8}$$

In this lesson we will build and identify equivalent fractions.

Analyze What one coin is equal to $\frac{2}{4}$ of a dollar?

Equivalent Fractions

Materials: **Lesson Activity 17,** fraction manipulatives

In this activity you will use your fraction manipulatives to show equivalent fractions. You will not cut apart Lesson Activity 17. Instead, you will place your fraction manipulatives on the Activity Master circles. Then you will count the parts covered to answer the following questions.

1. Find the circle that shows six equal parts. Each part is $\frac{1}{6}$ or one sixth. Fit a $\frac{1}{3}$ fraction on the circle. How many sixths equal $\frac{1}{3}$? Copy and complete this equation:
$$\frac{1}{3} = \frac{\square}{6}$$

2. Fit two $\frac{1}{3}$ fractions on the circle that shows sixths. How many sixths equal $\frac{2}{3}$? Copy and complete this equation:
$$\frac{2}{3} = \frac{\square}{6}$$

3. Find the circle that shows eight equal parts. Each part is $\frac{1}{8}$ or one eighth. Fit a $\frac{1}{4}$ fraction on the circle. How many eighths equal $\frac{1}{4}$? Copy and complete this equation:
$$\frac{1}{4} = \frac{\square}{8}$$

4. Fit three $\frac{1}{4}$ fractions on the circle that shows eighths. How many eighths equal $\frac{3}{4}$? Copy and complete this equation:
$$\frac{3}{4} = \frac{\square}{8}$$

When you are finished with the activity, color both sides of the fraction circles on Lesson Activity 17. Then cut them out and add them to your resealable plastic bag with your other fraction manipulatives for use in future lessons and problem sets.

Example 1

What equivalent fractions are represented by these rectangles?

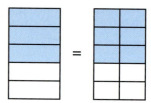

For the rectangle on the left 3 of 5 parts are shaded. For the rectangle on the right 6 of 10 parts are shaded. So, $\frac{3}{5}$ and $\frac{6}{10}$ are equivalent fractions.

$$\frac{3}{5} = \frac{6}{10}$$

Example 2

The first rectangle has three equal parts. We see that two parts are shaded. So, two thirds of the figure is shaded.

$$\frac{2}{3} = \frac{?}{6}$$

The second rectangle has six equal parts. Copy or trace the rectangles on your paper. Then shade the second rectangle to match the shaded part of the first rectangle. Study the rectangles to help you complete the equation:

$$\frac{2}{3} = \frac{\square}{6}$$

We copy and shade the rectangles to match.

$$\frac{2}{3} = \frac{4}{6}$$

The shaded rectangles show that $\frac{2}{3} = \frac{4}{6}$.

a. Use your fraction manipulatives to find and name three fractions equivalent to $\frac{1}{2}$.

b. Two quarters have the same value as five dimes. Write two equivalent fractions of a dollar represented by these two sets of coins.

c. Draw and shade two squares to show that $\frac{1}{2}$ is equivalent to $\frac{2}{4}$.

d. Multiple Choice Which shaded figure below illustrates a fraction equivalent to $\frac{1}{2}$?

A $\frac{2}{3}$ B $\frac{3}{4}$ C $\frac{2}{6}$ D $\frac{5}{10}$

Written Practice

Distributed and Integrated

1. In 1962, John Glenn, Jr., was the first American to orbit the Earth.
(39) In 1968, three American astronauts first orbited the moon. How many years were there between these two events?

2. The meal cost $25. The tax was $2. Murphy left a tip of $4.00.
(18, 21) What was the total price of the meal with tax and tip?

3. Randall gave Ivory 20 pencils. Then he had 48 pencils. How many
(40) pencils did Randall have before he gave pencils to Ivory? Write a some went away number sentence to find the answer.

4. (**Analyze**) Edward has 6 pairs of white socks, 5 pairs of black
(44) socks, and 3 pairs of blue socks. What fraction of his socks are white?

5. What fraction of Edward's socks in problem **4** is NOT white?
(43)

6. (**Represent**) Draw two parallel segments that are $1\frac{3}{4}$ inches long.
(35, Inv. 4)

7. The distance from Seattle to Boston is about two thousand, five
(32) hundred miles. Use digits to write that number.

8. The odometer showed this display.

    a. Write the number of miles with digits and a comma.

    b. Use words to write the number of miles shown.

9. **Multiple Choice** Which fraction is not equal to 1?

    A $\frac{2}{2}$ **B** $\frac{3}{3}$ **C** $\frac{4}{5}$ **D** $\frac{6}{6}$

10. **Multiple Choice** Which fraction equals $\frac{1}{2}$? Use your manipulatives to help you find the answer.

    A $\frac{2}{5}$ **B** $\frac{2}{3}$ **C** $\frac{2}{4}$ **D** $\frac{2}{6}$

11. Which number in the fraction $\frac{4}{6}$ tells the number of equal parts in the whole?

Add or subtract, as shown:

12. $800 - 149$

13. $932 - 30$

14. $\$5.76 + \$3.35$

15. $\$560 - \$320$

16. $84¢ + 96¢ + 28¢$

17. $\square - 35 = 40$

18. **Multiple Choice** How much money is $\frac{1}{4}$ of a dollar plus $\frac{3}{10}$ of a dollar?

    A 25¢   **B** 30¢   **C** 55¢   **D** 60¢

19. The door was 7 feet high. How many inches is 7 feet?

Feet	1	2	3	4	5	6	7
Inches	12	24	36				

20. The Garcias drove from Del Norte to Hooper to Alamosa and back
(18, 31) to Del Norte. How far did the Garcias drive?

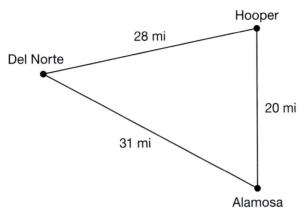

Tyrone's parents took him to Greg's Go Kart Track because he got all A's and B's on his report card. It cost $1.50 to drive 2 laps around the track. How much will it cost to drive 8 laps?

LESSON 48

• **Finding Fractions and Mixed Numbers on a Number Line**

facts   Power Up 48

jump start   Count up by 6s from 0 to 60.
                   Count up by 9s from 0 to 90.

 Write a fact family using the numbers 8, 8, and 16 in the workspace on your paper.

Write the number "nine hundred forty-six" using digits on your worksheet. What digit is in the tens place?

mental math   **a. Estimation:** Round $630 to the nearest hundred dollars.

b. Measurement: How many inches are in 3 feet?

c. Number Sense: $11 + 11$

d. Money: Find the value of these bills and coins:

problem solving   Bret has a total of 9 coins in his left and right pockets. He has 3 more coins in his right pocket than in his left pocket. How many coins does he have in each pocket?

We have used fractions to describe parts of a whole and parts of a set. We can also use fractions to name points on a number line.

On this number line, there are tick marks for 0 and 1. There are many points between 0 and 1 that can be named using fractions.

Suppose we divide the distance from 0 to 1 into two equal parts. Then the distance from zero to the middle mark is $\frac{1}{2}$.

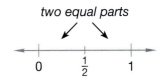

If we divide the distance from 0 to 1 into 3 equal parts, the marks between represent $\frac{1}{3}$ and $\frac{2}{3}$.

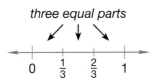

Notice that the denominator of each fraction is the total number of segments between 0 and 1. The numerator of the fraction is the number of segments from 0.

numerator ⟶ $\dfrac{2}{3}$ ⟶ Number of segments from 0.

denominator ⟶ $\phantom{\dfrac{2}{3}}$ ⟶ Number of segments between 0 and 1.

Example 1

Write fractions to name points A, B, and C on this number line.

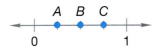

The three tick marks between 0 and 1 divide the distance from 0 to 1 into four segments. So 4 is the denominator of each fraction.

- Point A is 1 segment from 0, so A represents $\frac{1}{4}$.

- Point B is 2 segments from 0, so B represents $\frac{2}{4}$.

- Point C is 3 segments from 0, so C represents $\frac{3}{4}$.

Example 2

Copy this number line on your paper and draw a dot at the point that represents $\frac{2}{5}$. Write $\frac{2}{5}$ below the dot.

We copy the number line. We see that there are 5 segments between 0 and 1, so the denominator is 5. To find $\frac{2}{5}$ we count 2 segments from zero, draw a dot, and write the fraction.

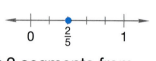

Analyze Use the number line above to answer this question: Which fraction is greater, $\frac{2}{5}$ or $\frac{4}{5}$? Explain your answer.

We can also locate and name mixed numbers on a number line. If a point is between two whole numbers on a number line, we use the smaller number as the whole part of the mixed number. Then we find and name the fraction part. We count the number of segments between the whole numbers to find the denominator. Then we count the number of segments from the smaller number to find the numerator.

Example 3

To what number is each arrow pointing?

a.

b.

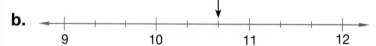

a. The arrow is pointing to a number between 6 and 7, so the whole number part is 6. There are four segments between each number and one segment between 6 and the arrow, so the fraction part is $\frac{1}{4}$. The arrow is pointing to **$6\frac{1}{4}$**.

b. The arrow is pointing to a number between 10 and 11. There are three segments between each number and two segments between 10 and the arrow. The mixed number is **$10\frac{2}{3}$**.

Fractions on the Number Line

Materials: **Lesson Activity 18**

Name the fractions and mixed numbers shown on **Lesson Activity 18.**

Lesson Practice Name the fractions shown on these number lines.

a.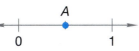

b.

c.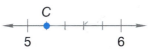

d.

e. What two equivalent fractions are illustrated by this pair of number lines?

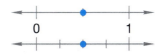

Written Practice *Distributed and Integrated*

Formulate Write number sentences for problems **1** and **2**. Then answer each question.

1. **Analyze** There are 24 hours in a day. At 7:00 a.m., how
(36, 3) many hours are left in the day? (*Hint:* A new day starts at midnight.)

2. The sale price of the pants was $29. With tax, the total was $31.
(36) How much was the tax?

3. What fraction of the students in your class are girls? What fraction
(44) are boys?

4. Tara finished her addition facts practice test in 28 seconds. Is
(17, 44) 28 seconds more than half of a minute or less than half of a minute? (*Hint:* There are 60 seconds in one minute.)

5. In 1912 Arizona became the 48th state. In 1960 Hawaii became
(39) the 50th state. Hawaii became a state how many years after
Arizona?

6. Which fraction is greater: $\frac{2}{5}$ or $\frac{3}{4}$?
(43)

7. Name the fraction shown on this number line.
(48)

8. Name a fraction equivalent to $\frac{1}{4}$.
(47)

9. Write $4\frac{5}{6}$ using words.
(46)

10. Find the missing number: $77 - \square = 9$
(40)

11. Draw and shade two rectangles to show that $\frac{1}{3}$ is equivalent to $\frac{2}{6}$.
(47)

Add or subtract, as shown:

12. $966 - 900$
(19)

13. $776 + 50$
(16)

14. $\$625 - \$375$
(19)

15. $49¢ + 94¢ + 55¢$
(21, 24)

16. $400 - 143$
(28)

17. $\$4.56 + \$5$
(22)

18. $83 - \square = 46$
(40)

19. Draw a number line from 600 to 700 with one tick mark every
(4, 33) 20 numbers. Label 600 and 700. Draw a point at 620.

20. (**Represent**) Sketch a map from this description. Then find the
(31) answer to the question.

> *Abilene is 52 miles west of Eastland. Baird is 32 miles west of*
> *Eastland on the road to Abilene. Which direction and how many*
> *miles is it from Baird to Abilene?*

LESSON 49

• Comparing Fractions, Part 2

facts

Power Up 49

jump start

 Count up by 4s from 0 to 40.

Count up by fourths from 0 to 2.

Write these money amounts in order from least to greatest:

$3.35 $2.95 $0.75

Draw a $1\frac{1}{4}$-inch line in the workspace on your worksheet.

mental math

a. Money: $1.00 − $0.90

b. Time: How many years are in 3 decades?

c. Number Sense: 30 − 9

d. Time: It is evening. What is the time 30 minutes after the time shown on the clock?

problem solving

Look for a pattern in these figures. Which figure does not belong? Explain your answer.

A   B   C   D

In recent lessons we have seen that two fractions may be equivalent (equal) or that one fraction may be less than or greater than another fraction.

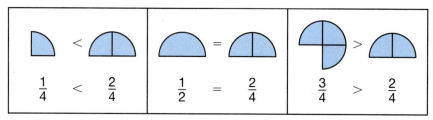

In this lesson we will continue comparing fractions using manipulatives and pictures.

Example 1

In one minute Erin finished $\frac{1}{2}$ of the facts practice worksheet and David finished $\frac{2}{5}$ of the worksheet. Which student finished more? (Use your fraction manipulatives to help you answer the question.)

Using fraction manipulatives we see that $\frac{1}{2}$ is greater than $\frac{2}{5}$.

This means that **Erin** finished more of the facts practice worksheet than David.

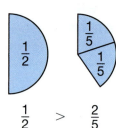

$$\frac{1}{2} \quad > \quad \frac{2}{5}$$

Example 2

Rodney and Rachel both have collections of toy vehicles.

Rodney's Collection   Rachel's Collection

a. **What fraction of Rodney's toy vehicles are trucks?**

b. **What fraction of Rachel's toy vehicles are trucks?**

c. **Who has the greater fraction of trucks?**

a. From the picture we see that 3 of Rodney's 6 vehicles are trucks, so $\frac{3}{6}$ are trucks.

b. We see that $\frac{2}{6}$ of Rachel's toy vehicles are trucks.

c. Since $\frac{3}{6}$ is greater than $\frac{2}{6}$, **Rodney** has the greater fraction of trucks in his collection.

Analyze One third of the trucks in Rodney's toy box are blue. Two thirds of the trucks are red. If Rodney takes a truck out of his toy box without looking, which color is he most likely to get? Why?

Lesson Practice

a. Angela walks $\frac{3}{4}$ of a mile to school. Byron walks $\frac{3}{5}$ of a mile to school. Who walks farther to school, Angela or Byron? Use manipulatives to model each fraction and find the answer.

b. What fraction of a dollar is three quarters? What fraction of a dollar is seven dimes? Compare the two fractions using a comparison symbol.

c. What fraction of the marbles in the bag are blue? What fraction of the marbles in the box are blue? Which container has the greater fraction of blue marbles?

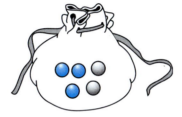 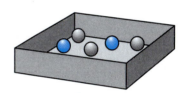

d. Use manipulatives or draw pictures to compare these two fractions.

$$\frac{2}{4} \bigcirc \frac{2}{3}$$

Written Practice

Distributed and Integrated

1. Jill has 84 baseball cards. Dakota has 72 baseball cards. Who has
(39) more baseball cards? How many more? Write a greater-lesser-difference number sentence to help you find the answer.

2. Talal bought paper for $2.00 and a folder for $0.75. If the total
(36) price for the paper and folder with tax was $2.95, how much was the tax?

3. There are 2 black cars, 3 white cars, and 5 red cars in the parking
(44, 49)
lot. What fraction of the cars are not red? Compare the fraction
of cars that are not red to the fraction of cars that are red using a
comparison symbol.

4. (**Represent**) Draw and shade $\frac{3}{4}$ of a circle.
(42)

5. Which fraction is greater: $\frac{1}{3}$ or $\frac{2}{4}$? You may draw pictures or use
(43, 49)
your fraction manipulatives to help you answer the question.

6. The artichoke cost 59¢. Jaime paid for it with three quarters. List
(14, 25)
the coins he should get back.

7. Find the missing number: $210 - \square = 99$
(40)

8. Look at this timeline to answer **a** and **b.**
(33, 39)

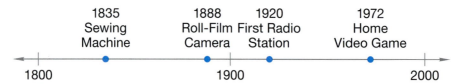

a. The first roll-film camera was made how many years before
the first home video game?

b. The first electronic guitar was made in 1948. Was that before
or after the first radio station?

9. The odometer showed this display.
(32)

a. How many miles are shown? Write the number using digits
and a comma.

b. Use words to write the number of miles shown.

10. Use your ruler to measure the segments:
(35)

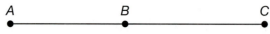

a. Point *A* to point *B*

b. Point *B* to point *C*

c. Point *A* to point *C*

11. (2) **Generalize** What number is missing in this sequence?

21, 28, _____, 42, 49, 56 ...

12. Name the fraction shown on this number line.
(48)

0   1

13. What fraction of a dollar is 3 nickels? What fraction of a dollar
(49) is 7 pennies? Compare the two fractions using a comparison
symbol.

Add or subtract, as shown:

14. 989 − 200
(19)

15. 38¢ + 84¢ + 45¢
(21, 24)

16. 1 ft. − 1 in. = _____ in.
(34)

17. 1 yd − 1 ft = _____ ft
(34)

18. Estimate the length in inches from the top to the bottom of this
(37) page. Then use your ruler to measure the length of this page to
the nearest inch.

19. Wilson rode his bike from Preston to Chauncey to Milton and then
(10, 18) back to Preston. How many miles did Wilson ride his bike?

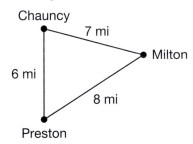

20. Tonya and Sherri each had a small loaf of homemade wheat
(47) bread. Tonya cut her loaf into three equal slices. Sherri cut her loaf
into six equal slices. How many of Sherri's slices are equal to one
of Tonya's slices? Use your fraction manipulatives to help you find
the answer.

• Probability, Part 2

Power Up

facts   Power Up 50

jump start   Count up by halves from 0 to 5.
                   Count up by 5s from 1 to 51.

                   🕐 It's afternoon. Draw hands on your clock to show 5:27.
                   Write the time in digital form.

                   ✏️ Write "four thousand nine hundred" using digits on your
                   worksheet.

mental math   **a. Number Sense:** 8 + 15

                   b. Number Sense: 17 + 9

                   c. Patterns: 5, 15, 25, 35, _____.

                   d. Number Line: Which point shows the number 101?

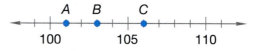

problem solving   Fayed has eight coins with a total value of 12¢. What are
                      the coins?

New Concept

When we spin this spinner, we
cannot be certain where it will stop.
However, we see that it is **more likely**
to stop on 1 than on 2. We can also
say it is **less likely** to stop on 2 than
on 1.

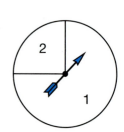

Some outcomes are **equally likely.** Since both area 3 and area 4 on this spinner are the same size, the spinner is equally likely to stop on 3 or 4.

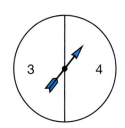

Example 1

Compare the following outcomes by using the terms *more likely, less likely,* **or** *equally likely.*

a. spinning 1 or spinning 2

b. spinning 2 or spinning 3

a. Since area 1 is larger than area 2, **spinning 1 is more likely than spinning 2.** We may also say that **spinning 2 is less likely than spinning 1.**

b. Areas 2 and 3 are the same size, so **spinning 2 and spinning 3 are equally likely.**

Example 2

Create a table that shows the number of each color of marble in this bag. If one marble is taken from the bag, which color is least likely to be picked? Which color is most likely to be picked?

First we draw the table and give it a title. Then we list the colors and numbers of marbles. Since there is only one white marble, the color that is least likely to be picked is **white.** Since there are more black marbles than any other single color, the color that is most likely to be picked is **black.**

Marbles in Bag

Color	Number
White	1
Gray	2
Black	4
Blue	3

Analyze Look at the table above to answer this question. If you put 2 more gray marbles in the bag, which color is more likely to be picked?

Lesson Practice

One marble will be picked from a bag with white, gray, black, and blue marbles. Look at these marbles to answer questions **a–c.**

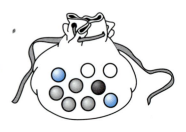

a. Which color is least likely to be picked?

b. Which color is most likely to be picked?

c. Which two colors are equally likely to be picked?

The spinner will be spun once. Look at the spinner to answer questions **d–f.**

d. The spinner is more likely to stop on what color?

e. The spinner is less likely to stop on what color?

f. How can we change the face of the spinner so that the spinner is equally likely to stop on either color?

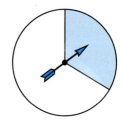

Written Practice *Distributed and Integrated*

Formulate Write number sentences for problems **1** and **2**. Then answer each question.

1. Two hundred seventy-four fans were in the stands when the
(20, 19) football game began. By halftime, 64 had gone home. How many fans were still in the stands at halftime?

2. The computer game costs $36 with tax. Jonathan has $21. How
(36) much more money does he need to buy the game?

3. There are thirteen stripes on the American flag. Seven of the
(44) stripes are red. What fraction of the stripes are white?

4. Which fraction is greater: $\frac{2}{3}$ or $\frac{1}{2}$?
(43)

5. Which fraction is smaller: $\frac{3}{4}$ or $\frac{3}{5}$?
(43)

6. Babe Ruth hit 60 home runs in 1927. Roger Maris hit 61 home
(39) runs in 1961. How many years were there from 1927 to 1961?

7. **Interpret** Look at the number line to answer **a** and **b**.
(27, 33)

a. Which point represents the number 6?

b. Which points represent numbers less than 5?

8. Copy this number line. Then draw point *T* on the number line to
(48) represent $7\frac{2}{3}$.

9. This map shows the towns of Monticello, Eatonton, and Sparta.
(Inv. 4) One inch represents a distance of ten miles. Use your ruler to find
the number of miles from:

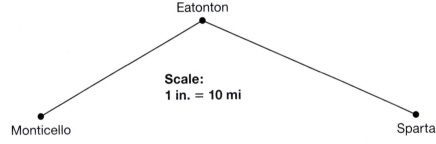

a. Monticello to Eatonton

b. Eatonton to Sparta

c. Monticello to Sparta through Eatonton

10. Name a fraction that is equal to $\frac{2}{4}$. Use your fraction manipulatives
(47) to find the answer.

11. Texas became a state in 1845. California became a state in 1850.
(39) How many years earlier did Texas become a state?

12. **Analyze** What coin is half the value of a dime?
(29)

13. (Conclude) What are the next three years in this sequence?
(2)

$$1980, 1990, 2000, \underline{\hspace{1cm}}, \underline{\hspace{1cm}}, \underline{\hspace{1cm}}, \dots$$

14. 99¢ + 62¢ + 10¢
(21, 24)

15. $7.50 − $2.50
(26)

16. $\square$ − 31 = 17
(40)

17. $140 − $75
(23)

18. a. Round $122 to the nearest hundred dollars.
(15, 30)

b. Round $189 to the nearest hundred dollars.

c. Estimate the sum of $122 and $189 using your answers to **a** and **b.**

19. Greta has 6 pencils in her desk. Don has 5 pencils in his. Greta
(44, 49) sharpened 3 of her pencils. Don sharpened 2 of his pencils.
a. What fraction of Greta's pencils are sharpened?

b. What fraction of Don's pencils are sharpened?

c. Use <, >, or = to compare your answers for **a** and **b.**

20. Jodie has a bag containing 4 blue marbles and 7 white marbles. Is
(50) Jodie more likely to pick a blue marble or a white marble?

Focus on

• Probability Games

In this investigation you will play three probability games using a dot cube. You will decide if the games are fair.

 **Activity**

Probability Games

Materials: dot cube, pencil and paper, Lesson Activity 19

Play the games with a partner. Each game needs a Player A and a Player B. Decide with your partner who will be A and who will be B. You will keep this letter for all three games. Each pair of players needs one dot cube.

Game 1

Take turns rolling a dot cube.

Rules:

- Player A gets a point if the number of dots is 1 or 6.
- Player B gets a point if the number of dots is 2, 3, 4, or 5.
- The first player with 10 points wins.

Keep track of points using tally marks (𝍷𝍷𝍷𝍷𝍷 𝍷𝍷).

Draw the table below on your paper and use it to keep score.

Player A	Player B

Game 2

Take turns rolling a dot cube.

Rules:

- Player A gets a point if the number of dots is even (2, 4, or 6).
- Player B gets a point if the number of dots is odd (1, 3, or 5).
- The first player with 10 points wins.

Draw the following table on your paper and use it to keep score.

Player A	Player B

1. Which game is more fair, Game 1 or Game 2? Why?

Game 3

With your partner, figure out a dot cube game you think would be fair.

Draw the following table on your paper and use it to keep score.

Player A	Player B

2. In Game 1, which player is more likely to win the game, Player A or Player B? Why?

3. In Game 2, which player is more likely to win the game, Player A or Player B? Why?

4. How did you design Game 3 so that the game was fair?

LESSON 51

• Rectangles

facts   Power Up 51

jump start

 Count up by 3s from 0 to 45.
Count up by 7s from 0 to 63.

Write these numbers in order from least to greatest:

457   375   407

 Draw a $4\frac{1}{2}$-inch segment on your worksheet. Record the length next to the segment.

mental math

a. Money: Marcus bought an eraser for $0.20. He paid $1.00. How much change did he receive?

b. Number Sense: $22 - 8$

c. Time: What is the time 2 hours after 4:05 in the afternoon?

d. Money: Find the value of these bills and coins:

problem solving

The first question on the quiz is multiple choice with three choices—A, B, or C. The second question is "true or false." Complete this tree diagram and list the possible combinations of answers.

1st question	2nd question
A	true
	false
B	___
	___
─	___
	___

Rectangles are all around us. Look around your classroom and you will see walls, windows, doors, book covers, and papers that are all the shape of rectangles.

How can you tell if a shape is a rectangle? Here are some things to look for.

- Rectangles are flat. A box is not a rectangle, but the sides of a box may be rectangles.

- A rectangle has four sides. Other shapes also have four sides, so just having four sides is not enough.

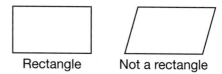

Rectangle   Not a rectangle

- A rectangle has four square corners.

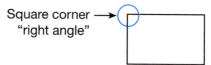

Square corner →
"right angle"

The square corners are called **right angles.** In fact, the word **rectangle** means right-angle shape.

- The first three descriptions are enough to identify a rectangle. We also see that the **opposite sides** of a rectangle are **parallel.** The sides that intersect are **perpendicular.**

Activity

Rectangle List

1. As a class, make a list of the rectangles you can see in your classroom. Some rectangles are long and narrow. Some rectangles are squares. A **square** is a special type of rectangle because it has four equal sides.

2. After you make your list of rectangles, describe how you know that a shape is a rectangle.

Identify each figure below as a rectangle or not a rectangle. If the figure is not a rectangle, state why it is not.

a.  □   b.  ▱   c. □   d. 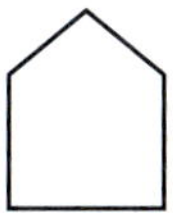 ⌂

a. The shape is a **rectangle**.

b. **The shape is not a rectangle because the corners are not right angles.**

c. A square is a specific kind of **rectangle**.

d. **The shape is not a rectangle because it does not have four sides.**

Verify   Is this statement true or false?

"Every square is a rectangle. Not every rectangle is a square."

Why or why not?

Lesson Practice   Identify each shape below as a rectangle or not a rectangle. If the shape is not a rectangle, write why it is not.

a.  ▭   b.  ▱

c. 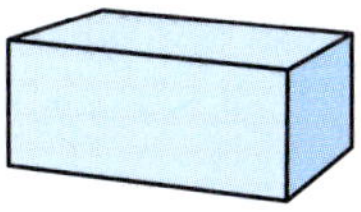   d.  □

e. Draw a rectangle that is not a square.

f. Draw a rectangle that is a square.

Written Practice   *Distributed and Integrated*

Formulate   Write number sentences for problem **1**. Write a complete sentence to answer the question.

1. The regular price of the sofa was $398. It was on sale for $50 off the
(19) regular price. What was the sale price of the sofa?

2. The price of the aquarium was $142. Tax was $12. Write the total
(12. 16)   price of the aquarium with tax using words.

3. One foot is what fraction of one yard?
(34, 44)

4. Draw a circle and divide it into thirds by imagining three hands of
(42)   a clock pointing to 12, 4, and 8. Then shade $\frac{1}{3}$ of the circle.

5. George Washington lived from 1732 to 1799. How many years did
(39)   he live?

6. Write 487 in expanded form.
(11)

7. (**Represent**)   Draw a rectangle. A rectangle has how many right
(51)   angles?

This map shows the location of the towns of Dakota City and
Belmond and Highways 3, 33, and 20. One inch on the map
represents a distance of ten miles. Use this map to help you
answer problems **8–10.**

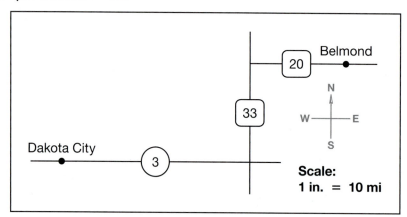

8. (**Analyze**)   Write directions to Belmond from Dakota City using
(31,
Inv. 4)   compass directions and miles.

9. About how many miles is the drive between Dakota City and
(Inv. 4)   Belmond? (1 inch = 10 miles)

10. a. Which road is parallel to Highway 3?
(Inv. 4)

   b. Which road is perpendicular to Highway 3?

11. If you double 1, the answer is 2. If you double 2, the answer is 4.
If you double 4, the answer is 8. Find the next two numbers in this doubling sequence.

(2)

$$1, 2, 4, 8, \underline{\hspace{1cm}}, \underline{\hspace{1cm}}, \dots$$

12. **Multiple Choice** Which shape is not a rectangle? Explain your answer.

(51)

A  B C

13. Cassie grew two bean plants for a science fair project. After three weeks, one measured 24 inches long and one measured 32 inches long. How much longer was the second bean plant? Write a greater-lesser-difference number sentence to find the answer.

(39)

Add or subtract, as shown:

14. $3 + 48¢ + 76¢

(21, 22)

15. $5.00 − $3.47

(28)

16. 562 + 348   **17.** 460 − 148

(16)   (19)

18. 3 + 3 + 3 + 3 + 3 + 3 + 3 + 3 + 3 + 3

(10)

19. a. Round $889 to the nearest hundred dollars.

(15, 30)

b. Round $61 to the nearest ten dollars.

c. Estimate the sum of the numbers in **a** and **b**.

20. **Represent** Draw two parallel line segments $2\frac{1}{2}$ inches long.

(35, Inv. 4)

• Length and Width

Power Up

facts

Power Up 52

jump start

 Count up by 4s from 0 to 40.
Count up by 8s from 0 to 80.

 Write the fraction "one half" using digits.

Write a fact family using the numbers 5, 7, and 12.

mental math

a. Money: Compare these money amounts using the symbol <, >, or =.

2 quarters ◯ 50¢

b. Money: 70¢ + 30¢

c. Time: A century is 100 years. How many years are in 2 centuries?

d. Fractions: What fraction of the circle is shaded?

problem solving

Karlos collects stamps. This table shows how many stamps Karlos has from each of several countries. If Karlos collects two more stamps from France and collects his first stamp from Mexico, how many stamps will he have in all?

Country	Number of Stamps
United States	40
Canada	6
France	2
Nigeria	2

New Concept

A rectangle has a **length** and a **width.** The measure of the longer side of a rectangle is called the length of the rectangle. The measure of the shorter side is called the width.

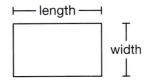

In this lesson, you will use your ruler to measure the lengths and widths of rectangles. For practice, use your ruler to measure the rectangle in the example to the nearest quarter inch.

Example

What are the length and width of this rectangle?

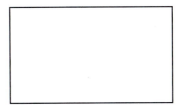

We place a ruler along two sides of the rectangle. The **length is $1\frac{3}{4}$ inches,** and the **width is 1 inch.**

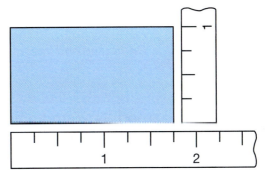

This means that the two longer sides are both $1\frac{3}{4}$ inches, and the two short sides are both 1 inch.

 **Activity**

Measuring Length and Width

Measure the lengths and widths of the rectangles on **Lesson Activity 20.**

(**Analyze**) One side of a rectangle is 3 inches long. How long is the opposite side?

Lesson Practice Use your ruler to find the length and width of each rectangle. On your paper, write the length and width.

a.

b.
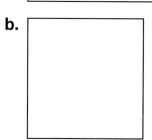

c. Draw a rectangle that is $1\frac{1}{2}$ inches long and 1 inch wide.

d. Draw a rectangle with four sides that are each 1 inch long. What kind of rectangle did you draw?

Written Practice *Distributed and Integrated*

1. Lisa had $2.40. She earned $4.25 more helping a neighbor in the
(18, 22) yard. Then how much money did Lisa have?

2. There are 28 students in room A and 31 students in room B.
(18) Altogether, how many students are in rooms A and B?

3. An inch is what fraction of a foot?
(34, 44)

4. Look at your answer to problem **3.** Which number is the
(41) numerator? Which number is the denominator?

5. The first postage stamp was issued in England in 1840. How many years ago was that?
(39)

6. Sketch a number line from 0 to 1 and divide the number line into fourths. Draw a dot on the number line at $\frac{3}{4}$ and write the fraction under the dot.
(48)

7. The two shaded rectangles below represent which two equivalent fractions?
(47)

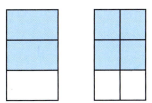

8. Julie lives four blocks from school. Write directions from Julie's home to school.
(31)

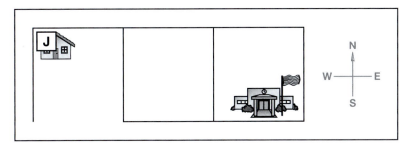

9. The odometer shows this display.
(32)

    a. How many miles are shown?

    b. Use words to write the number of miles shown.

10. Brent took ten big steps. With each big step, Brent traveled about one yard. About how many feet did Brent travel in ten big steps?
(34)

11. Multiple Choice Which figure is not a rectangle? Explain your answer.
(51)

  A   **B**    **C**

12. **Represent** Draw a rectangle that is two inches long and
one inch wide.
(34, 52)

13. $5.90 − $2.75
(26)

14. **Analyze** 1 ft. − 2 in. = _____ in.
(14, 34)

15. 450 − 125
(19)

16. 87 + 56 + 36
(24)

17. Veronica gave Paolo 15 pretzels. Then she had 18 pretzels left.
(40) How many pretzels did Veronica have before she gave pretzels
to Paolo? Write a some-went-away number sentence to find the
answer.

18. Write a fraction equal to 1 that has a denominator of 7.
(46)

19. On their vacation, the Lees drove from Cleveland to Washington,
(27) D.C., to New York and then back to Cleveland. Write the miles in
order from greatest to least.

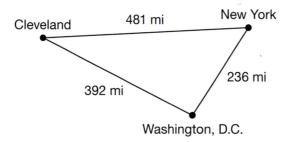

20. Use your ruler to find the length and width of this
(35, 52) rectangle.

Early Finishers

Real-World Connection

Suni uses four lemons to make a three-liter pitcher of lemonade.
How many lemons will Suni use to make 15 liters of lemonade?
How many pitchers will she need? You may use manipulatives to
find the answer.

• Rectangular Grid Patterns

Power Up

facts	Power Up 53
jump start	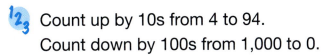 Count up by 10s from 4 to 94. Count down by 100s from 1,000 to 0.
	The alarm clock rang at 20 minutes after 6 in the morning. Draw hands on your clock to show this time. Write the time in digital form.
	The temperature in the mountains was 40°F. At the beach it was 50 degrees warmer. Mark your thermometer to show the temperature at the beach.
mental math	**a. Fractions:** Compare these fractions using the symbol $<$, $>$, or $=$.

$$\frac{3}{4} \bigcirc \frac{1}{4}$$

b. Number Sense: $25 - 9$

c. Number Sense: $400 + 30 + 3$

d. Patterns: What number is missing from the pattern shown below?

2	12	____	32	42

problem solving

Five shoppers were waiting in the checkout line. Then one more shopper got in line. To make the checkout quicker, the store opened a second checkout line. One half of the shoppers in the first line moved to the second line. How many shoppers moved to the second line?

We can draw rectangles on grid paper. We trace over the grid lines to make the size rectangle we want. To describe the size of the rectangle, we say **"units"** instead of "inches". We can count the units by looking at the grid. This rectangle is 3 units long and 2 units wide.

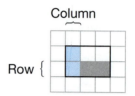

Inside the rectangle, we see small squares arranged in **columns** and **rows.** Columns go up and down. Rows go from side to side.

Example 1

What is the length and width of this rectangle?

Start at one corner and count the number of columns and the number of rows. This rectangle is **4 units long** and **3 units wide.**

Example 2

How many small squares are inside this rectangle?

We can find the number of squares a few ways. One way is to count them one by one.

Another way is to count four columns of 3 squares: 3, 6, 9, 12.

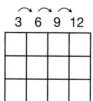

We can also count three rows of 4 squares: 4, 8, 12.

Whatever way we choose to count, the total is **12 small squares.**

Activity

Rectangular Patterns

Materials: **Lesson Activity 21** or grid paper

On grid paper, draw rectangles with the following lengths and widths.

1. 5 unit by 4 unit   **2.** 3 unit by 3 unit

3. 6 unit by 3 unit   **4.** 7 unit by 4 unit

Inside each rectangle, write the total number of small squares in the rectangle. For example, a 4 unit by 2 unit rectangle would look like this.

(**Generalize**) What shape could you draw on the grid paper that has the same number of columns and rows?

(**Lesson Practice**) Find the number of small squares inside each of these rectangles. You may use grid paper to draw the rectangles for problems **c** and **d,** or you may find the answer mentally.

a.    **b.**

c. 5 unit by 2 unit

d. 5 unit by 5 unit

e. How many columns of squares are in this rectangle?

f. How many rows of squares are In this rectangle?

1. The book had 194 pages. Nelson has read 54 pages. How many
(19, 20) pages does he need to read to finish the book?

2. Vernon saw 19 constellations at the planetarium. Suzanne saw
(39) 22 constellations. How many more constellations did Suzanne
see? Write a greater-lesser-difference number sentence to find the
answer.

3. Most of the ten digits from 0 to 9 are written with curves. What fraction
(44) of the digits are written without curves? What are those digits?

4. Use fraction manipulatives to build a model of $\frac{3}{5}$. Then draw a
(41, 42) picture of the model.

5. George Washington Carver lived from 1864 to 1943. How many
(39) years did he live?

6. a. How many units long is this rectangle?
(53)

b. How many units wide is this rectangle?

c. How many small squares are inside this rectangle?

7. (**Represent**) Draw a rectangle that is $2\frac{1}{2}$ inches long and $1\frac{1}{4}$ inches
(35, 52) wide.

8. Estimate the distance in inches from the left-hand side of your
(35, 37) desk to the right-hand side. Then use your ruler to measure the
distance across your desk to the nearest quarter inch.

9. (**Predict**) What is the 7th number in this sequence?
(2)
$$3, 6, 9, 12, \ldots$$

Add or subtract, as shown:

10. 1920 − 1620
(39)

11. 72 + 10 + 28
(24)

12. $5.00 − $3.85
(28)

13. $5.49 + $3.94
(22)

14. **Analyze** 1 yd − 12 in. = _____ in.
(14, 34)

15. 10 + 10 + 10 + 10 + 10 + 10 + 10 + 10 + 10 + 10
(10)

16. a. Round $27 to the nearest ten dollars.
(15, 30)

  b. Round $367 to the nearest hundred dollars.

  c. Estimate the sum of the numbers in **a** and **b**.

17. Pedro hit a home run. He ran from home to first base, to
(18, 24) second base, to third base, and to home. How many feet
did Pedro run?

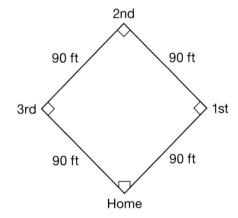

2nd

90 ft   90 ft

3rd   1st

90 ft   90 ft

Home

18. Sketch a number line from 0 to 1. Equally space four tick marks to
(48) divide the distance into five equal segments. Draw a dot at $\frac{2}{5}$ and
a dot at $\frac{3}{5}$. Below each dot write the fraction.

19. Use the number line in problem **18** to help you compare $\frac{2}{5}$ and $\frac{3}{5}$.
(49)

20. In a bag are five marbles. Two are red and three are blue. If one
(50) marble is taken from the bag without looking, which color is more
likely to be picked?

LESSON
54

• Multiplication as
Repeated Addition

facts　　　Power Up 54

**jump
start**

　Count down by 3s from 30 to 0.
Count down by 4s from 40 to 0.

It's afternoon. Draw hands on your clock to show 1:19.
Write the time in digital form.

The morning temperature was 65°F. It was 11 degrees
warmer in the afternoon. Mark your thermometer to
show the afternoon temperature.

**mental
math**

a. Number Sense: 60 + 70

b. Estimation: Round $27.00 to the nearest ten dollars.

c. Time: A decade is 10 years. How many years are in
4 decades?

d. Number Line: What number is represented by Point *F*?

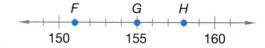

**problem
solving**

Anya is using square tiles to cover an
index card. She has already placed
7 tiles on the card. How many more
tiles does she need to cover the entire
index card?

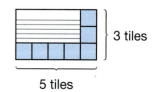

To find the total value of 6 nickels we can add.

5¢ + 5¢ + 5¢ + 5¢ + 5¢ + 5¢ = **30¢**

We can also count by fives.

5¢,   10¢,   15¢,   20¢,   25¢,   **30¢**

Another way to find the total is to **multiply.** We **multiply** when we combine equal groups.

$$6 \times 5¢ = 30¢$$

"6 times 5¢ equals 30¢"

"6 nickels is 30¢"

6 groups of 5 is 30

The $\times$ between the 6 and 5¢ is a **multiplication sign,** which we usually read by saying "times."

Example 1

Write 4×7 as an addition problem and find the total.

Since 4×7 means 4 sevens, we write four 7s and add.

$$7 + 7 + 7 + 7 = 28$$

This addition shows that $4 \times 7 = 28.$

Example 2

Write this addition as a multiplication and show the total.

$$3 + 3 + 3 + 3 + 3$$

We count five 3s, which total 15. So we write "5 times 3 is 15."

$$5 \times 3 = 15$$

We can use **multiplication** to find the number of small squares in a rectangle.

We see 4 columns with 2 squares in each column. We see 8 squares in all.

$$4 \times 2 = 8$$

Example 3

Write the multiplication and total shown by this rectangle.

There are 4 columns and 4 rows and a total of 16 squares.

$$4 \times 4 = 16$$

Discuss Could $3 + 4 + 6 + 3 = 16$ be written as a multiplication? Why or why not?

Lesson Practice

For problems **a–d**, write the multiplication as an addition, then write the total.

a. 3×5 **b.** 4 times 6

c. 2×8 **d.** 4×10

For problems **e** and **f**, write each addition as a multiplication, then write the total.

e. $2 + 2 + 2 + 2 + 2$ **f.** $4 + 4 + 4$

g. Write the multiplication and total shown by this rectangle.

Written Practice   *Distributed and Integrated*

Analyze The park shown here is 300 yards long and 200 yards wide. Use this information for problems **1, 2,** and **3.**

1. If Melody starts at the corner of Greenleaf and Park St., jogs east to the corner of Park St. and Whittier, and then south to the corner of Whittier and Main St., how many yards will she jog?

(31, 51, 52)

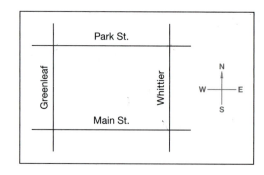

2. If Melody continues jogging to the corner of Main St. and
(16, 52) Greenleaf, how many yards will she jog altogether?

3. **Multiple Choice** Read problem **1** again. When Melody reaches
(47) the corner of Whittier and Main, what fraction of the distance
around the park has she jogged?

A $\frac{1}{2}$ **B** $\frac{2}{3}$ **C** $\frac{3}{4}$ **D** $\frac{3}{5}$

4. Jeremy bought a 500-page notebook. He used some of the
(40) pages for a book report. Then his notebook had 489 pages.
How many pages did Jeremy use for his book report? Write
and solve a some went away number sentence to find the
answer.

5. ⟨**Represent**⟩ Use a ruler to draw a rectangle that is $1\frac{1}{2}$ inches long
(35, 52) and $1\frac{1}{2}$ inches wide. What kind of a rectangle did you draw?

6. Write this addition as a multiplication and show the total.
(54)

$$4 + 4 + 4 + 4 + 4$$

7. Write the multiplication and the total shown by this
(53) rectangle.

8. Write this multiplication as an addition and show the total.
(54)

$$4 \times 5$$

9. On this map, how many inches is it from:
(35)
    a. Aubry to Reston?

    b. Reston to Hickory?

    c. Aubry to Hickory?

Aubry   Reston   Hickory

10. How many different numbers can you roll with one dot cube?
(44,
Inv. 5) What fraction of those numbers are less than 3?

11. Write 276 in expanded form.
(11)

12. Chad and Vic are playing a game with a dot cube. If a roll turns up
$\frac{(50,}{Inv. 5)}$ a 1 or a 2, Chad wins a point. If a roll turns up a number greater
than 2, Vic wins a point. If the cube is rolled once, which player is
more likely to win the point? Why?

Add or subtract, as shown:

13. $6.45 + $0.50
(22)

14. $3.65 − $3.48
(26)

15. 24 + 36 + 64
(24)

16. 1 foot − 8 inches
(34)

17. 2 + 2 + 2 + 2 + 2 + 2 + 2 + 2
(10)

18. (**Predict**) Find the eighth number in this sequence:
(2)

$$4, 8, 12, 16, \ldots$$

19. Find the missing addend: $8 + 6 + m + 5 = 25$
(9, 10)

20. Hector noticed a layer of ice on the road.
(4) He checked the thermometer. What was the
temperature?

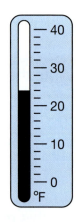

LESSON
55

• **Multiplication Table**

facts	Power Up 55
jump start	Count up by 8s from 0 to 80. Count up by 6s from 0 to 60.
	The bus arrives at school at 10 minutes to 8 in the morning. Draw hands on your clock to show this time. Write the time in digital form.
	The daily low temperature was 13°C. The daily high temperature was 15 degrees warmer. Mark the high temperature on your thermometer.
mental math	**a. Number Sense:** $7 + 16$
	b. Number Sense: $19 - 9$
	c. Calendar: How many days are in 4 weeks?
	d. Fractions: What fraction of the circle is shaded?

problem solving

Melia learned in science class that insects have six legs. She made a chart to find the total number of legs on 5 insects. Which number is incorrect in Melia's chart? What is the correct number? Explain your answer.

Insects	Legs
1	6
2	12
3	17
4	24
5	30

We can find the answer to a multiplication problem on a **multiplication table.** Notice that a multiplication table is a list of the numbers we say when we count by ones, twos, threes, fours, and so on.

	0	1	2	3	4	5	6	7	8	9	10	11	12
0	0	0	0	0	0	0	0	0	0	0	0	0	0
1	0	1	2	3	4	5	6	7	8	9	10	11	12
2	0	2	4	6	8	10	12	14	16	18	20	22	24
3	0	3	6	9	12	15	18	21	24	27	30	33	36
4	0	4	8	12	16	20	24	28	32	36	40	44	48
5	0	5	10	15	20	25	30	35	40	45	50	55	60
6	0	6	12	18	24	30	36	42	48	54	60	66	72
7	0	7	14	21	28	35	42	49	56	63	70	77	84
8	0	8	16	24	32	40	48	56	64	72	80	88	96
9	0	9	18	27	36	45	54	63	72	81	90	99	108
10	0	10	20	30	40	50	60	70	80	90	100	110	120
11	0	11	22	33	44	55	66	77	88	99	110	121	132
12	0	12	24	36	48	60	72	84	96	108	120	132	144

The two numbers that are multiplied are called **factors,** and the answer is the **product.**

$$6 \times 5 = 30$$

factor $\times$ factor $=$ product

To find a product, we look where a row and column meet. For example, to find the product of 6×5, we trace column 6 and row 5. Column 6 and row 5 meet at 30, so $6 \times 5 = 30$. We could also trace column 5 and row 6 and find the same answer.

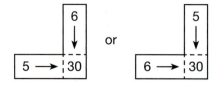

Example 1

Use the multiplication table to find the product of 7 and 8.

The product is the answer when we multiply. To find the product for 7×8, we look where a column and row with 7 and 8 meet.

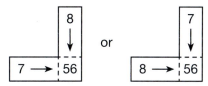

We see that $7 \times 8 = $ **56.**

Example 2

Use the multiplication table to find the number of small squares in this rectangle.

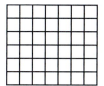

There are 7 columns and 6 rows. We find 7×6 on the table.

We see that $7 \times 6 = $ **42.**

The factors and products on a multiplication table are called **multiplication facts.** It is very important for you to memorize the multiplication facts. We will practice the multiplication facts so that you learn them well.

Activity

Using a Multiplication Table

Use the multiplication table in this lesson to find each product.

1. 6×8 **2.** 8×6

3. 9×9 **4.** 7×11

5. How many inches is 7 feet? Find 7×12.

6. How many feet is 8 yards? Find 8×3.

Discuss What patterns do you see on the multiplication chart?

Use a multiplication table to find each product.

a. 4 × 6
b. 6 × 3
c. 8 × 12
d. 9 × 7
e. What is the value of 8 nickels?
f. How many small squares are in an 8 unit by 4 unit rectangle?

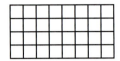

Written Practice   *Distributed and Integrated*

On a piece of grid paper, Paul drew a picture of a wall of his home showing door and a window. A side of each small square represents 1 foot. Use this picture to help you answer problems **1** and **2**.

1. a. How many feet long is the wall?
(53)

   b. How many feet high is the wall ?

2. Write a multiplication and total to show how many small squares
(54) are inside the rectangle for the window.

3. Sharon was born in 1999. How old was she on her birthday in
(39) 2007?

4. (**Represent**) The description below tells how Juan goes to
(31) Michael's house. Draw a map that matches the description.
Show both homes and school.

   From home, Juan walks 3 blocks west to school. From school, Juan walks 2 blocks north to Michael's home.

5. Look at the map you drew for problem **4**. How many blocks is
(44) it from Juan's home to Michael's home? What fraction of the distance to Michael's home has Juan walked when he is at the school?

6. Write an addition sentence and a multiplication sentence to show how
(54) to find the value of four nickels.

Use a multiplication table to find each product.

7. 7×9
(55)

8. 6×12
(55)

9. 8×8
(55)

10. 3×7
(55)

11. Wesley bought a carton of milk for 45¢ and paid with five dimes.
(14, 25) List the coins he should get back in change.

12. (Predict) What is the 6th number in this sequence?
(2)

$$12, 24, 36, 48, \ldots$$

Add or subtract, as shown:

13. $360 - 160$
(19)

14. $\$4.58 + \$4.84$
(22)

15. $75 + 89 + 98$
(24)

16. $\$5.25 - \$2.75$
(26)

17. $3 + 3 + 3 + 3 + 3 + 3 + 3 + 3 + 3 + 3$
(10)

18. Find the missing number: $48 - \square = 27$.
(40)

19. Marsha looked up from her breakfast to see the clock.
(3) What time was it?

20. Multiple Choice One hour is 60 minutes,
(47) so 15 minutes is $\frac{15}{60}$ of an hour. Which fraction
below is equivalent to $\frac{15}{60}$ of an hour?

A $\frac{1}{5}$ **B** $\frac{1}{4}$ **C** $\frac{1}{2}$ **D** $\frac{1}{10}$

LESSON 56

• Multiplication Facts: 0s, 1s, and 10s

facts Power Up 56

jump start  Count up by halves from 0 to 5.
Count up by fourths from 0 to 2.

 Write these numbers in order from least to greatest:

1,059   950   1,095

Label the number line by 10s from 0 to 100.

mental math

a. Number Sense: 6 + 16 + 4

b. Time: What is the time 2 hours after 9:30 in the morning?

c. Money: $1.00 − $0.85

d. Money: Find the value of these bills and coins:

problem solving Aunt Didi packed a cooler with drinks for the picnic. The cooler held 24 bottles altogether. There were 12 more bottles of water than bottles of juice. How many bottles of water were in the cooler? How many bottles of juice were in the cooler?

New Concept

There are 169 multiplication facts to learn from 0 × 0 through 12 × 12. Many of these facts can be learned quickly.

In the multiplication table below the blue columns and rows have 0, 1, or 10 as a factor. These are the facts we will learn in this lesson. When we know these 69 facts, there will be 100 facts left to learn.

	0	1	2	3	4	5	6	7	8	9	10	11	12
0	0	0	0	0	0	0	0	0	0	0	0	0	0
1	0	1	2	3	4	5	6	7	8	9	10	11	12
2	0	2	4	6	8	10	12	14	16	18	20	22	24
3	0	3	6	9	12	15	18	21	24	27	30	33	36
4	0	4	8	12	16	20	24	28	32	36	40	44	48
5	0	5	10	15	20	25	30	35	40	45	50	55	60
6	0	6	12	18	24	30	36	42	48	54	60	66	72
7	0	7	14	21	28	35	42	49	56	63	70	77	84
8	0	8	16	24	32	40	48	56	64	72	80	88	96
9	0	9	18	27	36	45	54	63	72	81	90	99	108
10	0	10	20	30	40	50	60	70	80	90	100	110	120
11	0	11	22	33	44	55	66	77	88	99	110	121	132
12	0	12	24	36	48	60	72	84	96	108	120	132	144

Look at the column and row with 0. Notice that when 0 is a factor, the product is 0 no matter what the other factor is.

$$0 \times 4 = 0$$

(Discuss) Why is the product always 0 when a factor is zero?

Now look at the column and row with 1. Notice that when 1 is a factor, the product equals the other factor.

$$1 \times 4 = 4$$

Finally, look at the column and row with 10. We see that when 10 is a factor, the product is the other factor with a zero to its right. Here are some examples.

$$10 \times 4 = 40 \qquad 10 \times 6 = 60 \qquad 10 \times 11 = 110$$

Zeros, Ones, and Tens

Practice the multiplication facts in this lesson with a partner. Ask each other multiplication questions with 0, 1, or 10 as a factor.

For example, you can ask "What is 0×8?" The answer is 0.

Lesson Practice Find each product.

a. 5×0 **b.** 9×10 **c.** 4×1

d. 10×3 **e.** 6×1 **f.** 0×11

g. 1×9 **h.** 12×0 **i.** 7×10

Written Practice   *Distributed and Integrated*

1. **Multiple Choice** The answer when numbers are multiplied is
(55) called the

    A sum.   **B** product.   **C** factor.   **D** difference.

2. What fraction of a dollar is two quarters? Five dimes is what
(47) fraction of a dollar? Are the two fractions you wrote equivalent? How do you know?

3. There are 169 multiplication facts to learn. There are 69 facts that
(19, 20) have 0, 1, or 10 as a factor. How many facts do not have 0, 1, or 10 as a factor?

4. Find the missing number: $357 - \square = 82$
(40)

5. Write the multiplication and total shown by this
(54) rectangle.

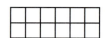

6. Write the multiplication and total shown by this
(54) rectangle.

7. Write a multiplication fact for finding the value of 6 dimes.
(54, 56)

8. Find each product.
(56)
    a. 1×8 **b.** 5×0 **c.** 0×12

9. Find each product.
(56)
    a. 1×8 **b.** 9×1 **c.** 1×11

10. Find each product.
(56)
    a. 10×6 **b.** 4×10 **c.** 10×11

11. **Formulate** How many feet are in 2 yards? Write an addition
(34, 54) sentence and a multiplication sentence to show the answer.

12. **Represent** Draw a rectangle that is $1\frac{1}{4}$ inches long and $\frac{1}{2}$ inch
(35, 52) wide.

Find these products on a multiplication table.

13. 6×7 **14.** 9×4 **15.** 11×11
(55)   *(55)*   *(55)*

Add or subtract, as shown.

16. 440 yd + 440 yd   **17.** $200 − $125
(16)   *(28)*

18. $9.90 + 10¢   **19.** 1 yd − 1 in. = _____ in.
(21, 22)   *(34)*

20. **Multiple Choice** Which of these shapes does not have four
(51) right angles?

    A   **B**   **C**

LESSON 57

• Arrays

facts   Power Up 57

jump start

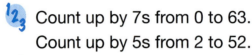

Count up by 7s from 0 to 63.
Count up by 5s from 2 to 52.

Write "one thousand two hundred sixty" using digits. What number is in the thousands place?

Draw a $3\frac{3}{4}$-inch segment on your worksheet. Record the length next to the segment.

mental math

a. Time: A **century** is 100 years. How many years are in 3 centuries?

b. Fractions: Compare these fractions using the symbol $<$, $>$, or $=$.

$$\frac{2}{2} \bigcirc \frac{3}{3}$$

c. Money: $26 + $9

d. Number Line: Which point represents 1,840?

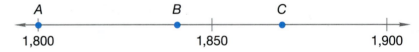

problem solving

There were 18 students on the school bus. One half of the students got off at the first stop. Then 6 students got off the bus at the second stop. How many students were left on the bus after the second stop?

An **array** is a rectangular pattern of items arranged in columns and rows.

Here we show 12 pennies arranged in an array. This array has 4 columns and 3 rows. It shows the multiplication fact $4 \times 3 = 12$.

Example 1

Write a multiplication fact shown by this rectangular array.

We see 5 columns of 3 stars. We also 3 rows of 5 stars. There are 15 stars in all. We can write two multiplication facts.

$$5 \times 3 = 15 \text{ or } 3 \times 5 = 15$$

Example 2

Draw a rectangular array of dots to represent 6 × 3. Then write the multiplication fact.

We make 6 columns of 3 dots (or 3 rows of 6 dots). We see 18 dots in all.

$$6 \times 3 = 18$$

Connect How can you use addition to verify that $6 \times 3 = 18$?

Activity

Arrays

Use counters or other objects to make an array for each pair of factors. For each array, write a multiplication fact on your paper that shows both factors and the product.

For example, for 4 × 2, make this array.

○ ○ ○ ○
○ ○ ○ ○

Then write this fact, 4 × 2 = 8.

1. 5 × 2 **2.** 6 × 4

3. 7 × 3 **4.** 3 × 8

Lesson Practice

For problems **a** and **b,** write a multiplication fact illustrated by each array.

a. X X X X X X X X X
    X X X X X X X X X
    X X X X X X X X X

b. ○ ○ ○ ○ ○ ○ ○
    ○ ○ ○ ○ ○ ○ ○
    ○ ○ ○ ○ ○ ○ ○
    ○ ○ ○ ○ ○ ○ ○

For **c** and **d,** draw a rectangular array of dots to represent each pair of factors. Then write the multiplication fact.

c. 6 × 2 **d.** 3 × 9

Written Practice   *Distributed and Integrated*

1. Jenna bought a picture frame, shown here. How many
(51) rectangles do you see?

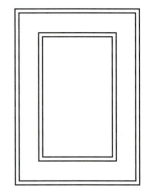

2. For **a** and **b** measure the smallest rectangle with your
(35, 52) ruler.

    a. What is the length of the rectangle?

    b. What is the width of the rectangle?

3. From 1912 to 1959, the United States flag had 48 stars.
(39) For how many years did the flag have 48 stars?

4. Write a multiplication fact illustrated by this array
(57) of stars.

5. Look at this timeline to answer the question below.
(33, 39)

For how many years did the United States flag have 15 stars?

6. (**Represent**) From 1822 to 1836, the stars on the flag were
(57) arranged in an array of 6 columns and 4 rows. Draw the array
with stars (or dots), and then write the multiplication fact for the
array.

7. Find the missing number: $811 - m = 299$.
(40)

8. Grace paid $50 for a $39 jacket. How much money should she
(14) get back?

9. Grace spent $3.90 on a metro ride. She donated $6.10 when she
(22) visited the Smithsonian Museum. How much did she spend in all?

10. Write a multiplication fact shown by this rectangle.
(53)

11. Find each product.
(56)
    a. 5×1 **b.** 7×0 **c.** 6×10

Use a multiplication table to find each product.

12. 8×7 **13.** 6×9 **14.** 12×12
(55)   *(55)*   *(55)*

Add or subtract as shown.

15. 880 yd + 88 yd   **16.** $200 − $172
(16)   *(28)*

Write a multiplication fact for each addition in problems **17** and **18.**

17. 2 + 2 + 2 + 2 + 2 + 2 + 2
(54)

18. 5 + 5 + 5 + 5 + 5 + 5 + 5
(54)

19. At sunset, the bus left for the airport. Marty looked at
(3)   the clock. What time was it?

20. How many pennies equal a dime? The value of a
(44)   penny is what fraction of the value of a dime?

*Real-World
Connection*

The Carrollton dirt bike track is 25 yards all the way around.
Sandra likes to ride the trail 4 times a day. How many yards does
Sandra ride in 6 days?

• Perimeter

Power Up

facts

Power Up 58

jump start

Count up by 3s from 0 to 45.
Count up by 9s from 0 to 90.

Write 3,455 as words.

Write two multiplication facts using the numbers 3, 10, and 30.

mental math

a. **Estimation:** Round $18 to the nearest ten dollars.

b. **Money:** 90¢ − 50¢

c. **Number Sense:** 12 + 12

d. **Time:** It is afternoon. The movie will begin 1 hour after the time shown on the clock. What time will the movie begin?

problem solving

Samir keeps a chart to show how much money he has at the end of each month. How much money do you predict Samir will have at the end of July?

Month	Money
January	$36
February	$48
March	$60
April	$72
May	$84

The distance around a shape is called its **perimeter.** To find the perimeter of a rectangle we add the lengths of the four sides.

Example

Visit www. SaxonMath.com/ Int3Activities for an online activity.

Chris walked the perimeter of the block. How far did he walk?

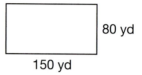

The perimeter is the distance around the block. We choose a corner and trace a path around the rectangle. Starting from point *A*, Chris walked 150 yards, then 80 yards, then 150 yards, and then 80 yards back to point *A*.

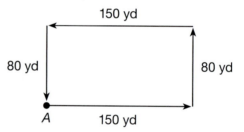

$$150 \text{ yd} + 80 \text{ yd} + 150 \text{ yd} + 80 \text{ yd} = 460 \text{ yd}$$

Chris walked **460 yd.**

Notice that when Chris reaches point *B,* he is halfway around the block. He has walked 230 yd. So another way to find perimeter is to double 230 yd.

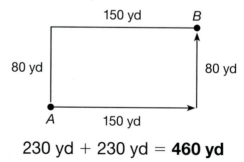

$$230 \text{ yd} + 230 \text{ yd} = \textbf{460 yd}$$

Analyze A square has a perimeter of 12 inches. What is the length of each side? (*Hint:* Think ____ + ____ + ____ + ____ = 12 or 4 × ____ = 12. You may use your multiplication table to find the missing number.)

Find the perimeter of each rectangle.

a.

12 in.

3 in.

b.

5 in.

5 in.

c. Trinh lives on a block that is 200 yards long and 100 yards wide. What is the perimeter of the block?

Written Practice — *Distributed and Integrated*

1. Morton is building fence around the pasture. What is
(58) the perimeter of the pasture?

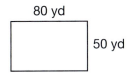

80 yd

50 yd

2. If one section of fence costs $4.25, then how much do
(18, 22) two sections of the fence cost?

3. Heidi planted trees in an array. Write the multiplication
(57) fact shown by this array.

4. **Connect** Look at the trees in problem **3.** Heidi says
(47) one row of trees is $\frac{5}{15}$ of the trees. Debbie says one row
of trees is $\frac{1}{3}$ of the trees. Which girl is right? Explain
your answer.

5. **Represent** Draw an array of dots to show the
(57) multiplication fact 5 × 4.

6. Which multiplication fact is shown by the squares in
(53, 54) this rectangle?

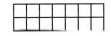

7. There are 169 multiplication facts from 0 × 0 to 12 × 12. There
(19) are 105 facts that have 0, 1, 2, 5, or 10 as a factor. How many
facts do not have these factors?

Use the map showing the park for problems **8–10.**

8. a. Name a street parallel to 1st Street.
(Inv. 4)

   b. Name a street perpendicular to 1st Street.

9. Each side of the park is 110 yards. What is the perimeter of the
(58) park?

10. (Verify) Is the park a rectangle? Is the park a square? How do
(51) you know?

11. The length of one side of the park in problem **10** is what fraction
(47) of the perimeter of the park?

Use a multiplication table to find each product.

12. 9 × 8   **13.** 9 × 12   **14.** 9 × 11
(55)   (55)   (55)

15. Find each product.
(56)
   a. 7 × 10   **b.** 7 × 1   **c.** 7 × 0

16. Find each product.
(56)
   a. 7 × 2   **b.** 2 × 9   **c.** 8 × 2

17. Find each product.
(56)
   a. 4 × 5   **b.** 8 × 5   **c.** 5 × 7

18. Write this addition as a multiplication. Show the product.
(54)
                    5 + 5 + 5 + 5 + 5

19. Write this multiplication as an addition. Show the sum.
(54)

$$3 \times 11$$

20. Multiple Choice In $6 \times 7 = 42$, both 6 and 7 are
(55)
    A addends.   **B** factors.   **C** products.   **D** sums.

Real-World Connection

Darnell and his friends went bowling. Darnell knocked down 7 of the 10 pins. Peter knocked down 4 of the 10 pins, and Mark knocked down 8 of the 10 pins. What fraction of the pins did each boy knock down? Who had the most pins still standing?

• Multiplication Facts: 2s and 5s

Power Up

facts   Power Up 59

jump start   Count up by 2s from 0 to 30 and back down to 0.
Count up by 5s from 0 to 60 and back down to 0.

Write 2,974 in expanded form.

Label the number line by halves from 0 to 5.

mental math

a. **Money:** 80¢ + 40¢

b. **Money:** Compare these money amounts using the symbol <, >, or =.

4 nickels ◯ 1 quarter

c. **Number Sense:** 27 − 8

d. **Fractions:** What fraction of the square is shaded?

problem solving

Focus Strategy: Work Backwards

Ginnie has a stack of $1 bills. She puts aside half of the bills. Then she uses the other half to make two equal groups of $5. How many $1 bills does Ginnie have in all?

(**Understand**) Ginnie has some $1 bills, but we do not know how many. We are asked to find how many $1 bills she has.

(**Plan**) We can *work backwards* to solve this problem.

(**Solve**) We know that Ginnie makes two equal groups of $5 each, which is $5 + $5 = $10. We are told that this amount is half of the bills. If $10 is one half, then the other half is also $10. So Ginnie has a total of $20.

Check We worked backwards to find that Ginnie has **20 $1 bills.** We know that our answer is reasonable, because two groups of $5 each is $10, and $10 is half of $20.

New Concept

In Lesson 56 we saw that 69 multiplication facts include 0, 1, or 10 as a factor. We have shaded these facts in the multiplication table below. The **blue** columns and rows show facts that have 2 or 5 as a factor.

	0	1	2	3	4	5	6	7	8	9	10	11	12
0	0	0	0	0	0	0	0	0	0	0	0	0	0
1	0	1	2	3	4	5	6	7	8	9	10	11	12
2	0	2	4	6	8	10	12	14	16	18	20	22	24
3	0	3	6	9	12	15	18	21	24	27	30	33	36
4	0	4	8	12	16	20	24	28	32	36	40	44	48
5	0	5	10	15	20	25	30	35	40	45	50	55	60
6	0	6	12	18	24	30	36	42	48	54	60	66	72
7	0	7	14	21	28	35	42	49	56	63	70	77	84
8	0	8	16	24	32	40	48	56	64	72	80	88	96
9	0	9	18	27	36	45	54	63	72	81	90	99	108
10	0	10	20	30	40	50	60	70	80	90	100	110	120
11	0	11	22	33	44	55	66	77	88	99	110	121	132
12	0	12	24	36	48	60	72	84	96	108	120	132	144

Until we memorize the facts, if 2 is a factor we can quickly find the product by doubling the other factor or by counting by 2s. If 5 is a factor we can find the product by counting by 5s.

Example 1

Find the product: 2 × 8

Here are two ways to find 2 × 8.

1. Double 8. Since 2 × 8 means 8 + 8, we know that 2 × 8 = **16.**

2. Count by 2s. We can count up by 2s to the 8th number.

2, 4, 6, 8, 10, 12, 14, 16 so 2 × 8 = **16**

Generalize What is another way to find 2 × 8?

> **Example 2**
>
> **Find the product: 7 × 5**
>
> We can quickly count by 5s to the seventh number.
>
> $$5, 10, 15, 20, 25, 30, 35$$
>
> So 7 × 5 = **35.**

Lesson Practice   Find each product.

a. 6 × 5   **b.** 6 × 2   **c.** 5 × 5   **d.** 5 × 2

e. 5 × 8   **f.** 2 × 8   **g.** 5 × 9   **h.** 2 × 9

Written Practice   *Distributed and Integrated*

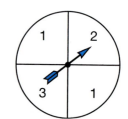

1. If the spinner is spun once, then is the spinner
(45, 50) most likely to stop on 1, on 2, or on 3?

2. If the spinner is spun once, then the spinner is equally
(45, 50) likely to stop on which two numbers?

3. **Analyze**   What fraction of the face of the spinner is labeled 1?
(43) What fraction of the spinner is labeled 2? Compare your two
fraction answers.

4. **Analyze**   Yoli walked once around the row of classrooms. What
(58) is the perimeter of the building? What is the perimeter of each
classroom?

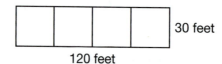
120 feet
30 feet

5. Diem has a half dollar, a quarter, a dime, and a nickel in his
(25) pocket. What is the total value of the four coins?

6. Find each product.
(56) **a.** 6 × 5   **b.** 6 × 10   **c.** 6 × 2

7. Change this addition to multiplication and find the total on a multiplication table.
(54, 55)

$$\$7 + \$7 + \$7 + \$7 + \$7 + \$7 + \$7 + \$7$$

8. George Washington was born in 1732. How old was he when he became president in 1789?
(39)

9. Molly made this rectangular shape with square tiles. The sides of each tile are one inch long.
(53)

    a. How long is this rectangle?

    b. How wide is this rectangle?

    c. How many tiles did she use?

10. Write a multiplication fact shown by the rectangle in problem **9.**
(54)

11. **Represent** Draw a rectangle that is $2\frac{1}{4}$ inches long and $1\frac{3}{4}$ inches wide.
(35, 52)

12. Find each product on a multiplication table.
(55)
    a. 3×6 **b.** 7×3 **c.** 3×9

13. Find each product.
(55)
    a. 9×1 **b.** 9×5 **c.** 9×0

Add or subtract, as shown.

14. $\$126 - \$95$
(19)

15. $\$4.58 + \$4.60$
(22)

16. $950 \quad 150$
(19)

17. $\$328 - \$258$
(19)

18. Find the missing addend:
(9)

$$100 = 50 + 25 + 10 + 5 + m$$

This map shows Braulio's house and school. Use this map as you answer problems **19** and **20**.

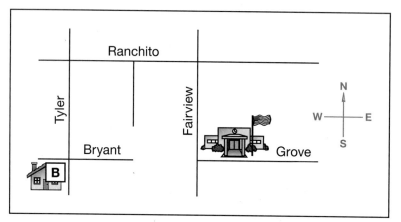

19. Write directions that describe how to get to Braulio's house from
(31)
school.

20. a. Name a street parallel to Tyler.
(Inv. 4)

b. Name a street perpendicular to Bryant.

LESSON 60

• Equal Groups
  Stories, Part I

Power Up

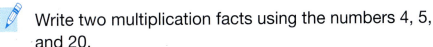

facts	Power Up 60

jump start

Count up by 8s from 0 to 80.
Count down by 25s from 200 to 0.

Write two multiplication facts using the numbers 4, 5, and 20.

Draw a $5\frac{1}{4}$-inch segment on your worksheet. Record the length next to the segment.

mental math

a. Time: A decade is 10 years. How many years are in 5 decades?

b. Number Sense: What is another way to write $10 + 10 + 10 + 10$? What is the total?

c. Money: Jamie took one dollar to the book fair. She bought a bookmark for 35¢. How much change did she receive?

d. Patterns: What number is missing from the pattern shown below?

56	50	44	38	_____

The width of the rectangular tennis court is 36 feet, as shown in the diagram. The length of the court is 78 feet. What is the perimeter of the tennis court?

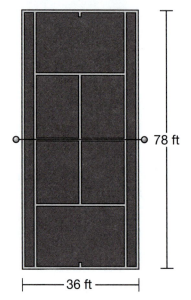

78 ft

36 ft

New Concept

Visit www.
SaxonMath.com/
Int3Activities
for a calculator
activity.

Stories about equal groups have a multiplication pattern. Here is an example of an equal groups story.

The teacher arranged the desks into 5 rows with 6 desks in each row. How many desks were there in all?

In this story, 5 is the number of groups, and 6 is the number in each group. Multiplying the number of groups times the number in each group gives us the total.

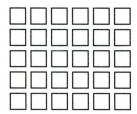

number of groups × number in each group = total

$$5 \times 6 = 30$$

There are 30 desks in all.

Example

There are 5 school days in each week. How many schools days are in 7 weeks?

We often see the word "each" in equal groups stories. In this story, 5 is the number in each group, and 7 is the number of groups.

number of groups × number in each group = total

$$7 \times 5 = 35$$

There are **35 school days** in 7 weeks without holidays.

Generalize Look at the factors in the example. What counting pattern would help you find the product?

Lesson Practice Write an equal groups number sentence for each story.

a. There are 3 feet in each yard. How many feet long is a rope 5 yards long?

b. There are 12 eggs in each dozen. How many eggs is 2 dozen?

c. Cory earns $9 each hour for helping a painter. How much money does Cory earn in 5 hours?

Written Practice *Distributed and Integrated*

Formulate Write an equal groups number sentence for problems **1–4** and then answer the questions.

1. Max is in class for 6 hours each day. How many hours is Max in
(60) class in 5 days?

2. Sherry saw 5 stop signs on the way to school. Each sign had
(60) 8 sides. How many sides were on all 5 stop signs?

3. The teacher arranged the desks in 7 rows with 5 desks in each
(60) row. How many desks were there in all?

4. Each movie ticket cost $8. Danielle's mom bought 5 tickets. What
(60) was the total price of the tickets?

5. Tamara arranged dimes in an array.
₍₅₇₎

What multiplication fact is illustrated by the array?

6. What is the value of the coins shown in problem **5?**
₍₂₅₎

7. Find each product on a multiplication table.
₍₅₅₎
    a. 8×4 **b.** 4×6 **c.** 8×6

8. Write this addition as a multiplication and find the total.
₍₅₄₎
    $4 \text{ mi} + 4 \text{ mi} + 4 \text{ mi} + 4 \text{ mi} + 4 \text{ mi} + 4 \text{ mi}$

9. (**Analyze**) What fraction of a dollar is $0.10?
₍₂₉₎

10. A square lawn that is 10 yards on each side has a
₍₅₈₎
narrow sidewalk around it. Cici walked around the
lawn. What is the perimeter of the lawn?

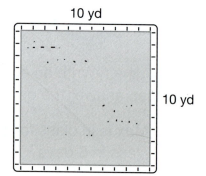

10 yd

10 yd

11. Find each product.
₍₅₆₎
    a. 9×2

    b. 9×5

    c. 9×10

12. Find each product using a multiplication table.
₍₅₅₎
    a. 6×6 **b.** 7×7 **c.** 8×8

Add or subtract, as shown:

13. $897 + $75
₍₁₆₎

14. 1 hour − 1 minute
₍₃₎

15. 56¢ + 48¢ + 79¢
_(21, 24)

16. $6.50 − $5.75
₍₂₆₎

17. **Conclude** Find the next three numbers in this sequence:
(2, 35)

$$1, 1\frac{1}{2}, 2, 2\frac{1}{2}, 3, \underline{\hspace{1cm}}, \underline{\hspace{1cm}}, \underline{\hspace{1cm}}, \ldots$$

18. Find the missing addend: $1 + 2 + 3 + 4 + m = 10$
(9)

19. How much money is 5 quarters, 6 dimes, 3 nickels, and 4 pennies?
(25)

20. Use your ruler to find the length and width of this rectangle.
(52)

 Real-World Connection The Crosbys are driving to the North Carolina coast for a long weekend vacation. The distance from their house to the coast is 562 miles. The Crosbys drove 248 miles before lunch. After lunch they drove 197 miles and then stopped for an afternoon break. How many more miles do they need to travel to reach the North Carolina coast? Write number sentences to show your answer.

Focus on

• More About Bar Graphs

Recall from Investigation 1 that a bar graph uses bars to match data. The bars may be vertical or horizontal. **Vertical** bars go up and down like columns. **Horizontal** bars go from side to side like rows.

Vertical bar graph

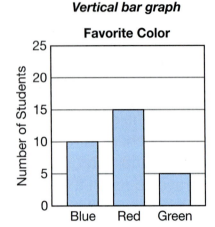

Horizontal bar graph

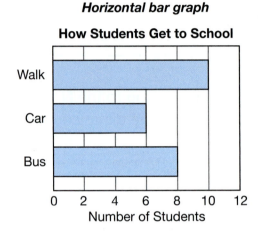

The title at the top tells what the graph is about. Labels along the bottom and the side tell what data is measured. The bottom or the side also has a scale. We compare the length of a bar to the scale to find how many or how much.

Look at the bar graphs above to answer problems **1–4**.

> **1.** What is the title of the vertical bar graph?
>
> **2.** How many students chose red as their favorite color?
>
> **3.** What is the title of the horizontal bar graph?
>
> **4.** How many more students ride the bus than ride in a car?

Before someone makes a bar graph, he or she gathers data. One way to gather data is to ask a lot of people the same question. This is called a **survey.** Some survey questions are multiple choice, such as, "Which of these three colors do you like best: blue, red, or green?" Other survey questions are open-ended, such as, "How do you get to school?"

In this investigation we will collect some data from the students in your class. Then you will choose two sets of data to make bar graphs.

Here are some survey questions you can ask. You may make up other survey questions. Record the results of the surveys on your paper. Then use the data from two surveys to make bar graphs on **Lesson Activity 22.** Choose numbers for the scales so that the data will fit on the graphs.

Survey Questions

- Which of these colors do you like best: blue, red, or green?
- How do you get to school most days?
- Which of these fruits do you like best: apples, oranges, or bananas?
- Siblings are brothers and sisters. How many siblings do you have?

- **Squares**
- **Multiplication Facts: Square Numbers**

Power Up

facts   Power Up 61

jump start   Count up by 7s from 0 to 70.
Count up by 10s from 5 to 95.

Write two multiplication facts using the numbers 2, 12, and 24.

Draw a rectangle that is 1 inch long and 1 inch wide.

mental math

a. Number Sense: 10 + 6 + 4

b. Time: It is 2:45 p.m. How many minutes is it until 3:00 p.m.?

c. Money: One yo-yo costs $0.45. Shantessa bought one yo-yo with $1.00. How much change did she receive?

d. Money: Find the value of these bills and coins:

problem solving

Jill listened to her favorite radio station from 4:00 p.m. to 5:00 p.m. During that hour, the radio station played 3 commercials. Each commercial lasted 4 minutes. Altogether, how many minutes of commercials did the radio station play between 4:00 and 5:00?

Squares

Tiles are often used to cover floors, shower walls, and counter tops. Many tiles are shaped like **squares.** Remember that a square is a special kind of rectangle with four sides of equal length. We can arrange square tiles to make larger squares.

Example 1

We can make square patterns using 1 tile, 4 tiles, or 9 tiles.

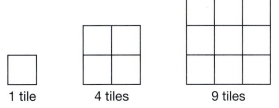

1 tile   4 tiles   9 tiles

How many tiles are needed to make the next square pattern in this sequence?

We add one more row and column of tiles. We count **16 tiles.**

Generalize Can you name another number of tiles that can make a square pattern?

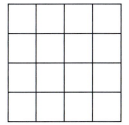

Multiplication Facts: Square Numbers

Numbers like 1, 4, and 9 are sometimes called square numbers. A **square number** is the product of two identical factors. We can write these numbers as multiplication facts.

$$1 \times 1 = 1 \qquad 2 \times 2 = 4 \qquad 3 \times 3 = 9$$

Activity

Squares on a Grid

Materials: color tiles

Use tiles to build squares that show all the square numbers from 1 to 25. You can start with the square numbers 1, 4, and 9. Write a multiplication fact for each square.

On a multiplication table, the square numbers appear diagonally across the table. Each square number is the product of two identical factors.

	0	1	2	3	4	5	6	7	8	9	10	11	12
0	0	0	0	0	0	0	0	0	0	0	0	0	0
1	0	1	2	3	4	5	6	7	8	9	10	11	12
2	0	2	4	6	8	10	12	14	16	18	20	22	24
3	0	3	6	9	12	15	18	21	24	27	30	33	36
4	0	4	8	12	16	20	24	28	32	36	40	44	48
5	0	5	10	15	20	25	30	35	40	45	50	55	60
6	0	6	12	18	24	30	36	42	48	54	60	66	72
7	0	7	14	21	28	35	42	49	56	63	70	77	84
8	0	8	16	24	32	40	48	56	64	72	80	88	96
9	0	9	18	27	36	45	54	63	72	81	90	99	108
10	0	10	20	30	40	50	60	70	80	90	100	110	120
11	0	11	22	33	44	55	66	77	88	99	110	121	132
12	0	12	24	36	48	60	72	84	96	108	120	132	144

Example 2

Find each product.

   a. 4 × 4   **b. 5 × 5**

We can make square patterns or use a multiplication table to find the products.

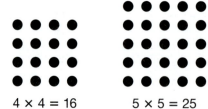

4 × 4 = 16   5 × 5 = 25

The square number 121 is the product of which two identical factors?

We see on the multiplication table that 121 is the product of **11 × 11.**

Lesson Practice

a. Copy and complete each multiplication fact below.

1 × 1	2 × 2	3 × 3	4 × 4
5 × 5	6 × 6	7 × 7	8 × 8
9 × 9	10 × 10	11 × 11	12 × 12

b. This square is made with 10 rows of 10 tiles. How many tiles are in this square?

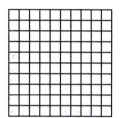

c. Here is a sequence of square numbers. What are the next three numbers in the sequence?

1, 4, 9, 16, ____, ____, ____, ...

Written Practice   *Distributed and Integrated*

1. Square tiles covered the front porch. How many tiles were used?
(53)

2. Write a multiplication fact for the array of tiles in problem **1.**
(57)

Formulate   Write number sentences for problems **3** and **4.** Then write a complete sentence to answer each question.

3. Fresh pies were on sale for $7.99. If the regular price was $9.87, how much is saved by buying them on sale?
(20, 26)

4. Ruben took six big steps to cross the room. About how many feet is it across the room? (Each big step is about a yard, which is three feet.)
(34, 60)

5. The odometer of John's car showed this display:
₍₃₂₎

    a. Write the number of miles shown using digits.

    b. Use words to state the number of miles the car has been driven.

6. **Multiple Choice** Which of these multiplications does *not*
_(56, 59) equal 16?

    A 16 × 1   **B** 8 × 2   **C** 8 × 8   **D** 4 × 4

7. Order these events from first to last. Then make a timeline from
₍₃₃₎ 1950 to 2000 to display the events.

    1976: Mars *Viking* probe   1997: Mars *Sojourner*
           launched   probe launched
    1969: Moon landing   1964: First space walk

8. What number is shown by the base ten blocks?
₍₁₁₎

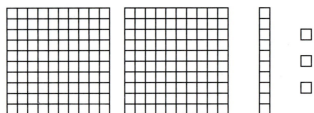

9. What fraction of the marbles in the bag are blue?
₍₄₄₎

10. If Chad picks one of the marbles in problem **9**
₍₅₀₎ without looking, which color is he more likely
to pick: white or blue?

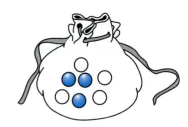

11. Compare these two fractions: $\frac{3}{7} \bigcirc \frac{4}{7}$
₍₄₉₎

12. （**Represent**）Draw a rectangle 3 inches long and 2 inches wide.
_(52, 58) What is the perimeter of the rectangle?

13. Find each product:
_(59, 61)
    a. 9 × 6   **b.** 9 × 5   **c.** 7 × 7

Add or subtract, as shown:

14. 38¢ + 75¢ + $1
(21, 22)

15. $450 − $375
(23)

16. $463 + $98
(16)

17. 11 × 11
(55, 61)

18. (Conclude) Find the next four numbers in this sequence:
(2, 32)

200, 400, 600, _____, _____, _____, _____, ···

19. Write 73,492 in expanded form.
(32)

20. A flock of 95 birds hopped around the park. Some flew away to
(40) find more food. Then there were 67 birds in the park. How many
birds flew away? Write and solve a subtraction number sentence
to find the answer.

*Real-World
Connection*

Roberto's team scored 59 points in a basketball game. Ian's team
scored fewer points than Roberto's team. Could the total number
of points scored by both teams be 123? Explain.

LESSON 62

• Area, Part 1

Power Up

facts   Power Up 62

jump start   Count down by 3s from 30 to 0.
Count down by 4s from 40 to 0.

Write the year "two thousand eleven" as digits.

Draw a $3\frac{1}{2}$-inch segment on your worksheet. Record the length next to the segment.

mental math   **a. Fractions:** Compare these fractions using the symbol <, >, or =.

$$\frac{2}{5} \bigcirc \frac{4}{5}$$

b. Money: $1.50 + $1.00

c. Number Sense: 22 + 11

d. Time: It is afternoon. Kim began reading a book at the time shown on the clock. She stopped reading 2 hours later. What time did she stop reading the book?

problem solving   A **dozen** is twelve. Ms. Kalinski arranged two dozen muffins in a 4 × 6 array. Then the children ate some of the muffins. This diagram shows the muffins that are remaining.

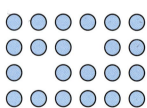

How many muffins did the children eat? How many muffins are left? Use a "some went away" pattern to solve the problem.

New Concept

In Lesson 58 we measured the perimeter of a rectangle. Recall that the perimeter of a rectangle is the distance around it. To measure perimeter, we add the lengths of the four sides of the rectangle.

In this lesson we will measure the **area** of a rectangle. The area of a rectangle is the amount of surface inside it. To measure area, we count the number of squares of standard size that fit inside the rectangle.

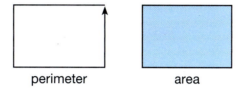

perimeter   area

Here we show the perimeter and area of a 3-inch by 2-inch rectangle.

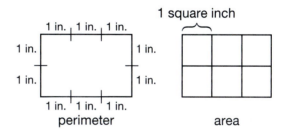

The perimeter of the rectangle is 10 inches, but the area is 6 square inches.

Notice that we use the words **square inches** to describe the area. Below we show an area equal to one square inch.

To measure small areas, we can use square inches. To measure larger areas, we can use square feet or square yards.

Activity

Area

On **Lesson Activity 23,** trace over grid lines to make the rectangles described below. Next to each rectangle, write its perimeter and area. Be sure to name the area in square inches.

1. Near the top of the grid, trace a 5-inch by 2-inch rectangle. What is its perimeter and area?

2. Trace a 6-inch by 3-inch rectangle. What is its perimeter and area?

(**Generalize**) Write a number sentence using the numbers 5, 2, and 10. Write another number sentence using the numbers 3, 6 and 18. What kind of sentences did you write? What do you think is another way to find the area of a rectangle besides counting squares?

Example

A 5-inch by 7-inch photograph has an area of how many square inches?

One way to find the area is to make 7 rows of 5 squares and count the number of squares. Another way to find the area of a rectangle is to multiply the length and width of the rectangle.

7 in. × 5 in. = **35 square inches**

5 in.

7 in.

Lesson Practice

a. **Multiple Choice** To measure area, we count

   A segments.   **B** squares.   **C** circles.   **D** rectangles.

b. Stan covered the front cover of a journal with 1-inch square stickers. What was the area of the front cover?

5 in.

6 in.

c. Silvia placed a stamp that was 1 square inch in the corner of a 3-inch by 5-inch envelope. Altogether, how many stamps would be needed to cover the front of the envelope?

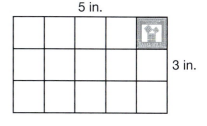
5 in.

3 in.

d. What is the perimeter and area of a 6-inch by 4-inch rectangle?

6 in.

4 in.

Written Practice
Distributed and Integrated

1. **Formulate** Miguel bought 8 boxes of tiles for $10 per box. What was the cost of all ten boxes? Write a number sentence. Then write a complete sentence to answer the question.
(56, 60)

2. a. What fraction of the tiles are blue?
(44)

b. What fraction of the tiles are white?

3. Compare the two fractions in problem **2.**
(49)

4. Barry made this rectangle out of one-inch square tiles.
(52, 62)

a. How long is the rectangle?

b. How wide is the rectangle?

c. How many tiles did he use?

d. What is the area of the rectangle?

5. What is the perimeter of the rectangle in problem **4?**
(58)

6. Multiple Choice Which of these multiplication facts equals 10?
(59, 61)

A 5 × 5 **B** 9 × 1 **C** 2 × 5 **D** 8 × 2

7. What number is shown by this model?
(11)

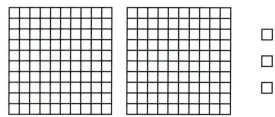

8. Multiply:
(56)
    a. 10×6 **b.** 10×12

9. What is the place value of the 6 in 825,630?
(32)

10. Point *A* represents what mixed number on this number line?
(48)

11. For a school fundraiser Roderick sold 132 key rings and
(39) 95 T-shirts. How many more key chains did Roderick sell than
T-shirts? Write and solve a greater-lesser-difference number
sentence to find the answer.

12. $\boxed{\textbf{Represent}}$ Draw the next square in this sequence:
(2, 61)

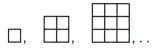

13. $\boxed{\textbf{Conclude}}$ The square numbers in problem **12** are 1, 4, 9, ...
(2, 61) What are the next two numbers in this sequence?

14. What multiplication fact is shown by this
(57) array?

                                         X X X X X X
                                         X X X X X X
                                         X X X X X X

15. $36¢ + 95¢ + \$2$ **16.** $\$300 - \$104$
(22)   (28)

17. Write the mixed number $4\frac{1}{2}$ using words.
(46)

18. Find the missing addend.
(9)
    a. $10 + m = 25$ **b.** $24 + n = 34$

19. Write 25,760 in expanded form.
(32)

20. Multiple Choice Which number sentence could you use to find
the amount of money Kurt spent on pencils?
(40)

Kurt had $10.75. He bought six pencils. Then he had $4.80.

A $10.75 + $4.80 = ☐   **B** $10.75 − ☐ = $4.80

C ☐ − $4.80 = $10.75   **D** $4.80 + $10.75 = ☐

Real-World Connection

Bryan's teacher asked him to sharpen 55 pencils. When he was finished, he handed out 32 pencils to his classmates and gave the rest to the teacher. The next day, Bryan sharpened another 55 pencils. This time he gave all of the pencils to his teacher. How many sharpened pencils did Bryan give his teacher altogether?

• **Area, Part 2**

Power Up

facts	Power Up 63
jump start	Count up by square numbers from 1 to 144. Count up by 100s from 0 to 2000. Draw an array to show the multiplication fact 2 × 3. Label the number line by 5s from 0 to 50.
mental math	**a. Estimation:** Round 289 to the nearest hundred. **b. Calendar:** How many days are in 5 weeks? **c. Money:** $1.20 − 40¢ **d. Fractions:** What fraction of the rectangle is shaded? 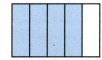
problem solving	If a coin is flipped, it can land showing either "heads" or "tails." Emilio will flip a quarter two times. One possibility is that the first flip will be heads and the second flip will also be heads.

1st flip   2nd flip

Another possibility is that the first flip will be heads and the second flip will be tails.

1st flip   2nd flip

What are the other possibilities Emilio can get by flipping a quarter two times? Copy and complete the tree diagram at right to help you find the combinations.

	1st Flip	2nd Flip	Result
		H	HH
	H	T	HT
	T	□	——
		□	——

New Concept

In Lesson 62 we used square inches to measure the areas of small rectangles. To measure larger areas, like the area of a floor, we often use **square feet** or **square yards.**

If a floor is covered with one-foot square tiles, we can find the area of the floor in square feet by counting tiles.

Example 1

The floor of a small room is covered with one-foot square tiles. Bill counted 10 tiles along one wall and 8 tiles along a perpendicular wall. How many tiles covered the whole floor? What was the area of the room?

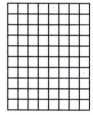

There are 8 tiles in each of the 10 rows. There are 10 × 8 = **80 tiles.** The tiles are one-foot squares, so the area of the floor is **80 square feet.**

Activity

Estimating Area in Square Feet

Use two one-foot squares to help you estimate the areas of some rectangular surfaces in the classroom, such as a desktop, tabletop, the inside surface of a door or window, or a bulletin board.

1. Name the object you measured on a piece of grid paper.

2. Draw a picture of its rectangular surface, with each square on the grid paper representing one square foot on the actual object.

3. Write its estimated area.

4. Describe how you found the area.

Carpeting is often sold by the square yard. A square that has sides 1 yard long has an area of one square yard.

(Analyze) There are 3 feet in one yard. How many square feet are in a square yard? How do you know?

Example 2

The picture shows a piece of carpet that is 3 yards long and two yards wide.

2 yd

3 yd

a. **The carpet covers an area of how many square yards?**

b. **The carpet covers an area of how many square feet?**

a. A 3-yard by 2-yard rectangle has an area of **6 square yards.**

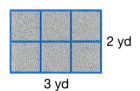
2 yd

3 yd

b. Each square yard equals 9 square feet. So 6 square yards is 6 × 9 square feet, which is **54 square feet.**

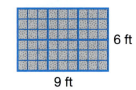
6 ft

9 ft

Lesson Practice

a. The floor of a small room is covered with one-foot square tiles. Bill counted 6 tiles along one wall and 8 tiles along a perpendicular wall. How many tiles cover the whole floor? What is the area of the room?

b. How many square yards of carpet are needed to cover the floor of a room that is 4 yards wide and 5 yards long? You can use color tiles to help you answer this question.

c. One square yard is 9 square feet. Copy and complete the table below.

Square yards	1	2	3	4	5	6
Square feet	9	18				

1. Monica walked from her garage to the street to estimate the
(37, 60) length of her driveway. She took ten big steps. Each big step was
about 3 feet. About how many feet long is her driveway?

2. (**Formulate**) Jimmy's great-grandfather is 84 years old. He retired
(36) when he was 65 years old. How many years has he been retired?
Write a number sentence. Then write a complete sentence to
answer the question.

One-foot square tiles covered the sidewalk. See the picture
at right to answer problems **3–5.**

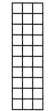

3. a. How long is the sidewalk?
(53)

    b. How wide is the sidewalk?

4. What is the area of the sidewalk?
(63)

5. What multiplication fact is shown by this array of squares?
(56, 57)

6. Multiple Choice Which of these multiplication facts equals 20?
(55)
    A 2×10 **B** 19×1 **C** 5×5 **D** 10×10

7. Multiple Choice Which shows five ones and six hundreds?
(11)
    A 56   **B** 560   **C** 650   **D** 605

8. Find the missing number: $\square - 398 = 245$.
(40)

9. Multiply:
(56)
    a. 6×10 **b.** 16×10

10. What is the place value of the 4 in 412,576?
(32)

Analyze Look at the square to answer problems **11** and **12**.

11. One yard is 3 feet. The picture shows one square yard. How many square feet is one square yard?
(63)

1 yd

1 yd

12. a. What is the perimeter of the square in yards?
(52, 58)

b. What is the perimeter of the square in feet?

13. Draw a picture to represent the mixed number $2\frac{1}{3}$.
(42, 46)

14. Write the two fractions shown by the shaded circles. Then compare the fractions.
(47)

15. Find each product on a multiplication table:
(55, 61)
a. 4×8 **b.** 3×9 **c.** 7×7

Add or subtract, as shown:

16. $498 + $679
(16)

17. $0.87 + $0.75 + $0.93
(22, 24)

18. $5.00 − $3.46
(26, 28)

19. $323 − $100
(19)

20. When Ismael came into class after lunch, he noticed the clock. Write the time in digital form.
(38)

LESSON 66

• Parallelograms

facts   Power Up 66

jump start    Count up by halves from 5 to 10.
Count up by fourths from 2 to 4.

Draw an array to show the multiplication fact 1×4.

Write these numbers in order from least to greatest.

625   695   655   595

mental math

a. Fractions: Compare these fractions using the symbol $<$, $>$, or $=$.

$$\frac{1}{2} \bigcirc \frac{2}{4}$$

b. Number Sense: $32 - 9$

c. Number Sense: $36 - 8$

d. Probability: CeeCee spins the spinner one time. What color is the spinner most likely to land on?

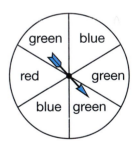

problem solving   Matt likes to solve crossword puzzles. He has a book of puzzles. He started at the beginning of the book and solves one puzzle each day. Matt solved Puzzle #4 on Monday. On what day did Matt solve Puzzle #1?

Waylon has some tiles shaped like this:

The tile has 4 sides.

Classify Is the shape a rectangle? How do you know?

Recall that a rectangle has four right angles. This shape does not have four right angles, so it is not a rectangle. We call this four-sided shape a parallelogram. A **parallelogram** is a four-sided flat shape that has two pairs of parallel sides.

One pair of
parallel sides

The other pair of
parallel sides

Classify Look at the figures below. Is a rectangle a parallelogram?

Example 1

Which of these figures is *not* a parallelogram?

A   B   C   D

A parallelogram has two pairs of parallel sides. We see two pairs of parallel sides in shapes **A, B,** and **C.**

A   B

C

However, shape **D** has only one pair of parallel sides.

Shape D is not a parallelogram.

Example 2

What is the perimeter of this parallelogram?

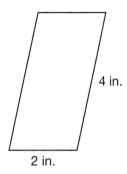

4 in.

2 in.

The parallel sides of a parallelogram are equal in length.

2 in. + 4 in. + 2 in. + 4 in. = 12 in.

The perimeter of the parallelogram is **12 in.**

We can name an angle of a parallelogram by the letter at its vertex. We can name a side by the letters at the ends of the line segment.

Example 3

a. Which angles of this parallelogram are acute and which are obtuse?

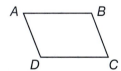

b. Which side is parallel to side AB?

a. Acute angles are less than right angles, so the acute angles are **angle A** and **angle C.** Obtuse angles are greater than right angles, so the obtuse angles are **angle B** and **angle D.**

b. The side parallel to side **AB** is side **DC.**

Lesson Practice

a. Draw a parallelogram that does *not* have right angles.

b. What is the perimeter of the parallelogram on the right?

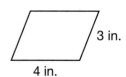
3 in.
4 in.

c. Multiple Choice Which shape below is *not* a parallelogram?

A   B   C   D

d. Which shapes in problem **c** are rectangles?

e. Which angles in this parallelogram are obtuse?

Q   R
T   S

f. Which side of this parallelogram is parallel to side *QT*?

Written Practice   *Distributed and Integrated*

1. **Formulate**   Gwen has 3 boxes of tiles with 40 tiles in each box.
(60, 24)   Write a number sentence to show how many tiles are in all 3 boxes.

2. Multiple Choice Gwen sees this tile pattern around the edge of
(2)   a shower. What are the next two tiles in the pattern?

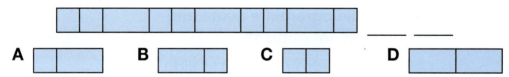
A   B   C   D

3. Write two addition facts and two subtraction facts using 7, 8,
(8)   and 15.

4. Multiple Choice Which shape is *not* a parallelogram?
(66)

A   B   C   D

5. One square yard equals 9 square feet. How many square feet is
(60, 64)   9 square yards?

For exercise, Sasha walks around the park every day. Look at the picture of the park for problems **6–9**.

6. What is the shape of the park?
(66)

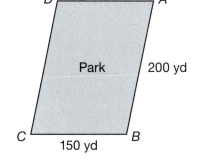

7. a. Which angles are acute?
(65)

   b. Which angles are obtuse?

8. What is the perimeter of the park?
(58)

9. Which side of the park is parallel to side *AB?*
(40, 66)

10. It takes Sasha 14 minutes to walk around the park twice. She started walking at 3:20 p.m. The clock shows the time she finished. Write the time in digital form.
(38)

11. Blaine opened a box of 40 tiles and used 28 of the tiles. How many tiles are left?
(20)

12. Use your inch ruler to measure the segments below to the nearest quarter inch.
(35)

   a. How long is segment *WX?*

   b. How long is segment *XY?*

   c. How long is segment *WY?*

13. There are three colors of marbles in a bag. Kyle picks one marble without looking. Which color is he least likely to pick?
(50)

Marbles in Bag

Color	Number
red	2
blue	3
green	5

14. Look at the table in problem **13** to answer **a** and **b**.
₍₄₄₎
  a. How many marbles are in the bag?

  b. What fraction of the marbles are blue?

15. $3.75 + $4.29
₍₂₂₎

16. $200 − $81
₍₂₈₎

17. 9 + 9 + 9 + 9 + 9 + 9 + 9 + 9
_(10, 54)

18. Write a fraction equal to 1 that has a denominator of 10.
₍₄₆₎

19. **Multiple Choice** Which fraction is *not* equal to $\frac{1}{2}$?
₍₄₇₎

  A $\frac{2}{4}$ **B** $\frac{3}{6}$ **C** $\frac{4}{7}$ **D** $\frac{5}{10}$

20. Point *A* represents what fraction?
₍₄₈₎

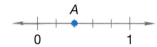

Real-World Connection

Tammy bought 7 pencils for 25 cents each. Then she bought 4 more pencils and gave 3 to her brother. How many pencils does Tammy have left? How much did she spend on the pencils altogether? You may use your manipulatives to help find the answer.

• **Polygons**

Power Up

facts

Power Up 67

jump start

 Count down by 7s from 70 to 0.

Count up by square numbers from 1 to 144.

 Write 6,562 in expanded form.

Draw a $2\frac{1}{4}$-inch segment on your worksheet. Record the length next to the segment.

mental math

a. **Number Sense:** $10 + 4 + 7$

b. **Number Sense:** $45 + 6$

c. **Money:** $10.00 - 4.50

d. **Measurement:** What is the perimeter of the square?

3 in.

problem solving

Focus Strategy: Work a Simpler Problem

Liz asked her father to download her 3 favorite songs from the Internet. Each song costs 99¢. How much will all 3 songs cost?

(**Understand**) We are asked to find the cost of 3 songs that are 99¢ each.

(**Plan**) We can *work a simpler problem.*

(**Solve**) The price 99¢ is close to $1. We can pretend that each song costs $1. This means 3 songs would cost $3. Each song is 1¢ less than a dollar, so 3 songs is 3¢ less than $3. We count backwards: $2.99, $2.98, **$2.97.**

Check We made our calculation with the amount $1 because it is a simpler number to work with than 99¢. Our answer makes sense, because $3 \times \$1 = \$3$, and $2.97 is a little less than $3.

A **polygon** is a closed, flat shape with straight sides.

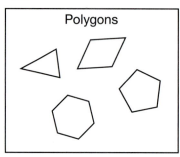   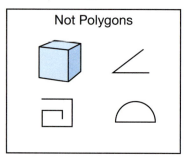

Discuss Is a polygon always a parallelogram? Why or why not?

Example 1

Explain why these shapes are *not* polygons.

a.    b. 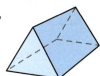   c.

a. **The shape is not closed.**

b. **The shape is not flat.**

c. **The shape is curved.**

In example 1, the figure in part **c** is a special curved figure we may know called a **circle.** A circle is a flat, closed shape, but it does not have straight sides. It is not a polygon.

Polygons are named by their number of sides.

Polygons

Name	Example	Number of sides
Triangle	△	3
Quadrilateral	▭	4
Pentagon	⬠	5
Hexagon	⬡	6
Octagon	⯃	8

Example 2

Kathleen arranged pattern blocks to make the design. What is the shape of each pattern block in the design?

Each pattern block in the design has 6 sides. A 6-sided polygon is a **hexagon.**

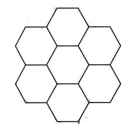

Example 3

a. Mrs. Lopez saw this sign and stopped at the intersection. What is the shape of the sign?

b. If each side of the stop sign is 12 inches long, what is the perimeter of the stop sign?

a. The sign has 8 sides. An 8-sided polygon is an **octagon.**

b. We add eight 12-inch sides or we multiply 12 inches by 8.

$$8 \times 12 \text{ in.} = 96 \text{ in.}$$

The perimeter of the stop sign is **96 inches.**

Example 4

These four shapes are all what type of polygon?

Each polygon has 4 sides. Any polygon with 4 sides is a **quadrilateral**.

Example 5

Simon ran the perimeter of the playground once. How far did he run?

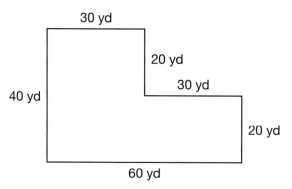

We add the length of each side to find the total distance around the playground.

60 yd + 20 yd + 30 yd + 20 yd + 30 yd + 40 yd = 200 yd

Simon ran **200 yards.**

Lesson Practice

a. Miguel arranged two kinds of polygons to make this pattern. Name the two types of polygons.

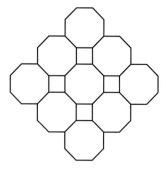

b. Draw a 3-sided polygon. What is the name for a polygon with 3 sides?

c. Multiple Choice Which of these figures is a polygon?

A B C D

d. Each side of the hexagon is 12 in. What is its perimeter?

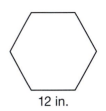

12 in.

e. What is the perimeter of the quadrilateral?

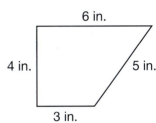

6 in.

4 in.   5 in.

3 in.

Written Practice
Distributed and Integrated

1. Paul finished two tile jobs. For the first job, he was paid $400. For the second job, he was paid $535. How much was he paid for both jobs?
(18)

2. How much more was Paul paid for the second job in problem **1** than for the first job?
(39)

3. **Estimate** Madison pays $590 each month for rent and $285 for her car. Estimate the total Madison pays for rent and for her car each month.
(30)

4. Jenny was born in 1998. How old will she be on her birthday in 2008?
(28, 39)

5. Gabe bought a postcard and gave the clerk a dollar. He got back two quarters, two dimes, and three pennies.
(25, 40)
    a. How much money did Gabe get back?

    b. How much did the postcard cost?

6. Arrange these numbers in order from least to greatest.
(27)
    263   326   362   236

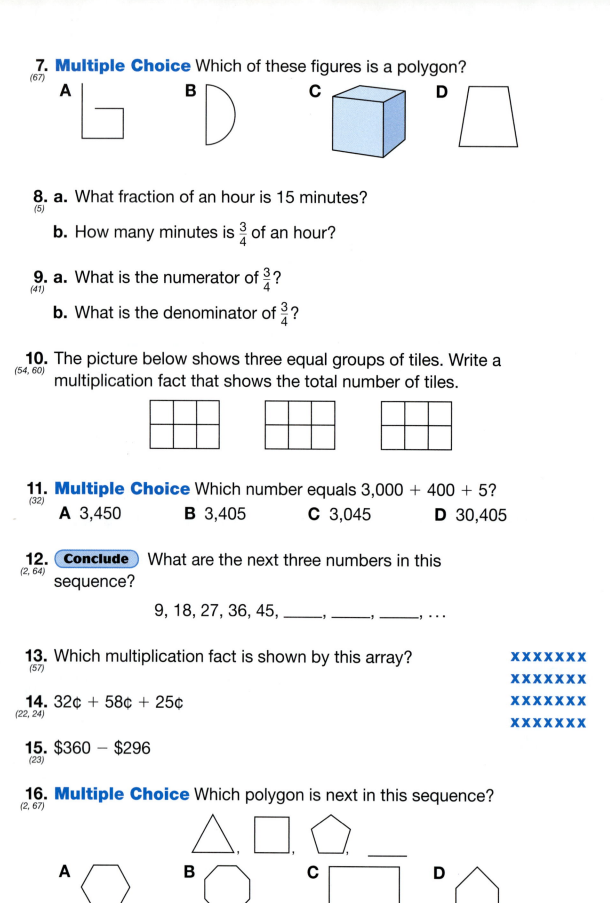

7. Multiple Choice Which of these figures is a polygon?
(67)

A   B   C   D

8. a. What fraction of an hour is 15 minutes?
(5)

b. How many minutes is $\frac{3}{4}$ of an hour?

9. a. What is the numerator of $\frac{3}{4}$?
(41)

b. What is the denominator of $\frac{3}{4}$?

10. The picture below shows three equal groups of tiles. Write a
(54, 60) multiplication fact that shows the total number of tiles.

11. Multiple Choice Which number equals 3,000 + 400 + 5?
(32)

   A 3,450   **B** 3,405   **C** 3,045   **D** 30,405

12. (Conclude) What are the next three numbers in this
(2, 64) sequence?

        9, 18, 27, 36, 45, _____, _____, _____, . . .

13. Which multiplication fact is shown by this array?
(57)

14. 32¢ + 58¢ + 25¢
(22, 24)

15. $360 − $296
(23)

        X X X X X X X
        X X X X X X X
        X X X X X X X
        X X X X X X X

16. Multiple Choice Which polygon is next in this sequence?
(2, 67)

A   B   C   D

17. Show how to write this addition as multiplication, and then find
_(54, 55) the total.

$$8 + 8 + 8 + 8 + 8 + 8 + 8$$

18. Which point best represents 16 on the number line?
₍₃₃₎

19. Use your inch ruler to find the length of this paper clip to the
₍₃₅₎ nearest quarter inch.

20. A square tile has sides 6 inches long.
_(58, 62)
    a. What is the perimeter of the tile?

    b. What is the area of the tile?

6 in.

6 in.

Early Finishers

Real-World Connection

Four friends ran a race. Tony ran faster than Bill. Bill ran faster than CJ. Ryan ran faster than Tony. Who won the race? Who came in last? Draw a picture to show how you got your answer.

• Congruent Shapes

Power Up

facts   Power Up 68

jump start   Count up by 4s from 0 to 40.
Count up by 8s from 0 to 80.

Write two multiplication facts using the numbers 8, 5, and 40.

Write the greatest 3-digit number that uses each of the digits 7, 5, and 8. What is the value of the digit in the ones place?

mental math

a. **Money:** $2.37 + $1.00

b. **Calendar:** How many days are in 10 weeks?

c. **Number Sense:** 700 + 700

d. **Fractions:** What fraction of the circle is shaded?

problem solving   The DVDs were priced at $9.99 each. At this price, how much would 2 DVDs cost? Explain how you found your answer.

If figures are the same size and shape, we say they are **congruent.**

Congruent Triangles

Not Congruent Triangles

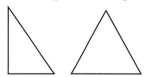

(**Discuss**) Two squares have the same perimeter. Will the two squares be congruent? Why or why not?

Example 1

Which pair of figures is not congruent?

A

B

C

D

The figures in **A, B,** and **C** are congruent. The figures in **D** are not congruent because they are not the same size.

If congruent figures are turned or flipped, they are still congruent. These three triangles are congruent.

Example 2

Which parallelogram below is not congruent to this parallelogram?

A

B

C

D

Recall that a parallelogram is a four-sided, flat shape that has two pairs of parallel sides. The parallelograms in A, B, and D are congruent to the figure in example 2 because they are all the same size and the same shape. Choice **C** is not congruent because it is a different size.

Congruent Shapes

Look around the room for two shapes or objects that are congruent. Name the shapes or objects on your paper. Sketch both of them.

Lesson Practice

a. What two words complete the definition?

Congruent figures are the same _____ and _____.

b. Draw a triangle that is congruent to this triangle.

c. **Multiple Choice** Which triangle below is congruent to the triangle in problem **b?**

A B C D

d. **Multiple Choice** Which pair of figures is *not* congruent?

A B

C D

Written Practice *Distributed and Integrated*

1. Mary wanted to buy a new rose bush. The red one cost $8.49.
(39) The yellow one cost $7.89. The red one cost how much more than the yellow one?

2. Mary decided to buy the yellow rose bush for $7.89. Tax was 55¢.
(18, 22) What was the total price including tax?

3. Mary gave the clerk $9.00 to pay for the rose bush in problem **2.**
(28, 25)
What coins did she probably get back in change?

Mary planted roses in her square rose garden. Look at the picture to help you answer problems **4–6.**

4. What is the perimeter of the garden?
(58)

5. What is the area of the garden?
(62)

6. The array of rose bushes in the garden represents what multiplication fact?
(57)

7 yd

7. The table below shows the numbers and colors of roses in Mary's garden.
(44)

Red	Pink	Yellow	White	Peach
6	5	3	2	4

What fraction of the roses in the garden are yellow?

8. Compare the fraction of roses that are red to the fraction that are pink.
(49)

9. Mary waters the roses for 20 minutes in the morning. The clock shows when she stopped watering. Write the time in digital form.
(38)

10. **Multiple Choice** Which shape below is *not* a polygon?
(67)

A   B   C   D

11. **Multiple Choice** Tran used tiles shaped like triangles and
(2, 67) parallelograms to make this border. What are the next two tiles in
the pattern?

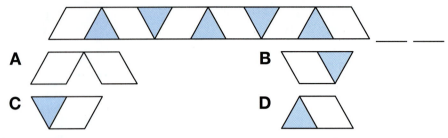

A   B

C   D

12. What is another name for this three-sided polygon?
(67)

13. **Conclude** These two triangles fit together to make
(66) what four-sided shape?

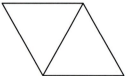

14. Use digits and symbols to write a fraction equal to
(46) 1 with a denominator of 8. Then write the fraction using words.

15. Find each product.
(56, 59)
   a. 5×0 **b.** 5×7 **c.** 7×10

16. Write the addition below as multiplication, and then find the
(54, 61) total.

$$7 + 7 + 7 + 7 + 7 + 7 + 7$$

17. $78 + 78 + 78$ **18.** $500 - 234$
(24)   (28)

19. **Represent** Draw a rectangle that is $1\frac{1}{2}$ inches long and $\frac{3}{4}$ inches
(35, 52) wide.

20. **Represent** Divide the rectangle you drew in problem **19** into
(42) three equal parts and shade $\frac{2}{3}$ of the rectangle.

• **Triangles**

facts   Power Up 69

jump start

 Count up by 12s from 0 to 120.
Count up by 10s from 6 to 96.

 Write "fourteen thousand, three hundred eighty" using digits. What digit is in the thousands place?

📏 Label the number line by 100s from 0 to 1,000.

mental math

a. Money: $1.30 + $0.40

b. Time: A **decade** is 10 years. How many years are in 10 decades?

c. Number Sense: 55 + 7

d. Measurement: What is the perimeter of the rectangle?

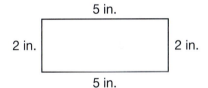

problem solving

Francesca and Sophie are going to the theater to see a movie. The movie is 1 hour 59 minutes long. The previews before the movie last 15 minutes. What is the total length of the previews and the movie? Explain how you found your answer.

New Concept

A **triangle** is a three-sided polygon.

Examples of triangles are shown in example 1.

Refer to the triangles to answer the questions below.

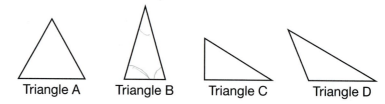

Triangle A   Triangle B   Triangle C   Triangle D

  a. Which triangle has a right angle?

  b. Which triangle has three equal sides?

  c. Which triangle has an obtuse angle?

  d. Which triangle has just two equal sides?

  a. **Triangle C** has a right angle.

  b. **Triangle A** has three equal sides.

  c. **Triangle D** has an obtuse angle.

  d. **Triangle B** has just two equal sides.

The table below shows some special kinds of triangles.

Types of Triangles

Name	Example	Characteristic
Equilateral		three equal sides
Isosceles		two equal sides
Right		one right angle
Scalene		all sides different lengths

Which triangle below is *not* congruent
to the triangle at right?

A   B   C   D

The triangle in example 2 is a right triangle with sides that are three different lengths. The triangles in A, B, and D are congruent to this triangle because they are all the same size and the same shape. The triangle in **C** is not congruent because it is a different shape.

 **Activity**

Make Equilateral and Right Triangles

Follow the directions on **Lesson Activity 24** to make triangles.

Lesson Practice

a. Kristin fit triangular pattern blocks together to make a hexagon. How many triangles did she use?

b. What type of triangles did Kristin use to make the hexagon?

c. Draw a right angle by tracing the side and bottom of a square tile. Then make a right triangle by drawing one more side.

d. Multiple Choice Which shape below is a triangle?

A   **B**   **C**   **D**

Written Practice   *Distributed and Integrated*

1. Multiple Choice Astra works 7 hours each day. How many
(60) hours does she work in 5 days?

   A 28 hrs   **B** 35 hrs   **C** 42 hrs   **D** 56 hrs

2. Write the fractions or mixed numbers shown on each number line.
(48)
  a.
         2   3   4

  b.
         0   1   2   3

3. Multiple Choice Donnell has a piece of tile in the shape of the figure at right. He wants to find a congruent shape among the scraps of tile. Which piece is congruent?
(68)

A **B** **C** **D**

Andersen laid 1-ft-square tiles on the floor of a room with this shape. Look at the picture to help you answer problems **4–6.**

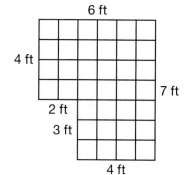

6 ft

4 ft

7 ft

2 ft

3 ft

4 ft

4. What is the perimeter of the room?
(58)

5. a. How many tiles did Andersen use?
(63)

    b. **Explain** What is the area of the room? Explain how you found the area.

6. a. The shape of the floor has how many sides?
(67)

    b. What is the name of a polygon with this number of sides?

There are blue marbles, white marbles, and gray marbles in a bag. Look at the picture and table to help you answer problems **7–10.**

7. What fraction of the marbles are gray?
(44)

8. Compare the fraction of the marbles that are white to the fraction that are blue.
(49)

9. Which color is most likely to be picked from the bag?
(50)

10. Which two colors are equally likely to be picked from the bag?
(50)

Marbles in Bag

Color	Number
Blue	4
White	3
Gray	3

11. The distance around the Earth is about 25,000 miles. Use words to write that number.
(32)

12. What is the place value of the 2 in 25,000?
(32)

13. What fraction of the circle at right is shaded?
(41)

14. **Represent** Draw a circle and shade $\frac{7}{8}$ of it.
(42)

15. Write a fraction equal to 1 that has a denominator of 9.
(46)

16. Find each product.
(61)
    a. 6×6 **b.** 7×7 **c.** 8×8

17. Find each product.
(64)
    a. 9×5 **b.** 9×10 **c.** 9×8

Look at the parallelogram and triangle to help you answer problems **18–20.**

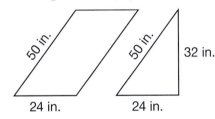

18. What is the perimeter of the parallelogram?
(58, 66)

19. What is the perimeter of the triangle?
(58, 69)

20. The perimeter of the parallelogram is how much greater than the
(39)   perimeter of the triangle?

Real-World Connection

Jamal made a spinner divided into four equal sections with a different number written in each section. He wrote the numbers 25, 15, 30, and 10 on the spinner. Draw a picture of the spinner. Is the spinner more likely, less likely, or equally likely to stop on an even number?

• Multiplication Facts: Memory Group

facts   Power Up 70

jump start
 Count down by 3s from 45 to 0.
Count down by 9s from 90 to 0.

 Draw a rectangle that is $1\frac{1}{2}$ inches long and 1 inch wide.

 Use these clues to find the secret number. Write the secret number on your worksheet.

• two-digit number

• perfect square

• product of the two digits is 6

mental math

a. **Number Sense:** 800 + 500

b. **Number Sense:** 45 − 9

c. **Time:** 120 minutes − 60 minutes

d. **Estimation:** Round the value of these bills to the nearest ten dollars.

problem solving   Draw the next two shapes in this pattern.

, ___, ___, . . .

The products of 20 facts we will practice in this lesson are marked in blue on the multiplication table. If we learn 10 of these facts, we will know all 20 facts.

For example, consider 8 × 7 and 7 × 8. If we memorize the product of 8 × 7, then we also know the product of 7 × 8.

The 8s column and the 7s row meet at 56.
The 7s column and the 8s row meet at 56.

	0	1	2	3	4	5	6	7	8	9	10	11	12
0	0	0	0	0	0	0	0	0	0	0	0	0	0
1	0	1	2	3	4	5	6	7	8	9	10	11	12
2	0	2	4	6	8	10	12	14	16	18	20	22	24
3	0	3	6	9	12	15	18	21	24	27	30	33	36
4	0	4	8	12	16	20	24	28	32	36	40	44	48
5	0	5	10	15	20	25	30	35	40	45	50	55	60
6	0	6	12	18	24	30	36	42	48	54	60	66	72
7	0	7	14	21	28	35	42	49	56	63	70	77	84
8	0	8	16	24	32	40	48	56	64	72	80	88	96
9	0	9	18	27	36	45	54	63	72	81	90	99	108
10	0	10	20	30	40	50	60	70	80	90	100	110	120
11	0	11	22	33	44	55	66	77	88	99	110	121	132
12	0	12	24	36	48	60	72	84	96	108	120	132	144

Represent Draw an array showing 8 × 7 and an array showing 7 × 8.

Activity

Flash Cards

Cut apart **Lesson Activity 25.** On the back of each flash card, write the product shown in the table. Practice the flash cards with a partner. Then clip the cards together and save them for practice.

Lesson Practice

Find each product.

a. 3
   × 4

b. 4
   × 6

c. 6
   × 7

d. 3
   × 7

e. 6
   × 8

f. 4
   × 8

g. 3
   × 6

h. 4
   × 7

i. 7
   × 8

j. 3
   × 8

1. What multiplication fact is represented by this rectangular pattern of tiles?
(53, 54)

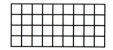

2. One foot is 12 inches. Glenna jumped 8 feet. Use a multiplication table to find how many inches Glenna jumped.
(55)

3. The tile factory makes tile in special shapes. Name each shape shown below.
(66, 67)

a.   **b.**   **c.**

4. Multiple Choice Which triangle below has a right angle?
(65, 69)

A   B   C   D

   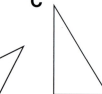   

5. a. A yard is how many feet?
(34, 63)

b. A square yard is how many square feet?

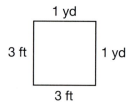

6. Multiple Choice Which pair of figures are congruent?
(68)

A   B

C      D

7. There were 89 students eating lunch in the cafeteria. Round 89 to the nearest ten.
(15)

8. Analyze Which point best represents 662?
(33)

9. Round 662 to the nearest hundred.
(15)

10. Find the missing number: $831 - \square = 294$.
(40)

11. **Analyze** Will measured the distance he could
(27, 32) ride his bike in 60 seconds. He recorded the
results in a table. Write the distances in order
from least to greatest.

Distance in 60 Seconds

Attempt	Feet
1st try	1,312
2nd try	1,320
3rd try	1,303
4th try	1,332

12. When dinner was over, Misha looked at the clock.
(38) Write the time in digital form.

13. **Conclude** Which two fractions below are equivalent?
(47)

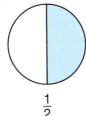   

$\frac{1}{2}$ $\qquad$ $\frac{1}{3}$ $\qquad$ $\frac{3}{8}$ $\qquad$ $\frac{2}{6}$

14. Compare: $\frac{1}{2}$ ◯ $\frac{3}{8}$
(49)

15. Find each product.
(70)
   a. 3×4 **b.** 3×6 **c.** 3×7

16. Find each product.
(70)
   a. 6×4 **b.** 6×7 **c.** 6×8

17. Find each product.
(70)
   a. 7×4 **b.** 7×8 **c.** 3×8

18. $1.98 + $3.65
(22)

19. $603 − $476
(23)

20. Which point on the number line best represents $2\frac{1}{2}$?
(48)

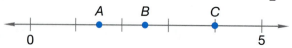

Early Finishers

Real-World Connection

Jackie bought 4 model tricycles and 7 model cars from Stan's Hobby Shop. Each model comes with a spare tire. How many tires came with the models altogether? You may draw pictures to help you find the answer.

Focus on

• Symmetry, Part 1

In nature we often see a balance in the appearance of living things. For example, when a butterfly folds up its wings, the two sides match. We call this kind of balance **symmetry.**

The line in the middle of this image of a butterfly is called the **line of symmetry.** The line of symmetry divides the butterfly into two equal halves. One half is a mirror image of the other half. If we hold a mirror along the line and look at the reflection, we see the complete image of the butterfly.

Visit www. SaxonMath.com/ Int3Activities for an online activity.

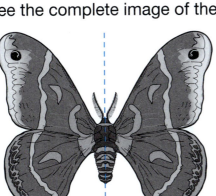

Miguel makes a pattern with tiles, as shown.

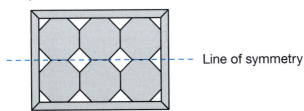

Line of symmetry

The tile pattern below the line of symmetry is a mirror image of the pattern above the line of symmetry.

(Discuss) Find another line of symmetry in the pattern above. Explain where the line of symmetry is.

Symmetry, Part 1

Materials: **Lesson Activity 26,** color tiles or pattern blocks

In the activity, you will make a symmetrical pattern using color tiles or pattern blocks. Place the tiles or blocks on both sides of the line of symmetry on **Lesson Activity 26.** Make sure both sides match. Then trace the pattern on paper. You may color the pattern so that the coloring is symmetrical. Here is an example.

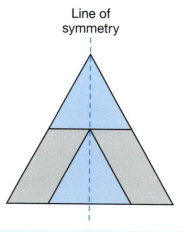

Line of symmetry

a. Cut pictures from newspapers and magazines of objects that have symmetry. Draw each picture's line of symmetry and paste the pictures on construction paper or cardboard to be displayed in the classroom.

• Rectangular Prisms

facts

Power Up 71

jump start

Count up by 25s from 0 to 250.
Count up by 7s from 0 to 77.

It is 5:05 in the morning. Draw hands on your clock to show the time in 15 minutes. Write the time in digital form.

The temperature in a restaurant kitchen was 28°C. It was 9 degrees cooler in the dining room. Mark your thermometer to show the temperature in the dining room.

mental math

a. Number Sense: 35 + 9

b. Number Sense: 5 + 4 + 4 + 5

c. Time: 45 minutes + 15 minutes

d. Fractions: What fraction of the marbles are white?

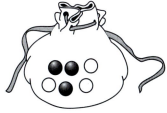

problem solving

Quinh plans to watch his favorite television show tonight. He told his mother that the show will begin in 14 minutes and will be over in 74 minutes. How long is Quinh's favorite television show?

Boxes come in different sizes and can be made of different materials. However, most boxes are alike in many ways. In this lesson we will study the shape of rectangular boxes. The shape of a rectangular box is called a **rectangular prism** or **rectangular solid.**

Rectangular prisms have flat sides shaped like rectangles. These flat surfaces are called **faces.** Two faces meet at an **edge.** Three faces meet at a point. These corner points are called *vertices.* Each corner point is a **vertex.**

Rectangular Prism

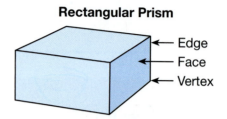

Some of the edges of a rectangular prism are **parallel** and some edges are **perpendicular.**

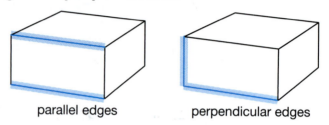

parallel edges   perpendicular edges

If we draw a "transparent" rectangular prism, we can see all the faces, edges, and vertices. First, we draw two overlapping rectangles that are **congruent.**

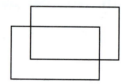

Then we connect the four vertices of one rectangle to the matching vertices of the other rectangle.

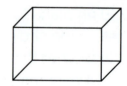

Represent   Practice drawing a rectangular prism.

Example 1

How many faces does a box have?

Place a box in front of you. See that it has a front and a back, a top and a bottom, and a left side and a right side. **A box has six faces.**

Example 2

Compare these two boxes. Describe how they are alike and how they are different.

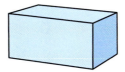

Both boxes are rectangular prisms. They each have 6 faces, 12 edges, and 8 vertices. Both boxes have rectangular faces. The boxes are different because the faces of the box on the left are longer than they are wide. The faces of the box on the right are all squares.

If every face of a rectangular prism is a square, then the figure is a **cube.** The box on the right in example 2 is a cube. All the edges of a cube are the same length.

Cube

Lesson Practice

a. Draw a picture of a transparent box.

b. How many vertices does a box have?

c. How many edges does a box have?

d. Describe a cube.

Written Practice

Distributed and Integrated

1. **Formulate** Molly counted the cars as the train rolled by the intersection. There were 103 cars, counting four engines and the caboose. How many cars were there not counting the engines and caboose? Write a number sentence. Then write your answer in a complete sentence.
(20, 28)

2. Hawkins bought two round-trip train tickets to Grant's Pass for $9.75 each. What was the cost for both tickets?
(22)

3. Hawkins paid for the two tickets in problem **2** with a $20 bill. How much money should he get back?
(26)

4. Multiple Choice Which picture below shows the mixed number $1\frac{4}{5}$?
(46)

A

B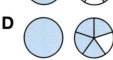

C

D

5. It is morning. The clock shows the time the train arrived in Chicago. Write the time in digital form.
(38)

6. Are the rails of train tracks parallel or perpendicular?
(Inv. 4)

7. The distance from the Upland Station to Burns Crossing is $17\frac{3}{10}$ miles. Use words to name $17\frac{3}{10}$.
(46)

8. Find each product.
(70)
    a. 8×7 **b.** 4×7 **c.** 6×7

9. Find each product.
(70)
    a. 3×8 **b.** 4×8 **c.** 6×8

10. Find each product.
(64)
    a. 9×4 **b.** 9×6 **c.** 9×8

11. (Represent) Follow the directions in this lesson to draw a rectangular prism.
(71)

12. A rectangular prism has how many faces?
(71)

13. Use your inch ruler to find the length of the sides of the right triangle.
(35, 69)
    a. side *AB*

    b. side *BC*

    c. side *CA*

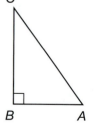

14. **Represent** On your paper draw a triangle congruent to the
_(68, 69) triangle in problem **13.**

15. **Multiple Choice** Which polygon shows a line of symmetry?
_(Inv. 7)

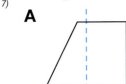 **A** 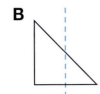 **B**   **C**   **D**

16. Martin has three quarters in his pocket. What fraction of a dollar is
₍₂₉₎ three quarters?

17. If every face of a rectangular prism is a square, then
₍₇₁₎ what is the name of the solid?

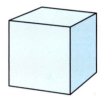

18. $32 + $68 + $124
₍₂₄₎

19. $206 − $78
_(26, 28)

20. Which number on the number line does point *M* represent?
₍₃₃₎

*Real-World
Connection*

Mr. Tuff is making a rectangular table that is 4 feet long and 3 feet
wide. Draw the table using the scale $\frac{1}{2}$ inch = 1 foot.

LESSON
72

• Counting Cubes

Power Up

facts Power Up 72

jump start Count up by 11s from 0 to 110. ✓
Count up by 5s from 3 to 53. ✓

Write 10,550 as words. *Ten thousand five hundred fifty*

Draw an isosceles triangle. Trace the sides that have equal length with a crayon.

mental math

a. Number Sense: Compare these numbers using the symbol <, >, or =

2,560 Ⓒ 2,690

b. Money: $10.00 ⫸ $5.25

c. Number Sense: 200 ⫸ 80

d. Time: It is afternoon. Marta went to the library at the time shown on the clock. She left 1 hour later. What time did she leave the library? *4:00*

problem solving A sheet of paper is folded in half and then cut with scissors as shown. How many pieces of paper will there be after the cut? *4*

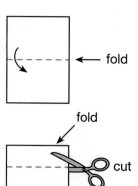

Andre uses a forklift to load boxes into a boxcar. Look at this stack of boxes. Can you count the number of boxes in the stack?

We cannot see all the boxes in the stack. One way to find the total is to first find the number of boxes in each layer.

Looking at the top of the stack, we see that there are nine boxes in the top layer.

Looking at the side, we see that there are three layers of boxes.

To find the total number of boxes, we can add: $9 + 9 + 9 = 27$. We can also multiply: $3 \times 9 = 27$.

(Formulate) If we add two more layers of boxes to the stack, how many boxes will we have altogether? Write a multiplication fact to show the answer.

Activity

Counting Cubes

Use cubes to build the stacks of cubes shown on **Lesson Activity 27.** Answer these questions for each stack of cubes.

- How many cubes are in one layer?
- How many layers are there?
- How many cubes are there in all?

Example 1

The picture shows a stack of cubes.

a. How many cubes are in each layer? 12

b. How many layers are there? 3

c. How many cubes are there in all? 36

a. There are **12 cubes** in each layer.

b. There are **three layers.**

c. Three layers with 12 cubes in each layer means there are **36 cubes in all.**

$$12 + 12 + 12 = 36 \text{ or } 3 \times 12 = 36$$

Lesson Practice   A box is filled with cubes, as shown at right.

a. How many cubes are in each layer? 6

b. How many layers are there? 5

c. How many cubes are there? 30

Written Practice   *Distributed and Integrated*

1. Sidney was on a 480-mile trip. When the train stopped in Omaha,
(20)   Sidney had traveled 256 miles. How much farther did Sidney have
to travel? 224

$$\begin{array}{r} 4\,8\,\cancel{0} \\ -\,2\,5\,6 \\ \hline 2\,2\,4 \end{array} \qquad \begin{array}{r} 2\,2\,4 \\ +\,2\,5\,6 \\ \hline 4\,8\,0 \end{array}$$

2. **Formulate**   It is 185 miles from Elam to Junction City. How far is
(18)   it from Elam to Junction City and back? Write a number sentence.

$$\begin{array}{r} 1\,8\,5 \\ +\,1\,8\,5 \\ \hline 3\,7\,0 \end{array} \qquad 185 + 185 = 370$$

3. Livestock were hauled east from Denver, Colorado, to Chicago,
(Inv. 4)   Illinois. Use the scale and your ruler to find the approximate
distance from Denver to Chicago.

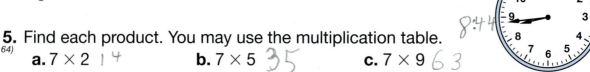

Denver ●————————————————————————● Chicago

1 inch = 200 miles   100 miles

4. It is morning in Chicago. Write the time shown at right in
(38)   digital form.

8:44

5. Find each product. You may use the multiplication table.
(59, 64)   **a.** 7×2 14   **b.** 7×5 35   **c.** 7×9 63

6. Find each product.
(70)   **a.** 8×4 32   **b.** 8×6 48   **c.** 8×7 56

7. Find each product.
(70)   **a.** 6×3 18   **b.** 6×4 24   **c.** 6×7 42

8. Find each product.
(64)

   a. 9×3 **b.** 9×7 **c.** 9×9

9. (**Represent**) In Lesson 71 we learned how to draw a rectangular
(71) prism. Use the same process to draw a cube. (*Hint:* Begin by drawing two overlapping squares.)

10. What is the shape of every face of a cube?
(71)

11. A rectangular prism has how many edges?
(71)

12. **Multiple Choice** Which polygon does *not* show a line of symmetry?
(Inv. 7)

A 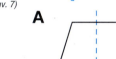   B   C   D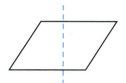

13. Harold put some small cubes together to make this larger
(72) cube. How many small cubes make the larger cube?

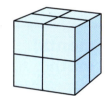

Use polygon *ABCD* and a ruler to answer problems **14–16.**

14. **a.** How long is each side of the polygon?
(35, 58)

   b. What is the perimeter of the polygon?

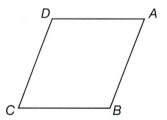

15. What is the shape of the polygon?
(66)

16. **a.** Which two angles are obtuse?
(65, 66)

   b. Which two angles are acute?

17. (**Conclude**) The numbers below make a pattern on a multiplication
(55, 61) table. What are the next three numbers in this pattern?

$$0, 1, 4, 9, 16, 25, \underline{\quad}, \underline{\quad}, \underline{\quad}, \ldots$$

18. 36¢ + 74¢ + $2   **19.** $2.00 − $1.26
(22, 24)   (26, 28)

20. A driveway is 10 yd long and 7 yd wide. What is the
(62, 63) area of the driveway?

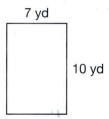
7 yd

10 yd

• Volume

facts   Power Up 73

**jump
start**   Count up by halves from 5 to 10.
            Count up by fourths from 2 to 4.

            Write two multiplication facts using the numbers 9, 7,
            and 63.

            Write these money amounts in order from least to
            greatest.

                $10.50 $10.95 $10.05 $11.50

**mental
math**   **a.** **Number Sense:** 38 + 8

           b. **Number Sense:** 3000 + 100 + 50 + 8

           c. **Measurement:** What is the perimeter of
           the triangle?

           d. **Geometry:** What type of triangle is
           shown in problem **c?**

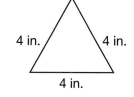

4 in.   4 in.

4 in.

**problem
solving**   Denair wrote an addition problem and then erased   2
            some of the digits. Find the missing digits in the   + 1 _
            problem.   2 7

New Concept

Visit www.
SaxonMath.com/
Int3Activities
for a calculator
activity.

One way to describe the size of a box is to say how much
space there is inside the box. If we fill up the box with cubes
we can describe the space inside the box in **cubic units.**
Instead of saying how many raisins or apples or oranges a
box can hold, we might say how many cubic inches it can
hold. We might describe the size of a boxcar by saying how
many cubic feet or cubic yards it can hold.

The amount of space an object occupies is called its **volume.** A cube with edges one inch long has a volume of one cubic inch.

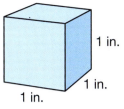

1 cubic inch

The activity below will help us understand volume. We will find the number of one-inch cubes needed to fill a box.

Volume

Materials: **Lesson Activity 28,** empty boxes such as shoe boxes or tissue boxes, rulers, one-inch cubes

For this activity, you will work together in small groups. Use your ruler to measure the length, width, and height of your box.

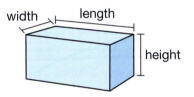

Record the length, width, and height in the table on **Lesson Activity 28.** Write the number of inches without a fraction. For example, if the length is $11\frac{3}{4}$ inches, just write 11 inches.

Dimensions of Box	
length	_____ in.
width	_____ in.
height	_____ in.

Next, figure out how many cubes are needed to make one layer on the bottom of the box. If you do not have enough cubes to cover the bottom of the box, you might need to multiply to find the number.

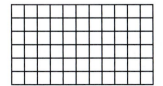

Record the number of cubes that will fit on the bottom of the box. This is the bottom layer. Then figure out how many layers the box could hold without going over the top. Finally, figure out the total number of cubes the box will hold. This is the approximate volume of the box in cubic inches.

Number of Cubes in Box	
number of cubes in bottom layer	_____
number of layers	_____
total number of cubes in box	_____

Write the approximate volume of the box as a number of cubic inches.

Example

Millie filled a small gift box with 1-inch cubes. The picture shows the top layer. There are two layers of cubes. How many cubes are in the box? What is the volume of the box in cubic inches?

We see the top layer. There are 4 rows of cubes and 5 cubes in each row.

$$4 \times 5 = 20$$

There are 20 cubes in the top layer. Since there are 2 layers, there are **40 cubes in the box.**

$$20 + 20 = 40$$

The volume of the box is **40 cubic inches.**

Discuss Could you find the volume of Millie's box in cubic feet? Why or why not?

Lesson Practice Jorge stores work supplies in 1-foot cubic boxes in his garage.

    a. What is the volume of each box?

    b. What is the volume of this stack of boxes?

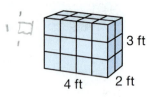

3 ft
4 ft 2 ft

1. A round-trip ticket to Topeka cost $149. Cory has $98. How much
(36) more money does he need to buy a ticket?

2. **Analyze** In a common year, June 30 is the 181st day of the year.
(40) How many days are there in the last six months of the year?

3. The railroad tie cutters worked 9 hours a day, 6 days a week. How
(60, 64) many hours did the tie cutters work in a week?

4. The ride to Pawtucket lasts an hour and a half. The
(39) train left the station at 8:45 a.m. The clock showed the
time it arrived in Pawtucket. Write the time in digital
form.

5. A pallet is loaded with boxes, as shown.
(72)   **a.** How many boxes are in each layer?

   b. How many layers are there?

   c. How many boxes are there?

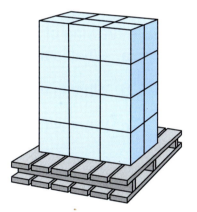

6. If each box in problem **5** is one cubic foot, then what
(73) is the volume of the stack of boxes?

7. Find each product:
(70)   **a.** 3×6 **b.** 3×8 **c.** 3×7

8. Find each product:
(64)   **a.** 5×9 **b.** 9×2 **c.** 9×9

9. Change this addition into multiplication and find the total:
(54)
$$\$5 + \$5 + \$5 + \$5 + \$5 + \$5$$

10. **Represent** Draw a cube.
(71)

11. A cube has how many vertices?
(71)

12. Which letter does not show a line of symmetry?
(Inv. 7)

C D E F

13. (**Connect**) Find the next three numbers in this sequence:
(2)

14, 21, 28, 35, _____, _____, _____, ...

14. Find each product:
(61, 70)
    a. 6×7 **b.** 7×7 **c.** 8×7

Add or subtract, as shown:

15. $800 - $724   **16.** $6.49 + $5.52
(28)   *(22)*

17. $9 + 9 + 9 + 9 + 9 + 9 + 9 + 9 + 9$
(10, 54)

18. Use words to write each fraction or mixed number.
(41, 46)
    a. $\dfrac{3}{7}$ **b.** $3\dfrac{1}{2}$ **c.** $\dfrac{9}{10}$ **d.** $2\dfrac{3}{4}$

19. A drawing of a box is shown at right.
(71)
    a. What is the length of the box?

    b. What is the width of the box?

    c. What is the height of the box?

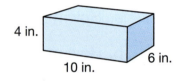
4 in.   6 in.   10 in.

20. What is the area of the top of the box in problem **19?**
(62)

Early Finishers
Real-World Connection

Mr. Crosby's mini van weighs 2,746 pounds. When he drives his daughter and four of her friends to softball practice the car weighs 3,273 pounds with the weight of the passengers. How much do the passengers of the car weigh altogether? Write 2,746 and 3,273 using words.

LESSON 74

• **Weight: Ounces, Pounds, and Tons**

facts   Power Up 74

jump start

 Count down by 4s from 40 to 0.
Count down by 8s from 80 to 0.

✏️ Draw an array to show the multiplication fact 4 × 2.

📏 Label the number line by 25s from 0 to 250.

mental math

a. **Number Sense:** 900 + 400 + 300

b. **Measurement:** How many inches are in 5 feet?

c. **Money:** $5.75 + $1.00

d. **Patterns:** What number is missing in the pattern below?

| 1 | 4 | 9 | _____ | 25 | 36 |

problem solving

Jim, Ron, and George were standing in line. There were 38 people in front of them and 3 people behind them. Altogether, how many people were standing in line?

New Concept

The **weight** of an object is a measure of how heavy it is.

Weight can be measured in ounces. A metal spoon weighs about one **ounce.**

Weight can also be measured in pounds. A playground ball might weigh about a **pound.** A pound is equal to 16 ounces.

Very heavy objects can be measured in tons. A small car weighs a **ton.** A ton is equal to 2,000 pounds.

Metal spoon   Playground ball   Small automobile

1 ounce   1 pound   1 ton

Units of Weight

1 pound = 16 ounces
1 ton = 2,000 pounds

Verify A 1-pound box of cereal costs the same as three 4-ounce boxes. Which is the better buy?

Example 1

Which of these objects would weigh about a pound?

A   Fork

B   Shoe

C   Van

Choice **B, a shoe,** weighs about a pound. A fork weighs about an ounce. A small van might weigh two tons.

Example 2

If a large car weighs about two tons, then it weighs about how many pounds?

A ton is 2,000 pounds. We can add to find the number of pounds in two tons.

2,000 pounds + 2,000 pounds = 4,000 pounds

A car that weighs about two tons weighs **about 4,000 pounds.**

 **Activity**

Weighing Objects

Use a scale to weigh various objects in the classroom. Make a table like the one below to record the name of each object and its weight. Can you find an object that weighs one ounce? Can you find an object that weighs one pound?

Weights of Objects

Name of Object	Weight

Lesson Practice

a. Would you describe the weight of a large dog in ounces, pounds, or tons?

b. **Multiple Choice** Which object weighs about an ounce?

A Birthday card **B** Box of cereal **C** Brick wall

c. The kitten weighed about two pounds. About how many ounces did the kitten weigh?

d. **Multiple Choice** The horse weighed about one half of a ton. About how many pounds did the horse weigh?

A 500 pounds **B** 1,000 pounds
C 1,500 pounds **D** 2,000 pounds

1. Jefferson sat by the window and watched the train go by.
(18) He counted thirty-eight coal cars and twenty-seven boxcars.
Altogether, how many coal cars and boxcars did he count?

2. **Formulate** The miners loaded 16 tons of ore in the morning.
(36) Their goal was 28 tons by nightfall. How many more tons of
coal did they need to load to reach their goal? Write a number
sentence

3. Automobiles were shipped west from Jonestown to Seagraves.
(Inv. 4) Use the scale to find the approximate distance from Jonestown to
Seagraves.

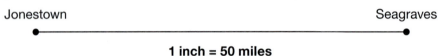

Jonestown   Seagraves

1 inch = 50 miles

4. It is noon in Detroit. Write the time in digital form.
(3)

5. Are the stripes on a United States flag parallel or perpendicular?
(Inv. 4)

6. The work crew was paid $16,000 for laying a mile of track on flat
(32) land. Use words to name $16,000.

7. How many ounces are equal to one pound?
(74)

8. The tunnel was four tenths of a mile long. Write four tenths as a
(41) fraction.

9. The first rail line connecting the east coast of the United States
(39) to the west coast was completed in 1869. How many years ago
was that?

10. Find each product.
(59)
    a. 6 × 2   **b.** 8 × 5   **c.** 5 × 6

11. Change this addition to multiplication and find the total.
(54)

$$3 \text{ ft} + 3 \text{ ft} + 3 \text{ ft} + 3\text{ft}$$

12. How many pounds are equal to
(74)
    a. one ton?   **b.** two tons?

13. Find each product.
(70)
    a. 6×7 **b.** 7×8 **c.** 6×8

Add or subtract, as shown:

14. $6.75 − $4.48
(26)

15. $1 − 1¢
(26, 28)

16. Find the missing addend: $10 + 20 + m = 100$
(9)

17. Dora made this rectangular prism using 1-inch cubes.
(72, 73)

    a. How many cubes did she use?

    b. What is the volume of the rectangular prism?

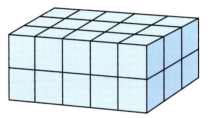

18. **Model** Each quarter inch on this map represents 10 miles.
(Inv. 4) How many miles is it from
    a. Calmer to Seaton?

    b. Calmer to Bayview?

    c. Bayview to Seaton?

19. **Multiple Choice** Which of these polygons does *not* have at
(65, 67) least one right angle? How can you tell?

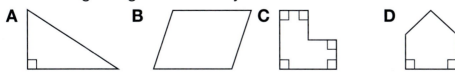

20. a. The polygon in problem **19,** choice **D** has how many sides?
(67)

    b. What is the name for a polygon with this number of sides?

• Geometric Solids

Power Up

facts   Power Up 75

jump start

 Count up by 6s from 0 to 60.
Count up by 12s from 0 to 120.

 Write "five and two fifths" using digits.

Use the clues below to find the secret number. Write the secret number on your worksheet.

- two-digit number
- perfect square
- sum of the digits is 7
- odd number

mental math

a. Estimation: Round 466 to the nearest hundred.

b. Number Sense: 44 + 11

c. Money: $1.60 − $0.80

d. Fractions: What fraction of the rectangle is *not* shaded?

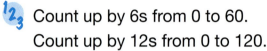

problem solving

Four students can sit at a square table (one student on each side). If two tables are joined together, six students can sit. (Notice that nobody can sit at the edges where the tables touch.)

Predict how many students can sit at four tables that are joined into one big square. To check your prediction, draw a diagram of the tables and place numbers where students can sit along the edges.

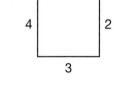

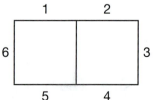

Geometric shapes that take up space are sometimes called **solids.** Cubes and other rectangular prisms are examples of **geometric solids.** The chart below shows some more geometric solids.

Geometric Solids

Shape	Name
	Cube
	Rectangular prism
	Triangular prism
	Pyramid
	Cylinder
	Cone
	Sphere

Classify Are rectangles, triangles, and circles solids? Why or why not?

Example 1

Which of these figures does *not* represent a solid?

A   B   C   D

Figure **C,** the pentagon, is a flat shape. It is not a solid.

The world around us is filled with objects that are shaped like solids and combinations of solids. In example 2 we show some common objects that are shaped like solids.

Example 2

Which object best represents a cylinder?

A

B

C

D

The object shaped most like a cylinder is choice **B**.

Activity

Solids

Find pictures in magazines or draw pictures of objects that are the shapes of the solids described in this lesson. Display the pictures on a classroom poster along with the names of the solid shapes.

Lesson Practice

Write the geometric name for the shape of each figure below.

a.

b.

c.

d.

e.

f.

1. **Analyze** Bill wants to load a crate so it weighs
(33, 36) 100 pounds. He placed the crate on a scale as shown
at right. How many more pounds can he put into the
crate?

2. Hector bought two matinee tickets to a movie. Each
(22) ticket cost $7.75. What was the total cost of both
tickets?

3. **Formulate** The train has seven boxcars. Each boxcar
(60, 70) has eight wheels. How many wheels are there on
all seven boxcars? Write a number sentence. Then
write your answer in a complete sentence.

4. Vegetables were sent north from San Francisco,
(Inv. 4) California, to Seattle, Washington. Find the
approximate distance from San Francisco to Seattle.

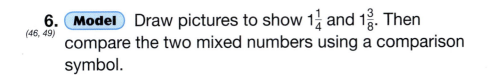

San Francisco   1 in. = 200 mi   Seattle

5. The clock shows the time the train arrived in Seattle
(38) Friday afternoon. Write the time in digital form.

6. **Model** Draw pictures to show $1\frac{1}{4}$ and $1\frac{3}{8}$. Then
(46, 49) compare the two mixed numbers using a comparison
symbol.

7. Find each product.
(64)
    a. 9×5 **b.** 7×9 **c.** 2×9

8. Find each product.
(56)
    a. 5×0 **b.** 9×1 **c.** 10×8

9. (Model) The drawing shows the top part of an old train rail. Use
(35) your ruler to find the distance across the top of the rail.

10. Teresa bought a pencil for 22¢ and paid for it with a dollar bill. What
(26, 28) coins should she get back in change?

11. How many pounds is
(74)   **a.** two tons?   **b.** four tons?

12. Find each product.
(70)   **a.** 6×3 **b.** 7×6 **c.** 8×7

13. $472 - $396   **14.** $354 + $263 + $50
(23)   (24)

15. $5 + 5 + 5 + 5 + 5 + 5 + 5 + 5 + 5 + 5$
(10, 54)

16. Find the missing addend: $36 = 12 + a + 16$
(9)

17. Wilson put 1-cubic-foot boxes into stacks like the one
(73, 74) shown at right.

   a. How many boxes are in a stack?

   b. What is the volume of a stack?

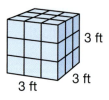
3 ft
3 ft
3 ft

18. For **a–c,** describe the weight of each animal as about an ounce,
(74) a pound, or a ton.

   a.   crow   **b.**   bison   **c.**   mouse

19. Name each solid in **a–c.**

(75)

a.
b.
c.

20. **Multiple Choice** Which figure below does *not* show a line of

(Inv. 7)

symmetry?

A
B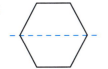
C
D

*Real-World
Connection*

Jerry and Phil took a math test on Wednesday. They scored 178 points altogether. Jerry scored ten points higher than Phil. What is each student's score?

• Multiplication Facts: 11s and 12s

Power Up

facts   Power Up 76

jump start   Count up by 11s from 0 to 110.
                  Count up by square numbers from 1 to 144.

                  Write these numbers in order from least to greatest.

                  1,025   12,050   12,500   1,250

                  Draw a square. Divide the square into 4 parts. Shade $\frac{3}{4}$ of the square. How much of the square is not shaded?

mental math   **a. Number Sense:** 18×10

                  b. Number Sense: $10 + 19 + 6$

                  c. Time: It is afternoon. Stella's birthday party began at the time shown on the clock. It ended 2 hours later. What time did the party end?

                  d. Calendar: How many days are in 6 weeks?

problem solving   This graph shows the amount of time Layne spent on his homework last week.

Altogether, how many hours did Layne spend on his reading and math homework last week?

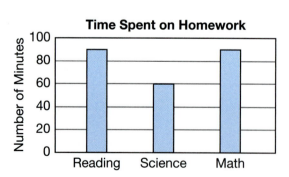

Since Lesson 56 we have been learning and practicing multiplication facts. In this lesson we will practice the remaining facts through 12 × 12.

	0	1	2	3	4	5	6	7	8	9	10	11	12
0	0	0	0	0	0	0	0	0	0	0	0	0	0
1	0	1	2	3	4	5	6	7	8	9	10	11	12
2	0	2	4	6	8	10	12	14	16	18	20	22	24
3	0	3	6	9	12	15	18	21	24	27	30	33	36
4	0	4	8	12	16	20	24	28	32	36	40	44	48
5	0	5	10	15	20	25	30	35	40	45	50	55	60
6	0	6	12	18	24	30	36	42	48	54	60	66	72
7	0	7	14	21	28	35	42	49	56	63	70	77	84
8	0	8	16	24	32	40	48	56	64	72	80	88	96
9	0	9	18	27	36	45	54	63	72	81	90	99	108
10	0	10	20	30	40	50	60	70	80	90	100	110	120
11	0	11	22	33	44	55	66	77	88	99	110	121	132
12	0	12	24	36	48	60	72	84	96	108	120	132	144

On the multiplication table, look down the 11s column and notice a pattern.

Analyze Describe the pattern you see.

Conclude Which 11s facts do you need to practice so that you can remember them?

Look down the 12s column. What patterns can you find?

Modeling 11s and 12s

We can model multiplying by 11 using $8\frac{1}{2}$-by-11-inch sheets of paper. On the floor or any other large surface, extend a tape measure to 66 inches.

Starting at the 0 mark, place a sheet of paper lengthwise along the tape measure. Make sure that the paper is lined up with the 0 tick mark and the 11 tick mark on the tape measure.

Continue placing sheets of paper end to end along the tape measure until you reach 66 inches. Name the total length in inches as you put each sheet of paper in place.

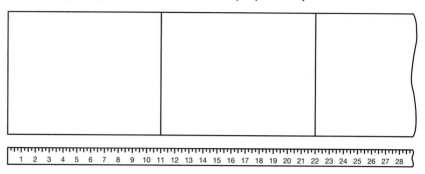

How many sheets of paper did you use?

Make a table showing the numbers of pages and inches for each page you placed.

Recall from Lesson 60 that multiplying the number of groups times the number in each group gives us the total.

number of groups × number in each group = total

So 6 sheets × 11 inches for each sheet = 66 inches.

We can model multiplying by 12 using 1-foot rulers. Extend a tape measure to 72 inches. Arrange the rulers end to end along the tape measure. Name the total length in inches as you put each ruler in place.

How many rulers did you use?

6 rulers × 12 inches for each ruler = 72 inches

Formulate Write a multiplication fact to represent each ruler you placed.

Example 1

Milton measured the total length of sheets of copy paper placed end to end. Each sheet of paper was 11 inches long. He recorded the results in a table. Make a table to show the total length of one through 12 sheets of paper.

We set up the table to show the number of sheets and the length in inches. We start with one sheet of paper with a length of 11 inches. We add 11 inches for each sheet of paper added to the row.

Number of Sheets	1	2	3	4	5	6	7	8	9	10	11	12
Length in Inches	11	22	33	44	55	66	77	88	99	110	121	132

Example 2

Use a multiplication table to find each product.

a. 3×12 **b.** 6×12 **c.** 12×12

a. $3 \times 12 = \textbf{36}$

b. $6 \times 12 = \textbf{72}$

c. $12 \times 12 = \textbf{144}$

Lesson Practice   Find each product.

a. 11×11 **b.** 11×12 **c.** 12×5

d. 12×6 **e.** 7×12 **f.** 8×12

g. 9×12 **h.** 12×10 **i.** 12×12

j. The word "dozen" means 12. John raises chickens and puts the eggs in cartons. Each carton contains a dozen eggs. Make a table to show the number of eggs in one through 12 cartons. How many eggs are in 9 cartons? How many eggs are in 12 cartons?

Written Practice   *Distributed and Integrated*

1. Jeff walked along the length of a rail. He took nine big steps. Each
(34, 60) big step was about 3 feet long. The rail was about how many feet long?

2. The California Gold Rush was in 1849. The first railroad across the
(39) country was complete in 1869. How many years were there from 1849 to 1869?

3. Fruit was shipped from Plains to Westcott . Find the approximate
(Inv. 4) distance from Plains to Wescott.

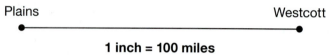

Plains   Westcott

1 inch = 100 miles

4. Name each shape below.
(75)
    a.   **b.**   **c.**

5. Find each product:
(64)
    a. 9×6 **b.** 4×9 **c.** 9×9

6. This picture is an old Santa Fe Railroad logo. Are the two
(Inv. 4) dark stripes inside the circle parallel or perpendicular?

7. The work crew was paid $48,000 for laying a mile
(32) of track in the mountains. Use words to name
$48,000.

8. Change this addition to multiplication and find the total.
(54, 76)
$$12 + 12 + 12 + 12 + 12 + 12$$

9. How many pounds are equal to
(74)
    a. three tons?   **b.** four tons?

10. The bridge is three tenths of a mile wide. Write three tenths as a
(41) fraction.

11. Find each product:
(70)
    a. 8×7 **b.** 4×6 **c.** 6×7

12. 85¢ + 76¢ + $10   **13.** $5.00 − $3.29
(22, 24)   (26, 28)

14. The hallway was 12 feet wide. How many inches are equal to
(60, 76) 12 feet?

15. Find each product:
(61, 76)
    a. 11×11 **b.** 11×12 **c.** 9×12

16. Boxes are stacked on the shelf as shown at right.
(72, 73)
    a. How many boxes are in the stack?

    b. What is the volume of the stack?

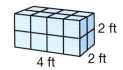

17. (**Formulate**) The rows of desks in the classroom
(57) formed an array. Write a multiplication fact for this array, which is shown at right.

18. Write the two fractions represented by the shaded
(41, 47) squares. Then compare the two fractions.

19. (**Model**) On this map, how many inches is it from
(35)
    a. Granville to Lexington?

    b. Lexington to Hampshire?

    c. Granville to Hampshire through Lexington?

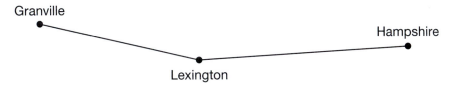

20. If each $\frac{1}{4}$ inch on the map in problem **19** represents 10 miles, how
(Inv. 4) many miles is it from Lexington to Hampshire?

Real-World Connection

Mrs. Lee is sorting items by their shapes. She made a pile for items that are shaped like cylinders. She made a second pile for items that are shaped like rectangular solids. She made a third pile for items that are shaped like spheres. Make a list of items Mrs. Lee can put in each pile.

LESSON 77

• Multiplying Three Numbers

facts   Power Up 77

jump start

 Count up by 7s from 0 to 77.
Count up by 12s from 0 to 120.

There are 5,280 feet in one mile. Write this number using words.

Write two multiplication facts using the numbers 6, 8, and 48.

mental math

a. **Money:** $10.00 − $6.75

b. **Number Sense:** 170 + 20

c. **Number Sense:** 20 × 10

d. **Time:** It is 7:35 a.m. How many minutes is it until 8:00 a.m.?

problem solving

Here we show examples of figures with a special made-up name, Snips. We also show nonexamples (figures that are not examples) of Snips. Study the examples and nonexamples.

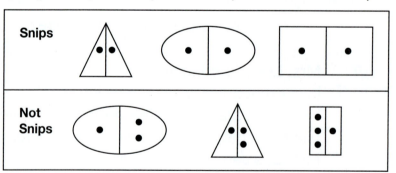

Which of these figures is a Snip? Explain your answer.

A 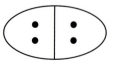   B   C

416 *Saxon Math Intermediate 3*

In Lesson 10 we learned how to add three numbers. In this lesson we will learn how to multiply three numbers.

To find the product of 2 × 3 × 4, we begin by multiplying two factors. We multiply 2 × 3. The product is 6.

2 × 3 × 4

6 × 4

Next we multiply 6 by the remaining factor, 4.

6 × 4 = 24

The product is **24.**

Example

Multiply: 4 × 2 × 7

First we multiply 4 × 2 to get 8. Then we multiply 8 × 7 to find the product of all three factors: 8 × 7 = **56.**

Multiplying to Find Volume

Materials: 1-inch cubes

In the activity in Lesson 73, we found the volume of a box by counting the total number of cubes the box would hold.

In this activity, we will use multiplication to find volume.

First, we will use cubes to build a rectangular prism. A rectangular prism has length, width, and height.

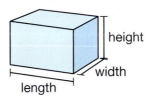

Build a rectangular prism that is 3 units long, 2 units wide, and 2 units high, as shown below.

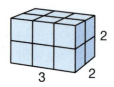

Count the number of cubes you used to build the rectangular prism. How many cubes are there in all?

What is the volume of the rectangular prism?

What is the length, width, and height of the rectangular prism?

What is the product when you multiply $3 \times 2 \times 2$?

Discuss What is the relationship between the length, width, and height of a rectangular prism and its volume?

Lesson Practice

Find each product in **a–d.**

a. $2 \times 2 \times 2$ **b.** $3 \times 3 \times 4$

c. $1 \times 2 \times 11$ **d.** $6 \times 2 \times 5$

e. What is the length, width, and height of this figure?

f. Find the volume of the figure by multiplying its length, width, and height.

Written Practice   *Distributed and Integrated*

1. **Formulate** The boxcar could carry 36 tons of cargo. Fifteen
(36) tons of cargo were already in the car. How many tons of additional cargo could the boxcar carry? Write a number sentence. Then write your answer in a complete sentence.

2. Four round tables were in the room. There were eight chairs around
(60, 70) each table. Altogether, how many chairs were there?

3. a. **Represent** Draw a picture of a cube.
(71)

   b. A cube has how many faces?

   c. A cube has how many vertices?

4. **Represent** Draw a rectangle that is 4 inches long and 1 inch wide.
(34, 52)

5. **a.** What is the perimeter of the rectangle you drew in problem **4?**
(58, 62)

b. What is the area of the rectangle?

6. How many pounds are equal to
(74)
   a. one ton?   **b.** two tons?   **c.** three tons?

7. Draw a picture to show the fraction $\frac{3}{7}$.
(42)

8. A large horse weighs about half of a ton. A half ton is equal to how many pounds?
(74)

9. The train was eight tenths of a mile long. Write eight tenths as a fraction.
(41)

10. Boxes were stacked on a pallet. Each box was one cubic foot.
(72, 73)

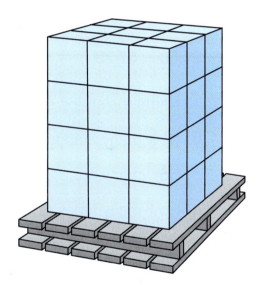

   a. How many layers of boxes were there in the stack?

   b. How many boxes were in each layer?

   c. How many boxes were there in the stack?

   d. What is the volume of the stack of boxes?

11. Draw an obtuse angle.
(65)

Judy saw these numbers on a boxcar. Refer to this illustration to answer problems **12** and **13**.

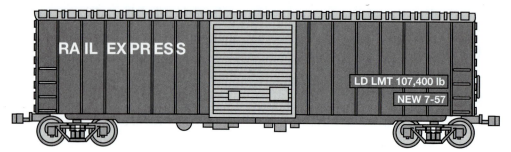

12. The "load limit" of this boxcar is 107,400 pounds. Use words to
(32) name this number.

13. On the boxcar, Judy saw NEW 7-57. This shows the month and
(1) year the boxcar was built. Name the month and full year this
boxcar was built.

14. $648 + $286
(16)

15. $7.50 − $7.29
(26)

16. 2 × 3 × 4
(77)

17. a. Name the shape shown.
(75)

   b. How many triangular faces does it have?

   c. How many rectangular faces does it have?

   d. How many faces does it have in all?

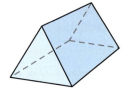

18. Find each product:
(76)
   a. 8 × 12   **b.** 9 × 12   **c.** 11 × 12

19. Multiple Choice Which pair of triangles are congruent?
(68, 69)

A   **B**   **C**   **D**

20. a. What fraction of the face of the spinner is blue?
(41, 45)

   b. If the spinner is spun once, is the arrow more likely
   to stop on blue or white?

LESSON 78

• Multiplying Multiples of Ten

Power Up

facts   Power Up 78

jump start   Count down by 3s from 45 to 0.
Count down by 6s from 60 to 0.

It is 2:20 in the afternoon. Draw hands on your clock to show the time in 2 hours. Write the time in digital form.

The high temperature on the first of the month was 48°F. The high temperature on the last day of the month was 7 degrees warmer. Mark your thermometer to show the high temperature at the end of the month.

mental math   **a. Time:** How many years are in 8 decades?

b. Number Sense: $10 + 18 + 5$

c. Money: Compare these money amounts using the symbol <, >, or =.

5 quarters ◯ 12 dimes

d. Measurement: What is the perimeter of the parallelogram?

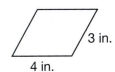

3 in.

4 in.

problem solving   Megan inserted 4 coins into the vending machine to purchase a snack bar that cost 65¢. The machine returned 1 nickel in change. What coins did Megan use in the vending machine?

The **multiples of ten** are the numbers that we say when we count by tens.

$$10, \quad 20, \quad 30, \quad 40, \quad 50, \ldots$$

Each multiple of ten can be written as a number times 10.

$$20 = 2 \times 10$$
$$30 = 3 \times 10$$
$$40 = 4 \times 10$$

One way to multiply multiples of ten is to multiply three factors. Below we multiply 4×30 by writing 30 as 3×10.

$$4 \times 30$$
$$\wedge$$
$$4 \times 3 \times 10$$

Next we multiply 4×3, which is 12. Then we multiply 12×10.

$$4 \times 3 \times 10$$
$$\vee$$
$$12 \times 10 = 120$$

A shortcut is to multiply the digit in the tens place and then attach a zero to the product. For 4×30, we multiply $4 \times 3 = 12$. Then we add a zero to the 12 to make 120.

$$④ \times ③0 = 120$$

Example 1

Diana has seven $20 bills. How much money is that?

Instead of adding seven 20s, we can multiply $20 by 7. We know that 7×2 is 14, so $7 \times \$20$ is **$140.**

Example 2

There are 40 cubes in each layer of this figure. How many cubes are there in all 4 layers?

Instead of adding four 40s, we multiply 40 by 4. Since 4×4 is 16, we know that 4×40 is 160. The figure contains **160 cubes.**

Lesson Practice

a. How much money is eight $20 bills?

b. If 5 classrooms each have 30 students, then how many students are in all 5 classrooms?

Find each product for problems **c–f.**

c. 4 × 60

d. 7 × 30

e. 8 × 40

f. 3 × 80

Written Practice   *Distributed and Integrated*

1. **Formulate** Clovis bought eight new railroad cars for his model
(60, 70) train. Each car cost seven dollars. How much did Clovis pay for all eight cars? Write a number sentence.

2. One hundred ninety people crowded into the model train show.
(36) The room could hold 240 people. How many more people could be in the room?

3. Lilly bought a ticket for $14.75. She paid for the ticket with two
(26, 28) $10 bills. How much money should Lilly get back?

4. What solid is the shape of a can of soup?
(75)

5. a. **Represent** Draw a picture of a rectangular prism.
(71)

   b. A rectangular prism has how many vertices?

   c. A rectangular prism has how many edges?

6. Judith made the rectangle at right with square tiles. The
(52, 62) sides of each tile are one inch long.

   a. How long is the rectangle?

   b. How wide is the rectangle?

   c. How many tiles did she use?

   d. What is the area of the rectangle?

7. What is the perimeter of the rectangle in problem **6?**
(58)

8. Find each product:
(59, 64)

    a. 7×0 **b.** 7×5 **c.** 7×9

9. Ten miles is 52,800 feet. Use words to write 52,800.
(32)

10. Find each product:
(76)

    a. 5×12 **b.** 6×12 **c.** 7×12

11. Find each product:
(64, 70)

    a. 6×7 **b.** 6×8 **c.** 6×9

12. Find each product:
(78)

    a. 3×20 **b.** 6×30 **c.** 4×40

13. $\$676 + \$234$ **14.** $\$1.00 - 73¢$
(16)   (26, 28)

15. $3 \times 3 \times 3$ **16.** 7×50
(77)   (78)

17. **Multiple Choice** A full-grown cat could weigh
(74)

    A 8 ounces.   **B** 8 pounds.   **C** 8 tons.

18. a. (**Connect**) How many ounces equal a pound?
(41, 74)

    b. An ounce is what fraction of a pound?

This map shows where Leslie and Monica live. Use this map to answer problems **19** and **20**.

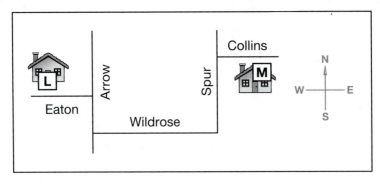

19. Name two roads perpendicular to Wildrose.
(Inv. 4)

20. Write directions that describe how to get to Monica's home from
(31)   Leslie's home.

LESSON
79

• **Length: Centimeters, Meters, and Kilometers**

facts Power Up 79

jump start

$^{1}2_{3}$ Count down by 4s from 40 to 0.
Count down by 8s from 80 to 0.

Write the largest 4-digit number that uses each of the digits 3, 2, 6, and 4. What is the value of the digit in the hundreds place?

Draw an isosceles triangle in the workspace on your worksheet. Then draw a line to show the triangle's line of symmetry.

mental math

a. Measurement: Which of these units would you use to measure a sheet of paper?

    feet   pounds   miles   inches

b. Number Sense: 26×10

c. Number Sense: 12×100

d. Algebra: The table below shows costs for a long-distance phone call. Find the missing money amount in the table.

Minutes	1	2	3	4	5
Cost	8¢	16¢	24¢	____	40¢

problem solving

Alex is half as old as Beyonce. Beyonce is 2 years older than Chandra. Chandra is 10 years old. How old is Alex?

Lesson 79   **425**

We have measured lengths in inches, feet, yards, and miles. These units are called customary units and are used mostly in the United States.

Nearly every other country uses the **metric system.** Metric units of length include **centimeters, meters,** and **kilometers.**

A ruler that is 12 inches long is about 30 centimeters long. A meter is 100 centimeters and is a little longer than a yard. A kilometer is 1000 meters and is a little more than half of a mile.

Metric Units of Length

Unit	Abbreviation	Reference
centimeter	cm	width of a finger
meter	m	one BIG step
kilometer	km	$\frac{6}{10}$ mile
1 meter = 100 centimeters 1 kilometer = 1000 meters		

Activity

Metric Units of Length

Most rulers have an inch scale on one side and a centimeter scale on the other side. Find the centimeter scale on your ruler. Use it to measure some objects at your desk in centimeters.

1. How wide is your paper?

2. How long is your paper?

3. How long is your pencil?

4. How long is this segment?

Work in small groups to measure with a meterstick.

5. About how many meters wide is the classroom door?

6. About how many meters high is the classroom door?

7. About how many meters long is the chalkboard or bulletin board in your classroom?

8. About how many meters long (or wide) is your classroom?

Example 1

Multiple Choice Which length could be the length of a pencil?

A 15 centimeters   **B** 15 meters

C 15 kilometers   **D** 15 feet

A **15 centimeters**

Example 2

The train engine pulled a line of 50 boxcars that was about a kilometer long. How many meters is a kilometer?

A kilometer is **1000 meters.**

Example 3

A 12-inch ruler is about 30 centimeters. If 3 rulers are laid end to end, about how many centimeters long would the 3 rulers be?

Since each ruler is about 30 cm long, 3 rulers would be 3×30 cm, which is about 90 cm long.

$$3 \times 30 \text{ cm} = 90 \text{ cm}$$

Analyze Is the length of 3 rulers more or less than a meter?

Example 4

Find the length and width of this rectangle in centimeters. Then find the perimeter of this rectangle in centimeters and find its area in **square centimeters.**

Using a centimeter ruler, we find the length and width.

Length	**4 cm**
Width	**3 cm**

We use these measures to find the perimeter and area.

Perimeter   4 cm + 3 cm + 4 cm + 3 cm = **14 cm**

Area   4 cm × 3 cm = **12 square cm**

Lesson Practice

a. Draw a segment 2 inches long. Then measure the segment in centimeters. Two inches equals about how many centimeters?

b. How many centimeters long is the cover of your math book?

c. A meter is how many centimeters?

d. It takes about 10 minutes to walk a kilometer. How many meters is a kilometer?

Refer to the rectangle to answer problems **e–h.**

e. How long is the rectangle in centimeters?

f. How wide is the rectangle in centimeters?

g. How many centimeters is the perimeter of the rectangle?

h. How many square centimeters is the area of the rectangle?

Written Practice   *Distributed and Integrated*

1. The passenger car on the train had nine rows of seats. Four
(60)   passengers could sit in each row. How many passengers could sit in the passenger car?

2. (Analyze)   In a common year, March 31 is the ninetieth day of
(1, 36)   the year. How many days are in the last nine months of the year? (*Hint:* Think of how many days are in a whole year.)

12. Find each product:
(70)
    a. 9×8 **b.** 7×8 **c.** 3×7

13. Here is a drawing of a brick:
(71)
    a. What is the length of the brick?

    b. What is the width of the brick?

    c. What is the height of the brick?

    d. What is the name for the shape of the brick?

10 cm   21 cm   6 cm

14. What is the area of the top of the brick in problem **13**?
(56, 62)

15. **Multiple Choice** Which figure is *not* a parallelogram?
(66)

 A   **B**   **C**   **D**

16. Find each product:
(77, 78)
    a. $2 \times 5 \times 4$ **b.** 6×50

17. Find each product:
(78)
    a. 4×70 **b.** 6×60 **c.** 9×40

Add or subtract, as shown below:

18. $\$10.00 - \$5.60$
(26, 28)

19. $\$95 + \$85 + \$75$
(24)

20. **a.** The spinner is least likely to stop on what number?
(44, 50)

    b. The spinner is most likely to stop on what number?

    c. What fraction of the face of the spinner has the number 2?

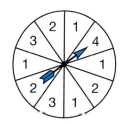

Early Finishers
Real-World Connection

Nancy practiced basketball for 1 hour and 45 minutes on Friday and 1 hour and 15 minutes on Saturday. Jenny practiced for 1 and one half hours on Friday and 120 minutes on Saturday. How many minutes did each girl practice over two days? Who practiced longer?

2. The class has collected 73 pounds of aluminum cans. The goal is
(28, 36) to collect 100 pounds. How many more pounds of cans does the
class need to collect to reach the goal?

3. (Connect) Write the next three numbers in the sequence below.
(2, 32)
2,000, 4,000, 6,000, _____, _____, _____, . . .

4. It's time for lunch. Write the time shown on the clock in
(3) digital form.

5. Multiple Choice Which of these multiplication facts
(55) equals 24? List all correct answers.

   A 3 × 6   **B** 2 × 12   **C** 1 × 24   **D** 4 × 6

6. What is the total value of five quarters, five dimes, five nickels,
(25) and five pennies?

7. Multiple Choice Which shows three tens and four thousands?
(32)
   A 34,000   **B** 4,003   **C** 4,030   **D** 30,004

8. (Analyze) Half of a dollar is equal to 50 cents. How many
(79) centimeters are equal to half of a meter?

9. Multiply:
(81)
   a. 2 × 24   **b.** 2 × 48

10. A box is filled with cubes as shown at right.
(72, 73)
   a. How many cubes are in each layer?

   b. How many layers are there?

   c. How many cubes are there?

   d. If each cube is one cubic inch, what is the volume of all of
      these cubes?

11. Write a fraction equal to one with a denominator of 5. Then write
(46, 49) the mixed number one and one fifth using digits and symbols.
Which number is greater?

Example 1

A ticket to the amusement park costs $34. How much would two tickets cost?

To find the answer, we can add $34 and $34, or we can multiply $34 by 2. Either way, we find the cost of two tickets is **$68.**

Add	Multiply
$34	$34
+ $34	× 2
$68	$68

Example 2

One yard is 36 inches. How many inches is two yards?

We can find the answer by adding or multiplying. Either way, we find that two yards is **72 inches.**

$$\begin{array}{r} \overset{1}{36} \\ + 36 \\ \hline 72 \end{array} \qquad \begin{array}{r} \overset{1}{36} \\ \times\ 2 \\ \hline 72 \end{array}$$

Lesson Practice   Find each product.

a. $14
     ×   2

b.   43
     ×   2

c. $27
     ×   2

d.   39
     ×   2

e. July and August each have 31 days. Altogether, how many days are in July and August? Find the answer by multiplying.

f. One pair of shoes costs $45. What would two pairs of the shoes cost? Find the answer by multiplying.

Written Practice   *Distributed and Integrated*

1. **Analyze**   The ceiling is 3 meters high. How many centimeters is
(60, 79)   3 meters?

 **Activity**

Doubling Money

Use your money manipulatives to solve these problems.

1. Mariya has $24. If she doubles her money, how much money will she have?

Step 1: Place 2 tens and 4 ones on your desk.

Step 2: Double the money by placing 2 more tens and 4 more ones on your desk.

Step 3: Combine the bills. What is the total?

2. Irena has $48. If she doubles her money, how much money will she have?

Step 1: Place 4 tens and 8 ones on your desk.

Step 2: Double the money by placing 4 more tens and 8 more ones on your desk.

Step 3: Combine the bills. Trade with the bank if you can.

Step 4: What is the total?

Here is how we multiply $24 by 2 using pencil and paper:

Set up.	Multiply 4 ones by 2.	Multiply 2 tens by 2.
$24	$24	$24
× 2	× 2	× 2
	8	$48

Here is how we multiply $48 by 2 using pencil and paper:

Set up.	Multiply 8 ones by 2.	Multiply 4 tens by 2.
	1	1
$48	$48	$48
× 2	× 2	× 2
	6	$96

When we multiply 8 ones by 2, the product is 16. Sixteen is 1 ten and 6 ones. We write the 6 in the ones place and the 1 ten above the 4 tens of 48.

When we multiply 4 tens by 2, the product is 8 tens. We add the 1 ten from 16 which makes 9 tens. The product is $96.

• Multiplying Two-Digit Numbers, Part 1

Power Up

facts   Power Up 81

**jump
start**   Count up by 12s from 0 to 120.
                     Count up by 5s from 4 to 94.

                     Write two multiplication facts using the numbers 3, 7,
                     and 21.

                     Draw a 7-centimeter segment on your worksheet.

**mental
math**   **a. Number Sense:** 56 + 27

                     b. Number Sense: 82 + 18

                     c. Number Sense: 450 − 400

                     d. Measurement: Which is the higher temperature, 32°F
                     or 5°C?

**problem
solving**   How many times does the minute hand go around a clock
                     in one day?

New Concept

When we double a number, we multiply the number by 2.
For example, when we double 6, we have 2 groups of 6,
or 12.

$$6 + 6 = 12$$

$$2 \times 6 = 12$$

We have learned multiplication facts for 2. In this lesson we
will practice multiplying two-digit numbers by 2.

(**Connect**) List some things that you use or see in real life
that come in pairs or doubles.

12. Multiple Choice What is the geometric name for this solid?

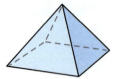

  A pyramid   **B** rectangular prism

  C triangular prism   **D** cube

Look around the classroom or around your house to find objects in the shape of each geometric solid we discussed in this investigation. Share the objects with the class, and choose an example of each to display.

• Mass: Grams and Kilograms

facts   Power Up 80

jump start

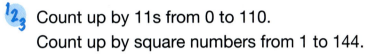 Count up by 11s from 0 to 110.
Count up by square numbers from 1 to 144.

Use these clues to find the secret number. Write the secret number on your worksheet.

- two-digit number
- between 20 and 40
- product of the digits is 14

Draw a 10-centimeter segment on your worksheet.

mental math

a. Calendar: How many months are in 3 years?

b. Number Sense: 23 + 40

c. Time: 50 minutes − 15 minutes

d. Number Line: What year is shown by point *G?*

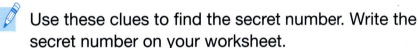

problem solving

Scott's basketball team will use two-digit numbers on their uniforms. Each player can choose a 1 or a 2 for the first digit. The second digit must be a 0, 1, or 2. What are the possible uniform numbers?

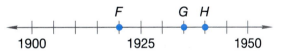
In the U.S. Customary System, ounces, pounds, and tons are units of weight. In the metric system, grams and kilograms are units of **mass.**

The mass of a dollar bill is about one gram. The mass of a large paper clip is also about one gram. A kilogram is 1,000 grams. The mass of your math textbook is about one kilogram. On Earth a kilogram weighs a little more than 2 pounds.

Metric Units of Mass

Unit	Abbreviation	Reference
gram	g	dollar bill or large paper clip
kilogram	kg	basketball
1 kilogram = 1,000 grams		

Metric Units of Mass

Copy the table below, and list two or three objects in each column of the table. Compare with a large paper clip to decide if an object is close to a gram or more than a gram. Compare with a basketball to decide if an object is more or less than a kilogram.

Mass of Objects

Close to a gram	More than a gram, less than a kilogram	More than a kilogram

Example 1

Which is the best estimate for the mass of a pencil?

12 grams   **12 kilograms**

The mass of a pencil is greater than a paper clip but much less than a basketball. So the mass is several grams but much less than a kilogram. The best estimate is **12 grams.**

Example 2

The mass of a pair of adult's shoes is about one kilogram. How many grams is a kilogram?

A kilogram is **1,000 grams**.

Analyze About how many grams is one shoe?

Lesson Practice

a. The mass of a dollar bill is about a gram. A kilogram of dollar bills would be about how many dollar bills?

b. Which is the best estimate for the mass of a month-old baby?

5 grams   5 kilograms

c. Arrange these objects in order from least mass to greatest mass:

your math book

your desk

a pencil

an eyelash

a paper clip

Written Practice   *Distributed and Integrated*

1. Rick and Antonia played a game with dot cubes. If they rolled a
(Inv. 5) 2 or 4, Rick got a point. If they rolled a 1, 3, 5, or 6, Antonia got a point. Was their game fair? Why or why not?

2. Conclude The train traveled across the prairie at a steady
(78) speed of 40 miles each hour. Copy and complete the table below to find how far the train traveled in 5 hours.

Hours	1	2	3	4	5
Miles	40	80			

3. The elevator had a weight limit of 4,000 pounds. How many tons
(74) is 4,000 pounds?

4. What is the name for a parallelogram that has four right angles?
(65, 66)

5. Write the fraction of each rectangle that is shaded. Then compare
(61, 70) the shaded rectangles.

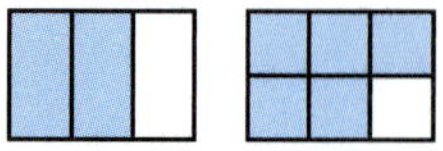

6. **Multiple Choice** Which of these multiplications does *not*
(61, 70) equal 12?

A 1 × 12　　　**B** 2 × 6　　　**C** 3 × 4　　　**D** 6 × 6

7. What is the total value of four quarters, eight nickels, two dimes,
(25) and a penny?

8. An odometer shows the following display:
(32)

a. Use numbers to write the miles shown.

b. Use words to state the number of miles the car has been
driven.

9. Name each figure below.
(67, 75)
a.

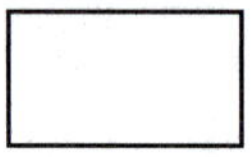

b.

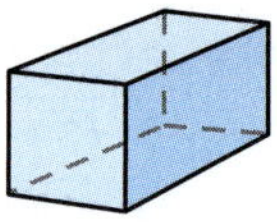

c.

d.

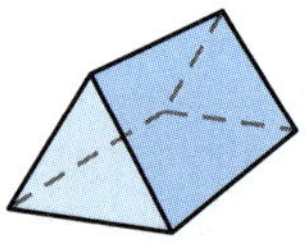

10. (Represent) Draw a picture of a cube. A cube has how many
(71) edges?

11. Alberto made this rectangular shape with
(52, 62) 1-centimeter square tiles.

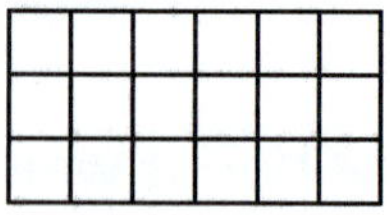

a. How long is the rectangle?

b. How wide is the rectangle?

c. How many tiles did he use?

d. What is the area of the shape?

12. Change this addition to multiplication and find the total:
(54, 76)

12 in. + 12 in. + 12 in. + 12 in. + 12 in. + 12 in.

13. Find each product:
(70)
    a. 8 × 7   **b.** 7 × 6   **c.** 3 × 7

14. Find each product:
(78)
    a. 4 × 30   **b.** 6 × 30   **c.** 8 × 30

15. A meter is 100 cm. A door that is 2 meters tall is how many
(79) centimeters tall?

16. $587 − $295   **17.** $5.45 + $3.57
(23)   (22)

18. What is the best estimate of the mass of a full-grown cat?
(80)

    4 kilograms   4 grams

19. Which letter does *not* show a line of symmetry?
(Inv. 7)

20. a. **Formulate** Show how multiplying three numbers helps you
(72, 77)   find the number of cubes in this stack.

    b. What is the volume of the stack of cubes?

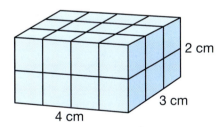

Focus on

• More About Geometric Solids

In Lesson 75 we learned the geometric names of several different solids. In this investigation we will practice identifying, classifying, and describing geometric solids.

Recall from Lesson 71 that rectangular prisms have faces, edges, and vertices.

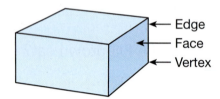

← Edge
← Face
← Vertex

Other geometric solids made of flat surfaces also have faces, edges, and vertices.

Give the geometric name for each of the solids in problems **1–4.** Describe the solid by its number and shape of faces. Then count the numbers of edges and vertices. Use the Relational GeoSolids to help you answer the questions.

1.

2.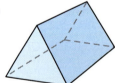

3.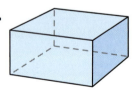

4.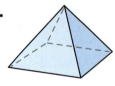

Some solids have surfaces that are not flat. Name each solid shown and described in problems **5–7.**

5.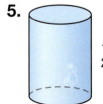

1 curved surface
2 flat surfaces
  shaped like circles

6.

1 curved surface
1 flat surface
  shaped like a circle

7.

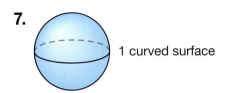

1 curved surface

Classifying Solids

Your teacher will show the class several objects labeled with letters from A–J. For each object, write its geometric name in the correct place on **Lesson Activity 29.** Then explain in your own words how you know that name is correct.

Use what you know about geometric solids and their attributes to answer problems **8–12.** Use your Relational GeoSolids to help answer the questions.

8. **Multiple Choice** Which geometric solid shown below does *not* belong? How do you know?

A

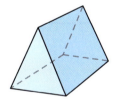

B

C

D

9. Multiple Choice Which object best represents a triangular prism?

A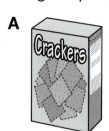

B

C

D

10. Multiple Choice Which geometric solid shown below has two flat surfaces and one curved surface?

A

B

C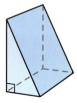

D

11. Multiple Choice Which geometric solid shown below has eight vertices?

A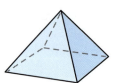

B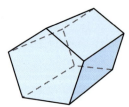

C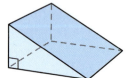

D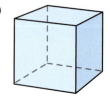

12. Multiple Choice What is the geometric name for this solid?

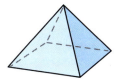

  A pyramid   **B** rectangular prism

  C triangular prism   **D** cube

Look around the classroom or around your house to find objects in the shape of each geometric solid we discussed in this investigation. Share the objects with the class, and choose an example of each to display.

• Multiplying Two-Digit Numbers, Part 1

facts   Power Up 81

**jump
start**   Count up by 12s from 0 to 120.
              Count up by 5s from 4 to 94.

              Write two multiplication facts using the numbers 3, 7,
              and 21.

              Draw a 7-centimeter segment on your worksheet.

**mental
math**   **a. Number Sense:** 56 + 27

              b. Number Sense: 82 + 18

              c. Number Sense: 450 − 400

              d. Measurement: Which is the higher temperature, 32°F
              or 5°C?

**problem
solving**   How many times does the minute hand go around a clock
              in one day?

New Concept

When we double a number, we multiply the number by 2.
For example, when we double 6, we have 2 groups of 6,
or 12.

$$6 + 6 = 12$$

$$2 \times 6 = 12$$

We have learned multiplication facts for 2. In this lesson we
will practice multiplying two-digit numbers by 2.

Connect List some things that you use or see in real life
that come in pairs or doubles.

Activity

Doubling Money

Use your money manipulatives to solve these problems.

1. Mariya has $24. If she doubles her money, how much money will she have?

 Step 1: Place 2 tens and 4 ones on your desk.

 Step 2: Double the money by placing 2 more tens and 4 more ones on your desk.

 Step 3: Combine the bills. What is the total?

2. Irena has $48. If she doubles her money, how much money will she have?

 Step 1: Place 4 tens and 8 ones on your desk.

 Step 2: Double the money by placing 4 more tens and 8 more ones on your desk.

 Step 3: Combine the bills. Trade with the bank if you can.

 Step 4: What is the total?

Here is how we multiply $24 by 2 using pencil and paper:

Set up.	Multiply 4 ones by 2.	Multiply 2 tens by 2.
$24	$24	$24
× 2	× 2	× 2
	8	$48

Here is how we multiply $48 by 2 using pencil and paper:

Set up.	Multiply 8 ones by 2.	Multiply 4 tens by 2.
	1	1
$48	$48	$48
× 2	× 2	× 2
	6	$96

When we multiply 8 ones by 2, the product is 16. Sixteen is 1 ten and 6 ones. We write the 6 in the ones place and the 1 ten above the 4 tens of 48.

When we multiply 4 tens by 2, the product is 8 tens. We add the 1 ten from 16 which makes 9 tens. The product is $96.

Example 1

A ticket to the amusement park costs $34. How much would two tickets cost?

To find the answer, we can add $34 and $34, or we can multiply $34 by 2. Either way, we find the cost of two tickets is **$68.**

Add	Multiply
$34	$34
+ $34	× 2
$68	$68

Example 2

One yard is 36 inches. How many inches is two yards?

We can find the answer by adding or multiplying. Either way, we find that two yards is **72 inches.**

$$
\begin{array}{r}
1 \\
36 \\
+\ 36 \\
\hline
72
\end{array}
\qquad
\begin{array}{r}
1 \\
36 \\
\times\ 2 \\
\hline
72
\end{array}
$$

Lesson Practice   Find each product.

a. $14
    × 2

b.   43
    × 2

c. $27
    × 2

d.   39
    × 2

e. July and August each have 31 days. Altogether, how many days are in July and August? Find the answer by multiplying.

f. One pair of shoes costs $45. What would two pairs of the shoes cost? Find the answer by multiplying.

Written Practice   *Distributed and Integrated*

1. **Analyze** The ceiling is 3 meters high. How many centimeters is
(60, 79) 3 meters?

2. The class has collected 73 pounds of aluminum cans. The goal is
_(28, 36) to collect 100 pounds. How many more pounds of cans does the
class need to collect to reach the goal?

3. (**Connect**) Write the next three numbers in the sequence below.
_(2, 32)
      2,000, 4,000, 6,000, _____, _____, _____, . . .

4. It's time for lunch. Write the time shown on the clock in
₍₃₎ digital form.

5. **Multiple Choice** Which of these multiplication facts
₍₅₅₎ equals 24? List all correct answers.

    A 3×6 **B** 2×12 **C** 1×24 **D** 4×6

6. What is the total value of five quarters, five dimes, five nickels,
₍₂₅₎ and five pennies?

7. **Multiple Choice** Which shows three tens and four thousands?
₍₃₂₎
    A 34,000   **B** 4,003   **C** 4,030   **D** 30,004

8. (**Analyze**) Half of a dollar is equal to 50 cents. How many
₍₇₉₎ centimeters are equal to half of a meter?

9. Multiply:
₍₈₁₎
    a. 2×24 **b.** 2×48

10. A box is filled with cubes as shown at right.
_(72, 73)
    a. How many cubes are in each layer?

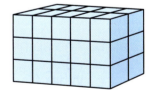

    b. How many layers are there?

    c. How many cubes are there?

    d. If each cube is one cubic inch, what is the volume of all of
        these cubes?

11. Write a fraction equal to one with a denominator of 5. Then write
_(46, 49) the mixed number one and one fifth using digits and symbols.
Which number is greater?

12. Find each product:
₍₇₀₎
    a. 9 × 8   **b.** 7 × 8   **c.** 3 × 7

13. Here is a drawing of a brick:
₍₇₁₎
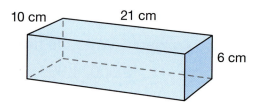
    a. What is the length of the brick?

    b. What is the width of the brick?

    c. What is the height of the brick?

    d. What is the name for the shape of the brick?

14. What is the area of the top of the brick in problem **13**?
_(56, 62)

15. **Multiple Choice** Which figure is *not* a parallelogram?
₍₆₆₎

  A   **B**   **C**   **D**

16. Find each product:
_(77, 78)
    a. 2 × 5 × 4   **b.** 6 × 50

17. Find each product:
₍₇₈₎
    a. 4 × 70   **b.** 6 × 60   **c.** 9 × 40

Add or subtract, as shown below:

18. $10.00 − $5.60   **19.** $95 + $85 + $75
_(26, 28)   ₍₂₄₎

20. a. The spinner is least likely to stop on what number?
_(44, 50)

    b. The spinner is most likely to stop on what number?

    c. What fraction of the face of the spinner has the number 2?

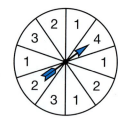

Real-World Connection

Nancy practiced basketball for 1 hour and 45 minutes on Friday and 1 hour and 15 minutes on Saturday. Jenny practiced for 1 and one half hours on Friday and 120 minutes on Saturday. How many minutes did each girl practice over two days? Who practiced longer?

LESSON 82

• Fair Share

Power Up

facts   Power Up 82

**jump
start**   Count up by halves from 0 to 5.
              Count up by fourths from 0 to 2.

              Write these numbers in order from least to greatest:

$$\frac{1}{2} \qquad 1\frac{1}{2} \qquad \frac{3}{4} \qquad 3$$

              Draw an equilateral triangle. Use a crayon to trace the
              sides that have equal length.

**mental
math**

a. **Money:** $1.65 + $2.00

b. **Number Sense:** 37 + 52

c. **Number Sense:** 620 − 100

d. **Probability:** Hector spins the
spinner one time. Which number is
the spinner most likely to land on?

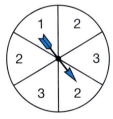

**problem
solving**

The area of Tandy's rectangular
bedroom window is 12 square feet. The height of her
window is 4 feet. What is the length of her window?

New Concept

We saw in Lesson 81 that when we double a number,
we multiply the number by 2. In this lesson, we will use
manipulatives and pictures to find half of a number. When
we find half of a number, we divide the number into two
equal parts and find the number in each part.

Below we show a **dozen** eggs in a carton. There are two rows of 6 eggs.

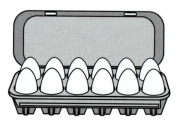

The picture shows that doubling 6 equals 12. The picture also shows that half of 12 is 6.

Fair Share

Materials: counters or tiles

1. Place 16 counters or tiles on your desk. Then separate the items into 2 equal groups. How many items are in each group?

2. Place 24 counters or tiles on your desk. Then separate the items into 2 equal groups. How many items are in each group?

There are two ways to show a number divided into 2 parts using pencil and paper.

$$24 \div 2 = 12 \qquad \qquad 2)\overline{24}^{\,12}$$

"24 divided by 2 equals 12."   "24 divided by 2 equals 12."

(Connect) If multiplication is the same as repeated addition, what do you think division is the same as?

Example 1

Draw a total of 14 Xs on your paper. Arrange the Xs in two rows like this:

X X X ...

X X X ...

How many Xs are in each row? Use digits and symbols to show two ways to write the division of 14 into 2 equal groups.

We write 14 Xs in 2 rows. There are **7** Xs in each row.

X X X X X X X

X X X X X X X

The pattern of Xs shows that 14 divided by 2 is **7**.

$$14 \div 2 = 7 \qquad 2)\overline{14} \quad {}^{7}$$

Example 2

Eighteen students line up in 2 equal rows. How many students are in each row? Use digits and symbols to show two ways to write the division of 18 into 2 equal groups.

We can use counters or draw pictures to help us divide 18 into 2 equal groups.

Since 18 divides into 2 equal groups of 9, there are **9 students** in each row.

$$18 \div 2 = 9 \qquad 2)\overline{18} \quad {}^{9}$$

Lesson Practice

a. We find half of a number by dividing by 2. We can use two open hands to show 10 divided by 2. What number is half of 10?

b. Use counters to find half of 12.

c. Draw a total of 8 Xs on your paper arranged in 2 equal rows. How many Xs are in each row? Show two ways to write the division of 8 into 2 parts.

d. Twenty students lined up in two equal rows. How many students were in each row?

1. Brandon ran 5 kilometers. How many meters is 5 kilometers?
(79)

2. Tamara bought a telescope for $189.00. Tax was $13.23. What
(22, 36) was the total price with tax?

3. (Analyze) On Monday Joni read 15 pages. On Tuesday Joni read
(81) twice as many pages as she read Monday. How many pages did
Joni read Tuesday?

4. Multiple Choice Which of these multiplication facts does *not*
(55) equal 18?

   A 3×6 **B** 9×9 **C** 18×1 **D** 2×9

5. Multiple Choice Bobby is five years old. Which of these could
(79) be his height?

   A 100 m   **B** 100 cm   **C** 100 km

6. What number is shown by this model?
(11)

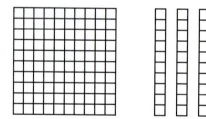

7. Marla arranged 16 counters to show half of 16. What
(82) number is half of 16?

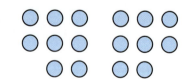

8. (Represent) Draw a square with sides 5 cm long.
(51, 79)

9. a. What is the perimeter of the square in problem **8?**
(58, 62)

    b. What is the area of the square?

10. Find each product.
(77, 81)

    a. $5 \times 4 \times 3$ **b.** 2×25

11. What is the place value of the 2 in 751,283?
(32)

12. Cubes are stacked as shown at right.
(72, 73)

    a. How many cubes are in each layer?

    b. How many layers are there?

    c. How many cubes are there?

    d. If each cube is one cubic centimeter, what is the volume of the stack of cubes?

13. Multiply:
(70, 78)

    a. 6×7 **b.** 7×80 **c.** 8×90

Add or subtract:

14. $4.58 + $8.97   **15.** $800 − $735
(22)   (28)

16. Find the missing addend: $24 + m = 100$.
(9, 28)

17. Write 57,240 in expanded form.
(32)

18. What is the name of each polygon?
(67)

    a.   **b.**   **c.**

19. What is the name of each solid?
(75)

    a. 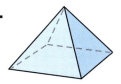   **b.**    **c.**

20. Which of the measures below is reasonable for the mass of a grape?
(80)

           6 grams   6 kilograms

LESSON
83

• **Finding Half of a Number**

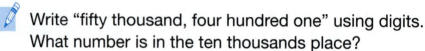

facts   Power Up 83

jump start   Count up by 7s from 0 to 77.
Count up by 100s from 0 to 2,000.

Write "fifty thousand, four hundred one" using digits.
What number is in the ten thousands place?

Label the number line by halves from 5 to 10. (Show these numbers: 5, $5\frac{1}{2}$, 6, $6\frac{1}{2}$, 7, $7\frac{1}{2}$, 8, $8\frac{1}{2}$, 9, $9\frac{1}{2}$, 10.)

mental math

a. Measurement: How many inches are in 4 feet?

b. Money: $10.00 − $9.25

c. Number Sense: 67 + 34

d. Fractions: What fraction of the circle is *not* shaded?

problem solving   Shawntel used pennies to make the patterns below. How many pennies does she need to build the next triangular pattern?

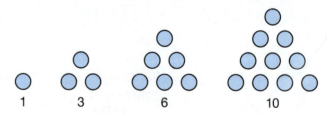

A multiplication table is a collection of multiplication facts. It is also a collection of division facts. In this lesson we will use a multiplication table to divide by 2.

	0	1	2	3	4	5	6	7	8	9	10	11	12
0	0	0	0	0	0	0	0	0	0	0	0	0	0
1	0	1	2	3	4	5	6	7	8	9	10	11	12
2	0	2	4	6	8	10	12	14	16	18	20	22	24
3	0	3	6	9	12	15	18	21	24	27	30	33	36
4	0	4	8	12	16	20	24	28	32	36	40	44	48
5	0	5	10	15	20	25	30	35	40	45	50	55	60
6	0	6	12	18	24	30	36	42	48	54	60	66	72
7	0	7	14	21	28	35	42	49	56	63	70	77	84
8	0	8	16	24	32	40	48	56	64	72	80	88	96
9	0	9	18	27	36	45	54	63	72	81	90	99	108
10	0	10	20	30	40	50	60	70	80	90	100	110	120
11	0	11	22	33	44	55	66	77	88	99	110	121	132
12	0	12	24	36	48	60	72	84	96	108	120	132	144

If we want to divide 12 by 2, we look at the row that begins with 2. Then we look across the row for 12. When we find 12, we look at the top of the column and find 6. We see that 12 divided by 2 is 6. We can write $12 \div 2 = 6$ or $2)\overline{12}$ with 6.

Connect What multiplication fact is related to $12 \div 2 = 6$?

Example 1

Use the multiplication table to find half of 22.

To find half of 22, we divide 22 by 2. We look across the 2s row for 22. We see 22 and look at the top of the column and find 11. Half of 22 is **11.**

Example 2

Drew and his sister bought a game that cost $18. They both paid half of the price. How much money did Drew pay?

We find half of $18 by dividing $18 by 2. We find 18 in the row for 2. We look at the top of the column and see 9. Drew paid **$9.**

Lesson Practice

a. One day is 24 hours. How many hours is half of a day?

b. Sixteen ounces equals a pound. How many ounces is half of a pound?

Find each answer on the multiplication table.

c. $2\overline{)14}$

d. $8 \div 2$

Written Practice   *Distributed and Integrated*

1. T-shirts were on sale for $2.00 off the regular price. If the regular
(20, 26) price was $8.95, what was the sale price?

2. **Analyze**   Michelle bought ten pens for 89¢ each. What was the
(21, 56) total price of the ten pens?

3. **Multiple Choice** Divide 12 into
(82, 83) two equal groups. What is half of 12?

A $\frac{1}{2}$ **B** 6

C 2   **D** 12

4. Computer chips were shipped from Fortner to Mesa. Use your
(35) ruler to find the distance from Fortner to Mesa.

Fortner   Mesa

1 in. = 100 miles

5. The clock shows the time that the computer chips
arrived in Mesa on Friday morning. Write the time in
digital form.

6. (Analyze) Two multiplication facts with a product of
8 are 1 × 8 and 2 × 4. Write two multiplication facts
using different factors that have a product of 6.

7. Write 560 in expanded form.

8. Multiply:
   a. 10 × 25¢   **b.** 7 × 40

9. **Multiple Choice** Marion sprinted as fast as she could and won
the race. Which of these is a likely distance for the length of the
race?

   A 100 m   **B** 100 cm   **C** 100 km

10. **Multiple Choice** Which addition is shown by the model below?

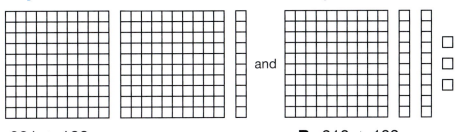

   A 201 + 123   **B** 210 + 123
   C 21 + 123   **D** 3 + 6

11. (Represent) Draw a picture of a rectangular prism. A rectangular
prism has how many
   a. faces?   **b.** vertices?

12. Find the fraction of each circle that is shaded. Then write the
fractions in order from least to greatest.

13. Carla made this rectangle out of floor tiles that were
(52, 62) one-foot squares.

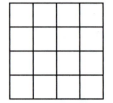

    a. How long is the rectangle?

    b. How wide is the rectangle?

    c. What is the area of the rectangle?

    d. What kind of rectangle is it?

14. Change the addition below to multiplication and find the total.
(54)

    10 cm + 10 cm + 10 cm + 10 cm + 10 cm

15. Find each product:
(78)
    a. 4 × 80   **b.** 3 × 90   **c.** 6 × 70

16. $35 + $47 + $176   **17.** $12.48 − $6.97
(24)   (26)

18. 2 × 57   **19.** 3 × 4 × 5
(81)   (77)

20. (**Model**) Use a centimeter ruler to measure the distances between
(79) these points:

    a. How many centimeters is it from point *A* to point *B*?

    b. How many centimeters is it from point *B* to point *C*?

    c. Use your answers to **a** and **b** to find the number of
    centimeters from point *A* to point *C*.

Real-World Connection

Aiesha has 2 bags of pretzels with 24 pretzels in each bag. She wants to share the pretzels with 5 friends. How many pretzels should Aiesha and her friends each have?

• **Multiplying Two-Digit Numbers, Part 2**

 **Power Up**

facts   Power Up 84

jump start   Count up by 25s from 0 to 250.
Count up by 10s from 7 to 97.

 Draw an array to show the multiplication fact
3 × 4.

Draw a 12-centimeter segment on your worksheet.

mental math
a. **Number Sense:** 55 + 35

b. **Time:** How many years are in 9 centuries?

c. **Measurement:** What is the perimeter of the triangle?

d. **Geometry:** What type of triangle is shown in problem **c?**

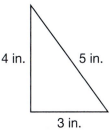

4 in.   5 in.

3 in.

problem solving
Kelly has 26 square tiles. There is one tile for each letter of the alphabet. Kelly will place the tiles in a box, mix them up, and then draw one tile. Which one of these outcomes is most likely to happen? Explain your reasoning.

A Kelly will draw the letter R.
B Kelly will draw a vowel.
C Kelly will draw a consonant.

In Lesson 81 we multiplied two-digit numbers by 2. In this lesson we will multiply two-digit numbers by other numbers.

We know that a quarter is 25¢ and that 3 quarters total 75¢.

Below we show the multiplication:

Set up.	Multiply 5 ones by 3.	Multiply 2 tens by 3.
25¢ × 3	¹25¢ × 3 **5**	¹25¢ × 3 **75¢**

When we multiply 5 ones by 3 the product is 15, which is 1 ten and 5 ones. We write 5 ones in the ones place and write the 1 ten above the 2.

When we multiply 2 tens by 3 the product is 6 tens. After multiplying we add the 1 ten for a total of 7 tens.

Analyze Write the multiplication above as addition.

Example 1

One foot is 12 inches. Mr. Simms is 6 feet tall. How many inches tall is Mr. Simms?

We find the number of inches in 6 feet by multiplying 12 inches by 6.

Set up.	Multiply 2 ones by 6.	Multiply 1 ten by 6.
12 × 6	¹12 × 6 **2**	¹12 × 6 **72**

Mr. Simms is **72 inches tall.**

The walls of a square classroom are 32 feet long. What is the perimeter of the room?

32 feet

Each side of the square is 32 feet. Instead of adding four 32s, we will multiply 32 ft by 4.

Set up.

32
× 4

Multiply 2 ones by 4.

32
× 4
8

Multiply 3 tens by 4.

32
× 4
128

The perimeter of the room is **128 feet.**

Find the product: 5 × 26

We write 26 above and 5 below with the 6 and 5 aligned in the ones place.

26
× 5

We multiply 6 ones by 5. The product is 30, which is 3 tens and 0 ones. We write 0 in the ones place and 3 above the 2.

3
26
× 5
0

Then we multiply 2 tens by 5. The product is 10 tens. Then we add the 3 tens for a total of 13 tens. We write 130, which is 1 hundred and 3 tens.

3
26
× 5
130

The product of 5 × 26 is **130.**

Lesson Practice   Find each product.

a. 12
    × 4

b. 21
    × 5

c. 15
    × 4

d. 35
    × 3

e. A foot is 12 inches. The ceiling is 8 feet high. How many inches high is the ceiling?

f. A pound is 16 ounces. Leon weighed 7 pounds when he was born. How many ounces is 7 pounds?

1. (Analyze) In each of the seven classrooms, there were 30 students. How many students were in all seven classrooms?
(60, 78)

2. Sixty-four students rode the bus for the field trip. The bus could hold 72 students. There was room on the bus for how many more students?
(36)

3. (Analyze) Denise bought ten 42¢ stamps. How much did she pay for the stamps?
(56, 60)

4. (Analyze) An African elephant can weigh 7 tons. How many pounds is 7 tons?
(74)

5. Name the fraction or mixed number shown on each number line below.
(48)

a.

b.

6. (Analyze) A pound is 16 ounces. How many ounces is half of a pound?
(74, 83)

7. Three multiplication facts that equal 12 are 1×12, 2×6, and 3×4. Write three multiplication facts that equal 18.
(55)

8. **Multiple Choice** The Olsens drove along the open highway. In one hour they could have traveled about how far?
(79)

   A 100 m   **B** 100 cm   **C** 100 km

9. Write an addition fact that is shown by this model:
(11)

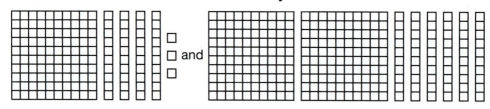

10. Find each product.
(78, 81)
    a. 2 × 30   **b.** 2 × 31

11. Find each product.
(84)
    a. 3 × 31   **b.** 4 × 31

12. One-inch cubes were used to build the rectangular
(72, 73)
prism at right.

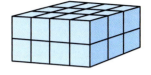

    a. How many inches long is it?

    b. How many inches wide is it?

    c. How many inches high is it?

    d. What is its volume?

13. Multiply:
(78)
    a. 7 × 80   **b.** 8 × 60   **c.** 7 × 60

Add or subtract, as shown below:

14. $20.00 − $12.87   **15.** 96¢ + 87¢ + 79¢
(26, 28)   (22, 24)

16. Use money to multiply 3 × $24.
(84)

17. a. The shaded circle at right represents which fraction
(42, 46)   name for 1?

    b. Draw and shade a circle to represent $\frac{4}{4}$.

18. Marsha glanced at the clock while she was eating dinner.
(38) Write the time in digital form.

19. Multiple Choice Which figure shows a triangle inside
(67) of a square?

    A   **B**   **C**   **D**

20. Multiple Choice Which word best names the shape of the Earth?
(75)
    A circle   **B** sphere   **C** rectangle   **D** cylinder

LESSON 85

• Using Manipulatives to Divide by a One-Digit Number

facts   Power Up 85

jump start   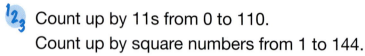 Count up by 11s from 0 to 110.
Count up by square numbers from 1 to 144.

It is 11:50 in the morning. Draw hands on your clock to show the time. Write the time in digital form.

In March the average daily high was 63°F. In January, the average high was 12 degrees cooler. Mark your thermometer to show the average high in January.

mental math   **a. Number Sense:** 54 + 60

b. Number Sense: 7 × 5 × 10

c. Money: $1.30 + 99¢

d. Estimation: Round the value of these bills and coins to the nearest dollar.

problem solving   Tom is thinking of a number that is greater than 20 but less than 30. The sum of the digits is 6. What is Tom's number?

New Concept

Using objects can help us understand the different meanings of **division.**

Activity

Equal Groups

Place 12 counters or tiles on your desk for problems **1** and **2.**

1. Tony has a collection of 12 rocks. He divided the rocks into 3 equal groups. How many rocks were in each group? (Act out the problem with your counters.)

2. Then Tony arranged the 12 rocks into groups with 3 rocks in each group. How many groups did he make? (Act out the problem with your counters.)

We saw two different meanings of division in the activity. In the first problem we were looking for the **number in each group.** In the second problem we were looking for the **number of groups.** In both problems, we started with one large group and separated it into smaller equal groups.

Connect When we divide, we separate a group into smaller equal groups. How does this relate to multiplication?

Example 1

Fifteen students lined up in 3 rows. How many students were in each row? Use manipulatives or draw a picture to represent the problem. Then show how to write the division.

We arrange 15 counters in 3 equal rows or draw a picture.

○ ○ ○ ○ ○
○ ○ ○ ○ ○
○ ○ ○ ○ ○

We see that there were **5 students** in each row. We write the division this way:

$$15 \div 3 = 5 \text{ or } 3\overline{)15}^{\,5}$$

Example 2

Fifteen students gathered in small groups of 3 students to work on the problem. How many groups were there? Use manipulatives or a picture to represent the problem. Then show how to write the division.

We separate 15 students into groups of 3.

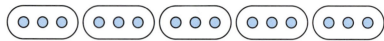

There are **5 groups** of students. We show the division this way:

$$15 \div 3 = 5 \text{ or } 3\overline{)15}^{\;5}$$

Lesson Practice

Use manipulatives or draw pictures to represent each problem. Then show how to write the division.

a. Eighteen books were stacked in three equal piles. How many books were in each pile?

b. Eighteen books were put in stacks with 3 books in each stack. How many stacks of books were there?

c. Todd has 20 quarters. He put 4 quarters in each stack. How many stacks did he make?

d. Becki cut a 12-inch-long ribbon into 4 equal pieces. How long was each piece of ribbon?

Written Practice   *Distributed and Integrated*

1. The new pencil was 18 cm long. Mark used one half of the pencil.
(79, 83) Then how long was the pencil?

2. Samantha bought some art supplies for $17.27 plus $1.22 sales
(22) tax. Write the total price.

3. The stamp cost 42¢. Jeremy gave the clerk a dollar bill. What
(25, 26) coins should Jeremy get back for change?

4. **Analyze** Darren used 10 tiles to make the rectangle at right. If he doubles the length of the rectangle, then how many tiles will he use in all?
(56)

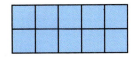

5. Robin and Ashley shared $14 equally. How much money was there for each girl?
(82, 83)

6. **Analyze** Multiply:
(84)
   a. $3 \times \$23$

   b. $4 \times \$23$

Model Use counters or draw a diagram to help you solve problems **7** and **8**.

7. Rob put 24 books in 3 equal stacks. How many books were in each stack?
(85)

8. Gwen put 24 books into stacks of 6 books. How many stacks were there?
(85)

9. Write an addition fact that is shown by the model below.
(11)

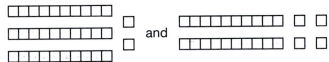

10. A box is filled with cubes as shown at right.
(72, 73)
   a. How many cubes are in each layer?

   b. How many layers are there?

   c. How many cubes are there?

   d. If each cube is 1 cubic inch, what is the volume of all the cubes?

11. Find each missing addend:
(9)
   a. $15 + m = 25$ **b.** $n + 12 = 20$

12. Find each product:
(78)
   a. 9×90 **b.** 8×80 **c.** 7×70

Add or subtract, as shown below:

13. $786 − $694
(23)

14. $3.50 + $0.97 + $0.85
(22, 24)

15. 5 × 33
(84)

16. 4 × 4 × 4
(77, 84)

17. **Multiple Choice** Which figure does *not* show a line of symmetry?
(Inv, 7)

 A   **B**   **C**   **D**

18. a. Draw a square with sides 6 cm long.
(58, 62, 79)

b. What is the perimeter of the square?

c. What is the area of the square?

19. Use the number line below to help you find the next four numbers
(2, 48) in this sequence:

$$2\frac{1}{2}, \ 2\frac{3}{4}, \ 3, \ 3\frac{1}{4}, \ 3\frac{1}{2}, \ \dots$$

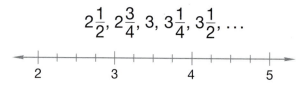

20. Draw two parallel line segments. Then draw two more parallel line
(Inv. 4) segments that cross the first two segments and are perpendicular
to them. What game can you play using this design?

*Real-World
Connection*

Martina is a carpenter. She has a wooden board that is 182 inches long. She is working on 2 projects. She uses 41 inches for the first project and 64 inches for the second project. How many inches of the board are left for Martina to use?

LESSON 86

- **Division Facts**
- **Multiplication and Division Fact Families**

Power Up

facts   Power Up 86

jump start   Count up by 2s from 0 to 30 and then back down to 0.
                   Count up by 5s from 0 to 60 and then back down to 0.

                   Write two multiplication facts using the numbers 5, 11, and 55.

                   Draw a 5-centimeter segment on your worksheet. About how many inches long is the segment?

mental math   **a. Calendar:** How many months are in 6 years?

                   b. Number Sense: 84 − 40

                   c. Number Sense: 77 + 25

                   d. Money: $3.49 + $7.00

problem solving In the problem solving exercise for Lesson 83, we found that we can use objects to make triangular patterns.

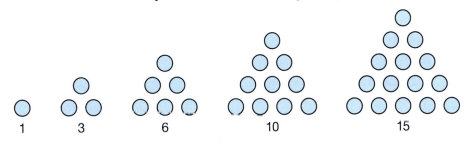

The numbers 1, 3, 6, 10, and 15 are examples of **triangular numbers.** Notice how the numbers increase:

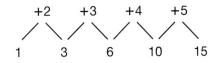

Continue the pattern to find the next two triangular numbers.

Division Facts

We can learn division facts while we are learning multiplication facts. The same three numbers that make a multiplication fact also make a division fact.

$$20 = 4 \times 5$$
$$20 \div 4 = 5$$

When we multiply, we know the two factors, and we are looking for the product. When we divide, we know the product and one of the factors, and we are looking for the other factor. When dividing we call these numbers the **dividend, divisor,** and **quotient.**

$$\text{dividend} \div \text{divisor} = \text{quotient} \qquad \text{divisor} \overline{)\text{dividend}}^{\text{quotient}}$$

Example 1

Find each quotient:

a. 24 ÷ 6   **b. 4)̄24**

a. We read 24 ÷ 6 as "Twenty-four divided by six." We may think, "Six times what number equals 24?" Since 6 × 4 = 24, the quotient is **4.**

b. We read 4)̄24 as "Twenty-four divided by four." We think, "What number times 4 equals 24?" Since 6 × 4 = 24, the quotient is **6.**

Multiplication and Division Fact Families

The three numbers that make a multiplication fact can also be used to make a division fact. Together, the multiplication facts and their related division facts make up a **fact family.**

Fact Family

Multiplication Facts	Division Facts
4 × 6 = 24	24 ÷ 6 = 4
6 × 4 = 24	24 ÷ 4 = 6

Example 2

Write two multiplication facts and two division facts using the numbers 6, 7, and 42.

The product is 42 and the factors are 6 and 7, which can be written in either order.

$$6 \times 7 = 42 \qquad\qquad 7 \times 6 = 42$$

By dividing 42 by 6 and by 7 we form two division facts.

$$42 \div 6 = 7 \qquad\qquad 42 \div 7 = 6$$

Example 3

Write two multiplication facts and two division facts shown by this array:

☆ ☆ ☆ ☆ ☆
☆ ☆ ☆ ☆ ☆
☆ ☆ ☆ ☆ ☆

There are 3 rows of 5 stars and 15 stars in all.

$$3 \times 5 = 15 \qquad\qquad 5 \times 3 = 15$$

$$15 \div 5 = 3 \qquad\qquad 15 \div 3 = 5$$

Analyze How many multiplication and division facts can be written to show an array of 3 rows of 3 stars?

Example 4

Find each missing factor.

a. $3 \times \square = 18$ b. $m \times 4 = 36$

To find a missing factor we divide the product by the known factor.

a. Because $18 \div 3 = 6$, we know that $3 \times \mathbf{6} = 18$.

b. Because $36 \div 4 = 9$, we know that $\mathbf{9} \times 4 = 36$.

Lesson Practice   Find each quotient.

a. $24 \div 3$ b. $3\overline{)18}$ c. $18 \div 9$

d. $2\overline{)8}$ e. $30 \div 5$ f. $4\overline{)20}$

g. Write two multiplication facts and two division facts using the numbers 56, 7, and 8.

h. Write two multiplication facts and two division facts represented by the array below.

☆ ☆ ☆ ☆ ☆ ☆ ☆
☆ ☆ ☆ ☆ ☆ ☆ ☆
☆ ☆ ☆ ☆ ☆ ☆ ☆

Find each missing factor.

i. $6 \times \square = 42$　　　　　**j.** $n \times 3 = 27$

Written Practice　　Distributed and Integrated

1. Oscar took his family to an amusement park. The fee to enter
(20, 28)　the park was $64. Oscar paid the fee with a $100 bill. How much money should he get back?

2. Marcie purchased 10 greeting cards for $0.35 each. How much
(21, 60)　did she pay for all 10 cards?

3. The odometer of the car showed this display:
(32)

　a. Write the number of miles shown using digits.

　b. Write the number of miles shown with words.

4. (**Model**) Use a centimeter ruler to help you answer the following
(69, 79)　questions about this triangle:

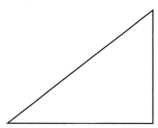

　a. How long are the three sides of the triangle?

　b. What is the perimeter of the triangle?

5. a. (**Represent**) Draw a triangle that is congruent to the triangle in
(68, 69) problem **4.**

b. What type of triangle did you draw?

6. What is the total value of ten quarters, ten dimes, ten nickels, and
(25) ten pennies?

7. Recall that a dozen is 12. How many eggs are equal to half of a
(83) dozen?

8. The bridge had a weight limit of 8 tons. How many pounds is
(74, 78) 8 tons?

9. Write two multiplication facts and two division facts using the
(86) numbers 7, 8, and 56.

10. Choose the best measure. The mass of a raisin is about
(80)   1 gram.   1 kilogram.

11. Multiple Choice This picture shows the answer to which
(11, 19) subtraction below?

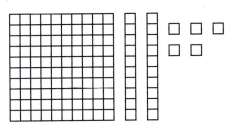

       A 375 − 250   **B** 125 − 50   **C** 750 − 200

12. Multiply:
(84)   **a.** 8 × 42

       b. 4 × 34¢

13. **Analyze** A box like the one shown below is completely filled with one-inch cubes.

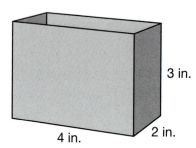

3 in.

2 in.

4 in.

a. How many cubes are needed for the bottom layer?

b. How many layers of cubes are needed to fill the box?

c. What is the volume of the box?

14. Find each product:
(78)
    a. 6 × 90   **b.** 4 × 80   **c.** 3 × 60

15. $300 − $166
(28)

16. $3.75 + $2.87
(22)

17. 8 × 9 × 10
(77)

18. Find the missing factor: 6 × n = 42
(86)

19. Write "four and three fourths" using digits.
(46)

20. **Multiple Choice** Which choice below best describes
(75)   the shape of a tent like the one shown at right?
    A pyramid   **B** rectangular prism
    C cone   **D** triangular prism

LESSON 87

• Capacity

facts   Power Up 87

jump start

Count down by 6s from 60 to 0.
Count down by 12s from 120 to 0.

Write two division facts using the numbers 3, 5, and 15.

Draw a rectangle and divide it into 8 parts. Then shade 3 parts. What fraction is not shaded?

mental math

a. **Money:** $2.60 + 99¢

b. **Number Sense:** 88 − 19

c. **Number Sense:** 7 × 3 × 10

d. **Algebra:** Jared made this table to show the number of pages he had read. Find the missing number in the table.

Pages read	10	20	30	40	50
Minutes	5	10	___	20	25

problem solving

Perry's school starts classes at half past eight in the morning. If it takes Perry 1 hour to get to school, at what time does Perry need to leave home?

New Concept

The amount of liquid a container can hold is called its **capacity.** To measure capacity in the Customary System, we use the units **fluid ounces, cups, pints, quarts,** and **gallons.** Some of these units have a doubles and halves relationship. On the following page we show some common containers.

Discuss How does the picture below show a doubles relationship? How does it show a halves relationship?

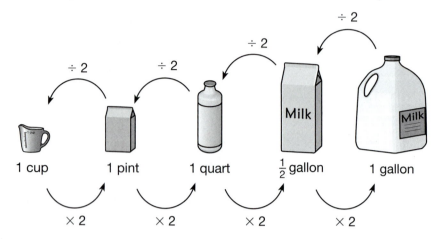

Measuring Capacity

Materials: measuring cup, one-pint bottle, one-quart bottle, half-gallon container, one-gallon container, water or rice

Do this activity in a small group or as a class.

1. Fill a measuring cup to the one-cup level and pour the contents into a one-pint bottle. Repeat until the bottle is full. How many cups were needed?

2. Empty the full one-pint bottle into the one-quart bottle. Repeat until the one-quart bottle is full. What is another name for half a quart?

3. Fill the half-gallon container from the one-quart bottle. What is another name for two quarts?

4. Then fill the one gallon container from the half-gallon container. How many quarts does it take to make a gallon?

Connect The word "quart" is in the word "quarter." In what way is a quart of water like a quarter of a dollar?

Analyze Doctors advise us to drink eight cups of water each day. What size liquid container equals eight cups?

Example 1

Multiple Choice Willow poured milk into her bowl of cereal. About how much milk did she pour?

    A 1 cup   **B** 1 quart   **C** 1 gallon

For a bowl of cereal, Willow would use about **one cup,** which is choice **A.**

Example 2

A cup is 8 ounces. How many ounces is a pint?

Two cups equal a pint; so a pint has twice as many ounces as a cup.

$$2 \times 8 \text{ ounces} = 16 \text{ ounces}$$

A pint is **16 ounces.**

A **liter** is used to measure capacity in the metric system. A liter is a little more than a quart.

   1 liter   1 quart   2 liters $\frac{1}{2}$ gallon

Example 3

Which is more, 2 liters of a beverage or $\frac{1}{2}$ gallon of a beverage?

Two quarts equal $\frac{1}{2}$ gallon. A liter is a little more than a quart; so 2 liters is close to, but **a little more than, $\frac{1}{2}$ gallon.**

Lesson Practice

  a. A gallon of milk is how many quarts?

  b. A pint is 16 ounces. How many ounces is a quart?

  c. **Multiple Choice** Which unit would describe the amount of juice in a container?

      A quart   **B** foot

      C pound   **D** meter

d. Multiple Choice Todd drank a glass of juice. Which measure below best describes the amount of juice in a glass?

A 10 ounces **B** 10 cups **C** 10 pints **D** 10 quarts

Written Practice

Distributed and Integrated

1. **Analyze** Gabriel filled the ice tray with water from the tap and
(4, 20) then put the ice tray in the freezer. If water from the tap is 62°F, how many degrees does it need to cool until it starts to freeze?

2. Joey and Jermaine shared 18 pretzels equally. How many pretzels
(82) did each boy get? Draw a picture to represent the problem.

3. **Conclude** Jayne rode her bike one mile on Monday, two miles
(81) on Tuesday, and four miles on Wednesday. Each day she rode twice as far as she rode the day before. How many miles did she ride on Saturday?

4. How many months is half of a year?
(83)

5. Steve paid two dollars for a toy that cost $1.39. What coins
(25, 26) should he get back in change?

6. Arrange these units in order of size from shortest to longest:
(79)
      meter   kilometer   centimeter

7. What fraction of a gallon is equal to a quart?
(44, 87)

8. **Multiple Choice** This picture shows the answer to which
(11, 84) multiplication below?

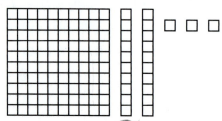

A 3×21 **B** 4×31 **C** 3×41 **D** 12×3

9. Multiply:
(84)

    a. 6 × 34   **b.** 3 × 46¢

10. **Multiple Choice** What is a reasonable estimate of the
(87) amount of water in a full pitcher?

    A 2 ounces   **B** 2 quarts

    C 2 gallons   **D** 2 cups

11. **Multiple Choice** A liter is closest in measure to a
(87)

    A pint.   **B** quart.

    C half-gallon.   **D** gallon.

12. Find the missing factor: $7 \times m = 28$.
(86)

$m = 4$

13. Look at the sequence below. Each number is twice as big as the
(81) number before it. Find the next three numbers in the sequence.

    1, 2, 4, 8, 16, <u>32</u>, <u>64</u>, <u>128</u>, ...

14. $8.96 + $4.78   **15.** $11.00 − $5.75
(22)   (26, 28)

16. 5 × 5 × 5   *125*   **17.** 6)‾42‾
(77, 84)   (86)

18. Write two multiplication facts and two division facts using the
(86) numbers 6, 7, and 42.

19. A rectangle was formed with tiles that were 1-foot squares.
(58, 62)

    a. How long is the rectangle?

    b. How wide is the rectangle?

    c. What is the area of the rectangle?

    d. What is the perimeter of the rectangle?

20. This paper clip is how many centimeters long?
(79)

• Even and Odd Numbers

facts   Power Up 88

jump start   Count up by 8s from 0 to 88.
Count up by 4s from 0 to 44.

Draw a rectangle that is 3 centimeters long and 3 centimeters wide.

Write the largest 4-digit number that uses each of the digits 1, 7, 8, and 5. What is the value of the digit in the thousands place?

mental math

a. **Number Sense:** $4 \times 4 \times 10$

b. **Number Sense:** $96 - 30$

c. **Number Sense:** 2, 7, 3, 8, 4, 9, _____

d. **Measurement:** What is the perimeter of the pentagon?

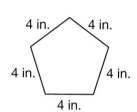

problem solving

Focus Strategy: Work a Simpler Problem

What day of the week is 71 days after Monday?

(**Understand**) We are asked to find which day of the week is 71 days after Monday.

(**Plan**) Instead of counting each of the 71 days, we can work a simpler problem.

(**Solve**) One week after Monday is Monday. Two weeks after Monday is also Monday. Each week is 7 days, so we can count up by 7s to reach 70, which is close to 71.

We know that 70 days after Monday is Monday. This means that 71 days after Monday is the next day, which is **Tuesday.**

(**Check**) Our answer is reasonable because 70 days is 10 weeks (10 × 7 days = 70 days). Ten weeks after Monday is Monday, so 10 weeks plus 1 day is Tuesday.

New Concept

If we can divide a number of objects into two equal groups, then the number is **even.** We see that 12 is an even number because 12 objects can be divided into two equal groups.

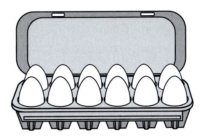

If a number of objects does not divide into two equal groups, the number is **odd.** So 11 is an odd number because it does not divide into two equal groups.

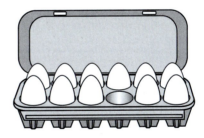

Activity

Even and Odd Numbers

Materials: counters

1. Place 10 counters on your desk. Can you divide 10 counters into two equal groups? Is 10 an even number or an odd number?

2. Place 9 counters on your desk. Can you divide 9 counters into two equal groups? Is 9 an even number or an odd number?

3. Place 8 counters on your desk. Divide the counters. Is 8 even or odd?

4. Place 7 counters on your desk. Is 7 even or odd? How do you know?

Example 1

Are the numbers we say when we count by twos even numbers or odd numbers?

2, 4, 6, 8, 10, …

Each of these numbers can be divided into two equal groups. When we count by twos from 2, we say **even numbers.**

The numbers 1, 3, 5, 7, 9... are odd numbers. They cannot be divided into two equal groups.

Generalize You can name every whole number as either even or odd. What is the rule for the pattern of even/odd numbers in the sequence 1, 2, 3, 4, 5, 6, 7, 8, 9, …?

Example 2

There are 21 students in the class. Can all the students line up into two equal rows?

The students can line up into two equal rows only if the number of students is even. Twenty-one is not an even number. It is an odd number.

21

No, 21 students cannot line up into two equal rows.

A quick way to tell if a counting number is even or odd is to look at the last digit of the number. If the last digit is even (0, 2, 4, 6, 8), then the number is even. If the last digit is odd (1, 3, 5, 7, 9), then the number is odd.

Example 3

There are 365 days in a common year. Is 365 even or odd?

The last digit of 365 is 5, which is odd. So 365 is **odd.**

Lesson Practice

a. Multiple Choice Which of these numbers is even?

A 3 **B** 13 **C** 23 **D** 32

b. Can 28 students line up into two equal rows? Explain your answer.

c. Simon has $7. Nathan has $7. If they put their money together, will they have an even number of dollars or an odd number of dollars?

d. Multiple Choice Which of these months has an even number of days?

A July **B** August

C September **D** October

Written Practice *Distributed and Integrated*

1. Ramon bought a half gallon of milk for $2.24, a loaf of bread for
(22, 60) $1.89, and a can of juice for $1.18. What was the total price of these groceries?

2. Ramon paid for the groceries in problem **1** with a $10 bill. How
(20, 28) much money should he get back?

3. From the Earth to the moon is about two hundred fifty thousand
(32) miles. Use digits to write that number.

4. How many inches are equal to half of a foot?
(83)

5. Draw a picture to represent $2\frac{1}{2}$.
(42, 46)

6. Double each number:
(81)
a. 100 **b.** 30

7. Find half of each number:

(83)

    a. 10   **b.** 30

8. **Multiple Choice** Which of the following numbers is an even

(88)

number?

    A 365   **B** 536   **C** 563   **D** 635

9. (**Explain**) Can John separate 15 counters into 2 equal

(88)

groups? Explain your answer.

10. Find each product.

(78, 84)

    a. 5 × 30   **b.** 4 × $24

11. a. How many pints are equal to a quart?

(87)

    b. What fraction of a quart is a pint?

12. Find each quotient.

(86)

    a. $8\overline{)48}$ **b.** 36 ÷ 4

13. Write 521,769 in expanded form.

(32)

14. (**Conclude**) In the sequence below each number is half as big as

(83)

the number before it. Find the next three numbers in the sequence.

$$64, 32, 16, \underline{\hphantom{00}}, \underline{\hphantom{00}}, \underline{\hphantom{00}}, \ldots$$

15. $496 + $467   **16.** $10.00 − $9.48

(16)   (26, 28)

17. 4 × 5 × 6   **18.** 3 × 36

(77, 78)   (84)

19. Find the missing factor: $9 \times n = 72$

(86)

20. (**Model**) Use a centimeter ruler to help you answer

(58, 62)

the following questions about this rectangle.

    a. What is the length of the rectangle?

    b. What is the width of the rectangle?

    c. What is the perimeter of the rectangle?

    d. What is the area of the rectangle?

LESSON 89

• Using a Multiplication Table to Divide By a One-Digit Number

Power Up

facts   Power Up 89

jump start   Count up by odd numbers from 1 to 25.
                   Count up by even numbers from 2 to 30.

                    Write two division facts using the numbers 4, 6, and 24.

                   Draw a 13-centimeter segment on your worksheet.
                   About how many inches long is the segment?

mental math   **a. Time:** What is the time 3 hours after 3:47 a.m.?

                   b. Measurement: How many inches are in 7 feet?

                   c. Money: $5.15 + $0.99

                   d. Money: Find the value of these bills and coins:

problem solving   Tristan's baby brother turned 13 months old in February.
                      In what month was Tristan's brother born?

In Lesson 83 we used a multiplication table to divide by 2. In this lesson we will use a multiplication table to divide by other numbers. Read the following problem.

For an art project, 24 students will sit at 6 tables. If the students are divided equally, how many students will sit at each table?

To answer the question, we divide 24 into 6 equal groups. To divide 24 by 6, we will use a multiplication table. We look in the 6 row for 24. At the top of the column, we see 4. This means $24 \div 6 = 4$. So, there are 4 students at each table.

Represent Draw a picture to show the solution to the problem above.

Multiplication Table

	0	1	2	3	4	5	6	7	8	9	10	11	12
0	0	0	0	0	0	0	0	0	0	0	0	0	0
1	0	1	2	3	4	5	6	7	8	9	10	11	12
2	0	2	4	6	8	10	12	14	16	18	20	22	24
3	0	3	6	9	12	15	18	21	24	27	30	33	36
4	0	4	8	12	16	20	24	28	32	36	40	44	48
5	0	5	10	15	20	25	30	35	40	45	50	55	60
6	0	6	12	18	24	30	36	42	48	54	60	66	72
7	0	7	14	21	28	35	42	49	56	63	70	77	84
8	0	8	16	24	32	40	48	56	64	72	80	88	96
9	0	9	18	27	36	45	54	63	72	81	90	99	108
10	0	10	20	30	40	50	60	70	80	90	100	110	120
11	0	11	22	33	44	55	66	77	88	99	110	121	132
12	0	12	24	36	48	60	72	84	96	108	120	132	144

Example 1

For Game Day the teacher divided the 32 students into 4 equal teams. How many students were on each team?

To find the answer to $4\overline{)32}$ on the table, we find 32 in the 4 row. Then we look at the top of the column and see 8. There were **8 students** on each team.

Example 2

The farmer planted an array of 42 trees in the orchard with 6 trees in each row. How many rows of trees did the farmer plant?

To find the quotient of 42 ÷ 6, we look in the 6 row for 42. We see 7 at the top of that column. The farmer planted **7 rows** of trees.

Lesson Practice

a. There are 12 inches in a foot. How many feet is 60 inches?

b. Derek placed 32 books in 4 equal stacks. How many books were in each stack?

Use a multiplication table to find each quotient.

c. 56 ÷ 8

d. 84 ÷ 7

e. $9\overline{)72}$

f. $6\overline{)54}$

Written Practice *Distributed and Integrated*

1. An eraser costs 32¢. How much would five erasers cost?
(60)

2. The record was 900 points. Jan had 625 points. How many more
(28, 36) points did Jan need to reach the record?

3. **Analyze** Half a dozen children were playing in the yard. Then
(83) half of them left. How many children were still in the yard?

4. How many centimeters is half of a meter?
(79, 83)

5. **Analyze** One way to mentally multiply by 4 is by "double
(78, 84) doubling" the other factor. That means to double the other factor,
then double the result.

a. 4 × 20

b. 4 × 21

6. Multiply:
(84)

a. 6 × $14

b. 7 × 14¢

7. **Multiple Choice** Which of the following coins has a value that
(88) is an even number of cents?

A penny   **B** nickel   **C** dime   **D** quarter

8. **Analyze** If a full gallon container of water is used to fill a
(87) half-gallon container and a quart container, then how much
water is left in the gallon container?

9. Write two multiplication facts and two division facts using the
(86) numbers 3, 9, and 27.

10. What number goes in the square to complete the
(86) multiplication fact?

$$\begin{array}{r} \square \\ \times\, 9 \\ \hline 54 \end{array}$$

11. **Multiple Choice** Which unit is best for measuring the mass of a
(80) barbell?

A kilograms   **B** feet   **C** meters   **D** ounces

12. **Multiple Choice** This picture shows the answer to which
(11, 84) multiplication?

A 12×2 **B** 10×24 **C** 4×51 **D** 20×4

13. The shirt was on sale for half price. If the regular price was $24,
(83) what was the sale price?

14. **Conclude** Find the next three numbers in this doubling
(81) sequence:

5, 10, 20, _____, _____, _____, ...

15. Find each quotient:
(86)
    a. 24 ÷ 4   **b.** 24 ÷ 6   **c.** 24 ÷ 8

16. $1 − 42¢   **17.** 38 + 47 + 163 + 9
(21, 28)   (24)

18. $63 − $45   **19.** 4 × 3 × 10
(23)   (77)

20. **Multiple Choice** Which multiplication or division fact
(85, 86) below is *not* illustrated by this diagram?

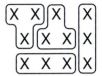

    A 12 ÷ 4 = 3   **B** 4 × 3 = 12
    C 12 ÷ 3 = 4   **D** 2 × 12 = 24

Real-World Connection

Roderick's baby sister drinks 3 cups of milk a day. How many cups of milk does his baby sister drink in a week? How many cups of milk would she drink in the month of April?

LESSON
90

• Equal Groups Stories, Part 2

Power Up

facts	Power Up 90
jump start	Count up by 3s from 0 to 45. Count up by 9s from 0 to 99.
	Draw a hexagon in the workspace on your worksheet.
	Use these clues to find the secret number. Write the secret number on your worksheet.

- two-digit number
- sum of digits is 9
- product of the digits is 20
- odd number

mental math

a. Number Sense: 17 + 16

b. Number Sense: 5 × 40

c. Geometry: How many sides do 3 hexagons have?

d. Time: It is afternoon. Keyanna's little sister took a nap at the time shown on the clock. She woke up 1 hour later. What time did she wake up?

problem solving

The school principal's office has a water cooler. The big bottle of water that sits on top of the cooler is labeled "5 gallons." Cheyenne is making a table to help her find how many cups of water are in 5 gallons. Copy this table and fill in the missing numbers. How many cups are in 5 gallons?

Gallons	Cups
1	16
2	
3	
4	
5	

Recall that an equal-groups story has three numbers.

If we know the number of groups and the number in each group, then we multiply to find the total.

Number of groups × Number in each group = Total

If we know the total and want to know the number of groups or the number in each group, we divide to find the answer.

Total ÷ Number of groups = Number in each group

Total ÷ Number in each group = Number of groups

Example 1

Twenty-eight children are going on a field trip. Seven cars are available to drive the children. If the children are divided into equal groups, how many children will ride in each car?

See how this story fits the equal groups pattern.

Number of groups × Number in each group = Total

7 cars   ×   ? in each car   = 28 children in all

This story has a missing factor.

7 × ? = 28

We can find a missing factor by dividing.

28 ÷ 4 = 7

We answer the question. **Four children** will ride in each car.

Example 2

Twenty-four people are coming to a party. They will sit at tables that will seat four people. How many tables will be needed to seat them all?

We see that the story fits the equal groups pattern.

Number of groups × Number in each group = Total

? tables   × 4 people at each table = 24 people in all

We know the total and the number in each group, but we do not know the number of groups.

$$? \times 4 = 24$$

We divide to find the missing factor.

$$4\overline{)24} \quad \begin{array}{c} 6 \end{array}$$

We find that **6 tables** are needed.

(**Represent**) Draw a picture to show the equal groups story in example 2.

Lesson Practice

a. Sylvester has 40 pennies. He puts them in stacks with 5 pennies in each stack. How many stacks does he make?

b. There are 30 desks in the room. The teacher wants to arrange the desks in 6 equal rows. How many desks will be in each row?

Written Practice — *Distributed and Integrated*

1. Simon took twelve big steps to cross the street. Each step is about 1 yard long. The street is about how many feet wide?
(34)

2. The television was on sale for $70 off the regular price. The regular price was $365. What was the sale price?
(20)

3. The population of the town is 16,000. Write the number using words.
(32)

4. a. Round $389 to the nearest hundred dollars.
(15)

b. Round $315 to the nearest hundred dollars.

5. Dixon bought a table for $389 and a chair for $315. Estimate the total cost of the desk and chair.
(30)

6. On Monday, Max finished the fact practice quiz in 80 seconds. On
(83) Wednesday, he finished in half that time. In how many seconds
did Max finish the quiz on Wednesday?

7. (**Analyze**) Mentally multiply by 4 by "double doubling" the other
(78, 84) factor.

   a. 4×30 **b.** 4×15

8. Thirty desks were arranged in rows with 5 desks in each row. How
(90) many rows of desks were there?

9. Multiple Choice Which illustration below shows an even number
(88) of counters?

      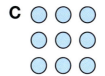

10. a. The shaded circle shows what fraction equivalent
(42, 47)   to $\frac{1}{2}$?

   b. (**Represent**) Draw and shade a circle to show a
   fraction equivalent to $\frac{1}{2}$ that has a denominator
   of 4. What is the fraction?

11. Multiply:
(84)   **a.** $6 \times \$25$ **b.** $7 \times 15¢$

12. Find the missing number: $48 - w = 29$.
(40)

13. (**Conclude**) In this sequence each number is half the number
(83) before it. Find the next three numbers in this sequence.

   160, 80, 40, _____, _____, _____, . . .

14. Find each quotient:
(85)   **a.** $25 \div 5$ **b.** $21 \div 3$ **c.** $20 \div 4$

15. $5 \times 6 \times 7$ **16.** $\$5.00 - \$2.34$
(77)   (26, 28)

17. Find each product:
(56, 78)
    a. 4 × 90   **b.** 7 × 90   **c.** 10 × 23

18. **Multiple Choice** Which polygon below does *not* have at least
(65, 67) one obtuse angle?

  A  **B**   **C** 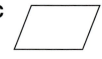   **D**

19. **Multiple Choice** Which figure shows a line of symmetry?
(Inv. 7)

  A    **B**   **C**    **D**

20. (**Represent**) Sketch a map that shows your school and your
(31) home. Make the top of the map north. Then write directions to
your home from school.

Early Finishers
Real-World Connection

Rosemary was making a costume. She sewed five buttons on
her costume. The red button was below the blue one. The green
button was above the blue one. The yellow button was between
the blue and red ones. The purple button was above the green
one. Which button is in the middle? Draw a picture to show your
answer.

Focus on

• Symmetry, Part 2

Recall from Investigation 7 that a line of symmetry divides a figure into mirror images.

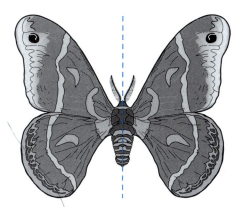

Visit www. SaxonMath.com/ Int3Activities for an online activity.

A figure may have one line of symmetry, two lines of symmetry, or more. A figure may also have no lines of symmetry.

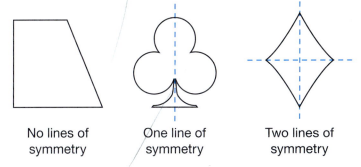

| No lines of symmetry | One line of symmetry | Two lines of symmetry |

A line of symmetry also shows where a figure could be folded in half so that one half exactly fits onto the other half. In the following activity, you will create shapes with one or two lines of symmetry by folding and cutting paper.

Activity 1

Creating Symmetrical Figures

Materials: two sheets of paper, scissors

Fold a sheet of paper in half. While the paper is folded, cut a shape out of the paper starting from one end of the folded edge to the other end.

Here we show a heart shape being cut from the folded paper:

Folded edge

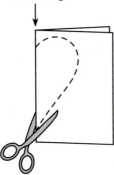

The opened figure you cut out has a line of symmetry along the fold.

Fold is line of symmetry

Repeat the activity with another sheet of paper folded twice.

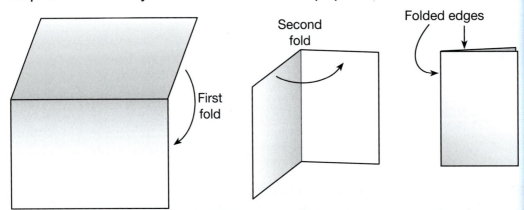

First fold

Second fold

Folded edges

Cut a shape from the twice-folded paper, beginning the cut from one folded edge and ending in the other folded edge.

The opened figure you cut out has two lines of symmetry along the folds.

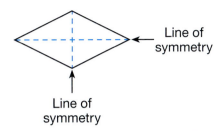

Recall from Investigation 7 that when we place an upright mirror on a line of symmetry, the reflection in the mirror completes the figure.

Place a mirror on the lines of symmetry in these figures to see the complete shape in the reflection.

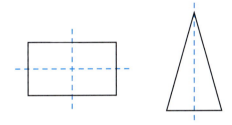

1. **Multiple Choice** Use a mirror to decide which of these letters has a line of symmetry.

2. **Multiple Choice** Which of these quadrilaterals shows a line of symmetry?

Activity 2

Lines of Symmetry

Materials: **Lesson Activity 30,** ruler, pencil

On **Lesson Activity 30,** there are four polygons. Three of the polygons have lines of symmetry. Draw at least one line of symmetry across each of those three polygons.

• Multiplying Three-Digit Numbers, Part 1

 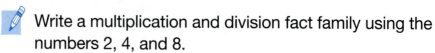

facts   Power Up 91

jump   Count up by 11s from 0 to 121.
start   Count up by 5s from 6 to 56.

Write a multiplication and division fact family using the numbers 2, 4, and 8.

Draw a $2\frac{1}{2}$-inch segment on your worksheet. Then make it $2\frac{1}{2}$ inches longer. What is the total length of the segment?

mental
math

a. **Number Sense:** 66 − 19

b. **Number Sense:** 24 + 38

c. **Calendar:** How many days are in 7 weeks?

d. **Estimation:** Round the value of these bills to the nearest ten dollars:

problem
solving

Dina arranged dominoes into a repeating pattern. Below we show the first ten dominoes in the pattern.

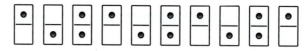

Draw the next two dominoes in the pattern.

New Concept

Gwen and Theo are guessing the number of pennies in a jar. They cannot empty the jar and count the pennies, so they think of other ways to estimate the number of pennies.

Sometimes we want to find the answer to a "how many" question when we cannot count. We can use math sense to estimate how many instead. In the next few lessons, we will practice different methods of estimating.

Gwen and Theo found an empty jar like the penny jar. They put 200 pennies in the jar. The jar was only partly filled.

Gwen and Theo estimated that they would need 8 times as many pennies to fill the jar completely. They multiplied 8 times 200 to estimate how many pennies would fill the jar.

$$\begin{array}{r} 200 \\ \times\ \ \ 8 \\ \hline 1{,}600 \end{array}$$

(**Analyze**) What fraction shows about what part of the second penny jar was filled?

Example 1

Find the product of 6 and 300.

Starting in the ones place, we multiply 0 ones by 6. The product is 0. Next, we multiply 0 tens by 6. The product is 0. Finally, we multiply 3 hundreds by 6. The product is 18 hundreds.

$$\begin{array}{r} 300 \\ \times\ \ \ 6 \\ \hline \mathbf{1{,}800} \end{array}$$

Example 2

Multiply: 7 × $250.

This multiplication is similar to multiplying a two-digit number. First, we multiply 0 ones by 7. The product is 0.

$$\begin{array}{r} \$250 \\ \times\quad 7 \\ \hline 0 \end{array}$$

Next, we multiply 5 tens by 7. The product is 35 tens, which is $350. We record the 5 tens in the tens place and write the 3 hundreds above the 2.

$$\begin{array}{r} 3 \\ \$250 \\ \times\quad 7 \\ \hline 50 \end{array}$$

Finally, we multiply 2 hundreds by 7. The product is 14 hundreds. We add the 3 hundreds, so the total is 17 hundreds.

$$\begin{array}{r} 3 \\ \$250 \\ \times\quad 7 \\ \hline \$1750 \end{array}$$

The final product is **$1,750.**

Estimation by Volume

Materials: **Lesson Activity 31,** jar filled with pennies, empty jar, extra pennies

Your teacher has filled a jar with pennies to help your class practice estimating. Guess the number of pennies in the jar and write your guess on **Lesson Activity 31.** You might want to talk about why you guessed your number.

Then watch and count as pennies are put into an empty jar like the penny jar.

1. How many pennies were put into the empty jar?

2. About what fraction of the jar is filled with pennies?

3. How many sets of pennies of this size would be needed to fill the jar?

4. What numbers would you multiply to estimate the number of pennies in the full jar?

5. If you would like to make a new estimate of the number of pennies in the full jar based on your work in this activity, record the new estimate on **Lesson Activity 31.**

Find each product.

    a. 7 × 400   **b.** 8 × $300

    c. 6 × 340   **d.** 4 × $750

Written Practice   *Distributed and Integrated*

1. Bertram divided 30 model cars into five equal groups. How many
(90) model cars were in each group?

2. Roderick has a bag of 18 marbles. Half of the marbles are red and
(50, 83) half are blue. Is drawing a red marble more likely, equally likely, or
less likely than drawing a blue marble?

3. What geometric solid has one curved surface and one flat surface
(Inv. 8) shaped like a circle?

4. Karen and Marie are sharing a bag of grapes. There are 18 grapes
(82) in the bag. If they share equally, how many grapes will there be for
each of the girls?

5. Find the next three numbers in this doubling sequence:
(2, 59)
$$\frac{1}{2}, 1, 2, \underline{\hspace{1cm}}, \underline{\hspace{1cm}}, \underline{\hspace{1cm}}, \dots$$

6. Multiply 76 by 2 using pencil and paper.
(81)

7. **Multiple Choice** This picture shows the answer to which
(11, 84) multiplication problem shown below?

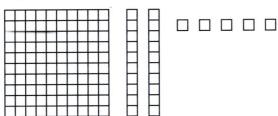

   A 25 × 10   **B** 25 × 5   **C** 21 × 5   **D** 20 × 6

8. A gallon of milk equals how many pints of milk?
(87)

9. **Formulate** A jar contains 200 pennies and is one fourth full.
(91) Write a multiplication number sentence to estimate about how many pennies would fill the jar.

10. Find m: $100 = 20 + 30 + 40 + m$
(9, 24)

11. Find each product:
(84)
    a. 60×3 **b.** 40×9

12. **Model** Draw a rectangle that is $1\frac{1}{4}$ inches long and $\frac{3}{4}$ inch wide.
(52, Inv. 9) Then draw its two lines of symmetry.

13. Find each quotient:
(86)
    a. $18 \div 3$ **b.** $18 \div 2$ **c.** $16 \div 8$

14. $\$6.75 - \$5.68$ **15.** $\$1 - 47¢$
(26)   (21, 26)

16. 132×2 **17.** 6×100
(91)   (91)

18. 5×32 **19.** 600×5
(84)   (91)

20. a. **Model** Use a pencil and ruler to draw a rectangle 4 inches
(52, 58, 63)   long and 3 inches wide.

    b. What is the perimeter of the rectangle?

    c. What is the area of the rectangle?

• **Parentheses**
• **Using Compatible Numbers, Part 1**

---

facts   Power Up 92

jump   Count up by odd numbers from 1 to 25.
start   Count up by even numbers from 2 to 30.

It is 6:35 in the morning. Draw hands on your clock to show the time in 2 hours. Write the time in digital form.

The temperature of the water at the beach was 76°F. The beach sand was 16 degrees warmer. Mark your thermometer to show the temperature of the beach sand.

mental   **a. Fact Family:** Find the missing number in this fact
math   family:

$$3 \times \square = 12 \qquad 12 \div \square = 3$$
$$\square \times 3 = 12 \qquad 12 \div 3 = \square$$

b. Number Sense: $46 + 22$

c. Number Sense: 15×100

d. Time: It is 10:28 p.m. How many minutes is it until 11:00 p.m.?

problem   The bookstore is advertising a special
solving   sale with this sign. The regular price
for one book is $9. How much would it
cost to buy 6 books while they are on
sale?

> **Sale!**
> Buy 2 books,
> get 1 free!

Parentheses

Addition, subtraction, multiplication, and division are called **operations.** To solve some problems, we do more than one operation. In the expression below, we see there are two operations. The **parentheses** show us which operation to do first.

$$12 - (6 + 2)$$

Since $6 + 2$ is in parentheses, we first add $6 + 2$, which equals 8. Then we subtract 8 from 12.

$$12 - 8 = 4$$

Example 1

Simplify: $12 - (6 - 2)$

We do the operation inside the parentheses first: $6 - 2$ equals 4. Then we subtract 4 from 12.

$$12 - (6 - 2)$$
$$12 - 4 = \mathbf{8}$$

Example 2

Which is greater, $(12 \div 6) \div 2$ or $12 \div (6 \div 2)$?

We work inside parentheses first.

$(12 \div 6) \div 2$	$12 \div (6 \div 2)$
$2 \div 2$	$12 \div 3$
1	4

We see that $\mathbf{12 \div (6 \div 2)}$ **is greater.**

Using Compatible Numbers, Part 1

When adding three numbers, it does not matter which two numbers we add first; the sum is the same.

$12 + (6 + 2)$	$(12 + 6) + 2$
$12 + 8$	$18 + 2$
20	20

A strategy to help add three or more numbers quickly is to look for **compatible numbers.** Compatible numbers are numbers that, together, are easy to work with. For example, numbers whose sums are round numbers are compatible numbers.

$$50 + 40 + 160$$

If we add from left to right, we first add 40 and 50 to get 90. Then we must add 90 and 160.

However, we might notice that $40 + 160 = 200$. If we add those numbers first, then our next addition is easy to perform mentally: $200 + 50 = 250$. We can use parentheses to show which addition we will perform first:

$$50 + (40 + 160)$$

Numbers that end in 25, 50, or 75 are also easy to work with because we can imagine counting with quarters.

Example 3

The supply closet has 75 crayons, 80 pens, and 25 pencils. How many writing tools are there altogether?

We recognize this as a "some and some more" story with three addends. We know that 75 and 25 total 100, so we choose to mentally add those addends first. Then we mentally add $100 + 80$ to get 180. There are **180 writing tools** altogether.

We can also use compatible numbers to estimate solutions to subtraction problems.

Example 4

Jasmine had $8.79. She spent $4.24 at lunch. About how much money does Jasmine have left?

To find the exact amount Jasmine has left, we would subtract $8.79 − $4.24. The amounts $8.79 and $4.24 are both very close to amounts we say when counting by quarters. We can rewrite the subtraction using compatible numbers this way: $8.75 − $4.25. We can perform this calculation quickly. **Jasmine has about $4.50 left.**

Lesson Practice

a. $12 - (6 \div 2)$

b. $(12 - 6) \div 2$

c. $12 \div (6 - 2)$

d. $(12 \div 6) - 2$

e. Compare: $(12 - 6) - 2 \bigcirc 12 - (6 - 2)$

For **f** and **g**, first write the pairs of compatible numbers. Then find the total.

f. $30 + 90 + 110$ **g.** $2 + 7 + 3 + 9 + 1$

h. Paolo spilled the puzzle pieces on the playground. The puzzle had 800 pieces but Paolo could only find 627. About how many puzzle pieces were lost? Write a subtraction number sentence using compatible numbers to find your answer.

Written Practice
Distributed and Integrated

1. The television cost $295. Sales tax was $20.65. What is the total
(18, 22)   price including tax?

2. **Model** Use your fraction manipulatives to fit three $\frac{1}{4}$-pieces
(43)   together to make $\frac{3}{4}$. Which is greater, $\frac{3}{4}$ or $\frac{1}{2}$?

3. The zookeeper wants to split a bag of peanuts between the zoo's
(82)   two elephants. There are 24 pounds of peanuts in the bag. If the elephants share equally, how many pounds of peanuts will there be for each of them?

4. Draw a regular prism. A rectangular prism has how many
(71)
   a. faces?   **b.** edges?   **c.** vertices?

5. Write 895,283 in expanded form.
(32)

6. Multiply to find the number of days in two common years. Use
(1, 91)   pencil and paper to show your work.

7. Rewrite this addition problem using compatible numbers, then
(92)   add to estimate the sum: $824 + 747$.

8. Patricia built this shape with 1-inch cubes.
(72)

    a. How many cubes are in each layer?

    b. How many layers are there?

    c. How many cubes were used to make this shape?

    d. What is the volume of the cube?

9. Estimate the sum of $395 and $598.
(30)

10. 4 × 60
(78)

11. 75 × 7
(85)

12. (Analyze) Michael paid $5 for a model that cost $4.39 with tax.
(20, 25) What coins should Michael get back in change?

13. (Formulate) Write a multiplication fact that shows how many
(63) small squares cover this rectangle.

14. Find the next two numbers in this sequence:
(2, 83)

          48, 24, 12, _____, _____, ...

15. Find each quotient:
(89)

    a. 30 ÷ 6   **b.** 35 ÷ 5   **c.** 32 ÷ 4

16. $100 − ($62 + $9)
(92)

17. $5.50 − $3.43
(26)

18. (7 × 80) + 40
(77, 92)

19. 5 × 12
(59)

20. The distance across a penny is about how many
(79) centimeters?

LESSON 93

• Estimating Products

facts   Power Up 93

jump   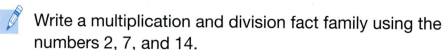 Count up by 7s from 0 to 84.
start   Count up by 10s from 8 to 98.

Write a multiplication and division fact family using the numbers 2, 7, and 14.

Madison had a $10 bill. She bought a stamp set for $8.80. What is the fewest bills and coins she could receive for change?

mental   **a. Money:** $78 + $50
math
                 b. Number Sense: 6 × 30

                 c. Number Sense: 2 × 3 × 4

                 d. Measurement: Mohini's desk at home is 3 feet long and 2 feet wide. What is the area of her desk?

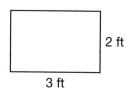

problem   The Pitzer family ordered an extra large pizza for dinner. The
solving   pizza was cut into 16 slices.

                 Mr. and Mrs. Pitzer ate 4 slices altogether. The oldest child, Clint, ate 3 slices. The other two children, Elisha and Jason, each ate 2 slices.

                 How many slices were left over? Did the family eat more than half of the pizza? Explain your answer.

In Lesson 30 we estimated sums and differences. In this lesson we will estimate products.

Manny and two of his friends went to the amusement park. Each ticket cost $18. About how much did the three tickets cost altogether?

By rounding numbers before we multiply, we can estimate the answer to a multiplication problem. We round $18 to $20 and multiply to find the estimate: $20 × 3 = $60. The three tickets cost about $60 altogether.

Example 1

Tickets to the professional basketball game were $38 each. Mr. Jones wanted to buy 4 tickets. Estimate the total price of the 4 tickets.

To estimate the total price we will round $38 to $40 before we multiply.

$$4 × \$40 = \$160$$

The total price of the tickets is about **$160.**

Formulate Write an estimating products story problem for the multiplication 4 × $40 = $160.

Example 2

Jamal counted 195 words on one page. About how many words would Jamal read on 5 pages?

We can round 195 to 200. If we assume that each page has about the same number of words, then each page has about 200 words. To estimate the number of words on 5 pages, we multiply 200 by 5.

$$5 × 200 = \mathbf{1,000}$$

Jamal would read **about 1,000 words** on 5 pages.

Lesson Practice

a. Estimate the total price of 4 water-park tickets at $19 each.

b. If tickets to the football game are $32 each, about how much would 5 tickets cost?

c. Every day Alida walks around the track 4 times. She counted 489 steps for one lap. About how many steps does she take walking 4 laps?

Written Practice · Distributed and Integrated

1. Leticia sleeps nine hours each night. How many hours does she sleep in one week?
(60)

2. Bruce put stamps totaling 75¢ on the package. However, it cost $1.12 to mail the package. How much postage did Bruce need to add to the package?
(26, 36)

3. Luis flew a total of 2,200 miles from Los Angeles to Seattle and back to Los Angeles. Use words to write the number of miles that Luis flew.
(32)

4. Multiple Choice Which of these measurements is a reasonable height for a ten-year-old person?
(79)

   A 140 km   **B** 140 m   **C** 140 cm

5. Write 3,000 + 700 + 40 in standard form.
(32)

6. Measure the length and width of this rectangle to the nearest quarter of an inch.
(35, 52)

7. List these units in order of size from smallest to largest:
(87)

   quart   gallon   pint   cup

8. The first box weighed 48 pounds. The second box weighed 52 pounds. The third box weighed 39 pounds. Use compatible numbers to find the total weight mentally.
(92)

9. (21 − 10) + 33
(92)

10. Multiply:
(84)
   a. 4 × 16   **b.** 6 × 24

11. Estimate the product of 4 and 683.
(93)

12. If 40 strawberries are placed equally in 5 bowls, how many
(90) strawberries will be in each bowl?

13. (**Model**) Fit two $\frac{1}{8}$-pieces together. What larger fraction piece do
(47) they match?

14. Find each quotient:
(86)
    a. 40 ÷ 8   **b.** 42 ÷ 7   **c.** 45 ÷ 5

15. 412 × 2   **16.** $12.25 − $9.89
(91)   (26)

17. 80 + (70 × 6)   **18.** (9 − 4) × 4
(92)   (92)

19. Use this map to answer the questions that follow:
(31,
Inv. 4)

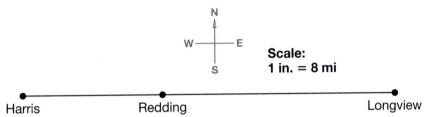

    a. Which town is east of Redding?

    b. How many miles is Longview from Harris?

20. (**Classify**) What is the geometric name for this figure?
(75) How many faces does it have?

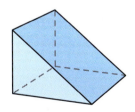

• **Using Compatible Numbers, Part 2**

facts   Power Up 94

jump start   Count up by 6s from 0 to 66.
                 Count up by 12s from 0 to 132.

                  Draw a rectangle and divide it into 8 parts. Then shade 6 parts. What fraction of the rectangle is shaded?

                  Write "six hundred thirty four dollars and seventy two cents" using digits and a dollar sign.

mental math **a. Estimation:** Round 525 to the nearest ten.

                 b. Number Sense: $591 - 300$

                 c. Number Sense: $65 + 45$

                 d. Time: It is afternoon. What will be the time 5 hours after the time shown on the clock?

problem solving Ms. Braden's third grade class is planning a picnic. The class will bring blankets to sit on at the picnic. Each blanket has enough space for 3 people to sit. There are 19 students in the class. How many blankets are needed so that all 19 students and Ms. Braden can have a place to sit?

In Lesson 92 we learned to use compatible numbers in addition and subtraction problems. We also used compatible numbers to help estimate answers to arithmetic problems. Remember that instead of rounding addends or factors, we can choose nearby numbers that are easy to work with.

	Problem		Easier Problem

Problem → **Easier Problem**

$$\begin{array}{r} 76 \\ + 73 \\ \hline \end{array} \qquad \rightarrow \qquad \begin{array}{r} 75 \\ + 75 \\ \hline \end{array}$$

$$\begin{array}{r} 26 \\ \times\ 4 \\ \hline \end{array} \qquad \rightarrow \qquad \begin{array}{r} 25 \\ \times\ 4 \\ \hline \end{array}$$

We can mentally double 75 instead of adding 76 and 73. We can mentally multiply 25 × 4 by thinking of counting quarters instead of multiplying 26 × 4 with pencil and paper.

Example 1

Use compatible numbers to estimate each sum or difference.

a. $10.78 + $2.24

b. 294 + 74 + 322

c. $10.00 − $5.72

a. We can rewrite the addition as $10.75 + $2.25. The sum is **about $13.00.**

b. We can rewrite the addition as 300 + 75 + 325:

$$\begin{array}{r} 300 \\ 75 \\ + 325 \\ \hline 700 \end{array}$$

c. The second amount is close to $5.75:
$10.00 − $5.75 = **$4.25.**

Example 2

Use compatible numbers to estimate the cost of 4 board games at $24 each.

The cost ($24) is close to $25. Multiplying $25 by 4 is easy because it is similar to counting quarters. Since 25 × 4 is 100, we estimate that the cost of the four games is about **$100.**

Use Compatible Number $25	Actual Problem

$$\begin{array}{r} \$25 \\ \times\ 4 \\ \hline \$100 \end{array} \qquad \begin{array}{r} \$24 \\ \times\ 4 \\ \hline \$96 \end{array}$$

Analyze What is the difference between the estimate and the actual product? Explain the difference.

Use compatible numbers to estimate in problems **a** and **b**.

a. Estimate the product of 249 × 4.

b. When Alida walks her dog, she travels one mile in 24 minutes. About how long would it take Alida to walk 2 miles?

c. Estimate the difference of $678 and $354.

Written Practice
Distributed and Integrated

1. Phil bought an aquarium for $62.97. Sales tax was $4.41. What was the total price with tax?
(18, 22)

2. Brad is thinking of a number between 1 and 10. He gives this hint: "If I multiply the number by itself, the product is 49." What is Brad's number?
(61)

3. Estimate the product of 82 and 4.
(93)

4. There are 5,280 feet in a mile. Find the number of feet in two miles.
(32)

5. What words go in the blanks?
(29, 87)

"Four _____ equal a dollar, and four _____ equal a gallon."

6. Janet placed 60 books on 5 shelves equally. How many books are on each shelf?
(90)

7. Is 254 closer to 200 or 300?
(15)

8. **Formulate** Rosa bought tickets to a concert. She paid $23 for each ticket. Use compatible numbers to estimate how much Rosa spent if she bought 5 tickets. Write a number sentence for the problem.
(94)

9. Multiply:
(84)
a. 4 × $25

b. 8 × 34

10. **Explain** How are a sphere and a cylinder different?
(75, Inv. 8)

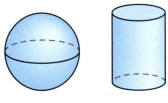

11. Name the place value of the 5 in each of these
(32) numbers:
  a. 45,321   **b.** 235

12. Find each product:
(78)
  a. 30 × 4   **b.** 6 × 90

13. **Multiple Choice** This picture shows the answer to which
(78) multiplication?

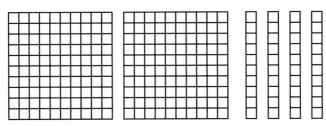

  A 6 × 40   **B** 20 × 7   **C** 2 × 12   **D** 2 × 40

14. Find each quotient:
(86)
  a. 48 ÷ 8   **b.** 49 ÷ 7   **c.** 42 ÷ 6

15. 7 × 2 × 5   **16.** 50 × 9
(77)   (78)

17. 3 × 7 × 9   **18.** 100 − (3 × 30)
(77, 84)   (78, 92)

19. Find *a*: 36 + *a* + 17 + 42 = 99
(9, 24)

20. **Model** Draw a rectangle 5 cm long and 4 cm wide. What is the
(52, 63) area of the rectangle?

• Using Estimation to Verify Answers

Power Up

facts	Power Up 95
jump start	Count up by 5s from 7 to 57. Count up by 4s from 0 to 44.

Draw a cube. How many vertices does a cube have?

Label the number line by fourths from 0 to $2\frac{2}{4}$. (Show these numbers: 0, $\frac{1}{4}$, $\frac{2}{4}$, $\frac{3}{4}$, 1, $1\frac{1}{4}$, and so on.)

mental math

a. **Number Sense:** $3 \times 3 \times 5$

b. **Number Sense:** $72 + 28$

c. **Number Sense:** $40 + 23 + 60$

d. **Time:** Sharla finished the sack race in 55 seconds. Kevin finished in 70 seconds. How many more seconds did it take Kevin to finish the race than Sharla?

problem solving

Talia arranged one dollar in pennies in a square array on the table. Then Talia scooped some of the pennies into her hand. This diagram shows the pennies that remained. Without counting, find the number of pennies on the table. (*Hint:* Imagine the array of pennies that Talia scooped into her hand, and write a subtraction number sentence.)

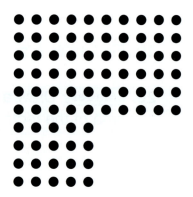

New Concept

We can use estimation to check whether a count, a measure, or a calculation is reasonable. Read the story on the following page and decide if Amber's total is reasonable.

Amber wants to buy 3 shirts for $28 each. She decides not to buy the shirts when she multiplies 3 × $28 and gets $624 for the total.

Amber could estimate to check if the total is reasonable. She could round $28 to $30. Then she could multiply 3 × $30 and find that the total price of the three shirts should be about $90. Since $624 is not close to $90, Amber's total is not reasonable.

(**Evaluate**) What mistake did Amber make when she multiplied 3 × $28 and got $624 for the total?

Example 1

Francine bought a bat for $32, a mitt for $49, and a pair of batting gloves for $13. She calculated that she would need $94 for all three items. Is her total reasonable?

Francine calculated a total price. We will use estimation to see if her answer is reasonable.

To estimate the total price, we round $32, $49, and $13 before we add.

$$\$30 + \$50 + \$10 = \$90$$

Our estimate is close to $94, so **Francine's total is reasonable.**

Example 2

Cody counted 213 words on one page. After reading 5 pages, Cody estimated that he had read 1050 words. Is Cody's estimate reasonable?

We can round 213 to 200. If we assume that each page has about the same number of words, then each page has about 200 words. To estimate the number of words on 5 pages, we multiply 200 by 5.

$$5 \times 200 = 1000$$

Since 1050 pages is close to 1000 pages, **Cody's estimate is reasonable.**

Lesson Practice

a. Roger bought a new bike seat for $31 and a helmet for $29. He calculated that he would need $90 to pay for both items. Is Roger's total reasonable? Explain your answer.

b. Jackson estimates that 5 tickets to the football game will cost more than $300. If tickets are $32 each, is Jackson's estimate reasonable? If not, about how much would 5 tickets cost?

c. Every day Alida walks around the track 5 times. She counted 489 steps for one lap. She estimates that she will walk 2,500 steps in 5 laps. Is her estimate reasonable? Explain your answer.

Written Practice
Distributed and Integrated

1. Estimate the cost of 7 uniforms at $62 each.
(93)

2. After using 36 of the 100 stamps, how many stamps did Sidney have left?
(40)

3. (Justify) Rachael bought 6 small bags of sunflower seeds. She found that there were 193 seeds in one bag. She estimated that there would be 1,800 seeds in all 6 bags. Is Rachael's estimate reasonable? Explain your answer.
(95)

4. Find each product.
(91)
    a. 3×400 **b.** $6 \times \$500$

    c. 7×430 **d.** $5 \times \$320$

5. What mixed number is halfway between 1 and 2?
(46, 48)

6. A yard is 36 inches. Multiply to find the number of inches in 2 yards.
(81)

7. A large bag of birdseed weighs about 38 pounds. Estimate the weight of 5 large bags of birdseed.
(93)

8. 1 quart = _____ cups
(87)

9. (Model) Draw a circle. Then divide the circle into fourths and shade one fourth of the circle.
(42)

10. Estimate the difference when $298 is subtracted from $602.
₍₃₀₎

11. Multiply:
₍₈₄₎
   a. 4 × $35   **b.** 3 × 21   **c.** 2 × 43

12. 5 × 700   **13.** 3 × 460
₍₉₁₎   ₍₉₁₎

14. 375 + 658 + 74   **15.** 370 − (9 × 40)
₍₂₄₎   _(78, 92)

16. (**Justify**) Each table in the restaurant can seat 6 people. Lori
₍₉₅₎ counted 31 tables in the restaurant. She estimates that the restaurant can only seat a total of 100 people. Is her estimate reasonable? Why or why not?

17. Find each quotient:
₍₈₆₎
   a. 28 ÷ 4   **b.** 36 ÷ 6   **c.** 48 ÷ 6

18. Use your ruler to find the length of this line segment to the nearest
₍₃₅₎ quarter of an inch.

—————————————————————

19. (**Conclude**) Counting by $\frac{1}{4}$s on a ruler, the order is
_(2, 35)

$$\frac{1}{4}, \frac{1}{2}, \frac{3}{4}, 1, \ldots$$

Find the next four numbers in this sequence:

$$\frac{1}{4}, \frac{1}{2}, \frac{3}{4}, 1, 1\frac{1}{4}, 1\frac{1}{2}, \underline{\quad}, \underline{\quad}, \underline{\quad}, \underline{\quad}, \ldots$$

20. This box is neatly filled with 1-centimeter cubes.
_(72, 73)

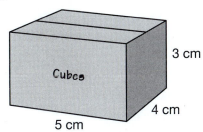

3 cm

Cubes

4 cm

5 cm

   a. How many cubes fit in the bottom layer?

   b. How many layers of cubes are there?

   c. How many cubes are used to fill the box?

   d. What is the volume of the box?

LESSON 96

• Rounding to the Nearest Dollar

Power Up

facts Power Up 96

jump start  Count up by odd numbers from 1 to 25.
Count up by even numbers from 2 to 30.

Write a multiplication and division fact family using the numbers 3, 6, and 18.

Draw a $3\frac{1}{2}$-inch segment on your worksheet. Then make it $1\frac{1}{4}$ inches longer. What is the total length of the segment?

mental math

a. Money: $7.80 + $1.99

b. Number Sense: 39 + 22

c. Number Sense: 8 × 60

d. Number Line: Which point shows the number 370?

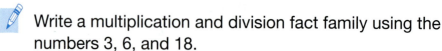

problem solving The third grade students at Lincoln School made this pictograph to show the number of books read by each class.

Use the pictograph to find how many more books the students must read to reach a total of 180 books.

Number of Books Read

Room 4	
Room 5	
Room 6	

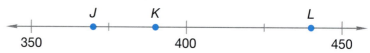

Key ☐ = 10 books

We can estimate with money by rounding dollars and cents to the nearest dollar.

What is the price of these two items rounded to the nearest dollar?

The price of the ball is between $2 and $3. Halfway between $2 and $3 is $2.50. Since $2.95 is greater than $2.50, the price is closer to $3.

The price of the puzzle is between $4 and $5. Halfway between $4 and $5 is $4.50. Since $4.39 is less than $4.50, the price is closer to $4.

Example 1

Brad saw a game at the toy store that cost $5.85. The price is between what two nearby dollar amounts? Round the price to the nearest dollar.

The price $5.85 is **between $5 and $6.** Halfway from $5 to $6 is $5.50. Since $5.85 is more than $5.50, the price to the nearest dollar is **$6.**

Example 2

The price of a box of crayons is $3.15 and a set of colored markers is $1.89. Estimate the total price of the two items.

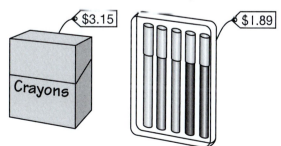

To estimate, we first round each price to the nearest dollar. Then we add to find the estimated total.

The $3.15 price rounds to $3.

The $1.89 price rounds to $2.

We add $3 and $2 and estimate that the total price is about **$5.**

Explain Explain why we rounded $3.15 down to $3.00.

Lesson Practice For problems **a–d,** round each dollar and cent amount to the nearest dollar.

a. $4.90

b. $6.25

c. $8.19

d. $6.79

e. Estimate the total price of a rubber ball that costs $2.95 and a plastic bat that costs $5.82.

f. Estimate the total price of a bottle of milk at $1.89, a box of cereal at $3.92, and a bag of fruit at $4.17.

Written Practice *Distributed and Integrated*

1. Bert is 150 cm tall. Lou is 118 cm tall. How many centimeters
(39) does Lou need to grow to be as tall as Bert?

2. Jenny bought ten cartons of eggs. There were a dozen eggs in
(60) each carton. How many eggs were there in ten cartons?

3. The price of a box of greeting cards is $4.50. This price is between
(96) what two nearby dollar amounts? Round $4.50 to the nearest dollar.

4. Add pairs of compatible numbers first to mentally find the total:
(92)
$$5 + 1 + 2 + 5 + 8 + 7$$

5. List the five odd numbers that are between 10 and 20.
(88)

6. Find each product:
(91)
    a. 4×500

    b. $3 \times \$800$

    c. 5×720

    d. $2 \times \$370$

7. $(50 + 21) + 17$
(92)

8. Kiondre and John put 300 pennies in the penny jar. They estimated
(91) that they would need 3 times that many pennies to fill the jar. About
how many pennies would Kiondre and John need to fill the jar?

9. (Model) Draw a triangular prism. Begin by drawing two
(75) congruent triangular faces.

10. A half gallon is the same as how many quarts?
(87)

11. What number is halfway between 3,000 and 4,000?
(33)

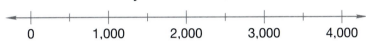

$$\begin{array}{ccccccc} 0 & 1,000 & 2,000 & 3,000 & 4,000 \end{array}$$

12. Counting by quarters on a ruler, the order is:
(35, 46)

$$\frac{1}{4}, \frac{1}{2}, \frac{3}{4}, 1$$

Find the next four numbers in this sequence:

$$2, 2\frac{1}{4}, 2\frac{1}{2}, \underline{\quad}, \underline{\quad}, \underline{\quad}, \underline{\quad}, \dots$$

13. Multiply:
(84)
   a. 4×15 **b.** 9×21 **c.** 8×45

14. One bouquet of flowers costs $12. Estimate the cost of
(93) 9 bouquets of flowers.

15. $20.00 − $1.99   **16.** $(63 + 37) \times 2$
(28)   (78, 92)

17. (Justify) It took 11 minutes for Jonathan to ride his bike one mile.
(93) He estimates that it will take him about an hour to ride his bike for
six miles. Is his estimate reasonable? Why or why not?

18. Use compatible numbers to estimate the products in **a** and **b.**
(94)   **a.** Estimate the product of 248×4.
   b. Estimate the product of 19×5.

19. Find each quotient:
(86)
   a. $27 \div 3$ **b.** $56 \div 7$ **c.** $63 \div 9$

20. Which of these numbers are even?
(88)
      152   365   438

• Multiplying Three-Digit Numbers, Part 2

facts   Power Up 97

jump start   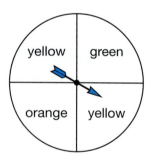 Count up by 25s from 0 to 250.
                   Count up by 10s from 0 to 110.

✏️ Aaron had a $10 bill. He bought a set of juggling balls for $4.65. Name the fewest bills and coins he could receive for change.

✏️ Use these clues to find the secret number. Write the secret number on your worksheet.

• two-digit number
• sum of digits is 8
• product of the digits is 0

mental math   a. **Number Sense:** $2 \times 4 \times 6$

                   b. **Number Sense:** $130 + 22 + 70$

                   c. **Measurement:** How many centimeters are in 3 meters?

                   d. **Probability:** Waverly spins the spinner one time. Which color is the spinner most likely to land on?

yellow | green
orange | yellow

problem solving   Josh watched the night sky from 9:00 to 10:00 during the meteor shower. He saw twice as many meteors after 9:30 as he saw before 9:30. Josh counted 24 meteors altogether. How many meteors did Josh see before 9:30?

To help them estimate the number of pennies in a full jar, Chad and Jodi filled up one jar with pennies. Then they put 234 pennies in a second jar that is similar in size.

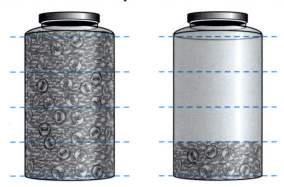

The second jar is only partly filled. Chad and Jodi estimate that they would need 4 times as many pennies to fill the second jar completely. So they estimate that the number of pennies in the full jar is about 4 × 234.

To multiply a 3-digit number with pencil and paper, we multiply the ones, then the tens, then the hundreds.

$$\begin{array}{r} {}^{1\,1}234 \\ \times\quad 4 \\ \hline 936 \end{array}$$

Discuss Look at the multiplication above. How many times do we need to regroup when we multiply 4 × 234? How can you tell?

Example 1

Find the product: 8 × 125

First, we multiply the 5 by 8. The product is 40. We record 0 in the ones place. We write the 4 tens of 40 above the 2.

$$\begin{array}{r} {}^{4}\ \\ 125 \\ \times\quad 8 \\ \hline 0 \end{array}$$

Next, we multiply 2 tens by 8. The product is 16 tens. We add the 4 tens. The total is 20 tens. We record 0 in the tens place and write 2 above the 1.

$$\begin{array}{r} {}^{24}\ \\ 125 \\ \times\quad 8 \\ \hline 00 \end{array}$$

Finally, we multiply 1 hundred by 8. The product is 8 hundreds. We add 2 hundreds. The total is 10 hundreds. The final product is **1,000.**

$$\begin{array}{r} {}^{24}\ \\ 125 \\ \times\quad 8 \\ \hline 1,000 \end{array}$$

Example 2

Chad compared the full penny jar with a jar that had 308 pennies. He thought the full jar had 7 times as many pennies, so he multiplied 308 by 7 to estimate the total. What was the product?

First, we multiply 8 by 7. The product is 56. We record the 6 in the ones place and write the 5 of 56 above the 0 in the tens place.

$$\begin{array}{r} 5 \\ 308 \\ \times \quad 7 \\ \hline 6 \end{array}$$

Next, we multiply 0 tens by 7. The product is 0. We add 5 and record 5 in the tens place.

$$\begin{array}{r} 5 \\ 308 \\ \times \quad 7 \\ \hline 56 \end{array}$$

Finally, we multiply 3 hundreds by 7. The final product is **2,156.**

$$\begin{array}{r} 5 \\ 308 \\ \times \quad 7 \\ \hline 2{,}156 \end{array}$$

Lesson Practice

a. 6×135

b. 7×213

c. $4 \times \$275$

d. $3 \times \$232$

e. 8×706

f. $9 \times \$204$

Written Practice *Distributed and Integrated*

1. **Model** Write the uppercase form of the ninth letter of the
(Inv. 9) alphabet. Then draw its lines of symmetry.

2. Tamara bought a dress for $39.95. Sales tax was $2.60. What was
(18, 22) the total price with tax?

3. Estimate the sum of $4.67 and $7.23 to the nearest dollar.
(30, 96)

4. **Multiple Choice** Which measurement is most likely the length of
(79) Vincent's pencil?

   A 15 cm   **B** 15 m   **C** 15 km

5. Stuart stacked seventeen books in two piles as equally as
(82) possible. How many books were in each stack?

6. The window was twice as wide as it was high. If the window was
(81) 35 inches high, then how wide was it?

7. (**Justify**) Susan estimated that 3 tickets to the baseball game will
(95) cost about $60. If tickets are $22 each, is her estimate reasonable?
Why or why not?

8. (**Analyze**) What words should be used in place of *w*, *y*, and *z* in
(87) this description?

> Doubling a cup makes a __*w*__. Doubling a __*w*__ makes
> a __*y*__. Doubling a __*y*__ makes a __*z*__. Doubling a
> __*z*__ makes a gallon.

9. (**Formulate**) Tyrone walks to school every day. He walks a total of
(93) 18 miles each month. Estimate the number of miles Tyrone walks
in 5 months. Write a number sentence.

10. Kumar used 1-inch cubes to build a rectangular solid
(73) like the one shown at right. How many 1-inch cubes did
Kumar use to build the solid?

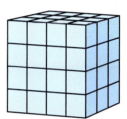

11. Multiply:
(84, 97)
    a. 4×210 **b.** 7×34

12. Divide:
(86)
    a. $2\overline{)12}$ **b.** $3\overline{)12}$

13. Round $5.38 to the nearest dollar.
(96)

14. 190×4 **15.** 230×5
(97)   (97)

16. $65 + $350 + $9   **17.** $6 + (5 \times 80)$
(24)   (78, 92)

18. Find each quotient:
(86)
    a. $42 \div 7$ **b.** $36 \div 4$ **c.** $64 \div 8$

19. Name the mixed numbers represented by points *A* and *B*.
(48)

20. **Model** Draw a rectangle that is 5 cm long and 3 cm wide.
(58, 63)

    a. What is the perimeter of the rectangle?

    b. What is the area of the rectangle?

Real-World Connection

Tony wants to paint his clubhouse. He has $15 to spend on supplies. At the paint store, he chose one can of blue paint for $9.99, a paint brush for $4.82, and a pack of reptile wall stickers for $3.62. Does Tony have enough money to buy all of the supplies he chose? Explain your answer.

LESSON 98

• Estimating by Weight or Mass

Power Up

facts Power Up 98

jump start   Count up by 9s from 0 to 108.
Count up by 5s from 8 to 58.

✏️ Write a multiplication and division fact family using the numbers 4, 4, and 16.

✏️ Draw a rectangle and divide it into 6 parts. Then shade 1 part. What fraction is *not* shaded?

mental math
a. **Money:** $200 − $136

b. **Number Sense:** 29 + 52

c. **Measurement:** What is the perimeter of this polygon? All sides are equal in length.

3 in.

d. **Geometry:** Name the polygon that is shown in problem **c.**

problem solving Ms. Hudson will pay to park her car in the parking garage. The cost is $3.50 for the first hour and $1.00 for each additional hour. Copy and complete this table to find the cost of parking a car in the garage for 6 hours.

Hours	Cost
1	$3.50

Gwen and Theo weighed the penny jar to help them estimate the number of pennies in the jar. They found that the mass of the jar was about 5 kilograms. Then they measured the mass of eight rolls of pennies. They found that the mass of eight rolls of pennies, or 400 pennies, was about 1 kilogram.

Use the information above to solve example 1.

Example 1

Create a table to help you estimate the number of pennies in 5 kilograms. Assume that 400 pennies has a mass of 1 kilogram.

Since the mass of 400 pennies is about 1 kilogram, we count up by 400 pennies for each kilogram.

Number of Pennies	400	800	1,200	1,600	2,000
Mass of Pennies	1 kg	2 kg	3 kg	4 kg	5 kg

We estimate that 5 kilograms of pennies is about **2,000 pennies.**

Analyze How many rolls of pennies can you make from 2,000 pennies?

Example 2

Alison knows that a pint of water weighs about a pound. She weighs a pitcher of water and finds that it weighs 7 pounds. The empty pitcher weighs 3 pounds. How many pints of water are in the pitcher?

Since the empty pitcher weighs 3 pounds and the filled pitcher weighs 7 pounds, we know that there are 4 pounds of water in the pitcher.

7 pounds	filled pitcher		4 pounds	water
− 3 pounds	empty pitcher		+ 3 pounds	empty pitcher
4 pounds	water		7 pounds	filled pitcher

Since one pint of water weighs about one pound, we estimate that **4 pints** of water are in the pitcher.

Activity

Estimating by Mass

Materials: full penny jar and **Lesson Activity 31** from Lesson 91, extra penny rolls, balance scale

Find the mass of the penny jar. Then find how many rolls of pennies have a mass of 1 kilogram. Use the information to help you estimate the number of pennies in the jar. You may use the results to improve your estimate on **Lesson Activity 31.**

Lesson Practice

a. An empty bucket weighs 1 pound. When filled with water, the bucket weighs 9 pounds. A pint of water weighs about 1 pound. About how many pints of water were in the bucket?

b. If 1 kilogram of pennies is about 400 pennies, then 6 kilograms of pennies is about how many pennies? Make a table of number pairs to find the answer.

Written Practice *Distributed and Integrated*

1. Sal wants to buy a radio that costs $31.76 with tax. He has $23.50. How much more money does Sal need to buy the radio?
(39)

2. A 5-gallon bucket is filled with water. How many quarts of water are in the bucket?
(87)

3. Find the products:
(97)
   a. 8×136 **b.** $9 \times \$151$

4. Find the missing number: $20 - n = 8$
(40)

5. The price of a pack of balloons is $5.49. The price of a pack of party hats is $3.29. Estimate the total price of the two items.
(96)

6. Find the missing factor: $5 \times m = 40$
(86)

7. A half gallon of milk is enough to fill how many cups?
(87)

8. What number is halfway between 2,000 and 3,000?
(33)

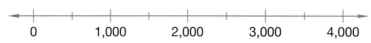

0   1,000   2,000   3,000   4,000

9. Katie is paid $7.75 per hour. Estimate how much Katie is paid for working 6 hours.
(96)

10. **Formulate** If one pound of apples is about 4 small apples, then 6 pounds of apples is about how many apples? Make a table to help find the answer.
(98)

11. Multiply:
(91)
   a. 4×150 **b.** 3×630 **c.** 35×7

12. Divide:
(86)
   a. $4\overline{)12}$ **b.** $6\overline{)12}$

13. **Multiple Choice** This picture below shows the answer to which multiplication expression?
(84, 91)

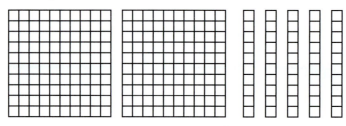

   A 25×5 **B** 50×5 **C** 20×5 **D** 100×3

14. Find each quotient:
(86)
   a. $28 \div 4$ **b.** $42 \div 6$ **c.** $54 \div 9$

15. $12.45 - $5.75
(26)

16. 215×3
(97)

17. $(70 \times 5) - 50$
(78, 92)

18. $470 + 63 + 7 + 86$
(24)

19. Refer to this rectangle to answer the questions that follow:

(58, 63)

a. The rectangle is how many centimeters long?

b. The rectangle is how many centimeters wide?

c. What is the area of the rectangle?

d. What is the perimeter of the rectangle?

20. Mark and two friends want to use the swing during a 15-minute
(89) recess. To find out how long each of them could use the swing, Mark divided 15 minutes by 3. What should Mark's answer be?

Real-World Connection

Carlos wants to buy a bottle of apple juice from the vending machine. A bottle of apple juice costs $0.75. He has five coins that total exactly $0.75. What five coins does Carlos have? You may use money manipulatives to help you find the answer.

LESSON 99

• Effects of Estimation

facts   Power Up 99

jump start   Count up by 4s from 0 to 48.
                 Count up by 8s from 0 to 96.

                 It is night. The plane will depart at 13 minutes before 9:00. Draw hands on your clock to show the departure time. Write the time in digital form.

                 The daily high on Wednesday was 32°C. That night, the low temperature was 17 degrees cooler. Mark your thermometer to show the low temperature.

mental math

a. Number Sense: $50 - 18$

b. Time: The music lesson lasted 35 minutes. The science lesson lasted 35 minutes. Altogether, how many minutes were the two lessons?

c. Number Sense: 9×50

d. Money: Fiona had $8.50. Then she spent $1.30. How much money did Fiona have left?

problem solving

During a storm, we hear thunder after we see lightning. We can tell how far away lightning is by how long it takes us to hear the thunder after we see the lightning. The sound of thunder travels about 1 mile every 5 seconds. Make a table to show how many seconds it takes the sound of thunder to travel 1, 2, 3, and 4 miles. Use the table to find how far away lightning occurs if we hear thunder 20 seconds after we see lightning.

Miles	Seconds
1	5

When we estimate an arithmetic answer, we often need to know whether our estimate is a little more than or a little less than the exact answer.

Example 1

Deb bought 4 gallons of milk for $2.89 per gallon. To estimate the total cost, Deb multiplied 4 × $3. Will Deb's estimate be greater than or less than the exact cost?

Deb rounded up the price of the milk. The rounded price is greater than the exact price.

$$\$3.00 > \$2.89$$

Therefore, **Deb's estimate will be greater than the exact price.**

$$
\begin{array}{ccc}
\text{Estimate} & > & \text{Exact} \\
\$3.00 & & \$2.89 \\
\underline{\times \qquad 4} & & \underline{\times \qquad 4} \\
\$12.00 & & \$11.56 \\
\end{array}
$$

Example 2

There are 26 students in each of the three classrooms. Nelson estimates that the total number of students in the classrooms is about 75 since 3 × 25 = 75. How does Nelson's estimate compare with the exact number of students?

Nelson used compatible numbers to estimate the total number of students. To multiply he chose a number less than the actual number of students in each classroom.

$$25 < 26$$

Therefore, **Nelson's estimate is less than the actual number of students.**

$$
\begin{array}{ccc}
\text{Estimate} & < & \text{Exact} \\
25 & & 26 \\
\underline{\times \; 3} & & \underline{\times \; 3} \\
75 & & 78 \\
\end{array}
$$

Evaluate Sam wants to buy four books for $3.29 each. He estimates that he will need $12 for the books. If Sam has $12, will he have enough money to buy all 4 books? Explain your answer.

Lesson Practice

a. Sal bought a gallon of milk for $2.89 and a box of cereal for $3.95. He added $3 and $4 to estimate the total price. Is Sal's estimate greater than or less than the exact price?

b. Thom is paid $9.15 per hour. Estimate how much Thom is paid for working 8 hours. Is your estimate greater than or less than Thom's exact pay?

Written Practice Distributed and Integrated

1. From goal line to goal line on a football field is 100 yards. How
(34, 91) many feet is 100 yards?

2. Formulate Write a multiplication fact that shows
(53) how many small squares cover this rectangle.

3. Analyze John bought a pair of sunglasses for $7.99
(99) and a bottle of sunscreen for $8.90. He added $8 and $9 to estimate the total price. Is John's estimate greater than or less than the exact price?

4. A plastic bag full of sweatshirts weighs 10 pounds. Two sweatshirts
(98) weigh about a pound. About how many shirts are in the bag?

5. Multiply:
(97)
  a. 2 × 227   **b.** 3 × $260

6. $8.95 + $2.89 + 43¢
(22, 24)

7. Multiple Choice Which pair of fractions below is not
(47) equivalent?

  A $\frac{1}{2}, \frac{2}{4}$ **B** $\frac{2}{3}, \frac{3}{4}$ **C** $\frac{2}{6}, \frac{1}{3}$ **D** $\frac{3}{6}, \frac{1}{2}$

8. A gallon of punch is how many cups of punch?
(87)

9. Estimate the difference when $2.95 is subtracted from $12.05.
(96)

10. How many small cubes were used to make this big cube?
(73)

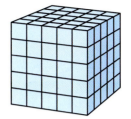

11. Use compatible numbers to estimate the products in parts **a** and **b**.
(94)

    a. Estimate the product of 252 × 2.

    b. Estimate the product of 23 × 3.

12. Multiply:
(84)

    a. 4 × 40   **b.** 6 × 62

13. Trace this figure. Then draw two lines of symmetry.
(Inv. 9)

14. (25 + 75) × 4   **15.** 75 × 3
(92)   (84)

16. 1,306 − 567   **17.** 708 × 6
(28)   (97)

18. Find each quotient:
(86)

    a. 56 ÷ 8   **b.** 45 ÷ 9   **c.** 63 ÷ 7

19. Find the lengths of these segments to the nearest centimeter:
(79)

    a. ————————————

    b. ——————————————

20. Write a fraction with a numerator of 2 and a denominator of 5. Then use words to name the fraction you wrote.
(41)

• Multiplying Dollars and Cents

 **Power Up**

facts	Power Up 100
jump start	Count up by 6s from 0 to 72. Count up by 12s from 0 to 144.

Write these amounts of liquid in order from least to greatest:

2 pints   2 gallons   2 cups   2 quarts

$\underline{012}$ Label the number line by tenths from 0 to 1. (Show these numbers: 0, $\frac{1}{10}$, $\frac{2}{10}$, $\frac{3}{10}$, $\frac{4}{10}$, and so on.)

mental math

a. Number Sense: 54 + 60

b. Geometry: One cube has 6 faces. How many faces do 3 cubes have?

c. Estimation: Round 355 to the nearest ten.

d. Patterns: Find the missing number in this pattern:

144	132	120	_____	96	84

problem solving

Look for a pattern in these figures. Which figure does *not* belong? Explain your answer.

 A   B   C   D

In Lesson 92 we learned how to multiply three-digit numbers. We multiply dollars and cents the same way. After multiplying, we must remember to write the dollar sign and decimal point in the product.

Example 1

Sergio bought 3 tickets to the movie for $7.75 each. What was the total price of the 3 tickets?

We can find the total by adding or by multiplying.

$$
\begin{array}{r}
\overset{2\ 1}{\ \$7.75} \\
\$7.75 \\
+\ \$7.75 \\
\hline
\$23.25
\end{array}
\qquad
\begin{array}{r}
\overset{2\ 1}{\$7.75} \\
\times\qquad 3 \\
\hline
\$23.25
\end{array}
$$

Notice that we write the dollar sign and the decimal point as part of the answer. The total was **$23.25.**

Example 2

Gwen put 430 pennies in a jar. She estimated that she would need 6 times as many pennies to fill the jar completely. She multiplied $4.30 by 6 to estimate the value of the pennies in the jar. What is the product?

We multiply 0 pennies by 6. The product is 0, which we record. Next, we multiply 3 dimes by 6. The product is 18 dimes, which is 1 dollar and 8 dimes.

$$
\begin{array}{r}
\overset{1}{\$4.30} \\
\times\qquad 6 \\
\hline
80
\end{array}
$$

Finally, we multiply 4 dollars by 6. The product is 24 dollars. We add the dollar of dimes to make 25 dollars. The final product is **$25.80.**

$$
\begin{array}{r}
\overset{1}{\$4.30} \\
\times\qquad 6 \\
\hline
\$25.80
\end{array}
$$

Analyze Gwen estimated that the value of the pennies in the jar would be $25.80. How many pennies would be equal to $25.80?

Find each product.

a. 6 × $4.00   **b.** 7 × $3.05

c. 5 × $3.40   **d.** 4 × $2.35

Written Practice   *Distributed and Integrated*

1. There were 32 books on the table arranged in four equal stacks.
(90)   How many books were in each stack?

2. Rob bought 5 bottles of juice for $2.29 per bottle. To estimate the
(99)   total cost, Rob multiplied 5 × $2. Will Rob's estimate be greater
than or less than the exact cost?

3. **Formulate** Change this addition to a multiplication and find
(54)   the total:

$$4 \text{ qt} + 4 \text{ qt} + 4 \text{ qt} + 4 \text{ qt} + 4 \text{ qt}$$

4. **Model** The upper case letter A has one line of
(Inv. 9)   symmetry. Write the upper case letter B and show
its line of symmetry.

5. Estimate the difference of $14.92 and $7.21.
(96)

6. Use a pencil and a centimeter ruler to draw a segment 5 cm long.
(79)   Then measure the segment with an inch ruler. The 5-cm segment
is about how many inches long?

7. What is the geometric name for this solid? Describe
(75,   the shape of its top and bottom faces.
Inv. 8)

8. $1.51 × 4
(100)

9. **Represent** Use symbols to write the mixed number
(46)   two and two thirds.

10. If 5 × 12 = 60, then what does 12 × 5 equal?
(55)

11. Gia is looking at a map. Each inch on the map represents 5 miles.
(Inv. 4) Two schools that are 4 inches apart on the map are how many
miles apart?

12. What length is halfway between 1 inch and $1\frac{1}{2}$ inch? Use your
(35) ruler to find the answer.

13. One plane ticket costs $415. Estimate the cost of two plane
(93) tickets.

14. Multiply:
(78, 97, 100) **a.** 5 × 40   **b.** 3 × 260   **c.** 4 × $1.25

15. (Analyze) Use mental math to find the sum. Begin by adding
(92) pairs of compatible numbers.

$$50 + 90 + 110$$

16. Find each quotient:
(86) **a.** 32 ÷ 4   **b.** 48 ÷ 6   **c.** 63 ÷ 9

17. 4 × 60
(78)

18. 376 + 28 + 205 + 9
(24)

19. Find the missing number: $n - 3 = 15$
(40)

20. If 1 box of pens has a mass of about 100 grams, then 6 boxes of
(98) pens have a mass of about how many grams? Make a table to
help find the answer.

Focus on

• Evaluating Estimates

In Lesson 99 we learned one way to evaluate estimates we make. In this investigation, we will talk about other ways to evaluate estimates, and we will evaluate the estimates we made on **Lesson Activity 31.**

Ian counted 198 words on one page of his science lesson.

1. How could he estimate the number of words in the whole lesson if it is six pages long?

Jerry, Talia, and Ian each estimated the number of words in the entire lesson. Their estimates are shown below:

Student	Estimate
Ian	1,200
Jerry	1,300
Talia	1,000

2. How can they find who made the closest estimate?

The students counted the words on all six pages of the science lesson and found that there are 1,245 words altogether.

3. Whose estimate was closest?

Evaluating Estimates

In this activity, we will count the pennies in the penny jar we first saw in Lesson 91 and compare the estimates we made on **Lesson Activity 31** to the actual number of pennies.

4. Before counting pennies, make your last estimate of the number of pennies in the jar. Record the estimate on your activity sheet. Also write your name and last estimate on a piece of scrap paper and give it to your teacher.

5. Work in pairs to count the pennies your teacher gives you. Put groups of 50 pennies into penny rolls. Neatly stack or organize any extra pennies.

6. A volunteer should write the numbers of pennies counted by each pair of students on the board or overhead. Then add them together as a class to find the total number. How many pennies were in the jar altogether?

7. With the class, sort the numbers in the "First Estimate" envelope until you find the closest estimate to the actual count.

8. Repeat the sorting for the "Last Estimate."

9. Which collection of estimates is closer to the actual count, the first estimate or the last estimate?

10. Look at **Lesson Activity 31.** Which one of your estimates was closest to the actual count?

11. (**Justify**) How do you decide which number is closest?

12. Which estimation strategy helped you improve your estimate the most?

LESSON 101

• Dividing Two-Digit Numbers

facts   Power Up 101

jump start
Count up by halves from 5 to 10.
Count up by fourths from 4 to 6.

Write a multiplication and division fact family using the numbers 8, 4, and 32.

Draw a $3\frac{1}{4}$-inch segment on your worksheet. Then make it $2\frac{1}{4}$ inches longer. What is the total length of the segment?

mental math

a. Number Sense: $98 - 39$

b. Number Sense: $83 + 47$

c. Calendar: How many months are in 7 years?

d. Algebra: This table shows costs for bookmarks at the school fair. How much do 5 bookmarks cost?

Bookmark	1	2	3	4	5
Cost	11¢	22¢	33¢	44¢	___

problem solving

The number 10 is a triangular number because 10 objects can be arranged in the shape of a triangle. Notice how the number of objects in each row of the triangle increases:

```
       ●              1 dot
------------------------------
     ●   ●            2 dots       1 + 2 + 3 + 4 = 10
------------------------------
   ●   ●   ●          3 dots
------------------------------
 ●   ●   ●   ●        4 dots
------------------------------
```

Use this pattern to find the number of dots in a triangular shape with 8 rows of dots.

Visit www.
SaxonMath.com/
Int3Activities
for a calculator
activity.

To sort a number of objects into equal groups, we can divide. In previous lessons, we learned how to divide using pictures, manipulatives, and the multiplication table. In this lesson, we will learn how to divide two-digit numbers using pencil and paper.

Think about how to answer the question in the following story:

Dan has a stack of 90 baseball cards. He wants to put the cards into a photo album. Each page of the album can hold 6 cards. How many pages can he fill?

As Dan begins putting 6 cards on each page of the photo album, the number of cards in the stack becomes less and less.

$$
\begin{array}{r}
90 \\
-6 \\
\hline
84 \\
-6 \\
\hline
78 \\
-6 \\
\hline
72 \\
\end{array}
\begin{array}{l}
\\
\text{6 cards on first page} \\
\\
\text{6 cards on second page} \\
\\
\text{6 cards on third page} \\
\\
\end{array}
$$

We could continue subtracting 6 cards until all the cards have been put into the album. A faster way to subtract the same number over and over is to divide. Here is how we can write the division:

$$6\overline{)90}$$

First, we look at the digit in the tens place. We think, "How many groups of 6 are there in 9?"

$$\overset{1}{6\overline{)90}}$$

We see that we can make 1 group of 6. So we write a 1 above the 9.

We also see that we have 3 circles left over. We show this by subtracting 6 from 9.

$$
\begin{array}{r}
\overset{1}{6\overline{)90}} \\
-6 \\
\hline
3 \\
\end{array}
$$

Next, we bring down the digit in the ones place.

$$
\begin{array}{r}
1 \\
6{\overline{\smash{)}90}} \\
\underline{-6\downarrow} \\
30
\end{array}
$$

We think, "How many groups of 6 are there in 30?"

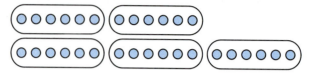

$$
\begin{array}{r}
15 \\
6{\overline{\smash{)}90}} \\
\underline{-6} \\
30
\end{array}
$$

We see that we can make 5 groups of 6. So we write a 5 in the quotient.

We also see that there are no circles left over. We show this by subtracting 30 from 30.

$$
\begin{array}{r}
15 \\
6{\overline{\smash{)}90}} \\
\underline{-6} \\
30 \\
\underline{-30} \\
0
\end{array}
$$

The quotient is 15. This means that Dan can fill 15 pages. We can be sure we are correct by multiplying 6 × 15.

$$
\begin{array}{r}
3 \\
15 \text{ pages} \\
\times \quad 6 \text{ cards per page} \\
\hline
90 \text{ cards}
\end{array}
$$

Formulate Write another story problem for the division 6$\overline{\smash{)}90}$.

Example 1

Maria is putting a collection of 48 postcards into a photo album. Each page can hold 3 postcards. How many pages can she fill?

We can find the number of pages Maria can fill by dividing 48 by 3. We find that the number of pages is **16.** To make sure our answer is correct, we multiply:

$$
\begin{array}{r}
16 \\
3{\overline{\smash{)}48}} \\
\underline{-3\downarrow} \\
18 \\
\underline{-18} \\
0
\end{array}
$$

$$
\begin{array}{r}
1 \\
16 \text{ pages} \\
\times \quad 3 \text{ postcards per page} \\
\hline
48 \text{ postcards}
\end{array}
$$

Example 2

Rob has a handful of nickels that total 80¢. How many nickels does Rob have?

To find the number of nickels, we divide 80 by 5. We find that Rob has **16 nickels.** We can multiply or quickly count by 5s to 80 to be sure that 16 nickels is 80¢.

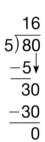

$$\begin{array}{r} 16 \\ 5\overline{)80} \\ -5\downarrow \\ \hline 30 \\ -30 \\ \hline 0 \end{array}$$

Lesson Practice

a. To display his rock collection Juan glues 5 rocks on each card. How many cards does he need for 75 rocks?

b. Shelley collected 54 shells that she will store in plastic bags. If she puts 3 shells in each bag, how many bags of shells will she have?

c. If 76 horn players line up in 4 rows, how many players will be in each row?

Written Practice   *Distributed and Integrated*

1. Hanna arranged 36 books in stacks of nine books each. How many stacks of books did Hanna make?
(90)

2. **Analyze** Lora wants to buy 3 folders for $2.39 each. She has $8. Estimate the total price of all three folders using compatible numbers. Does Lora have enough to pay for all three folders?
(94, 99)

3. 78 ÷ 6
(101)

4. 54 ÷ 3
(101)

5. Find the missing number: $24 - w = 3$
(40)

6. Use a pencil and a ruler to draw a segment 4 inches long. Measure the segment with a metric ruler. A 4-inch segment is about how many centimeters long?
(35, 79)

7. **Conclude** Simon began counting by hundreds:
(2, 32)

"100, 200, 300, 400, 500, . . ."

What will be the fifteenth number Simon says?

8. **Formulate** Write two multiplication facts and two division facts
(86)   using the numbers 8, 4, and 32.

9. What length is halfway between $1\frac{1}{4}$ inches and $1\frac{3}{4}$ inches?
(35)

10. A bike shop bought four *Midas Mountaineer* bicycles from the
(60, 97)   factory for $248 each. What was the total cost of the four bikes?

11. Draw a square with sides $\frac{1}{2}$ inch long. Then trace around the
(35, 58)   square with your pencil. How far is it around the square?

12. Marlinda is putting photos in a family album. She places
(90)   36 photos equally on 6 pages. How many photos does she
     place on each page?

13. How many small cubes were used to build this
(72)   rectangular solid?

14. From 1492 to 1992 was how many years?
(39)

15. Multiply:
(84,
100)   **a.** 6 × 24   **b.** 5 × $2.30

16. Half of a circle is also called a semicircle. Copy this
(Inv. 7)   semicircle and show its line of symmetry.

17. Find each quotient.
(86)   **a.** 28 ÷ 7   **b.** 56 ÷ 8   **c.** 36 ÷ 9

18. Estimate the sum of $5.17, $6.98, and $8.89.
(96)

19. Write these fractions in order from least to greatest:
(49)
$$\frac{3}{4} \qquad \frac{1}{2} \qquad \frac{2}{3}$$

20. **Multiple Choice** Which symbol goes in the box: 24 □ 2 = 12?
(86)   **A** +   **B** −   **C** ×   **D** ÷

• Sorting

Power Up

facts

facts   Power Up 102

jump start
Count up by 11s from 0 to 132.
Count up by 5s from 9 to 59.

Write these fractions in order from least to greatest:

$$\frac{1}{3} \qquad \frac{1}{4} \qquad \frac{4}{5} \qquad \frac{1}{2}$$

A pair of shin guards costs $2.89. Marcy wants to buy 3 pairs. Write a number sentence to estimate the cost of the 3 pairs altogether.

mental math

a. Measurement: Which of these units would you most likely use to measure the amount of lemonade in a glass?

   ounces   pounds   gallons   feet

b. Number Sense: $40 + 35 + 7$

c. Number Sense: $480 - 110$

d. Time: It is afternoon. The first clock shows the time the spelling bee began. The second clock shows the time the bee ended. How many minutes did the spelling bee last?

problem solving

A *palindrome* is a number or word that is the same whether it is written forward or backward. The word "noon" is a palindrome. The number 11 is also a palindrome.

Predict the number of two-digit palindromes that are between the numbers 10 and 100. Then list the palindromes to check your prediction.

People who have collections usually organize their collections in a logical way. They sort their collections by deciding what is similar and what is different.

Example 1

Sharon collects buttons. She has sorted the buttons into three groups. What rule does Sharon use to sort the buttons? In which group will she place the new button?

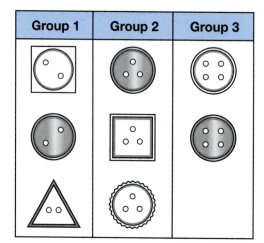

We look at the buttons in each group to see what is the same. We look at the buttons in different groups to see what is different. We see that the buttons in the same group have the same number of holes, and that the buttons in different groups have a different number of holes.

Sharon puts a button in Group 1 if it has 2 holes.

She puts a button in Group 2 if it has 3 holes.

She puts a button in Group 3 if it has 4 holes.

So, Sharon will place the **new button in Group 2.**

Example 2

Sort the following numbers into two groups: even numbers and odd numbers.

26, 73, 54, 49, 31, 80

All even numbers end with a ones digit that is even. We make two lists.

Even numbers: 26, 54, 80

Odd numbers: 73, 49, 31

(List) List five more numbers that belong in the even numbers group. List five more numbers that belong in the odd numbers group.

Lesson Practice

a. Describe the sorting rule for the numbers in these two groups.

Group A: 10, 60, 40, 20, 70

Group B: 12, 23, 74, 31, 58

b. Jill has a collection of action figures. Describe some ways she could sort the figures.

Written Practice   *Distributed and Integrated*

1. Twenty-four children separated into three teams with an equal
(90) number of children on each team. How many children were on each team?

2. (Classify) Sort these numbers into two groups: even numbers
(88, 102) and odd numbers.

75, 23, 98, 43, 82, 11, 90, 86

3. $(275 + 375) - 200$
(92)

4. (Analyze) The recipe called for one cup of milk. If the recipe is
(87) doubled, how many pints of milk should be used?

5. Use your pencil and a ruler to draw a segment $\frac{2}{4}$ of an inch long.
(35, 47) What is another fraction name for $\frac{2}{4}$ of an inch?

6. **Model** Draw an array of 27 Xs with 3 Xs in each row. How many
(57, 86) Xs are in each column of your array?

7. Polly calculated that $3 \times (4 \times 5) = 60$. What is $(3 \times 4) \times 5$?
(92)

8. Write 875,632 in expanded notation.
(11)

9. What number is halfway between 300 and 600?
(33)

10. **Explain** Kiondre and John have two large jars that are the same
(91) size. One jar is full of pennies. The other jar has 300 pennies and
is about $\frac{1}{4}$ full. How can Kiondre and John estimate the number of
pennies in the jar that is full? Estimate the number of pennies in
the full jar.

11. Randall has 3 extra large boxes of crayons. Each box contains
(60, 97) 108 crayons. How many crayons does Randall have in all?

12. $3 \times 5 \times 8$
(77)

13. Describe the sorting rule for the numbers in these two groups.
(102)

                Group A: 0, 1, 4, 5, 8

                Group B: 10, 32, 35, 57, 79

14. From 1776 to 1826 was how many years?
(39)

15. Multiply:
(84,
100) **a.** 7×14 **b.** $3 \times \$2.50$

16. Estimate the cost of 7 sleeping bags for $78 each.
(93)

17. Find each quotient.
(86)
    a. $30 \div 6$ **b.** $40 \div 5$ **c.** $64 \div 8$

18. $76 \div 2$ **19.** $81 \div 3$
(101)   (101)

20. Cheryl bought a gallon of milk for $3.19 and two boxes of cereal
(96) for $4.89 each. Estimate the total cost of the three items.

• **Ordering Numbers Through 9,999**

Power Up

facts	Power Up 103
jump start	Count up by odd numbers from 1 to 25. Count up by even numbers from 2 to 30.
	It is 19 minutes after 8 in the morning. Draw hands on your clock to show the time. Write the time in digital form.
	The temperature in the school library is 21°C. It is 14 degrees cooler on the playground. Mark your thermometer to show the temperature on the playground.
mental math	**a. Time:** The school lunch period lasts 35 minutes. Recess after lunch lasts 25 minutes. Altogether, how long are lunch and recess?
	b. Number Sense: $3 \times 4 \times 4$
	c. Money: $3.30 − 99¢
	d. Measurement: Lindsey is making a lid for her jewelry box. The lid is 9 inches long and 5 inches wide. What is the area of the lid?

5 in.

9 in.

problem solving	Sera made up a riddle to tell people her age. She says that she is 14 years younger than the number of months in 2 years. How old is Sera?

We arrange numbers in order when we write or say the numbers from least to greatest (or from greatest to least). We use place value to help us order numbers.

Example 1

Write these numbers in order from least to greatest.

| 3,672 | 3,712 | 372 |

Writing the numbers in a column can help us order the numbers. We line up digits with the same place values.

Thousands	Hundreds	Tens	Ones
3	6	7	2
3	7	1	2
	3	7	2

We see that 372 is least. Both 3,672 and 3,712 have 3 in the thousands place; so we compare the digits in the hundreds place. Since 6 is less than 7, the order is:

| 372 | 3,672 | 3,712 |

Example 2

A mail carrier might arrange mail for a street using these two rules:

1. **Order mail with even-numbered addresses from least to greatest.**

2. **Order mail with odd-numbered addresses from greatest to least.**

Follow these two rules to arrange these "addresses" into an even numbered column and an odd-numbered column.

| 5327 | 5342 | 5353 | 5339 | 5352 | 5348 |

We start by sorting the addresses into an even-numbered group and an odd-numbered group.

Even: 5342, 5352, 5348

Odd: 5327, 5353, 5339

Then we order the even numbers in a column from least to greatest. Finally, we order the odd numbers in a column from greatest to least.

Even Addresses	Odd Addresses
5342	5353
5348	5339
5352	5327

Lesson Practice

a. The birth years in Roger's family are as follows:

1998   2002   1976   1974

Arrange these years from earliest to latest.

b. In 2000, the population of Blanco County was 8,418. The population of Castro County was 8,285. The population of Archer County was 8,854. List the names of the 3 counties in order from least population to greatest.

c. Robinson compared the price of a game at three different stores. Here are the prices:

$18.85 $19.25 $17.98

Arrange the prices in order from least to greatest.

Written Practice   *Distributed and Integrated*

1. Burgess arranged twenty-four quarters into stacks with
(90)   four quarters in each stack. How many stacks of quarters did Burgess form?

2. Draw a polygon with six sides. What is the geometric name for
(67)   the figure you drew?

3. $75 \div 5$
(101)

4. $88 \div 4$
(101)

5. Write an uppercase D and show its line of symmetry.
(Inv. 9)

6. Compare an inch ruler with a metric ruler. A 1-foot-long ruler is
(35, 79)   about how many centimeters long?

7. There are 25 textbooks on the shelf. Can the books be separated
(88) into two equal stacks?

8. $84 \div 7$ **9.** $56 \div 8$
(86)   *(86)*

10. Arrange these numbers from least to greatest:
(103)

$$2{,}654 \quad 2{,}913 \quad 2{,}987 \quad 2{,}398$$

11. Use words to write the sum of $750 and $840.
(16, 32)

12. Nadia collected 294 soda cans for a class recycling project.
(93) Raul collected about 3 times as many cans as Nadia collected.
Estimate the number of cans Raul collected.

13. Draw a rectangle that is one inch long and $\frac{1}{2}$ inch wide. Trace
(52, 58) around the rectangle. How many inches is it around the
rectangle?

14. Find the missing numbers:
(9)
  a. $6 + a = 24$ **b.** $6 \times c = 24$

15. Multiply: $6 \times \$4.20$
(100)

16. Draw a cube and a rectangular prism. How are the figures alike?
(Inv. 8) How are they different?

17. Find each quotient.
(86)
  a. $27 \div 3$ **b.** $45¢ \div 5$ **c.** $\$36 \div 6$

18. $\$10.00 - (\$5.85 + 89¢)$
(28, 92)

19. Shaundra ran a 3-kilometer race. How many meters are in
(79) 3 kilometers?

20. Describe the sorting rule for the numbers in these two groups:
(102)

Group A: 11, 25, 36, 48, 59

Group B: 125, 238, 374, 431, 578

- **Sorting Geometric Shapes**

Power Up

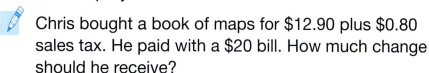

facts   Power Up 104

jump start   Count up by square numbers from 1 to 144.
Count up by 10s from 9 to 99.

Chris bought a book of maps for $12.90 plus $0.80 sales tax. He paid with a $20 bill. How much change should he receive?

Write a multiplication and division fact family using the numbers 5, 9, and 45.

mental math

a. Estimation: Jerry will buy 4 bars of soap for 97¢ each. Estimate the total cost to the nearest dollar.

b. Number Sense: $900 - 450$

c. Number Sense: 400×2

d. Measurement: How many quarts are in a gallon?

problem solving   The kickoff to start the football game was at 1:00 p.m. During halftime, Tyrone looked at his watch and saw that it was 2:30 p.m.

Start of game

Halftime

What is a reasonable prediction for the time the football game will end? Explain how you made your prediction.

We sort or **classify** shapes by how they are alike or different. Look at the shapes below.

Discuss How are they alike? How are they different? How could we sort them into two different groups?

Example 1

Sort these figures into polygons and figures that are not polygons. Then describe your sorting rule.

We separate the figures into two groups.

Polygons   Not Polygons

Polygons are flat, closed shapes with straight sides. Shapes with curved sides are not polygons.

Example 2

These three-dimensional figures are sorted into two groups. Describe the sorting rule.

Solids

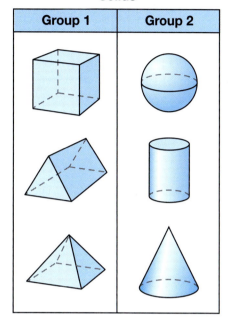

The solids in Group 1 have straight edges, and every face is a polygon. The solids in Group 2 have at least one curved surface.

Classify What is another rule we could use to sort these figures?

Lesson Practice

a. Sort these polygons into two groups: triangles and quadrilaterals.

b. Describe how the solids in Group 1 are alike. Describe how the solids in Group 1 are different than the solids in Group 2.

Group 1	Group 2

Written Practice — *Distributed and Integrated*

1. In Millie's backyard, 48 stalks of corn grow in 6 equal rows with an equal number of stalks in each row. How many stalks grow in each row?
(90)

2. Last year Kevin was 114 cm tall. This year he is 121 cm tall. How many centimeters did Kevin grow in a year?
(39)

3. Draw an array of 20 dots with 4 dots in each column. How many dots are in each row?
(57)

4. Estimate each answer by rounding each number to the nearest hundred dollars before you add or subtract.
(30)
    a. $396 + $419   **b.** $587 − $259

5. Find the missing number: $18 - m = 3$
(40)

6. How many grams equal one kilogram?
(80)

7. **Conclude** Simon began counting by thousands:
(2, 32)

1,000, 2,000, 3,000, 4,000, …

What will be the fifteenth number Simon says? Use words to write the answer.

8. **Multiple Choice** Which of the following equals one quart?
(87)

A 3 cups   **B** 4 pints   **C** 2 pints   **D** 2 cups

9. If 56 ÷ 7 = 8, then what does 56 ÷ 8 equal?
(86)

10. This rectangle is partly covered with small squares.
(63) Altogether, how many small squares would cover the rectangle?

11. **Justify** Roderick has a bag of 10 marbles. There are 5 blue
(50) marbles. The rest of the marbles are red. Is drawing a red marble less likely, equally likely, or more likely than drawing a blue marble? How do you know?

12. A year is 365 days. Find the number of days in 4 years by
(97) multiplying 365 by 4. Then add one day for a leap year. Show your work.

13. (24 + 80) − 44
(92)

14. **Model** Angela planted 24 flowers in 4 rows. How many flowers
(85) were in each row? Draw a picture to represent the problem.

15. Multiply:
(100)   **a.** 5 × $0.24   **b.** 4 × $0.24

16. There are 70 crackers in each package. Each box contains
(78) 4 packages. How many crackers are in one box?

17. Find each quotient.
(86)   **a.** 36¢ ÷ 4   **b.** 36 ÷ 6   **c.** 35 ÷ 7

18. Write 6,877 in expanded form.
(32)

19. Use compatible numbers to estimate the total price of 8 sandwiches
(94) for $2.56 each.

20. Multiply: 721 × 2
(97)

Real-World Connection

Li entered a reading contest every year for four years. He read one book each month for the first year. If he read the same number of books each year, how many books did he read in four years?

LESSON
105

• **Diagrams for Sorting**

facts   Power Up 105

jump start   Count up by 3s from 0 to 45 and then back down to 0.
Count up by 9s from 0 to 108 and then back down to 0.

Write these years in order from earliest to latest:

1977   1899   1957   1999

Draw a rectangular prism on your worksheet. How many vertices does a rectangular prism have?

mental math   **a. Fact Family:** Find the missing number in this fact family:

$$5 \times \square = 20 \qquad 20 \div \square = 5$$
$$\square \times 5 = 20 \qquad 20 \div 5 = \square$$

b. Number Sense: $687 - 200$

c. Measurement: How many yards are equal to 9 feet?

d. Number Sense: Which point below represents the number $8\frac{1}{2}$?

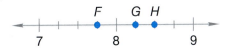

problem solving   Twenty-three students are taking a field trip to the zoo. Each car can hold 4 students. How many cars will be needed for all 23 students? Will all the cars carry the same number of students? Explain your answer.

New Concept

Visit www.
SaxonMath.com/
Int3Activities for
an online activity.

We can use circles to help us sort collections of things.

Example 1

Draw two circles. Label one circle "Even numbers" and the other circle "Odd numbers." Then write these numbers in the correct circles.

15, 26, 7, 14, 30, 21

We draw and label the circles and write the numbers.

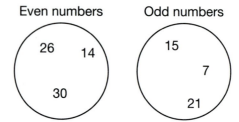

A **Venn diagram** is a special type of sorting circle. The circles in a Venn diagram overlap. The overlap part shows what the groups have in common.

Example 2

Copy the Venn diagram and write the following numbers in the correct parts of the circles.

15, 18, 20, 24, 25

First, we sort the numbers into two groups.

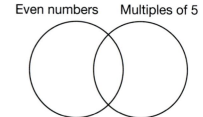

Even Numbers	18, **20**, 24
Multiples of 5	15, **20**, 25

Notice that 20 belongs in both groups. On the Venn diagram, we write 20 in the space where the two circles overlap. Then we place the other numbers in the correct circle.

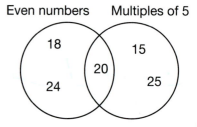

Example 3

Copy the Venn diagram and then draw the following polygons in the correct parts of the circle. One circle is labeled "P" for parallel sides and one circle is labeled "R" for right angle.

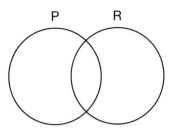

 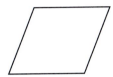

The triangle has a right angle but no parallel sides. The parallelogram has parallel sides but no right angles. Since the square has parallel sides and right angles, it is in both circles.

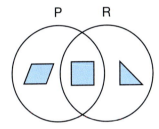

Analyze Where would you place an isosceles triangle in this diagram?

Lesson Practice

a. Draw two circles that do not overlap. Label one circle "Quadrilaterals" and the other circle "Triangles." Then draw these shapes in the correct circles.

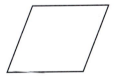

b. Draw a Venn diagram. Label one circle "Q" for quadrilaterals and the other circle "R" for shapes that have a right angle. Then draw these shapes in the correct parts of the circles.

Written Practice *Distributed and Integrated*

1. If each foot of molding costs 75¢, then what is the cost for each
(100) yard of molding?

2. Forty-one students stood in two lines as equally as possible. How many students were in each line?
(88)

3. Write an uppercase H. Show its two lines of symmetry.
(Inv. 9)

4. The mass of one large paper clip is about one gram. The mass of two dozen large paper clips is about how many grams?
(80, 98)

5. Round $395 to the nearest hundred dollars.
(15)

6. What is the geometric name for the shape of the object at right?
(75)

7. Estimate the total price of a salad for $5.62, soup for $3.18, and juice for $1.20.
(96)

8. In what place is the 7 in each of these numbers?
(32)
   a. 3,674   **b.** 367

9. What number is halfway between 500 and 1000?
(33)

500 600 700 800 900 1000

10. Patrick wants to buy 4 yo-yos. Each yo-yo costs $3.23. He estimates that the total price will be $12.00. How does Patrick's estimate compare to the actual price? How do you know?
(99)

11. Draw a square with sides 2 cm long. Trace around the square. All the way around the square is how many centimeters?
(58, 79)

12. Change this addition to a multiplication and find the total:
(54, 78)
       60 sec + 60 sec + 60 sec + 60 sec + 60 sec

13. Find the missing factor: $6 \times n = 48$
(86)

14. 365×3
(97)

15. 400×8
(91)

16. $81 \div 9$
(89)

17. $92 \div 2$
(101)

18. Find each quotient.
(86)
    a. 81 ÷ 9   **b.** 32 ÷ 4   **c.** 42 ÷ 7

19. Find the next three numbers of this sequence:
(2, 91)

             5, 10, 20, 40, _____, _____, _____, · · ·

20. A rectangular floor like the rectangle shown at right will
(63) be covered with square tiles that are 1 foot on each
side. How many tiles will cover the floor?

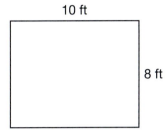

10 ft

8 ft

*Real-World
Connection*

One python is 27 feet long and another is 22 feet long. Is the
total length of the two pythons longer than an anaconda that is
44 feet long? What is the total length of all three snakes? Write
number sentences and use a comparison symbol to show your
answers.

LESSON 106

• Estimating Area, Part 1

 **Power Up**

**jump
start**

 Count up by 4s from 0 to 48 and then back down to 0.
Count up by 8s from 0 to 96 and then back down to 0.

 A board game costs $13.50. A small jigsaw puzzle
costs $6.15. Write a number sentence to estimate how
much they cost altogether.

 Draw a $3\frac{3}{4}$-inch segment on your worksheet. Then
make it $\frac{3}{4}$ inch longer. What is the total length of the
segment?

**mental
math**

a. Number Sense: 25×3

b. Money: $13.40 − $1.99

c. Measurement: Patrick jogged 700 meters and then
walked 190 meters. How many meters did Patrick jog
and walk altogether?

d. Estimation: Use compatible numbers to estimate
47×4.

**problem
solving**

This checkerboard pattern has
9 squares altogether. Five of the
squares are dark and 4 of the squares
are light.

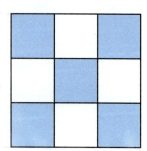

Find the number of dark squares
and light squares in a checkerboard
pattern that has 16 squares
altogether.

A grid of squares can help us estimate the area of a shape. Below we show a figure on a centimeter grid. Each square on the grid is one square centimeter. We can count squares to find the area of the figure.

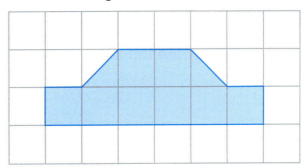

We count 8 whole squares and 2 half squares in the figure. The 2 half squares together equal 1 whole square. So the area of the figure is 9 square centimeters.

Example 1

In this diagram each square equals one square foot. What is the area of the figure on the grid?

We count 10 whole squares and 4 half squares. The 4 half squares together equal 2 whole squares. So we add 10 whole squares and 2 whole squares and get 12 whole squares. The area is **12 square feet.**

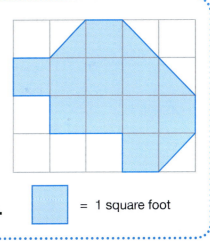

= 1 square foot

Shapes do not always have straight edges or fit exactly onto grids. Monica drew this shape on a piece of centimeter grid paper:

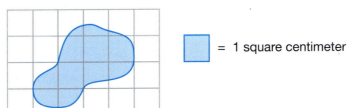

= 1 square centimeter

If a square is fully or mostly shaded, we count it as one whole square. If a square is about half shaded, we count it as a half square. If a square is only barely shaded, we do not count it. We see 5 squares that are whole or almost whole and 4 squares that are about half shaded. The area of Monica's shape is about 7 square centimeters.

Example 2

In this diagram, each square equals one square meter. Estimate the area of the surface of the pond.

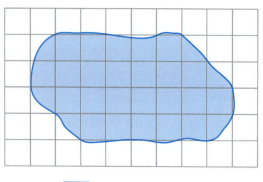

☐ = 1 square meter

To estimate the area, we count each nearly whole square in the figure as a whole square. We count each nearly half square as a half square. We do not count a square if only a small part is in the figure. Altogether, we count 24 whole squares and 6 half squares. The 6 half squares together equal 3 whole squares. The area of the pond is about **27 square meters.**

Lesson Practice   **a.** Find the area of this figure:

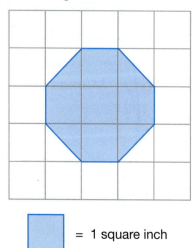

☐ = 1 square inch

b. Estimate the area of this figure:

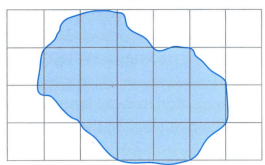

⬜ = 1 square yard

Written Practice
Distributed and Integrated

1. Robert carried the football and gained 11 yards, making a first
(34) down. How many feet is 11 yards?

2. 72 ÷ 3
(101)

3. 575 × 3
(97)

4. Find the next three numbers in this sequence.
(2)
... 600, 700, 800, _____, _____, _____, ...

5. (Connect) Write a multiplication fact that shows the number of
(76) inches in 8 feet.

6. What length is halfway between $1\frac{1}{2}$ inches and 2 inches?
(35)

7. Estimate the product of 487 and 3.
(93)

8. a. Estimate the sum of $608 and $487.
(16, 30)

b. Calculate the sum of $608 and $487.

9. If 11 × 12 = 132, then what does 12 × 11 equal?
(55)

10. Which digit is in the thousands place in each of these numbers?
(32)
a. 23,478   **b.** 375,129

11. **Represent** Draw a picture of a cube. A cube has how many
(75) vertices?

12. A common year is 365 days. Write 365 in expanded form.
(11)

13. Draw a rectangle that is 2 cm long and 1 cm wide.
(58, 63)
     a. What is the perimeter of the rectangle?

     b. What is the area of the rectangle?

14. Multiply:
(100)
     a. 7 × $1.45   **b.** 4 × $0.45

15. Find each quotient.
(86)
     a. 16 ÷ 2   **b.** 36 ÷ 6   **c.** 24 ÷ 3

16. 173 × 7   **17.** 322 × 8
(97)   (97)

18. 500 × 7
(91)

19. Find the next three numbers in this sequence:
(2)
              200, 225, 250, _____, _____, _____, …

20. **Analyze** Find the area of the figure at right.
(106)

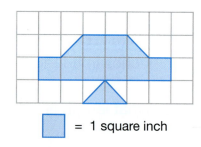

= 1 square inch

Early Finishers
Real-World Connection

Leon asked his brother to find out how many dollars he has in his
pocket by solving a riddle. The first clue is that he has less than
$30. The other clues are that the sum of the digits is four, and
half of the total amount is an odd number of dollars. How much
money does Leon have in his pocket?

• **Drawing Enlargements**

Power Up

facts   Power Up 107

jump start   Count up by 6s from 0 to 72 and then back down to 0.
                   Count up by 12s from 0 to 144 and then back down to 0.

                   It is evening. The train will arrive at 18 minutes before 7.
                   Draw hands on your clock to show the time the train will
                   arrive. Write this time in digital form.

                   The ice at the hockey rink is 22°F. The temperature in
                   the arena is 33 degrees warmer. Mark your thermometer
                   to show the temperature in the arena.

mental math   **a. Number Sense:** $510 + 210$

                   b. Number Sense: 80×9

                   c. Probability: Gracie spins the
                   spinner one time. On which
                   number is the spinner most likely
                   to land?

                   d. Fractions: What fraction of the
                   spinner is labeled with the number 2?

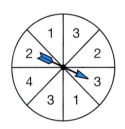

problem solving   Jessica had a long piece of ribbon. She cut an 8-inch
                      length from one end of the ribbon. Then she cut the rest of
                      the ribbon into four equal lengths of 12 inches each. How
                      long was the original piece of ribbon?

Overhead projectors, movie projectors, and photograph laboratories produce a larger image. The larger image is called an *enlargement.* In this activity you will draw an enlargement using two different-sized grids.

Brenda placed a small-grid transparency over the picture of a horse. Then she copied on a large grid what she saw on the small grid. She copied one square at a time until she was done.

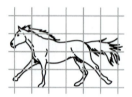 

Activity

Drawing Enlargements

Materials: **Lesson Activity 23,** small-grid transparency, a picture you wish to copy

Tape or clip the small-grid transparency over a picture. Then copy the picture one square at a time onto **Lesson Activity 23.**

Estimate Each square on **Lesson Activity 23** has an area of one square inch. About how many square inches is the area of your enlargement?

Written Practice

Distributed and Integrated

1. Bea drew a marble from the bag without looking.
(45) Is she more likely to draw a blue marble or a black marble?

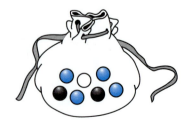

2. The table shows the years in which Matt and his siblings were
(103) born. Write the names in order from oldest to youngest.

Name	Birth Year
Jessica	1993
Matt	1980
Samantha	2000
Paul	1997

3. Draw a square with sides $1\frac{1}{2}$ inches long. What is the perimeter of
(58) the square?

4. Multiple Choice Which of the following does *not* equal 15?
(6, 56)
    A $15 + 0$ **B** $15 - 0$ **C** 15×0 **D** 15×1

5. $90 \div 5$
(101)

6. 111×3
(97)

7. Divide 39 by 3.
(101)

8. Gina puts 10 pennies in each pile. How many piles can Gina make
(90) with 100 pennies?

9. In what place is the 5 in each of these numbers?
(32)
    a. 524   **b.** 36,452

10. Draw a rectangle 3 cm long and 2 cm wide. What is its area?
(63)

11. (**Classify**) Sort these figures into polygons and figures that are
(104) not polygons.

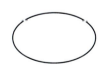 

12. Round $5.58 to the nearest dollar.
(96)

13. 7.50×5
(100)

14. 1.20×3
(100)

15. Find each quotient.
(86)
    a. 56 ÷ 7   **b.** 63 ÷ 7   **c.** 24 ÷ 4

16. (**Classify**) Draw two circles that do not overlap. Label one circle
(105)
"Even Numbers" and the other circle "Odd Numbers." Then write
each of these numbers in the correct circle.

34 88 17 61 81 22 98 23

17. (50 + 50) − 25   **18.** (99 + 1) × 4
(92)   (92)

19. (**Represent**) Draw an obtuse triangle. How many of its angles are
(65, 69)
obtuse? How many are acute?

20. Betty ran 3 miles in 21 minutes. About how long did it take her to
(89)
run one mile?

*Real-World
Connection*

Curt, Bob, and Lee each made a pile of snowballs. Together they
made 15 snowballs. Bob made two more than Lee. Lee made
two more than Curt. How many snowballs did each boy make?
Draw a picture showing what their piles of snowballs would look
like.

LESSON 108

• Estimating Area, Part 2

facts   Power Up 108

jump start    Count up by 5s from 0 to 60 and then back down to 0. Count up by 10s from 0 to 120 and then back down to 0.

Write a multiplication and division fact family using the numbers 9, 8, and 72.

Draw an equilateral triangle. Then draw a line of symmetry.

mental math

a. Number Sense: $5,000 + 900 + 70 + 5$

b. Number Sense: $300 - 199$

c. Number Sense: Each tent uses 6 stakes to hold it to the ground. How many stakes are needed for 4 tents?

d. Measurement: Dana's backyard deck is 8 yards long and 4 yards wide. What is the area of the deck?

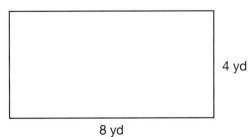

4 yd

8 yd

problem solving   Julian opened a package of printer paper. He put 300 sheets into the black-and-white printer. He put half as many sheets into the color printer. Julian placed the remaining 50 sheets in his desk. How many sheets were in the package of printer paper that Julian opened?

New Concept

We may use transparency grids to help estimate the area of figures.

Justin placed a centimeter grid on a parallelogram and estimated its area. Kylie placed an inch grid on a triangle and estimated its area.

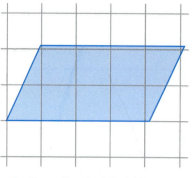

Justin estimated that the area was 8 square centimeters.

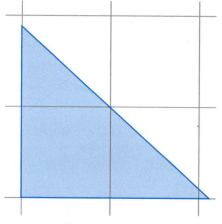

Kylie estimated that the area was 2 square inches.

Analyze Lucy estimated the area of a rectangle using a centimeter grid and again using an inch grid. Was the number of square units greater using the centimeter grid or the inch grid?

Activity

Estimating Area with a Grid

Materials: **Lesson Activity 33,** inch-grid transparency, centimeter-grid transparency

Use transparency grids to help you estimate the area of each figure on **Lesson Activity 33.**

Extension Use transparency grids to find the areas of other shapes in your books or in magazines.

Written Practice
Distributed and Integrated

1. On what number is the spinner least likely to stop?
(50)

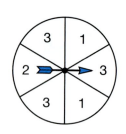

2. The third grade at Larson elementary collected aluminum cans for a recycling drive. Room A collected 312 cans, Room B collected 624 cans, and Room C collected 511 cans. Estimate the total number of cans collected by the third grade.
(30)

3. (Analyze) Is the estimate you made for problem **2** greater than or less than the actual total number of cans?
(99)

4. Use a pencil and a ruler to draw a rectangle that is $1\frac{1}{2}$ inches long and $1\frac{1}{4}$ inches wide. Then show its two lines of symmetry.
(52, Inv. 9)

5. Joel compared the prices of teddy bears at three different stores.
(103)

$18.95 $12.95 $17.95

Arrange the prices in order from least to greatest.

6. A roll of pennies is 50 pennies. A roll of dimes is 50 dimes. A roll of dimes is equal in value to how many rolls of pennies?
(21)

7. A pint is 16 ounces. How many ounces is two quarts?
(84, 87)

8. (Explain) Describe the sorting rule for the fractions in these two groups.
(102)

Group A: $\frac{2}{2}, \frac{3}{3}, \frac{4}{4}, \frac{5}{5}, \frac{6}{6}$

Group B: $\frac{1}{2}, \frac{1}{3}, \frac{1}{4}, \frac{1}{5}, \frac{1}{6}$

9. $(10 + 15) \div 5$
(92)

10. $68 \div 2$
(101)

11. Write these three numbers in order from least to greatest
(103)

1,376   2,147   1,859

12. How many small cubes were used to build this rectangular prism?
(73)

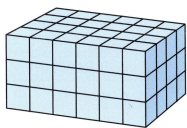

13. 700 × 3
(91)

14. 36 × 4
(84)

15. $0.75 × 6
(100)

16. Cesar counted 153 raisins in a large box. Estimate the number of
(93) raisins that would be in 5 large boxes.

17. $4.50 × 3
(100)

18. 451 × 2
(97)

19. $61 - m = 24$
(40)

20. ⬤ Represent Draw a triangular prism. How many vertices does
(75) it have?

Real-World Connection

Pedro walks 13 blocks every morning to get to school. When he gets to the seventh block, he meets his friend Zack and they walk the rest of the way together. When Pedro and Zack get to the eleventh block, they meet Alyssa and all three walk to school together. How many blocks do Pedro and Zack walk together? Does Pedro walk more blocks alone or with his friends? You may use manipulatives or draw a picture to help you find the answer.

• Points on a Grid

Power Up

facts   Power Up 109

jump start

Count up by 7s from 0 to 84 and then back down to 0.
Count up by 11s from 0 to 132 and then back down to 0.

A fishing rod costs $11.35. Write a number sentence to estimate the cost of 4 fishing rods to the nearest dollar.

Use your ruler to draw a square with a perimeter of 8 inches.

mental math

a. Number Sense: 25×5

b. Number Sense: $87 + 37$

c. Number Sense: $50 \div 2$

d. Patterns: Find the missing number in this pattern:

248	252	256	___	264	268

problem solving

Emma made a pattern with three different shapes. What two shapes are missing in the pattern?

If we number the lines on a grid, we can name any point on the grid with two numbers.

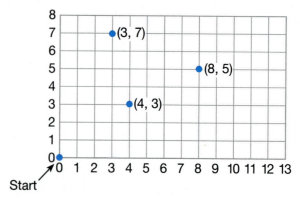

The two numbers in parentheses are called **coordinates.** Coordinates are like the address of a point. They tell us how to get to a point starting from (0, 0). The first number tells us how many spaces we move to the right. The second number tells us how many spaces we move up.

For example, to get to point (4, 3), we move sideways from (0, 0) to the 4. Then we move up 3 spaces. Starting from (0, 0), practice going to the right and then up to (3, 7) and to (8, 5).

Example 1

Write the coordinates of points _A, B,_ and _C_ on this grid.

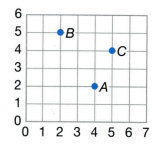

To find the first number of the coordinates, we place our finger on the point and move it straight down until we get to the number on the bottom of the grid. To find the second number of the coordinates, we place our finger on the point again and move it to the left until we get to the number on the side. We write the coordinates in parentheses.

_A_ (4, 2)   **_B_ (2, 5)**   **_C_ (5, 4)**

Example 2

Name the letter of the point that has these coordinates:

   a. (6, 3)

   b. (2, 4)

To find (6, 3) we start at (0, 0) and go sideways to 6. Then we go up 3 spaces. We see point **R.**

To find (2, 4) we go sideways to 2. Then we go up 4 spaces. The letter of the point is **P.**

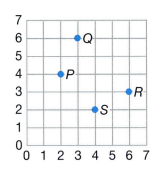

Lesson Practice

Write the coordinates of the following points:

   a. Point *A*

   b. Point *B*

   c. Point *C*

   d. Point *D*

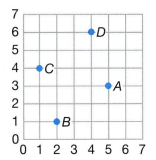

Name the letter of the point that has these coordinates.

   e. (6, 3)

   f. (1, 4)

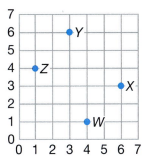

Written Practice   *Distributed and Integrated*

1. Vincent is reading a book that is 286 pages long. He has 72 pages
(40) left to read. How many pages has Vincent already read?

2. Ginger ran to the fence and back twice. If it is 75 yards to the
(84) fence, how far did Ginger run?

3. The distance from Olga's house to school on a map is 2 inches.
(Inv. 4) If each inch on the map represents a distance of 4 miles, how many miles is Olga's house from school?

4. $8 \times 5 \times 7$
(77, 78)

5. **Multiple Choice** Which of the following is the best choice to
(30) estimate $579 - 329$?

    A $600 - 300$ **B** $500 - 300$ **C** $600 - 400$ **D** $500 - 400$

6. Is $8.65 closer to $8 or $9?
(96)

7. **Analyze** A pint of water weighs about one pound.
(87, 98)
    a. About how many pounds does a gallon of water weigh?

    b. About how many pounds does the water in a filled five-gallon
    aquarium weigh?

8. Use compatible numbers to mentally find the sum of 50, 90, 150,
(92) 20, and 10. List the pairs of compatible numbers you added first.

9. Use a comparison symbol in place of the circle to show
(17) each comparison.

    a. 123 ◯ 132   **b.** $5 + 7$ ◯ $7 + 5$

10. How many centimeters are in a meter?
(79)

11. How many small cubes were used to build this
(73) rectangular solid?

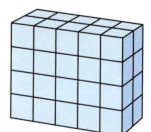

12. **Formulate** Change this addition to a
(54, 76) multiplication and find the total.

    12 in. + 12 in. + 12 in. + 12 in. + 12 in. + 12 in.

13. Write these numbers in order from least to greatest:
(103)

    1,152   1,215   1,125

14. $78 \div 3$ **15.** 420×4
(101)   (97)

16. Find each quotient.
(86)
    a. $27 \div 3$ **b.** $28 \div 7$ **c.** $42 \div 6$

17. 94 × 2
(84)

18. 52 ÷ 4
(101)

19. Multiply:
(100)
    a. 4 × $2.50

                    b. 8 × $2.50

20. (**Explain**) Describe the sorting rule for the numbers in these
(102)
two groups.

                        Group A: 0, 2, 4, 6, 8

                        Group B: 1, 3, 5, 7, 9

Real-World Connection

Sonya played on a soccer team that practiced every day from the first of June through the end of October. How many days did Sonya's team practice in all?

• **Dot-to-Dot Design**

Power Up

facts	Power Up 110
jump start	Count up by 25s from 0 to 250. Count up by 100s from 0 to 2,000.
	Write a multiplication and division fact family using the numbers 11, 6, and 66.
	Use these clues to find the secret number. Write the secret number on your worksheet.

  • three-digit number
  • less than 150
  • perfect square
  • palindrome

mental math

a. Number Sense: $100 \div 4$

b. Number Sense: $201 - 199$

c. Measurement: How many feet are equal to 48 inches?

d. Money: Masa, Marta, and Naomi paid $24 altogether for tickets to the history museum. How much money did each ticket cost?

problem solving

It took Jack 25 minutes to walk from the U.S. Capitol to the White House. Then it took him 20 minutes to walk from the White House to the Lincoln Memorial. Jack arrived at the Lincoln Memorial at 2:50 p.m. At what time did Jack leave the U.S. Capitol?

In this lesson you will draw a design on a grid by drawing line segments from point to point.

For example, we can draw an arrow on grid paper by first graphing these points:

1. (10,5)	2. (9,7)	3. (16,4)	4. (9,1)
5. (10,3)	6. (5,3)	7. (4,1)	8. (2,1)
9. (3,3)	10. (2,3)	11. (2,5)	12. (3,5)
13. (2,7)	14. (4,7)	15. (5,5)	16. (10,5)

To draw the lines, we start at point 1. From point 1, we draw a segment to point 2. From point 2, we draw a segment to point 3. We continue drawing segments from point to point in order. The drawing begins and ends at the same point.

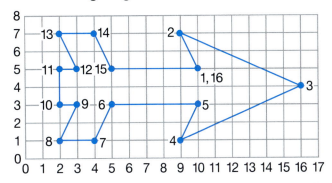

Classify The design above is a closed figure made up of line segments. What do we call a closed, flat shape with straight sides?

Activity

Dot-to-Dot Design

Materials: **Lesson Activity 34**

On **Lesson Activity 34,** draw segments from point to point to complete the drawing.

1. Sammy bought three pizzas for $7.50 each. What was the total cost of the pizzas?
(100)

2. Write these numbers from least to greatest:
(103)
$$7,862 \quad 5,798 \quad 9,365$$

3. What is the geometric name for this shape? How many edges does it have? How many vertices?
(75)

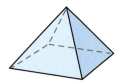

4. **Classify** Mick sorted geometric shapes into Group A and Group B. Where should he put the shape shown in problem **3?**
(104)

Group A	Group B

5. Round $7.75 to the nearest dollar.
(96)

6. Estimate the difference when 395 is subtracted from 504.
(30)

7. Copy the figure at right and draw its line of symmetry.
(Inv. 9)

8. Use a ruler to draw a square with sides 2 inches long. What is the perimeter of the square?
(58)

9. **Represent** Use a comparison symbol to show each
(27) comparison. Then write the comparison in words.

  a. 2×3 ◯ 3×2 **b.** \$0.05 ◯ 50¢

10. If $60 \div 5 = 12$, then what does $60 \div 12$ equal?
(86)

11. A leap year contains 366 days. Write 366 in expanded form.
(11)

12. Estimate the product of 92 and 9.
(93)

13. **Multiple Choice** If $1 \diamondsuit 1 = 1$ and $2 \diamondsuit 2 = 1$, then $\diamondsuit$ stands for which
(86) symbol?

  A $+$ **B** $-$ **C** $\times$ **D** $\div$

14. $38 \div 2$ **15.** 51×3
(101)   (84)

16. Multiply: $4 \times \$1.25$
(100)

17. Find each quotient.
(86)
  a. $64 \div 8$ **b.** $63 \div 9$ **c.** $60 \div 10$

18. $5 \times 9 \times 2$
(77)

19. **Connect** Use your ruler to help you find the next three numbers
(2, 35) in this sequence:

$$2, 2\frac{1}{4}, 2\frac{1}{2}, \underline{\quad}, \underline{\quad}, \underline{\quad}, \cdots$$

20. **Formulate** Write a multiplication fact that shows how
(53) many small squares cover this rectangle.

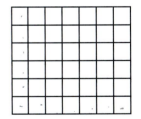

Early Finishers

Real-World Connection

Jalicia went out for lunch. She spent half of the money she had on
her meal. After she finished lunch and paid the bill, she had \$2.25
left. How much money did she have before lunch?

Focus on

• Planning a Design

In Lesson 110, we followed directions to draw a dot-to-dot design. In this investigation we will create a simple design and write directions for drawing the design.

1. Practice writing directions with your class. Look at the design at right. We can start the directions from any point. We will pick point (1,1) as the first point. We name (5,1) as the second point. Then we will continue around the figure, naming the point where each new segment ends. Below are the first three points.

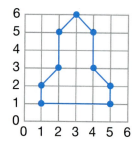

Continue naming the points in order all the way back to (1,1). You should have 10 points on your list when you are done.

1. (1, 1)

2. (5, 1)

3. (5, 2)

2. Practice drawing and writing directions by drawing a triangle on **Lesson Activity 35.** Begin by drawing three dots where grid lines intersect. Be sure the three dots are not lined up. Then draw segments between the dots to make a triangle.

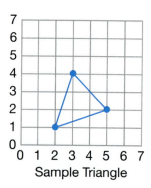

Sample Triangle

Now you are ready to write directions for someone else to make your triangle.

For number 1, write the coordinates of one point (vertex) of your triangle.

For number 2, write the coordinates of the second point of your triangle.

For number 3, write the coordinates of the third point of your triangle.

For number 4, write the coordinates of the first point of your triangle again so that the person following your directions will draw the third side of the triangle.

For our sample triangle, the directions look like this:

1. (5, 2)   **3.** (2, 1)

2. (3, 4)   **4.** (5, 2)

3. On **Lesson Activity 36,** you can draw your own dot-to-dot design. Then you can write directions for another student to follow so that they can make your design. Follow these rules:

- Use only segments—no curves.

- Make all segments end at points where lines on the grid intersect.

- Write the coordinates in order.

- Begin and end at the same point.

- Check your work by following your own directions.

A

acute angle
(65)

An angle whose opening is smaller than a right angle.

acute angle   not **acute angles**

*An **acute angle** is smaller than both a right angle and an obtuse angle.*

ángulo agudo

Un ángulo cuya abertura es más pequeña que un ángulo recto.

*Un **ángulo agudo** es menor que un ángulo recto y que un ángulo obtuso.*

---

addend
(6)

Any one of the numbers in an addition problem.

$2 + 3 = 5$ *The **addends** in this problem are 2 and 3.*

sumando

Cualquiera de los números en un problema de suma.

$2 + 3 = 5$ *Los **sumandos** en este problema son el 2 y el 3.*

---

addition
(6)

An operation that combines two or more numbers to find a total number.

$7 + 6 = 13$ *We use **addition** to combine 7 and 6.*

suma

Una operación que combina dos o mas números para encontrar un número total.

$7 + 6 = 13$ *Usamos la **suma** para combinar el 7 y el 6.*

---

a.m.
(3)

The period of time from midnight to just before noon.

*I get up at 7 **a.m.,** which is 7 o'clock in the morning.*

a.m.

Período de tiempo desde la medianoche hasta justo antes del mediodía.

*Me levanto a las 7 **a.m.** lo cual es la 7 de la mañana.*

---

angle
(65)

The opening that is formed when two line segments intersect.

*These line segments form an **angle**.*

ángulo

Abertura que se forma cuando se intersecan dos segmentos de recta.

*Estos segmentos de recta forman un **ángulo.***

---

area
(62)

The number of square units needed to cover a surface.

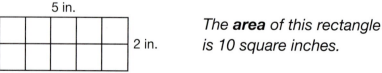

5 in.

2 in.

*The **area** of this rectangle is 10 square inches.*

área

El número de unidades cuadradas que se necesita para cubrir una superficie.

*El **área** de este rectángulo es de 10 pulgadas cuadradas.*

array
(57)

A rectangular arrangement of numbers or symbols in columns and rows.

X X X
X X X *This is a 3-by-4 **array** of Xs.*
X X X *It has 3 columns and 4 rows.*
X X X

matriz

Un arreglo rectangular de números o símbolos en columnas y filas.

*Esta es una **matriz** de Xs de 3 por 4. Tiene 3 columnas y 4 filas.*

B

bar graph
(Inv. 1)

A graph that uses rectangles (bars) to show numbers or measurements.

Rainy Days

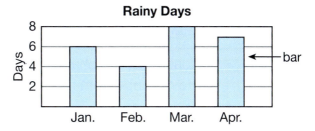

This **bar graph** shows how many rainy days there were in each of these four months.

gráfica de barras

Una gráfica que utiliza rectángulos (barras) para mostrar números o medidas.

*Esta **gráfica de barras** muestra cuántos días lluviosos hubo en cada uno de estos cuatro meses.*

C

calendar
(1)

A chart that shows the days of the week and their dates.

\	SEPTEMBER 2009					
S	M	T	W	T	F	S
		1	2	3	4	5
6	7	8	9	10	11	12
13	14	15	16	17	18	19
20	21	22	23	24	25	26
27	28	29	30			

calendar

calendario

Una tabla que muestra los días de la semana y sus fechas.

capacity
(87)

The amount of liquid a container can hold.

*Cups, gallons, and liters are units of **capacity.***

capacidad

La cantidad de líquido que puede contener un recipiente.

*Tazas, galones y litros son medidas de **capacidad.***

Celsius *(4)*	A scale used on some thermometers to measure temperature. *On the **Celsius** scale, water freezes at 0°C and boils at 100°C.*
Celsius	Escala que se usa en algunos termómetros para medir la temperatura. *En la escala **Celsius**, el agua se congela a 0°C y hierve a 100°C.*

centimeter *(79)*	One hundredth of a meter. *The width of your little finger is about one **centimeter**.*
centímetro	Una centésima de un metro. *El ancho de tu dedo meñique mide aproximadamente un **centímetro**.*

century *(57)*	A period of one hundred years. *The years 2001–2100 make up one **century**.*
siglo	Un período de cien años. *Los años 2001–2100 forman un **siglo**.*

circle *(67)*	A closed, curved shape in which all points on the shape are the same distance from its center.

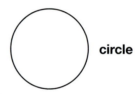

circle

círculo	Una figura cerrada y curva en la cual todos los puntos sobre la figura están a la misma distancia de su centro.

column *(1, 53)*	A vertical arrangement of numbers, words, or objects in a calendar, table, or array.

column

column

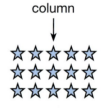

columna	Un arreglo vertical de números, palabras u objetos en un calendario, tabla o matriz.

common year *(1)*	A year with 365 days; not a leap year. *The year 2000 is a leap year, but 2001 is a **common year**. In a **common year** February has 28 days. In a leap year it has 29 days.*
año común	Año con 365 días; no un año bisiesto. *El año 2000 es un año bisiesto, pero el año 2001 es un **año común**.* *En un **año común** febrero tiene 28 días. En un año bisiesto tiene 29 días.*

comparison symbol *(17)*	A mathematical symbol used to compare numbers. ***Comparison symbols** include the equal sign (=) and the "greater than/less than" symbols (> or <).*
símbolo de comparación	Un símbolo matemático utilizado para comparar números. *Los **símbolos de comparación** incluyen al símbolo de igualdad (=) y los símbolos "mayor que/menor que" (> o <).*
compatible numbers *(92)*	Numbers that are close in value to the actual numbers and are easy to add, subtract, multiply, or divide.
números compatibles	Números que están cerca en valor a los números reales y que son fáciles de sumar, restar, multiplicar o dividir mentalmente.
cone *(75)*	A three-dimensional solid with one curved surface, one flat, circular surface, and a pointed end. 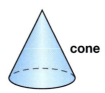
cono	Un sólido tridimensional con una superficie curva, con una superficie circular plana y con un extremo puntiagudo.
congruent *(68)*	Having the same size and shape. 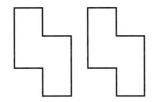 *These polygons are **congruent.** They have the same size and shape.*
congruente	De igual tamaño y forma. *Estos polígonos son **congruentes.** Tienen igual tamaño y forma.*
coordinates *(109)*	A pair of numbers used to locate a point on a grid. 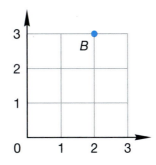 *The **coordinates** of point B are (2, 3).*
coordenadas	Un par de números que se utilizan para ubicar un punto sobre una cuadrícula. *Las **coordenadas** del punto B son (2, 3).*

counting numbers (4)	The numbers used to count; the numbers in this sequence: 1, 2, 3, 4, 5, 6, 7, 8, 9, ... *The numbers 12 and 37 are **counting numbers,** but 0.98 and $\frac{1}{2}$ are not.*
números de conteo	Los números que se utilizan para contar; los números en esta secuencia: 1, 2, 3, 4, 5, 6, 7, 8, 9, ... *12 y 37 son **números de conteo** pero 0.98 y $\frac{1}{2}$ no lo son.*
counting patterns (2)	*See **sequence.***
patrones de suma	*Ver **secuencia.***
cube (71)	A three-dimensional solid with six square faces.

cube

cubo	Un sólido tridimensional con seis caras cuadradas.
cubic unit (73)	A cube with edges of designated length. Cubic units are used to measure volume.

*The shaded part is 1 **cubic unit.** The volume of the large cube is 8 **cubic units.***

unidad cúbica	Un cubo con aristas de una longitud designada. Las unidades cúbicas se usan para medir volumen. *La parte sombreada es de 1 **unidad cúbica.** El volumen del cubo mayor es de 8 **unidades cúbicas.***
cylinder (75)	A three-dimensional solid with two flat surfaces shaped like circles and one curved surface.

cylinder

cilindro	Un sólido tridimensional con dos superficies planas como círculos y con una superficie curva.

D

data (Inv. 1)	Information gathered from observations or calculations. *82, 76, 95, 86, 98, 97, 93* *These **data** are average daily temperatures for one week in Utah.*
datos	Información reunida de observaciones o cálculos. *Estos **datos** son el promedio diario de las temperaturas de una semana en Utah.*

decade (69)	A period of ten years. *The years 2001–2010 make up one **decade.***
década	Un período de diez años. *Los años 2001–2010 forman una **década.***

decimal point (21)	A symbol used to separate dollars from cents in money. $34.15 **decimal point**
punto decimal	Un símbolo que se utiliza para separar los dólares de los centavos en dinero.

degree (°) (4)	A unit for measuring temperature. 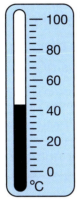 Water boils. Water freezes. *There are 100 **degrees** (100°) between the freezing and boiling points of water on the Celsius scale.*
grado (°)	Una unidad para medir temperatura. *Hay 100 **grados** (100°) de diferencia entre los puntos de ebullición y congelación del agua en la escala Celsius, o escala centígrada.*

denominator (41)	The bottom number of a fraction; the number that tells how many parts are in a whole. $\frac{1}{4}$ *The **denominator** of the fraction is 4. There are 4 parts in the whole circle.*
denominador	El número inferior de una fracción; el número que indica cuántas partes hay en un entero. *El **denominador** de la fracción es 4. Hay cuatro partes en el círculo entero.*

difference (7)	The result of subtraction. $12 - 8 = 4$ *The **difference** in this problem is 4.*
diferencia	El resultado de una resta. *La **diferencia** en este problema es 4.*

digit (11)	Any of the symbols used to write numbers: 0, 1, 2, 3, 4, 5, 6, 7, 8, 9. *The last **digit** in the number 2587 is 7.*
dígito	Cualquiera de los símbolos que se utilizan para escribir números: 0, 1, 2, 3, 4, 5, 6, 7, 8, 9. *El último **dígito** en el número 2587 es 7.*
dividend (86)	A number that is divided. $12 \div 3 = 4$ $3\overline{)12}$ with quotient 4 $\dfrac{12}{3} = 4$ *The **dividend** is 12 in each of these problems.*
dividendo	Número que se divide en una división. *El **dividendo** es 12 en cada una de estas operaciones.*
division (85)	An operation that separates a number into a given number of equal parts or into a number of parts of a given size. $21 \div 3 = 7$ *We use **division** to separate 21 into 3 groups of 7.*
división	Una operación que separa un número en un número dado de partes iguales o en un número de partes de una medida dada. *Usamos la **división** para separar 21 en 3 grupos de 7.*
divisor (86)	A number by which another number is divided. $12 \div 3 = 4$ $3\overline{)12}$ with quotient 4 $\dfrac{12}{3} = 4$ *The **divisor** is 3 in each of these problems.*
divisor	Número que divide a otro en una división. *El **divisor** es 3 en cada una de estas operaciones.*
dozen (62)	A group of twelve. *The carton holds a **dozen** eggs.* *The carton holds 12 eggs.*
docena	Un grupo de doce. *El cartón contiene una **docena** de huevos.* *El cartón contiene 12 huevos.*

E

edge (71)	A line segment formed where two faces of a solid intersect. *The arrow is pointing to one **edge** of this cube. A cube has 12 **edges**.*
arista	Segmento de recta que se forma donde se intersecan dos caras de un sólido. *La flecha está apuntando hacia una **arista** de este cubo. Un cubo tiene 12 **aristas**.*

equally likely *(50)*	Two events that have the same probability of happening. 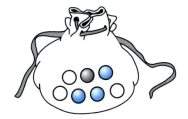 *Drawing a blue marble and drawing a white marble are* ***equally likely.***
igualmente probables	Dos eventos que tienen la misma probabilidad de ocurrir. *Sacar una canica azul y sacar una canica blanca son **igualmente probables.***
equals *(6)*	Has the same value as. *12 inches **equals** 1 foot.*
es igual a	Con el mismo valor. *12 pulgadas **es igual a** 1 pie.*
equilateral triangle *(69)*	A triangle in which all sides are the same length. *This is an **equilateral triangle.** All of its sides are the same length.*
triángulo equilátero	Un triángulo que tiene todos sus lados de la misma longitud. *Éste es un **triángulo equilátero.** Sus tres lados tienen la misma longitud.*
equivalent fractions *(47)*	Different fractions that name the same amount. 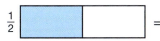  $\frac{1}{2}$ *and* $\frac{2}{4}$ *are **equivalent fractions.***
fracciones equivalentes	Fracciones diferentes que representan la misma cantidad. $\frac{1}{2}$ *y* $\frac{2}{4}$ *son **fracciones equivalentes.***
estimate *(30)*	To find an approximate value. *He **estimates** that the sum of 203 and 304 is about 500.*
estimar	Encontrar un valor aproximado. *Puedo **estimar** que la suma de 203 más 304 es aproximadamente 500.*
even numbers *(46)*	Numbers that can be divided into 2 equal groups; the numbers in this sequence: 0, 2, 4, 6, 8, 10, ... ***Even numbers** have 0, 2, 4, 6, or 8 in the ones place.*
números pares	Números que se pueden dividir en grupos iguales; los números en esta secuencia: 0, 2, 4, 6, 8, 10, ... *Los **números pares** tienen 0, 2, 4, 6 u 8 en el lugar de las unidades.*

exchanging *(Inv. 2)*	*See* **regrouping.**
intercambiar	*Ver* **reagrupar.**

expanded form *(11)*	A way of writing a number that shows the value of each digit. *The **expanded form** of 234 is 200 + 30 + 4.*
forma desarrollada	Una manera de escribir un número que muestra el valor de cada dígito. *La **forma desarrollada** de 234 es 200 + 30 + 4.*

F

face *(71)*	A flat surface of a geometric solid. *The arrow is pointing to one **face** of the cube. A cube has six **faces.***
cara	Una superficie plana de un sólido geométrico. *La flecha apunta hacia una **cara** del cubo.* *Un cubo tiene seis **caras.***

fact family *(8)*	A group of three numbers related by addition and subtraction or by multiplication and division. *The numbers 3, 4, and 7 are a **fact family.** They make these four facts:* $3 + 4 = 7 \quad 4 + 3 = 7 \quad 7 - 3 = 4 \quad 7 - 4 = 3$
familia de operaciones	Grupo de tres números relacionados por sumas y restas o por multiplicaciones y divisiones. *Los números 3, 4 y 7 forman una **familia de operaciones.** Forman estas cuatro operaciones:* $3 + 4 = 7 \quad 4 + 3 = 7 \quad 7 - 3 = 4 \quad 7 - 4 = 3$

factor *(55)*	Any one of the numbers multiplied in a multiplication problem. $2 \times 3 = 6$ *The **factors** in this problem are 2 and 3.*
factor	Cualquiera de los números que se multiplican en un problema de multiplicación. $2 \times 3 = 6$ *Los **factores** en este problema son el 2 y el 3.*

Fahrenheit *(4)*	A scale used on some thermometers to measure temperature. *On the **Fahrenheit** scale, water freezes at 32°F and boils at 212°F.*
Fahrenheit	Escala que se usa en algunos termómetros para medir la temperatura. *En la escala **Fahrenheit,** el agua se congela a 32°F y hierve a 212°F.*

fluid ounce *(87)*	*See* **ounce.**
onza líquida	*Ver* **onza.**

| **fraction** | A number that names part of a whole. |
| (5) | |

$\frac{1}{4}$ of the circle is shaded.

$\frac{1}{4}$ is a **fraction.**

| **fracción** | Un número que representa una parte de un entero. |

$\frac{1}{4}$ del círculo está sombreado. $\frac{1}{4}$ es una **fracción.**

G

| **geometric solid** | A shape that takes up space. |
| (75) | |

geometric solids　　　　not **geometric solids**

cube　cylinder　　circle　rectangle　hexagon

| **sólido geométrico** | Un figura geométrica que ocupa espacio. |

| **graph** | A diagram that shows data in an organized way. *See also* **bar graph** *and* **pictograph.** |
| (Inv. 1) | |

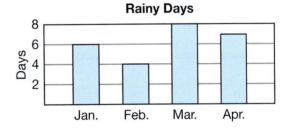

bar **graph**

| **gráfica** | Un diagrama que muestra datos de manera organizada. *Ver también* **gráfica de barras** *y* **pictograma.** |

| **greater than** | Having a larger value than. |
| (17) | *Five is **greater than** three (5 > 3).* |

| **mayor que** | Con valor mayor. |
| | *Cinco es **mayor que** tres (5 > 3).* |

H

| **half** | One of two equal parts that together equal a whole. |
| (5) | |

| **mitad** | Una de dos partes iguales que juntas equivalen a un entero. |

hexagon (67)	A polygon with six sides.
	hexagon
hexágono	Un polígono con seis lados.

horizontal (Inv. 6)	Side to side; perpendicular to vertical.
	horizontal line vertical line not **horizontal** lines
horizontal	Lado a lado; perpendicular a la vertical.

I

intersect (Inv. 4)	To share a common point or points.
	*These two lines **intersect**.* *They share the common point M.*
intersecar	Compartir uno o más puntos en común.
	*Estas dos rectas **se intersecan**. Tienen el punto M en común.*

isosceles triangle (69)	A triangle with at least two sides of equal length.
	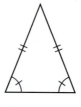 *Two of the sides of this **isosceles triangle** have equal lengths.*
triángulo isósceles	Un triángulo que tiene por lo menos dos lados de igual longitud.
	*Dos de los lados de este **triángulo isósceles** tienen igual longitud.*

K

key
(Inv. 1)

An expression on a pictograph that shows how many objects are represented by each picture.

Fish in the Class Aquarium	
Angelfish	🐟🐟🐟🐟
Guppies	🐟🐟🐟🐟🐟🐟
Goldfish	🐟🐟🐟

Key
🐟 = 2 fish

clave
Una expresión en un pictograma que muestra cuántos objetos están representados por cada imagen.

---

kilometer
(79)

A metric unit of length equal to 1000 meters.

*One **kilometer** is approximately 0.62 mile.*

kilómetro
Una unidad métrica de longitud igual a 1000 metros.

*Un **kilómetro** es aproximadamente 0.62 milla.*

L

leap year
(1)

A year with 366 days; not a common year.

*In a **leap year** February has 29 days.*

año bisiesto
Un año con 366 días; no es un año común.

*En un **año bisiesto** febrero tiene 29 días.*

---

length
(34, 52)

1. A measure of the distance between any two points.

├─────────── 3 in. ───────────┤

*The **length** of this nail is 3 inches.*

2. The measure of one of the longer sides of a rectangle. *See also* **width.**

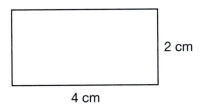

2 cm

4 cm

*The **length** of this rectangle is 4 centimeters.*

longitud
1. Una medida de la distancia entre dos puntos cualesquiera.

*La **longitud** de este clavo es de 3 pulgadas.*

2. La medida de uno de los lados más largos de un rectángulo. *Ver también* **ancho.**

*La **longitud** de este rectángulo es de 4 centímetros.*

less likely *(45)*	An event whose probability is less than another event.  *Drawing a white marble is **less likely** than drawing a black marble.*
menos probable	Un suceso cuya probabilidad es menor que la de otro suceso. *Sacar una canica blanca es **menos probable** que sacar una canica negra.*
less than *(17)*	Having a smaller value than. *Three is **less than** five (3 < 5).*
menor que	Con un valor menor. *Tres es **menor que** cinco (3 < 5).*
line of symmetry *(Inv. 7)*	A line that divides a figure into two halves that are mirror images of each other. *See also* **symmetry.** **lines of symmetry** not **lines of symmetry**
eje de simetría	Recta que divide una figura en dos mitades, en la cual una mitad es la imagen especular de la otra. *Ver también* **simetría.**
line segment *(Inv. 4)*	A part of a line with two distinct endpoints. A ———— B $\overline{AB}$ is a **line segment.**
segmento de recta	Parte de una recta con dos puntos extremos específicos. $\overline{AB}$ es un **segmento de recta.**
liter *(87)*	A metric unit of capacity or volume. *A **liter** is a little more than a quart.*
litro	Una unidad métrica de capacidad o volumen. *Un **litro** es un poco más que un cuarto.*

M

mass *(80)*	The amount of matter an object contains. A kilogram is a metric unit of mass. *The **mass** of the bowling ball is 7 kilograms.*
masa	La cantidad de materia que un objeto contiene. Un kilogramo es una unidad métrica de masa. *La **masa** de la bola de boliche es de 7 kilogramos.*

meter
(79)

The basic unit of length in the metric system.

*A **meter** is equal to 100 centimeters, and it is slightly longer than 1 yard.*

*Many classrooms are about 10 **meters** long and 10 **meters** wide.*

metro

La unidad básica de longitud en el sistema métrico.

*Un **metro** es igual a 100 centímetros y es ligeramente más largo que una yarda. Muchos salones de clase miden como 10 **metros** de largo y 10 **metros** de ancho.*

---

metric system
(79)

An international system of measurement in which units are related by tens. Also called the *International System.*

*Centimeters and kilograms are units in the **metric system.***

sistema métrico

Un sistema internacional de medición en cual las unidades se relacionan por dieces. También es llamado el *Sistema internacional.*

*Centímetros y kilogramos son unidades del **sistema métrico.***

---

midnight
(3)

12:00 a.m.

***Midnight** is one hour after 11 p.m.*

medianoche

12:00 a.m.

*La **medianoche** es una hora después de las 11 p.m.*

---

more likely
(45)

An event whose probability is greater than another event.

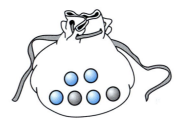

*Drawing a blue marble is **more likely** than drawing a gray marble.*

más probable

Un suceso cuya probabilidad es mayor que la de otro suceso.

*Sacar una canica azul es **más probable** que sacar una canica gris.*

---

multiple
(78)

A product of a counting number and another number.

*The **multiples** of 3 include 3, 6, 9, and 12.*

múltiplo

El producto de un número de conteo por otro número.

*Los **múltiplos** de 3 incluyen 3, 6, 9 y 12.*

---

multiplication
(54)

An operation that uses a number as an addend a specified number of times.

$7 \times 3 = 21$ *We can use **multiplication** to*
$7 + 7 + 7 = 21$ *use 7 as an addend 3 times.*

multiplicación

Una operación que usa un número como un sumando cierto número de veces.

$7 \times 3 = 21$ *Podemos usar la **multiplicación** para usar*
$7 + 7 + 7 = 21$ *7 como un sumando 3 veces.*

multiplication table *(55)* **tabla de multiplicación**	A table used to find the product of two numbers. The product of two numbers is found at the intersection of the row and the column for the two numbers. Una tabla que se usa para encontrar el producto de dos números. El producto de dos números se encuentra en la intersección de la fila y la columna de los dos números.
multiply *(54)* **multiplicar**	*See* **multiplication.** *Ver* multiplicación.

N

noon *(3)* **mediodía**	12:00 p.m. **Noon** *is one hour after 11 a.m.* 12:00 p.m. *El* **mediodía** *es una hora después de las 11 a.m.*
number line *(4)* **recta numérica**	A line for representing and graphing numbers. Each point on the line corresponds to a number. 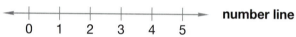 Una recta para representar y graficar números. Cada punto de la recta corresponde a un número.
number sentence *(6)* **enunciado numérico**	A complete sentence that uses numbers and symbols instead of words. *See also* **equation.** *The* **number sentence** *4 + 5 = 9 means "four plus five equals nine."* Una oración completa que usa números y símbolos en lugar de palabras. *Ver también* **ecuación.** *El* **enunciado numérico** *4 + 5 = 9 significa "cuatro más cinco es igual a nueve".*
numerator *(41)* **numerador**	The top number of a fraction; the number that tells how many parts are counted. $\frac{1}{4}$ *The* **numerator** *of the fraction is 1. One part of the whole circle is shaded.* El número de arriba en una fracción; el número que indica cuántas partes se cuentan. *El* **numerador** *de la fracción es 1. Una parte del círculo completo está sombreada.*

O

obtuse angle
(65)

An angle whose opening is bigger than a right angle.

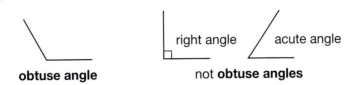

obtuse angle   not **obtuse angles**

*An **obtuse angle** is larger than both a right angle and an acute angle.*

ángulo obtuso

Un ángulo cuya abertura es mayor que un ángulo recto.

*Un **ángulo obtuso** es más grande que un ángulo recto y que un ángulo agudo.*

octagon
(67)

A polygon with eight sides.

octagon

octágono

Un polígono de ocho lados.

odd numbers
(46)

Numbers that have 1 left over when divided into 2 groups; the numbers in this sequence: 1, 3, 5, 7, 9, 11, ...

***Odd numbers** have 1, 3, 5, 7, or 9 in the ones place.*

números impares

Números que cuando se dividen en 2 grupos iguales tienen residuo 1; los números en esta secuencia: 1, 3, 5, 7, 9, 11, ...

*Los **números impares** tienen 1, 3, 5, 7 ó 9 en el lugar de las unidades.*

opposite sides
(51)

Sides that are across from each other.

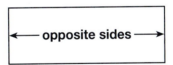

◄─── opposite sides ───►

lados opuestos

Lados que están uno enfrente del otro.

ordinal numbers
(1)

Numbers that describe position or order.

*"First," "second," and "third" are **ordinal numbers.***

números ordinales

Números que describen la posición u orden.

*"Primero", "segundo" y "tercero" son **números ordinales.***

ounce
(74, 87)

A unit of weight in the customary system. Also a measure of capacity.

*Sixteen **ounces** equals a pound. Sixteen **ounces** equals a pint.*

onza

Una unidad de peso en el sistema usual. También es una unidad de capacidad.

*Dieciséis **onzas** es igual a una libra. Dieciséis **onzas** es igual a una pinta.*

P

---

parallel lines
(Inv. 4)

Lines that stay the same distance apart; lines that do not cross.

parallel lines

rectas paralelas — Rectas que siempre están a la misma distancia; rectas que no se cruzan.

---

parallelogram
(66)

A quadrilateral that has two pairs of parallel sides.

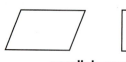

parallelograms

not a
parallelogram

paralelogramo — Un cuadrilátero que tiene dos pares de lados paralelos.

---

parentheses
(92)

A pair of symbols used to show which operation to perform first: ( ).

$$15 - (12 - 4)$$

*In the expression 15 − (12 − 4), the **parentheses** mean that 12 − 4 should be calculated first. Then that difference should be subtracted from 15.*

paréntesis — Un par de símbolos que se utilizan para mostrar que operación se debe de hacer primero: ( ).

*En la expresión 15 − (12 − 4) los **paréntesis** significan que 12 − 4 debe ser calculado primero. Después esa diferencia se debe de restar de 15.*

---

pentagon
(67)

A polygon with five sides.

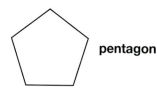

pentagon

pentágono — Un polígono con cinco lados.

---

perimeter
(58)

The distance around a closed, flat shape.

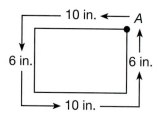

*The **perimeter** of this rectangle (from point A around to point A) is 32 inches.*

perímetro — Distancia alrededor de una figura cerrada y plana.

*El **perímetro** de este rectángulo (desde el punto A alrededor del rectángulo hasta el punto A) es 32 pulgadas.*

perpendicular lines
(Inv. 4)

Two lines that intersect at right angles.

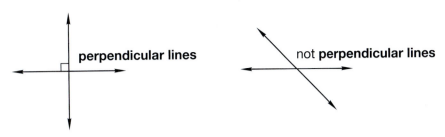

perpendicular lines   not **perpendicular lines**

rectas perpendiculares

Dos rectas que se intersecan formando ángulos rectos.

---

pictograph
(Inv. 1)

A graph that uses symbols to represent data.

Stars We Saw	
Tom	☆ ☆ ☆ ☆ ☆
Bob	☆ ☆
Sue	☆ ☆ ☆ ☆
Ming	☆ ☆ ☆ ☆ ☆
Juan	☆ ☆ ☆ ☆ ☆ ☆

*This is a **pictograph.**
It shows how many
stars each person saw.*

pictograma

Una gráfica que usa símbolos para representar datos.

*Éste es un **pictograma.** Muestra el número de estrellas que vio cada persona.*

---

place value
(11)

The value of a digit based on its position within a number.

$$
\begin{array}{r}
341 \\
23 \\
+\quad 7 \\
\hline
371
\end{array}
$$

*Place value tells us that 4 in 341 is worth "4 tens." In addition problems we align digits with the same **place value.***

valor posicional

El valor de un dígito basado en su posición dentro de un número.

*El **valor posicional** nos dice que 4 en 341 vale "4 dieces". En problemas de suma alineamos los dígitos con el mismo **valor posicional.***

---

p.m.
(3)

The period of time from noon to just before midnight.

*I go to bed at 9 **p.m.**, which is 9 o'clock at night.*

p.m.

Período de tiempo desde el mediodía hasta justo antes de la medianoche.

*Me voy a dormir a las 9 **p.m.**, lo cual es las 9 de la noche.*

---

point
(4, 109)

An exact location on a line or grid.

•A   *This dot represents **point** A.*

punto

Un lugar exacto en una línea o cuadrícula.

*Esta marca representa el **punto** A.*

polygon (67)	A closed, flat shape with straight sides. polygons not **polygons**
polígono	Una figura cerrada y plana que tiene lados rectos.

pound (74)	A customary measurement of weight. One **pound** is 16 ounces.
libra	Una unidad usual de peso. Una **libra** es igual a 16 onzas.

probability (45)	A way of describing the likelihood of an event. The **probability** of the spinner landing on C is the greatest (it is the most likely).
probabilidad	Una manera de describir la posibilidad de ocurrencia de un suceso. La **probabilidad** de que la flecha se detenga en C es la mayor (es la más probable).

product (55)	The result of multiplication. $5 \times 3 = 15$ The **product** of 5 and 3 is 15.
producto	El resultado de una multiplicación. $5 \times 3 = 15$ El **producto** de 5 por 3 es 15.

pyramid (75)	A three-dimensional solid with a polygon as its base and triangular faces that meet at a vertex. pyramid
pirámide	Un sólido tridimensional con un polígono en su base y caras triangulares que se encuentran en un vértice.

Q

quadrilateral (67)	Any four-sided polygon. Each of these polygons has 4 sides. They are all **quadrilaterals.**
cuadrilátero	Cualquier polígono de cuatro lados. Cada uno de estos polígonos tiene 4 lados. Todos son **cuadriláteros.**

quarter *(5)*	A term that means one-fourth.
cuarto	Un término que significa un **cuarto.**

quotient *(86)*	The result of division.

$$12 \div 3 = 4 \qquad 3\overline{)12} \qquad \frac{12}{3} = 4$$

*The **quotient** is 4 in each of these problems.*

cociente	El resultado de una división.
	*El **cociente** es 4 en cada una de estas operaciones.*

R

rectangle *(51)*	A quadrilateral that has four right angles.

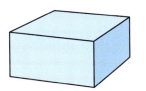

rectangles   not **rectangles**

rectángulo	Un cuadrilátero que tiene cuatro ángulos rectos.

rectangular prism *(71)*	A geometric solid with 6 rectangular faces.

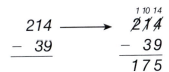

rectangular prism

prisma rectangular	Un sólido geométrico con 6 caras rectangulares.

rectangular solid *(71)*	*See* **rectangular prism.**
sólido rectangular	*Ver* **prisma rectangular.**

regrouping *(14)*	To rearrange quantities in place values of numbers during calculations.

$$214 \longrightarrow \overset{1\ 10\ 14}{\cancel{2}\cancel{1}\cancel{4}}$$
$$-\ 39 \qquad\qquad -\ \ 39$$
$$\overline{1\,7\,5}$$

*Subtraction of 39 from 214 requires **regrouping.***

reagrupar	Reordenar cantidades de acuerdo a los valores posicionales de los números cuando se hacen cálculos.
	*La resta de 39 de 214 requiere de **reagrupación.***

right angle
(51)

An angle that forms a square corner. It is often marked with a small square.

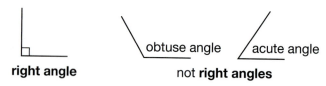

right angle   not **right angles**

*A **right angle** is larger than an acute angle and smaller than an obtuse angle.*

ángulo recto

Un ángulo que forma una esquina cuadrada. Se indica con frecuencia con un pequeño cuadrado.

*Un **ángulo recto** es mayor que un ángulo agudo y menor que un ángulo obtuso.*

---

right triangle
(69)

A triangle with one right angle (square corner).

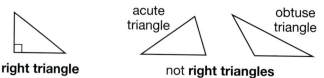

right triangle   not **right triangles**

triángulo rectángulo

Un triángulo con un ángulo recto (esquina cuadrada).

---

round
(15)

To express a calculation or measure to a specific degree of accuracy.

*To the nearest hundred dollars, $294 **rounds** to $300.*

redondear

Expresar un cálculo o medir con cierto grado de precisión.

*A la centena más cercana, $294 se **redondea** a $300.*

---

rows
(1, 53)

A horizontal arrangement of numbers, words, or objects in a calendar, table, or array.

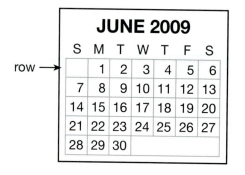

filas

Un arreglo horizontal de números, palabras u objetos en un calendario, tabla o matriz.

scale
(4)

A type of number line used for measuring.

| cm | 1 | 2 | 3 | 4 | 5 | 6 | 7 |

*The distance between each mark on this ruler's **scale** is 1 centimeter.*

escala

Un tipo de recta numérica que se usa para medir.

*La distancia entre cada marca en la **escala** de esta regla es 1 centímetro.*

scale map
(Inv. 4)

A map where each unit on the map stands for a different number of units on the actual object or location.

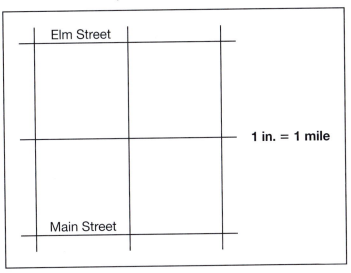

*On this **scale map** of city streets, Main Street and Elm Street are 2 inches apart.*

mapa a escala

Un mapa donde cada unidad en el mapa representa un número diferente de unidades en el objeto o lugar real.

*En este **mapa a escala** de las calles de la ciudad, la calle Main y la calle Elm están a 2 pulgadas de distancia.*

scalene triangle
(69)

A triangle with three sides of different lengths.

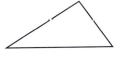

*All three sides of this **scalene triangle** have different lengths.*

triángulo escaleno

Un triángulo con todos sus lados de diferente longitud.

*Los tres lados de este **triángulo escaleno** tienen diferente longitud.*

segment
(Inv. 4)

See **line segment.**

segmento

Ver **segmento de recta.**

sequence
(2)

A list of numbers arranged according to a certain rule.

*The numbers 5, 10, 15, 20, ... form a **sequence**. The rule is "count up by fives."*

secuencia

Una lista de números ordenados de acuerdo a una regla.

*Los números 5, 10, 15, 20, ... forman una **secuencia**. La regla es "contar hacia adelante de cinco en cinco".*

---

side
(65)

A line segment that is part of a polygon.

*The arrow is pointing to one **side**. This pentagon has 5 **sides**.*

lado

Un segmento de recta que es parte de un polígono.

*La flecha está apuntando hacia un **lado**. Este pentágono tiene 5 **lados**.*

---

solid
(75)
sólido

See **geometric solid**.

*Ver **sólido geométrico**.*

---

sphere
(75)

A round geometric solid with one curved surface.

sphere

esfera

Un sólido geométrico redondo con una superficie curva.

---

square
(51)

1. A rectangle with all four sides of equal length.

12 in.

12 in. 12 in.

12 in.

*All four sides of this **square** are 12 inches long.*

2. The product of a number and itself.

*The **square** of 4 is 16.*

cuadrado

1. Un rectángulo con cuatro lados iguales.

*Los cuatro lados de este **cuadrado** miden 12 pulgadas de longitud.*

2. El producto de un número por sí mismo.

*El **cuadrado** de 4 es 16.*

---

square centimeter
(79)

A measure of area equal to that of a square with sides 1 centimeter long.

square centimeter

1 cm

1 cm

centímetro cuadrado

Una medida de área que es igual a la de un cuadrado con lados de 1 centímetro de largo.

square inch *(62)*	A measure of area equal to that of a square with 1-inch sides. **square inch** 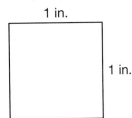
pulgada cuadrada	Una medida de área que es igual a la de un cuadrado con lados de 1 pulgada de largo.
square number *(61)*	The product when a whole number is multiplied by itself. *The number 9 is a **square number** because $9 = 3^2$.*
número al cuadrado	El producto de un número multiplicado por sí mismo. *El número 9 es un **número al cuadrado** porque $9 = 3^2$.*
square unit *(62)*	An area equal to the area of a square with sides of designated length. *The shaded part is 1 **square unit**. The area of the large rectangle is 8 **square units**.*
unidad cuadrada	Un área igual al área de un cuadrado con lados de longitud determinada. *La parte sombreada es 1 **unidad cuadrada**. El área del rectángulo grande es igual a 8 **unidades cuadradas**.*
straight angle *(65)*	An angle that forms a straight line. 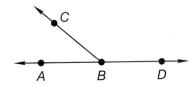 *Angle ABD is a **straight angle**. Angles ABC and CBD are not **straight angles**.*
ángulo llano	Un ángulo que forma una línea recta. *El ángulo ABD es un **ángulo llano**. Los ángulos ABC y CBD no son **ángulos llanos**.*
subtraction *(7)*	The arithmetic operation that reduces a number by an amount determined by another number. *We use **subtraction** to take 12 away from 15.* $15 - 12 = 3$
resta	La operación aritmética que reduce un número por una cantidad determinada de otro número. *Usamos la **resta** para tomar 12 de 15.*
sum *(6)*	The result of addition. $2 + 3 = 5$ *The **sum** of 2 and 3 is 5.*
suma	El resultado de sumar. $2 + 3 = 5$ *La **suma** de 2 y 3 es 5.*

survey	A method of collecting data about a particular population.
(Inv. 6)	*Mia conducted a **survey** by asking each of her classmates the name of his or her favorite television show.*
encuesta	Un método para recolectar datos acerca de una población en particular.
	*Mia hizo una **encuesta** entre sus compañeros para averiguar cuál era su programa favorito de televisión.*

| **symmetry** | Correspondence in size and shape on either side of a dividing line. *See also* **line of symmetry.** |
| (Inv. 7) | |

These figures have **symmetry.**   These figures do not have **symmetry.**

| **simetría** | Correspondencia en tamaño y forma entre cada lado de una línea divisoria. *Ver también* **eje de simetría.** |

T

| **table** | A way of organizing data in columns and rows. |
| (Problem Solving Overview) | |

Our Group Scores

Name	Grade
Group 1	98
Group 2	72
Group 3	85
Group 4	96

*This **table** shows the scores of four groups.*

| **tabla** | Una manera de organizar datos en columnas y filas. |
| | *Esta **tabla** muestra las puntuaciones de cuatro grupos.* |

| **tally mark** | A small mark used to help keep track of a count. |
| (Problem Solving Overview) | |

卌   *I used **tally marks** to count cars. I counted five cars.*

| **marca de conteo** | Una pequeña marca que se usa para llevar la cuenta. |
| | *Usé **marcas de conteo** para contar carros. Yo conté cinco carros.* |

| **tick mark** | A mark dividing a number line into smaller portions. |
| (4) | |

| **marca de un punto** | Una marca que divide a una recta numérica en partes más pequeñas. |

timeline
(33)

A type of number line for which each tick mark represents a date.

Flight Timeline

1903	1927	1947	1969
Wright Brothers' powered flight	Lindberg's transatlantic flight	Yeager's supersonic flight	Armstrong/ Aldrin moon landing

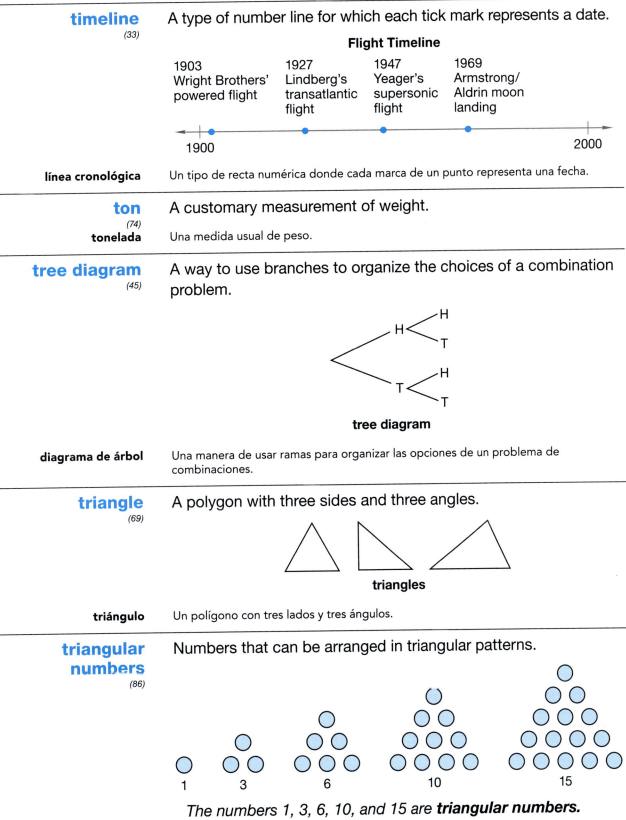

1900   2000

línea cronológica   Un tipo de recta numérica donde cada marca de un punto representa una fecha.

---

ton
(74)
tonelada

A customary measurement of weight.

Una medida usual de peso.

---

tree diagram
(45)

A way to use branches to organize the choices of a combination problem.

tree diagram

diagrama de árbol   Una manera de usar ramas para organizar las opciones de un problema de combinaciones.

---

triangle
(69)

A polygon with three sides and three angles.

triangles

triángulo   Un polígono con tres lados y tres ángulos.

---

triangular numbers
(86)

Numbers that can be arranged in triangular patterns.

1   3   6   10   15

*The numbers 1, 3, 6, 10, and 15 are **triangular numbers.***

números triangulares   Números que pueden ser ordenados en un patrones triangulares.

*1, 3, 6, 10 y 15 son **números triangulares.***

triangular prism (75)	A geometric solid with 3 rectangular faces and 2 triangular faces.

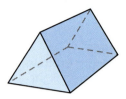

prisma triangular	Un sólido geométrico con 3 caras rectangulares y 2 caras triangulares.

U

unit (53)	Any standard object or quantity used for measurement. *Grams, pounds, liters, gallons, inches, and meters are all **units**.*
unidad	Un objeto o cantidad estándar que se usa para medir. *Gramos, libras, litros, galones, pulgadas y metros son **unidades**.*

U.S. Customary System (34)	A system of measurement used almost exclusively in the United States. *Pounds, quarts, and feet are units in the **U.S. Customary System**.*
Sistema usual de EE.UU.	Un sistema de medición que se usa casi exclusivamente en EE.UU. *Libras, cuartos y pies son unidades del **Sistema usual de EE.UU.***

V

Venn diagram (105)	A type of diagram that shows how objects, numbers, or words are sorted.

Venn diagram

Even numbers   Multiples of 5

18   20   15

24   25

diagrama de Venn	Un tipo de diagrama que muestra cómo y cuántos objetos, números o palabras se separan.

vertex (65, 71)	(Plural: *vertices*) A point of an angle, polygon, or solid where two or more line segments meet.

*The arrow is pointing to one **vertex** of this cube. A cube has eight **vertices**.*

vértice	Punto de un ángulo, polígono o sólido donde se unen dos o más segmentos de recta. *La flecha está apuntando hacia un **vértice** de este cubo. Un cubo tiene ocho **vértices**.*

vertical	Upright; perpendicular to horizontal.
(Inv. 6)	

vertical line not **vertical** lines

vertical	Hacia arriba; perpendicular a la horizontal.

volume	The amount of space a solid shape occupies. Volume is
(73)	measured in cubic units.

*This rectangular prism is 3 units wide, 3 units high, and 4 units deep. Its **volume** is 3 · 3 · 4 = 36 cubic units.*

volumen	La cantidad de espacio ocupado por una figura sólida. El volumen se mide en unidades cúbicas.

*Este prisma rectangular tiene 3 unidades de ancho, 3 unidades de altura y 4 unidades de profundidad. Su **volumen** es 3 · 3 · 4 = 36 unidades cúbicas.*

W

weight	The measure of the force of gravity on an object. Units of weight
(74)	in the customary system include ounces, pounds, and tons.

*The **weight** of the bowling ball is 12 pounds.*

peso	La medida de la fuerza de gravedad sobre un objeto. Las unidades de peso en el sistema usual incluyen onzas, libras y toneladas.

*El **peso** de la bola de boliche es 12 libras.*

width	The measure of one of the shorter sides of a rectangle. *See also*
(52)	**length.**

2 cm

4 cm

*The **width** of this rectangle is 2 centimeters.*

ancho	La medida de uno de los lados más cortos de un rectángulo. *Ver también* **longitud.**

*El **ancho** de este rectángulo es de 2 centimetros.*

Y

yard	A customary measurement of length.
(34)	
yarda	Una medida usual de longitud.

Symbols

Symbol	Meaning	Example
<	Less than	2 < 3
>	Greater than	3 > 2
=	Equal to	2 = 2
°F	Degrees Fahrenheit	100°F
°C	Degrees Celsius	32°C
∟	Right angle	⊡
…	And so on	1, 2, 3, …
×	Multiply	9 × 3
·	Multiply	3 · 3 = 9
÷	Divide	9 ÷ 3
+	Add	9 + 3
−	Subtract	9 − 3
$\overline{)}$	Divided into	3$\overline{)9}$

Símbolos/Signos

Símbolo/Signo	Significa	Ejemplo
<	Menor que	2 < 3
>	Mayor que	3 > 2
=	Igual a	2 = 2
°F	Grados Fahrenheit	100°F
°C	Grados Celsius	32°C
∟	Ángulo recto	⊡
…	Y más, etcétera	1, 2, 3, …
×	Multiplica	9 × 3
·	Multiplica	3 · 3 = 9
÷	Divide	9 ÷ 3
+	Suma	9 + 3
−	Resta	9 − 3
$\overline{)}$	Dividido entre	3$\overline{)9}$

Abbreviations

Abbreviation	Meaning
ft	Foot
in.	Inch
yd	Yard
mi	Mile
m	Meter
cm	Centimeter
km	Kilometer
L	Liter
ml or mL	Milliliter
lb	Pound
oz	Ounce
kg	Kilogram
g	Gram
qt	Quart
pt	Pint
c	Cup
gal	Gallon

Abreviaturas

Abreviatura	Significa
pie	pie
pulg	pulgada
yd	yarda
mi	milla
m	metro
cm	centímetro
km	kilómetro
L	litro
mL	mililitro
lb	libra
oz	onza
kg	kilogramo
g	gramo
ct	cuarto
pt	pinta
tz	taza
gal	galón

Circles, 362

Clocks
analog, 17–19, 29–31, 207–208
digital, 17–19, 207

Column addition, 131–132, 535. *See also* **Addition**

Columns
in arrays, 307
in calendars, 9–10, 14

Comma, in large numbers, 175–177

Common years, 8

Comparing numbers
comparison symbols (<, >, =), 93–95, 142, 177, 234–235, 266–267, 502, 531
fractions, 234–235, 266–267
money, 93–95, 146–147, 551
stories about, 212–213
whole numbers, 93–95, 147, 177, 500, 502, 531–532, 538–539

Comparison symbols (<, >, =), 93–95, 142, 177, 234–235, 266–267, 502, 531

Compatible numbers, 500–502, 508–510, 531

Cones, 405–406, 436–439

Congruent shapes, 369–370, 374–375, 386

Coordinates, 578–579, 583, 586–587

Counting patterns. *See* **Patterns**

Cubes, 387, 405–406, 436–439. *See also* **Rectangular prisms**

Cubic units, 394–396. *See also* **Volume**

Cup, 471–474

Customary System. *See* **U.S. Customary System**

Cylinders, 405–406, 436–439

D _____

Data, 56–58
collecting, 167–168, 326–327
displaying, 57–58, 167–168, 327

Dates
reading and writing, 8–11
on timelines, 181–182, 212

Decimal point (.), 115–117

Degrees (°), 23–25

Denominator, 224–225, 240, 250, 261–262

Differences, 39–41, 212–213, 217. *See also* **Subtraction**
estimating, 162–163, 501–502, 509–510

Digital clocks, 17–19, 207

Digits, 60, 65–67, 76–77, 85–89, 103–105, 116–117, 131–132, 174–177, 478

Directions, writing, 169–171, 222

Distance, 186–188
estimating, 201–203
measuring, 186–188, 191–194, 202
measuring on maps, 193–194, 221–222

Dividend, 466. *See also* **Division**

Division
by 2, 445–447, 451–452
dividend, 466
divisor, 466
equal groups stories, 487–488, 541–543
fact families, 466–468
facts, 451–452, 466–468
halving, 445–447, 451–452
modeling, 445–447, 461–462, 477–479, 541–542
multiplication table and, 451–452, 482–483
quotient, 466

Divisor, 466. *See also* **Division**

Dollars ($), 60–62, 115–117. *See also* **Money**

Dot-to-dot design, 582–583, 586–587. *See also* **Coordinates**

Doubling numbers, 440–441, 472, 509

E _____

Edges, 386–387, 436, 555

Enlargements, 570

Equal groups stories, 322–323, 487–488, 510, 513–514, 522, 531–532, 535

Equal sign (=), 34–35, 93

Equilateral triangles, 374–375

Equivalent fractions, 254–257, 263

K

Keys, in pictographs, 56, 166–168

Kilogram, 431–433

Kilometer, 426–428

L

L (liter). *See* **Liter**

Later – earlier = difference stories, 210–211

lb (pound). *See* **Pound**

Leap years, 8

Length
estimating, 186, 187, 201–203
measuring, 186–188, 191–194, 202, 283–284, 426–428
of rectangles, 263–264, 288–289
units of, 186–187, 426–428

Less than (<), 93–95. *See also* **Comparing**

Lines of symmetry, 383–384, 491–493

Liter (L), 473

M

m (meter). *See* **Meter**

Maps. *See* **Scale maps**

Mass, 431–433
estimating, 432–433, 526–527

Measuring
area, 335–337
capacity, 472
length, 186–188, 191–194, 202, 283–284, 426–428
mass, 431–433
perimeter, 312–313, 427–428
volume, 394–396
weight, 401

Meter (m), 426–428

Metric system, 426–428, 431–433

Midnight, 18

Minus sign (–), 39–41

Mirror images (symmetry), 363–364, 491–493

Missing numbers, 49–50, 198–199, 217–218, 467–468

Mixed numbers, 251, 262–263
on number lines, 262–263

Money
adding, 70–73, 85–90, 112–113, 120–121, 131–132
comparing, 93–95, 147
counting, 135–138
decimal point and, 115–117
estimating with, 81–82, 517–518
exchanging, 112–113, 115–116
fractions and, 157–158
modeling, 60–63, 70–73, 76–77, 86–90, 93–95, 103–106, 112–113, 115–117, 120–121, 125–127, 135–137, 141–143, 147–148, 153–154, 441
multiplying, 441–442, 509, 522, 535–536
naming, 115–117
place value and, 60–62, 70–73
rounding, 80–82, 517–518
subtracting, 76–77, 103–105, 109–110, 112–113, 124–127, 153–154

Months, 8–11, 39–40, 41
days in, 8–11

Multiples of ten, 422, 495–497, 505–506

Multiplication
× (multiplication sign), 293–294
by 0, 303–304
by 1, 303–304
by 2, 317–318
by 5, 317–318
by 9, 346–348
by 10, 303–304
by 11, 411–413
by 12, 411–413
arrays and, 307–308
of dollars and cents, 535–536
equal group stories, 322–323, 487–488, 510, 513–514, 522, 531–532, 535
estimating products, 505–506, 509–510, 531–532
fact families, 466–468
facts, 299, 303–304, 317–318, 329–331, 346–348, 378–379, 411–413
memory group, 378–379
missing factors, 467–468
modeling, 288–289, 294, 307–308, 330–331, 411–412, 417–418, 441–442
of money, 441–442, 509, 522, 535–536

by multiples of ten, 422–423, 495–497, 505–506

as repeated addition, 293–294, 307

square numbers, 329–331

table, 298–300, 303, 317, 330, 346, 379, 411, 451, 482

of three numbers, 417–418

of three-digit numbers, 495–497, 521–522

of two-digit numbers, 440–442, 456–457, 509–510

Multiplication facts, 299, 466–468

0s, 303–304

1s, 303–304

2s, 317–318

5s, 317–318

9s, 346–348

10s, 303–304

11s, 411–413

12s, 411–413

memory group, 378–379

square numbers, 329–331

Multiplication table, 298–300, 303, 317, 330, 346, 379, 411, 451, 482

INDEX

Problem solving strategies, *continued*
    make an organized list, 6, 244–245
    make it simpler, 5, 6, 361–362, 476–477
    use logical reasoning, 5, 6, 161–162
    work backwards, 5, 6, 316–317
    write a number sentence, 5, 6, 108

Products, 298–300, 303–304, 317–318,
323, 329–331, 346–348, 378–379, 413,
417–418, 422–423, 441–442, 457,
521–522, 535–536
    estimating, 505–506, 509–510,
      513–514, 531–532

Pyramids, 405–406, 436–439

Q

Quadrilaterals, 363–365, 555

Quart, 471–474

Quarter ($\frac{1}{4}$), 29–31, 191–193. *See also* **Fourth**

Quotient, 466–467, 483. *See also* **Division**

R

Rectangles, 278–279, 356, 358
    area, 335–336
    length and width, 283–284
    perimeter, 312–313, 335–337

Rectangular prisms, 385–387, 405–406,
436–439
    volume, 394–396

Rectangular solids. *See* **Rectangular prisms**

Regrouping
    in addition, 71–73, 87–90, 112–113,
      162–163, 120–121
    in multiplication, 521–522, 535–536
    in subtraction, 76–77, 112–113, 141–144,
      162–163

Right angles, 278–279, 351–352, 356,
374–375

Right triangles, 374–375

Rounding
    money, 80–82, 162–163, 505, 513–514,
      517–518
    whole numbers, 80–82, 162–163, 505–506,
      513–514

Rows
    in arrays, 307
    in calendars, 9–10

Rulers, 186–188, 191–194, 202, 221–222,
283–284

S

Scales, 23–24, 58, 207, 326–327

Scale maps, 221–222

Scalene triangles, 374

Sequences, 13–15. *See also* **Patterns**

Shapes. *See* **Polygons**; **Circles**

Skip counting, 13–15, 18, 19, 207

Solids. *See* **Geometric solids**

"Some and some more" stories, 98–99,
197–199, 501, 513

"Some went away" stories, 109–110,
141–144, 217–218

Sorting, 546–547, 560–561
    diagrams for, 559–561
    geometric shapes, 554–556, 561
    Venn diagrams, 560–561

Spheres, 405–406, 436–439

Square corners. *See* **Right angles**

Square numbers, 329–331

Square units, 335–337, 341–342, 347,
565–567, 573–574. *See also* Area

Squares, 278–279, 329, 561
    perimeter, 312–313

Story problems
    about comparing, 212–213
    equal groups, 322–323, 487–488,
      513–514, 522, 531–532, 535
    greater – lesser = difference, 212–213
    later – earlier = difference, 212–213
    some and some more, 98–99, 197–199,
      501, 513
    some went away, 109–110, 141–144,
      217–218

Straight angles, 351

INDEX